W9-BEF-865

3 1489 00637 9554

DISCARDED BY
FREEPORT
MEMORIAL LIBRARY

Principles *of* Helicopter Flight

Second Edition

W.J. Wagtendonk

Aviation Supplies & Academics, Inc.
7005 132nd Place SE
Newcastle, WA 98059-3153

Principles of Helicopter Flight

Walter J. Wagtendonk OBE

Second U.S. Edition, Revised 2006

Aviation Supplies & Academics, Inc.
7005 132nd Place, SE
Newcastle, Washington 98059-3153 U.S.A.

First published in New Zealand by Walter J. Wagtendonk, 1992

©2006 Walter J. Wagtendonk
All rights reserved.
Second edition, published 2006 by Aviation Supplies & Academics, Inc.
No part of this manual may be reproduced in any manner whatsoever including
electronic, photographic, photocopying, facsimile, or stored in a retrieval
system, without the prior written permission of the publisher.

Nothing in this manual supersedes any operational documents or procedures
issued by the Federal Aviation Administration, aircraft and avionics
manufacturers, flight schools, or the operators of aircraft.

Cover photo © iStockphoto.com/Johan Ramberg

Published in the United States of America

10   9 8 7 6 5 4 3

ASA-PHF-2
ISBN 1-56027-649-5
    978-1-56027-649-4

Library of Congress Cataloging-in-Publication Data:

Wagtendonk, Walter J,. 1929
        Principles of helicopter flight / Walter J. Wagtendonk.
            p.   cm.
        Includes index.
        ISBN 1-56027-649-5
        1. Helicopters—Aerodynamics. 2. Helicopters—Piloting
    1. Title.
    TL716.W32 1995
    629.132' 5252—dc20   95-52965
                                                          CIP

Acknowledgments

United States

Amy Laboda, Editor

Don Fairbanks
Cardinal Helicopter Training,
Batavia, Ohio

Associate Professor W. (Bill) Hopper
Dept. of Aerospace and Technology,
Parks College of St Louis University
Cahokia, Illinois

Connie Reeves, Major (ret) US Army,
Dowell, Maryland

McDonnel Douglas
Seattle, Washington

Special thanks to Raymond W. Prouty
Westlake Village, California, for valuable
advice and permission to use copyright
material.

New Zealand

Flight Lieutenant Phil Murray,
Royal New Zealand Air Force (ret)

John Reid, MBE

Peter Tait
Helicopters NZ Ltd

Colin Bint

Andy Smith
Nelson Aviation College

Keith Broady, Nelson

Bill Conning
Helicopter Operations Ltd

Ann Wagtendonk

Air Commodore Stewart Boys CBE AFC
Royal New Zealand Air Force (ret)

Contents

23. Mountain Flying 221

24. Helicopter Icing 237

Foreword

A helicopter in flight is a working demonstration of all of the basic physical laws of the universe in action: Newton's first three laws of motion, Bernoulli's Principles, the whole lot. The complexity of the theory behind why a helicopter flies is understandably daunting to the novice pilot. No matter how well he learns to fly the craft, however, he remains a novice pilot until he truly comes to understand the physical principles behind the workings of its controls and rotor mechanisms, for it is those principles that define the very limits of his machine.

There is much more to helicopter flight than "beating the air into submission." The Principles of Helicopter Flight was written for the pilot and budding aerodynamicist who is ready to learn why a helicopter flies the way it does and how its flight envelope was developed.

This book contains much more than a simple explanation of the four basic forces of flight – lift, drag, thrust and weight – and much more than a generalized breakdown of helicopter control functions, though both topics are covered in detail over the course of several chapters. Instead what the author, W. J. Wagtendonk, offers his reader is a building block approach to helicopter aerodynamics and operations, beginning with an in-depth examination of basic physics and building through to the subtleties of advanced operations such as high mountain flying, flying sling loads and confined area, high performance maneuvering.

The difference between this book and other helicopter text books is that by the time the reader arrives at the chapters encompassing advanced helicopter flight operations, he or she understands clearly why the helicopter behaves as it does. Terms such as ground resonance, loss of tail rotor effectiveness, vortex ring state and abnormal vibration have deeper meanings for pilots who comprehend the sophisticated aerodynamics involved; it is this depth of knowledge that helps them resolve potentially devastating problems before they occur. For pilots this deeper understanding of why helicopters fly also translates into the ability to more precisely fly the aircraft right up to the outside limits of its capabilities. For the aerodynamicist the understanding gained from reading this text is an invitation to designing new machines with even wider envelopes of operation, or more docile handling characteristics.

If you really want to know helicopters, go ahead, turn the page.

Amy Laboda
1995

Preface

Many years of teaching he basics of helicopter aerodynamics have instilled in me a degree of sympathy with my students about the lack of reference material which should have been available to provide the fundamentals of the subject in a logical and practical fashion.

All textbooks on helicopter aerodynamics currently available have undisputed value, but few, if any, cover the subject in a manner which assists the learner for the recreational or professional helicopter license in line with the syllabus common to most countries. My attempt, through this training manual, is to fill in the gaps and to provide students with a useful reference which is complementary to existing texts and which deals with most theory aspects required for the basic licenses.

There is no doubt that the complexity of helicopter principles of flight will always provide many and varied points of view. Inaccurate terminology, often borrowed from fixed wing theory, has been one of the main culprits in furthering this trend. I believe there is a great need for the adoption of universally accepted terms and understandings because the lack of these hinder a student's ability to study a variety of manuals in order to gain the widest possible knowledge.

In spite of my sincere attempts to ensure that this manual contains no mistakes and that the manner in which I have dealt with the principles will have the concurrence of most experts in the field, I am certain that the odd explanation may produce comment. It has been my aim to keep explanations as simple as possible, even to the extent where some may feel that one or two matters have been over-simplified. My experience "in front of the class" over many years has taught me however, that the method I have developed function most successfully in making students understand the complex issues involved. This notwithstanding, constructive comments and useful suggestions will no doubt form part of future editions of this manual.

W.J.W.
1995

Physics

If you want to fully understand the principles of helicopter aerodynamics, you must understand certain terms, laws and theorems in physics. This chapter deals with principles of physics that have a direct bearing on helicopter flight.

Newton's Laws

Sir Isaac Newton theorized three basic laws, all of which pertain to flying helicopters.

Newton's First Law

All bodies at rest or in uniform motion along a straight line will continue in that state unless acted upon by an outside force.

Newton's first law defines the principle of *inertia*, which means that bodies tend to keep doing what they are doing. If they are "doing" anything at all while in motion, the path the body travels is a straight line. If change is required, then a force must be applied to achieve that change. For example, getting a locomotive moving down a track requires a force which would be greater than the force required to get a small car rolling along a level road. The fundamental physical difference between a locomotive and a compact car is their mass. Mass means the amount (or quantity) of matter in a body; it is directly proportional to inertia. Thus to change the state of rest of any body, a force is required that must be proportional to the mass of that body. The larger the mass and thus the greater its inertia, the greater the force required.

A body's inertia does not change unless its mass changes. A helicopter at sea level or at altitude, flown fast or slow, has the same inertia, provided its mass does not change.

The term inertia is often confused with momentum. Momentum considers not only the mass of the body concerned, but also the velocity at which it travels. Bodies at rest cannot have momentum, although they do have inertia. For a given mass within a body, the faster it travels, the greater its momentum.

Momentum is formulated as:

$$Momentum = m \ x \ V$$

where *m* represents mass and *V* represents velocity.

When a helicopter travels faster, its momentum increases and a greater force is required to bring it to a halt. Alternatively, if its velocity stays the same, but there are more people on board, then momentum increases, this time because of the increase in mass and again, a greater force is required to bring the aircraft to a stop.

> **The greater the mass of a body, the greater its inertia and the greater the force required to change its state of rest or uniform motion along a straight line.**

This principle applies no matter where the body is or whether it is moving fast, slow or not at all.

For a given mass, however, if it has velocity it will have momentum as well as inertia.

> **The greater the velocity, the greater the momentum and the greater the force required to change its state of uniform motion along a straight line.**

In short, all bodies have mass and inertia, but not all bodies have momentum. Only those bodies that have velocity have momentum, too.

There are many instances in everyday flying where inertia and momentum play an important part in operating a helicopter. Once you understand their influences you can better anticipate the magnitude of control inputs needed to make required changes within a safe distance or time. For example, if a pilot makes an approach into a confined area when the aircraft is at its maximum gross weight and at a high rate of descent, then the helicopter's inertia is high because of its large mass and its momentum is high because of its high vertical velocity. The pilot must arrest the momentum downward with another force, usually involving power, to prevent the ground impact from being the force that arrests the momentum!

Newton's Second Law

> **Force is proportional to Mass x Acceleration.**

To accelerate a body at a given rate, the force used must be proportional to the mass of that body. Alternatively, if a given mass must be accelerated at a higher rate, then the force required must be greater.

The accelerated air (the induced flow) through a rotor system, which produces the required force for sustained flight, is a good example of this law in action. If the amount of air is increased, then its mass is greater, and as a result the acceleration required can be reduced to provide the same upward force. Alternatively, if the aircraft is heavier and the force required to keep it airborne is greater, then for the same mass of air processed through the rotor disc, its acceleration needs to be greater.

Newton's Third Law

> **For every action there is an equal and opposite reaction.**

Newton's third law is often misused by assuming that the word action means force. One force is not always equally opposed by another. Only when no acceleration takes place, either in terms of speed or direction, could one say that all forces are equal and opposite and only then could one say that to each force there is an equal and opposite force.

When a helicopter hovers at precisely one height, all actions (and in this case "forces") have equal and opposite reactions, but this applies only so long as there is no accelerated movement up/down, left/right or fore/aft.

Conclusion

Newton's laws have a fundamental influence on all aspects of helicopter flight. Throughout this book many of these aspects can be referenced to this chapter and it is therefore important that you have a good understanding of the principles.

Mathematical Terms

In explaining Newton's laws (and those that follow) everyday words are used, such as velocity and acceleration. Although these words appear to be simple and straightforward, in mathematical terms they are somewhat more complex and may require re-learning.

Velocity

Velocity means: speed and direction. The problem here is the inclusion of the term "direction" as an integral part of the word velocity. To say that one's car, traveling at 50 mph, has a velocity of 50 mph is wrong unless a direction value is included. You could only say that a car has a velocity of 50 mph if the vehicle travels at that speed in a given direction, for example, due north. Although this aspect is not of earth-shattering importance on its own merits, the issue is vital when other terms are considered that relate to velocity, such as acceleration.

Acceleration

Acceleration is simply the rate of change of velocity. If the term velocity is understood correctly, it is clear that by changing either the speed part of velocity or the direction part of velocity, one has changed velocity and because of that, acceleration has been established.

Imagine a helicopter maintaining exactly 50 knots in a steady turn to the right. Although the aircraft's speed is unchanged, its direction is not; in fact its direction is constantly changing. The aircraft is accelerating because of this continuous change in direction.

> **Understand then, that by altering either the speed of an object or its direction, or both, the object is accelerating.**

In this context, slowing down (commonly referred to as deceleration) is also acceleration, but in a negative sense.

Equilibrium

Equilibrium means: a state of zero-acceleration. When an object travels in a straight line at a constant speed, its velocity is constant (since there is no change in either speed or direction). It can then be said that the object is in equilibrium. If an object travels at a steady 50 mph on a curve, however, it must be accelerating because its direction is constantly changing and it can then not be in equilibrium.

The terms *equilibrium* and *balanced forces* are often confused. Whenever a body travels at a steady speed on a curve, it cannot possibly be in equilibrium because direction is continuously changing. If the curve on which it travels has a perfect and constant radius, however, then all the forces acting on it will be equal and opposite (this assumes there is centrifugal force). Thus it is possible to have balanced forces, yet no equilibrium. To illustrate, a helicopter doing perfect steep turns at a constant altitude, speed and radius is not in equilibrium, but forces acting upon the aircraft are balanced.

Gravitational Forces

Nature's laws dictate that an attractional force exists between all masses. The greater the masses, the greater the force of attraction is between them. In addition to the size of the masses, the distance between them also has an influence: the greater the distance between masses, the less the attractional force.

This law is not always easy to see because any two adjacent masses, or objects, do not always move towards each other. Just because that movement is not evident, however, does not mean that the attractional force isn't there. In most cases, the drag between the objects and the surface they are resting on is greater than the force of attraction between them and so movement is prevented.

The earth is essentially an object of great mass that exerts a large attractional force on any other object in its proximity. The result of this attractional force on any given mass, or object, is called *weight*. The earth's gravitational force originates from its core and acts on the core of any other mass nearby. The farther the object from the earth's core, the less affected it is by the earth's gravity. Since the result of this attraction is called weight, it follows that the mass further removed must have less weight. Indeed, when the distance between earth and a body becomes so large that the attractional force between them becomes negligible, the body is said to be weightless. To say in this instance that it has no weight at all would be technically incorrect because there is still an earth attractional force, but it is now so small as to be unrecognizable.

Earth attractional force has the symbol g, while the mass it acts on has the symbol m. Thus weight can be formulated as:

Weight $= m \times g$

This means that the greater the mass for a given "g" the greater the weight or, the greater the distance away from earth for a given m, the less the weight. Remember that mass does not vary if the number of molecules is not altered, but the weight of this mass will change with significant changes in altitude.

Centripetal Force

Newton's first law states that bodies in motion travel along a straight line and that a force is required when this straight line is to be changed into a curve. This force is called *centripetal force*. Since this force causes constant direction changes that change the body's velocity, it follows that centripetal force must be an accelerating force.

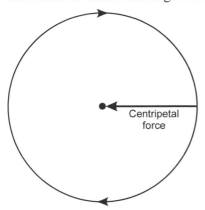

Figure 1-1. *Centripetal force acting to the center of the circle.*

If the mass of an object is large, it is hard to move it from a straight path to a curved one. If the object's velocity in terms of speed is high, it is also tough to move onto a curve. In both cases the changing force must be great. The force to make the object follow a wide curve (large radius) is less than the force required to make the object follow a tight curve (small radius).

Thus centripetal force is directly proportional to the mass of the object and the velocity at which it travels. It is however, inversely proportional to the radius (*r* in the formula below) of the curve. The force can be formulated as:

$$Centripetal\ force\ (CPF)\ =\ \frac{m\ x\ V^2}{r}$$

This formula is used extensively when dealing with forces involved in turns and recoveries from descents.

Vector Quantities

A vector quantity is defined as that which has *magnitude* and *direction*. *Magnitude* means quantity or amount. Forces that have magnitude and direction, such as vector quantities, can be added and subtracted.

Figure 1-2 shows how two vectors, A and B, acting from a common point, produce a resultant vector, C. To solve vector quantities, place your pencil at the end of vector A, parallel vector B, then repeat this for vector A until the two lines you've drawn intersect. The resultant vector, C, acts in the direction of the intersection of the two parallel (dashed) lines you drew, and the magnitude of the resultant is determined by measuring its length. This solution is called a *parallelogram vector solution,* and it is used extensively throughout following chapters.

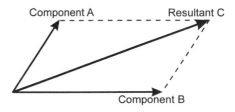

Figure 1-2. *Parallelogram of forces. Component A and component B produce resultant C.*

Figure 1-3. *Clockwise moment about point X.*

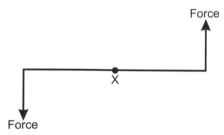

Figure 1-4. *Couple with potential to rotate counterclockwise around X.*

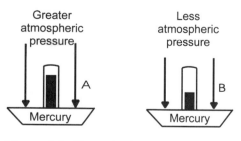

Figure 1-5. *Moment of a couple.*

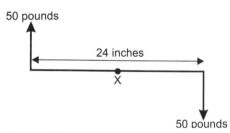

Figure 1-6. *Atmospheric pressure effect on pressure energy. Situation A at sea level has greater pressure than situation B at altitude.*

In general terms, anything that has velocity involved, directly or indirectly, is a vector quantity, whereas anything that has only mass involved directly or indirectly, is not a vector quantity. For example:

Momentum = mass x velocity.

Since *V* is directly involved, momentum must be a vector quantity. By the same token, inertia is only related to mass, so inertia cannot be a vector quantity.

Moments And Couples

Moments

The *moment* of a force about a given point is the product of that force and the right-angle distance from that point to the line of action of the force. This means that a moment is the product of a force over a given linear distance. The potential of a moment is rotation (Figure 1-3).

Couples

A *couple* consists of two equal, parallel and opposite forces. When these forces act around the point equidistant between the forces, a couple produces rotation (torque) (Figure 1-4). Both moments and couples can produce rotation, clockwise or counterclockwise, as determined by the orientation of forces.

The *moment of a couple* (torque strength) is determined by one of the two forces multiplied by the distance between the forces:

one force x arm of the couple = moment of couple.

Figure 1-5 is an example of a couple having a force of 50 pounds at each end and an arm of 24 inches (2 feet). The moment of this couple is 2 x 50 = 100 foot-pounds.

Energy

A body that possesses energy can do work. There are many types of energy, such as light energy, sound energy and dynamic energy. In aerodynamics only two energies are of concern, pressure energy and dynamic (kinetic) energy. All the remaining energies are put to one side and considered a "constant."

Pressure Energy

Pressure energy can be related to atmospheric pressure; it has the potential to do work. Air at sea level has a greater pressure energy than air at say, 10,000 feet. A good example of pressure energy yielding work is the barometer (Figure 1-6). A tube filled with mercury and inverted in a bath of mercury will, at sea level, support an approximately 30 inch column of mercury within it. The barometer functions because the air pressure, pressing on the surface of the mercury in the bath, has the ability to hold this 30 inch column up, so atmospheric pressure carries out work. There are many similar examples indicating that pressure energy does in fact produce work or has the potential to do work.

Principles of Helicopter Flight

Dynamic Energy (also known as Kinetic Energy)

Dynamic energy results from motion which implies that any object not in motion cannot have dynamic energy. Alternatively, when in motion, a body possesses dynamic energy whether it likes it or not. Dynamic energy is formulated as:

Dynamic Energy = ½ m V²

This means that:

1. A greater mass at a given velocity has more dynamic energy; and/or

2. A mass having a higher velocity will have a greater dynamic energy.

The velocity is squared, so that if the velocity is increased by a factor of two, the dynamic energy increases four times. Furthermore, a velocity increase by a factor of five results in a dynamic energy increase of $(5 \times 5) = 25$.

The ½ factor of the formula is a mathematical constant and in practical terms has little significance. Its origin lies in the fact that dynamic energy obtained by a body is a function of the velocity it has at the beginning of the equation and the velocity attained at the end. The total dynamic energy possessed by the body is the average of the velocities. An average can be calculated by adding the beginning to the end and multiplying by ½.

Understanding dynamic and pressure energies is fundamental to the principles of flight.

Units of Measurement

The following units of measurement are used throughout this text:

Time	Seconds or Minutes
Distance	Meter or Foot
Mass	Pound (lb) or Kilogram (kg)
Weight	Pound (lb) or Kilogram (kg)
Force	kgf (force) or lbf (force) or Newton
Work	1 Joule = work done by 1 N acting over 1 meter)
Power	Watt. Power is the rate of doing Work, 1 Joule per second = 1 Watt
Energy	Joule (ability to do Work)
Moment and Couple	Inch-pound, Foot-pound or meter Newton (mN)
Standard Atmospheric pressure at sea level	29.92 in. Hg (1013.2 "hectopascals", hPa)
Standard Temperature	59° F (15° C)
Temperature lapse rate	3.5° F (2° C) per 1,000 feet elevation (approximately)

Inches of mercury (in.Hg) and hectopascals (known as "*millibars*" in the past), and Celsius and Fahrenheit are used interchangeably throughout the text. It is good practice to be familiar with and be able to manipulate both metric and English standards of measurement.

Graphs

This text book contains a number of graphs. A graph consists of an X-axis (the horizontal baseline) and a Y-axis (the vertical baseline). Within the confines of these axes are "curves" or "information lines" that can be straight or rounded depending on the relationship between the values represented on the X and Y axes. The intersection of the X and Y axes is the "origin."

To keep things simple, the graphs in Figure 1-7 relate the price of a fluid in liters against the price in dollars. In A the graph is a straight line indicating a direct proportion between liters and dollars. This example shows that the more liters one buys, the greater the cost in dollars on 1-for-1 basis, so there is no difference in price per liter no matter how many liters are purchased. In B, however, the graph shows a parabola-like relationship, indicated by the curved line. As more liters are purchased, the price per liter increases.

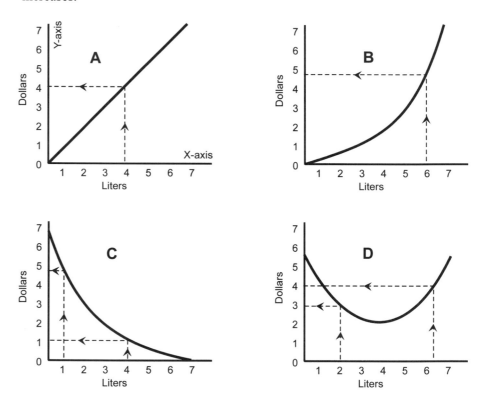

Figure 1-7. *Simplified examples of graphs.*

For instance, the cost of two liters is one dollar (50 cents/liter) while six liters cost close to five dollars (83 cents/liter). To establish this answer, draw a line straight up from six liters on the X-axis, strike the curve and then draw a horizontal line to the Y-axis.

In C, a hyperbola-like curve shows that one liter costs about four dollars whereas four liters cost less than one dollar. Again, this answer was found by drawing a line straight up from one liter, striking the curve and drawing a horizontal line to the Y-axis. Repeating this for four liters, it can be seen that the Y-axis is intersected at just below the one dollar mark. In D, a parabola-like curve indicates that from one to four liters, the price in dollars falls, while beyond four liters, the price per liter increases.

The principle of graphs is to use the known factor of the X or Y axis, and, after constructing the curve, ascertain the value of the unknown factor on the other axis. Although the above examples worked from the X axis to the Y axis, the same procedure in reverse can be used at will. You can draw a horizontal line from a value on the Y axis to the curve and then a vertical line down to the X axis.

Review 1

> **Note**: Unless otherwise stated, all Review questions throughout this book assume a counterclockwise rotating rotor when viewed from above.

1. The inertia of a body is determined by its _____, changes in altitude (do/do not) affect inertia.

2. When a helicopter climbs at increasing airspeed, its inertia (does/does not) change but its momentum (increases/ decreases/ remains constant).

3. When the mass of air through a rotor system becomes less, the downward acceleration must be (greater/smaller) to provide the same opposing force to weight.

4. When a helicopter is in a steady rate turn at a constant airspeed, the aircraft (is / is not) accelerating because it is constantly changing its _____.

5. During a constant-radius/steady-rate turn at a constant airspeed, all forces acting on the helicopter (are/are not) balanced and the aircraft (is/is not) in equilibrium.

6. Ignoring fuel burn-off, as an aircraft continues to gain altitude, its mass (does/does not) vary, earth attractional force becomes (stronger/ weaker) and the aircraft's weight becomes less/more).

7. Assuming the mass of an aircraft and its airspeed remain constant, the centripetal force required to turn it on a reducing radius must be (greater/ smaller).

8. A couple consists of _____ equal, parallel and opposite forces, and when these forces act around a point equal distance between the forces, the couple tends to produce _____.

9. The strength of a moment is (increased/ decreased) when the lever arm increases.

10. Assuming your helicopter has a constant mass, its kinetic energy (doubles/quadruples) when its airspeed doubles.

The Atmosphere

Helicopter flight performance is directly related to the density of the atmosphere. Air density is primarily influenced by:

- atmospheric pressure
- air temperature
- moisture content of air (loosely referred to as the air's humidity)

Atmospheric Pressure

Air consists of molecules, primarily nitrogen, oxygen (and variable quantities of water vapor) that are attracted by the earth's gravitational force. In Chapter 1 you learned that any mass attracted by the earth's gravity has weight, which confirms that air also has weight, the amount depending on the mass of air molecules and its distance from the earth center. Since there are more air molecules at lower levels in the atmosphere, the total mass is greater there. Gravity's pull is stronger closer to the earth's core, so the weight of the air is greatest close to sea level and decreases with altitude. Because atmospheric pressure is the result of the weight of a column of air above a given datum (measuring point, or reference point) it follows that the higher the datum (the higher the altitude), the less the air's pressure.

Atmospheric pressure has a strong influence on air density, which is the number of air molecules per volume. The greater the number of molecules in a given volume, the greater the density. When air pressure is high, such as at sea level, air molecules are more compressed and as a result, density is high. Similarly, when air pressure is low, such as at high altitude, the same given volume has less air molecules within it, and its density is low.

As you go higher, then, air pressure decreases, as does air density. Similarly, descending to lower altitudes involves increasing pressure that increases density.

Air pressure and air density are directly proportional.

Air Temperature

The atmosphere is warmed from below by a "hot plate" action from the earth's surface when it is warmed by the sun. The warmest air temperatures are typically found near the surface and progressively colder temperatures are experienced as one goes higher up in the atmosphere.

Air temperature has an effect on density because molecules move further apart when they are warmed and closer together when they are cooled. With a gain in altitude, temperature generally decreases, which attempts to cause an increase in density. In reverse, when descending, air temperature increases which attempts to cause density to decrease.

Air temperature and air density are *inversely* proportional.

Combined Effects

You can now see that air density is affected by two factors, atmospheric pressure and air temperature, and that these two factors have opposing effects on density.

1. With altitude, pressure falls off, which reduces density.
2. With altitude, temperature falls off, which tends to increase density.

Because the pressure effect has by far the stronger influence it can be said that with altitude, density decreases, but it does so at a slightly reduced rate because of the opposing temperature factor.

Moisture Content

The mass of a molecule of water vapor is less than the mass of a molecule of "dry air." Thus if an abundance of water vapor is present in a parcel of air ("humid" air), its total density is less.

The ability of air to hold moisture depends largely on temperature, the warmer the air, the greater its ability to hold moisture. Because temperature decreases with altitude, the humidity of air decreases as height is gained. Therefore, reduced density due to moisture content is more applicable closer to sea level.

The Standard Atmosphere (International Standard Atmosphere - ISA)

Previous paragraphs have shown that changes in pressure, temperature and moisture content have a strong influence on air density, which has a fundamental influence on flight. Since density is rarely constant, it follows that a helicopter's performance varies from day to day.

To make it easier to anticipate aircraft performance in any given atmospheric conditions, a set of atmospheric values has been agreed upon and may be used as "the average" so that, when actual conditions are less than, equal to, or better than the average, the helicopter's capabilities can be estimated. The "average" values are contained in the *standard atmosphere* (or *International Standard Atmosphere*), which assumes that:

1. Sea level pressure is 29.92 inches of mercury (in.Hg) - equal to 1013.2 hPa, formerly known as millibars (mb). Also known as QNE.
2. Sea level air temperature is 59° Fahrenheit (15° Celsius).
3. Temperature lapse rate is 3.5° Fahrenheit/1,000 feet (1.98° Celsius per 1000 feet) up to 36,090 feet, above which temperature is assumed to be constant at −56.5° Celsius

Ignoring (for now) the influence of moisture content, the standard atmosphere shows that the main considerations in determining aircraft performance are *pressure* and *temperature* (which determine density). Clearly, if actual conditions on a given day are better than the criteria contained within the standard atmosphere values, one can assume that the aircraft's performance will be better than average, and if conditions are less than standard atmosphere values, performance will be less than average.

Pressure Altitude

Pressure altitude makes allowance for actual sea level pressure (also known as QNH) being different from the standard atmosphere value of 29.92 in.Hg (1013.2 hPa). When the sea level pressure is less than 29.92 in.Hg (less than 1013.2 hPa) the air is less compressed, so pressure (and therefore density) is less, and the helicopter does not perform as well as in standard conditions. This situation is known as a *high pressure altitude* because the reduced pressure associated with the condition is akin to finding oneself at greater altitudes, where less pressure is found.

Alternatively, if the barometric pressure is greater than 29.92 in.Hg (greater than 1013.2 hPa), the air has greater pressure (and therefore greater density) and performance is better. This condition is referred to as a *low pressure altitude* because greater pressure is associated with lower altitudes.

Density Altitude

Density altitude allows for temperature being less than, equal to, or greater than that at pressure altitude in standard conditions.

If the temperature at any given pressure altitude is warmer than "average" (standard atmosphere), the density of air is reduced. This leads to a *high density altitude* because the reduced density situation is akin to being at a greater altitude. In reverse, temperatures colder than average at any pressure altitude result in a *low density altitude*.

Summary

The effects of pressure altitude, density altitude and humidity of air in general terms:

> **A high density altitude** occurs when
> - the barometric pressure is less than 29.92 in.Hg (less than 1013.2 hPa);
> - temperature is warmer than standard atmosphere conditions; and
> - the air is moist.
>
> **High density altitude results in decreased aircraft performance.**
>
> **A low density altitude** occurs when
> - barometric pressure is greater than 29.92 in.Hg (greater than 1013.2 hPa);
> - the temperature is colder than standard atmosphere conditions; and
> - the air is dry.
>
> **Low density altitude results in better than average aircraft performance.**

Operational Considerations

In helicopter operations, an intimate appreciation of pressure altitude, density altitude and humidity is a prerequisite for safe and professional flying. Prior to flight, set the altimeter and note the barometric pressure, check the outside air temperature gauge and compare it to standard conditions, and last, note the humidity of the surrounding air. If the readings show a low barometric pressure, a high temperature and humid conditions, be aware that the performance of your helicopter will be reduced. Your hover ceiling will be lower, you may have to off-load cargo to reduce your gross weight, and/or modify your climb-out procedure. The helicopter simply does not fly as well as on a cool, dry day.

Chapter 25, Helicopter Performance, deals with the practical application of atmospheric conditions to helicopter performance charts and real world operations.

Review 2   The Atmosphere

1. The three elements that determine air density are _____ , _____ and _____

2. Air pressure is the result of the _____ of a column of air above _____ .

3. With increasing altitude, air pressure _____ which causes air density to _____ .

4. The atmosphere is warmed (from above/from below).

5. With increasing altitude, air temperature (increases/decreases) and this tends to (increase/decrease) air density.

6. The combined effect of pressure and temperature changes with increasing altitude causes air density to (increase/decrease).

7. The standard atmosphere (ISA) assumes that sea level pressure is _____ in.Hg (or _____ hPa), sea level air temperature is _____ °F (or _____ °C) and temperature lapse rate is ._____°F (or ___°C) per thousand feet.

8. A low density altitude results when pressure is _____, temperature is _____ and the moisture content of air is _____. Helicopter performance under these circumstances is (good/poor).

Lift 3

Definitions

The following chapters refer to a number of terms that are critical for comprehension. Those which require thorough knowledge at this stage are listed below. For further reference, see the Glossary at the back of the book.

> **chord (line).**
> The straight line between the blade's leading edge and its trailing edge.
>
> **blade angle.**
> The angular difference between the chord of the blade and the plane of rotation (POR). This angle may be altered by the pilot through movement of the collective lever or through the cyclic control.
>
> **angle of attack.**
> The angular difference between the chord of the blade and the relative airflow (also known as the relative wind).
>
> **feathering axis.**
> The straight line axis between the root of the blade and its tip about which the blade can alter its blade angle.
>
> **feathering.**
> The movement of the blade about its feathering axis (which results in blade angle, or pitch angle, changes).

Most explanations in this book are based on counterclockwise-rotating rotors viewed from above. But many helicopters have rotors that spin clockwise which will affect the direction in which certain reactions work. In some instances the text explains how this difference in rotation affects a particular situation, but in the absence of such text you should determine the consequence of clockwise rotation yourself.

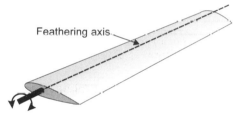

Feathering axis

Since flight involves an aircraft rising on its own above the earth's surface a force must exist that overcomes the weight of the aircraft. Although at first glance it appears that helicopters are kept aloft by lift, this is not strictly true. Helicopters clearly need lift to fly, but the lift force from the rotor blades, as conventionally defined in aerodynamics, is only a part of the force that opposes weight, as we shall see shortly.

To help understand the concept of lift, consider Figure 3-1. An airflow is shown moving horizontally across the page until it disappears behind screen A. When it re-appears, it flows precisely the same as it did prior to being lost from sight and this implies that: either nothing was done to the airflow while it was out of sight, or, if something was done to the airflow behind the screen, the change was rectified so that there was no net change.

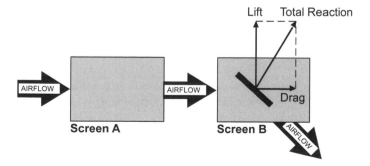

Figure 3-1. *The basic concept of lift production.*

The flow then disappears behind screen B and on reappearing it can be seen that the airflow has been deflected downwards. Newton's third law states that for every action there is an equal and opposite reaction. Accordingly, if something deflected the airflow down behind screen B, the object must have received an equal and opposite reaction, that is, it must have been subjected to an upward force. The vector quantity *total reaction* depicts that force. Notice that this total reaction acts more or less at right angles to the object, assumed to be a flat plate in this case.

Considering the airflow and the plate on which the total reaction acts, the total reaction can be divided into two components:

1.   **Lift**, which acts at right angles to the airflow.

2.   **Drag**, which acts in line with the airflow.

When the airflow was behind A it cannot have been subjected to a total reaction because there had been no net downward deflection, and there cannot have been any net lift. Yet when it passed screen B, a net deflection had occurred, total reaction, lift and drag must have taken place behind screen B.

Thus we can conclude that whenever air is deflected, lift is produced and when air is not deflected, or if no net deflection takes place, lift is zero.

The production of lift through deflection of the *relative airflow* (RAF) as it passes an object is the result of changes in the atmospheric pressure which occur around the surface of that object. Nature demands that when a streamlined flow (one that is not turbulent) is made to speed up to "get past" a body, the atmospheric pressure in that area will decrease and the opposite will occur in those areas where the flow is made to slow down. This is consistent with Bernoulli's theorem which, in essence, states:

In a streamlined flow of fluid, the sum of all energies is a constant.

A moving airflow contains potential energy (because of height), heat energy, pressure energy and dynamic energy (from its velocity). Unless the speed of the flow is very high, the changes in potential and heat energy are so small they can be ignored. In a streamlined flow at low speed, Bernoulli's theorem can therefore be stated as:

Pressure energy + dynamic energy = a constant.

Hence, when the dynamic energy of an airflow is increased by an increase in speed, the pressure energy (in other words, atmospheric or static pressure) reduces, and vice versa.

A simple demonstration of Bernoulli's theorem is the flow of a streamlined fluid through a convergent/divergent duct, commonly referred to as a *venturi* (Figure 3-2). On the left, prior to entering the venturi, the air has a certain atmospheric pressure (say sea level pressure of 29 in.Hg or 1010 hPa) and because of this, the airflow possesses a given amount of pressure energy (say 800 units). Because the airflow is moving (at say 75 knots) it possesses a given amount of dynamic energy (say 600 units). Thus the total energy contained within the flow amounts to 1,400 units.

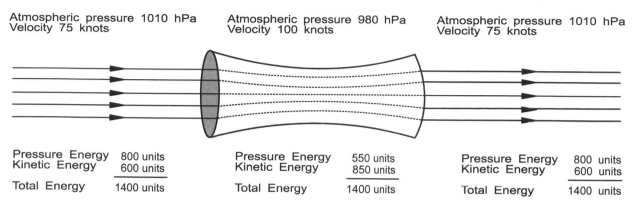

Figure 3-2. *Venturi effect showing decrease in atmospheric pressure when the velocity of the streamlined flow increases.*

If the flow remains streamlined (not turbulent) and if the air molecules are to retain their approximate relative position to each other, the speed of the flow must increase on entering the venturi (the center section of the diagram) and at the narrowest part of the duct, the velocity must be at its greatest.

Since a greater flow velocity must mean an increase in dynamic energy (say it has increased to 850 units) it follows that the pressure energy must reduce by an equivalent amount if the total energy within the flow is to remain a constant. The pressure energy must therefore change to 550 units to maintain the total energy at 1,400 units. Atmospheric pressure relates to pressure energy; so a lower pressure energy must mean less air pressure (say 550 units represent 27 in.Hg or 990 hPa of pressure). As the airflow exits the venturi (on the right of the diagram), it slows down to pre-entry values and the atmospheric pressure reverts back to 29 in.Hg (or 1010 hPa).

This demonstrates the fact that increasing flow velocities must produce a reduction in air pressure provided the airflow remains streamlined.

Figure 3-3 shows the same behavior of air over an airfoil. The fact that the top half of the venturi is not present in no way means that the principle does not apply. The relative airflow is deflected by the airfoil in such a way that a net downwash occurs behind the airfoil (the down flow at the rear is greater than the up flow at the front). For the airflow to remain streamlined, the molecules of air over the top of the airfoil have to travel faster than those beneath the airfoil. In similar fashion as in the venturi, energy resulting from motion (dynamic energy) increases, and the pressure within the streamlined flow decreases.

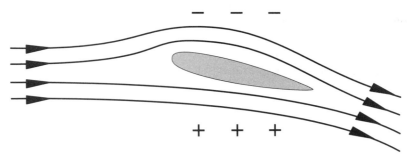

Figure 3-3. *Deflection of the relative airflow causes less pressure above the airfoil compared to that below.*

Under some circumstances, the airflow beneath the airfoil slows down, thus the dynamic energy in that flow decreases. In accordance with Bernoulli's theorem, the decreased dynamic energy must result in an increase in pressure in the airflow.

It can therefore be concluded that when a streamlined airflow is deflected downwards by an airfoil, the air pressure above becomes less than the pressure below. The airfoil responds to this difference in pressure and will move into the area of lower pressure. An upward force is produced, which we call *lift*.

Notice the way in which a flat plate and a symmetrical airfoil deflect an airflow. When flat-on to the flow, the deflection of the airflow above is precisely the same as the deflection below. There is no net deflection (remember screen A) and therefore there can be no net lift. Accordingly, any symmetrical airfoil (and many helicopters blades are of symmetrical shape) that is asked to produce practical lift must be inclined to some extent to the relative airflow so that the air's deflection over the top of the airfoil is greater than that underneath. The inclination of the airfoil to the airflow is known as the airfoil's *angle of attack* (more about which follows).

The Lift Formula

$$Lift = C_L \; ^1\!/_2 \; \rho \; V^2 \; S$$

Although this formula looks somewhat forbidding at first glance, when each factor is isolated and explained it is easier to understand. If you understand the construction of the lift formula, the study of helicopter aerodynamics is considerably simpler. Without understanding the lift formula (and a few others as well), it is virtually impossible to grasp the intricacies of helicopter flight.

C_L represents *lift coefficient*. In simple terms, this factor depicts the ability of an object to deflect, or bend, an airflow. Consider a chair, a book, a cube, and an airfoil. They all possess an ability to deflect air. Most of these items of different shape accomplish this deflection in an inefficient manner, however. The chair would be the least suitable item, closely followed by the cube. Since both produce erratic and disturbed eddies as the airflow moves past, streamlined airflow isn't maintained. The book makes a slightly better job, but even then, its sharp edges do not enhance a smooth deflected flow. Clearly, the airfoil has the best shape to bend air, and it does its job with minimum interference to the smoothness of the flow, thereby enhancing the retention of a streamlined flow.

This illustrates that *shape* is one of the primary ingredients that determines the lift coefficient.

It was stated earlier in this chapter that a symmetrical airfoil, when flat-on to the relative airflow, produces no net lift, that is to say that the deflection above is equaled by the deflection below. If the symmetrical shape is to be a positive producer of lift, it must be able to deflect the air to a greater extent over the top than underneath. This can be achieved if the airfoil is placed at an angle to the relative airflow. The angle between the chord of the airfoil (straight line between the leading edge and trailing edge) and the relative airflow is the *angle of attack* (Figure 3-4).

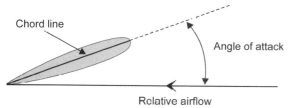

Figure 3-4. *Angle of attack is the angle between the chord line and the relative airflow.*

The greater the angle of attack, the higher the value of the lift coefficient, and the smaller the angle of attack, the less the value of the lift coefficient. When the angle of attack is zero on the symmetrical shape, the value of the lift coefficient is zero. It is of interest to note that airfoil shapes other than symmetrical, usually referred to as conventional airfoils, can have workable lift coefficients at 0° angle of attack. Their zero lift coefficient angle of attack can even be around the −4° value.

The graph in Figure 3-5 shows the value of the lift coefficient with changes in angle of attack of a symmetrical airfoil. The coefficient progressively increases at a constant rate as the angle of attack increases. There is, however, an angle of attack where the value of the lift coefficient is maximum. Beyond that angle of attack the lift coefficient decreases rather abruptly. That angle of attack is known as the *critical angle of attack*, or the *stall angle of attack* of the airfoil. At the stall angle, the airfoil operates at its maximum lift coefficient or C_{Lmax}.

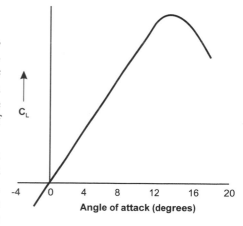

Figure 3-5. *Effect of angle of attack on C_L of a symmetrical airfoil.*

The main reason for the sharp drop-off in the lift coefficient beyond the stall angle is the turbulent nature of the airflow that then exists because the airfoil has ceased to be an efficient deflector of air.

We can summarize by saying that the lift coefficient is that part of lift that represents the ability of an airfoil to deflect air. The lift coefficient depends on the *shape of the airfoil* and the *angle of attack.*

Dynamic Energy (Dynamic Pressure) - $\frac{1}{2} \rho V^2$

This part of the lift formula constitutes dynamic energy. Lift production requires an airflow passing an airfoil and that implies that there must be motion of air. Whenever there is motion there will be dynamic energy and it is to be expected, then, that dynamic energy is represented in the lift formula.

Within dynamic energy, ρ represents air density. The ρ has taken the place of m (for mass) in the original dynamic energy formula because mass of air is essentially its density. It is important that air density is represented in the lift formula since this relates to its variable quantity. The function of the density factor is that, for a given velocity, a decrease in ρ will give a decrease in dynamic energy and that may decrease the amount of lift produced. Therefore, leaving all other factors constant, flight at higher altitudes results in less lift.

V represents *true air speed* (*TAS*), the speed at which the airfoil flies through the air. In helicopter terms, V represents the rotor rpm because it is the angular velocity of the blade that determines the speed at which the air passes each given section of the blade. Again, assuming all other factors of the lift formula to be a constant, an increase in V will increase lift. Note the "squared" function of velocity. This means that lift varies, not on a one-for-one basis with velocity, but as the square of the velocity. For instance, a three-fold increase in velocity increases lift nine times, assuming other lift formula factors are a constant.

S represents the surface area of the airfoil. This implies that the larger the area, the greater the lift produced and the smaller the area, the less lift produced by the airfoil. In practical terms, S may be considered a constant in helicopter aerodynamics because a given helicopter blade does not alter its area, unlike a wing, which can have its area affected by extension of flaps and leading edge devices.

Summary

Lift, as represented by the lift formula $C_L \frac{1}{2} \rho V^2 S$ is the result of a number of factors. To produce lift, you must have an object that can deflect air in the smoothest possible way. It must move through air of some density. It must move through that air at some velocity and the area of the object must be of some magnitude.

It would be a mistake to assume that by changing one of the factors of the lift formula, the total amount of lift changes in the same fashion. It's not always true. For instance, increase the lift coefficient of the airfoil (larger angle of attack), but at the same time decrease V, and the overall effect may be a decrease in lift. Therefore, a change in one of the lift formula factors only produces a corresponding change in lift if the remaining formula factors remain unaltered.

Indicated Airspeed and True Airspeed

Explanations in following chapters require an understanding of the difference between *indicated airspeed* (*IAS*) and *true airspeed* (*TAS*), a function of dynamic energy. This difference will be better understood if we examine the airspeed indicator (the ASI) which measures the dynamic pressure resulting from aircraft speed and displays this as Indicated Airspeed in knots.

A forward facing open-ended tube (called the *pitot tube*) brings moving air completely to rest. The resulting pressure is the sum of dynamic pressure (due to aircraft speed) and static pressure due to the atmospheric pressure surrounding the aircraft. Tubing channels this pressure to an expansion capsule in the instrument.

Static pressure enters the instrument from a static intake which is positioned somewhere on the aircraft where speed has no influence. For instance, some static intakes are in the cabin which is normally vented to outside air.

With static + dynamic in the capsule and static in the instrument case it follows that static pressure cancels out. Therefore, the degree of expansion of the capsule is due solely to dynamic pressure.

With the ASI needle activated by the capsule through a system of gears it follows that a given expansion presents a given airspeed, eg. 68 knots as shown in Figure 3-6.

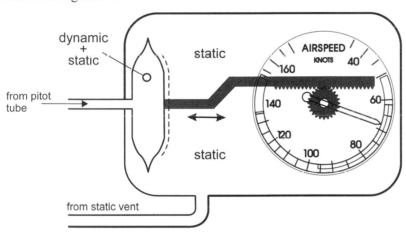

Figure 3-6. *Principle of operation of the Airspeed Indicator (ASI).*

Dynamic pressure equates to dynamic energy which, as explained, is represented by $\frac{1}{2} \rho V^2$. Ignoring the $\frac{1}{2}$ factor this means that the reading of the airspeed indicator is determined by the density of the surrounding air (ρ) and the actual, True Airspeed (V) at which the aircraft moves.

Consider a helicopter flying at sea level at an IAS of 100 knots; the capsule is expanded by a given amount. If the aircraft then goes into a climb at the same speed the density of the air will begin to decrease and the capsule will contract. (If there were no density at all, ie in space, the capsule would have nil expansion.) So, while maintaining the same TAS with an increase in altitude, the IAS will reduce. Turning this round, if the IAS is maintained, then the TAS increases as altitude is gained.

This topic crops up a few times as you progress through this book.

Center Of Pressure

The *center of pressure* is to lift what *center of gravity* is to weight.

> The *center of gravity* of an object may be defined as the point through which all the weight forces are said to act. Consequently, the *center of pressure* may be defined as the point (on the chord line) through which all the aerodynamic forces are said to act.

Since these forces are lift and drag (the two components of the total reaction), it is correct to say that the center of pressure is the point through which lift acts.

The position of the center of pressure and its movement depends totally on the shape of the airfoil and the angle of attack at which it meets the relative airflow. These two factors determine how the relative airflow around the airfoil is deflected and that in turn, determines the distribution of pressures around the airfoil.

Non-symmetrical airfoils allow for substantial movement in center of pressure with changes in the angle of attack, especially when the curvature (camber) of the airfoil is great. The symmetrical shape, however, has its center of pressure *more or less fixed* (the importance of this feature is highlighted further on).

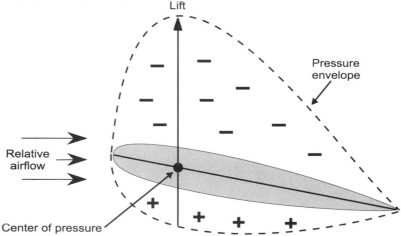

Figure 3-7. *Position of Center of Pressure is determined by the shape and size of the negative pressure envelope above and the positive pressure envelope below the airfoil. For a given **symmetrical** airfoil, center of pressure position is essentially fixed with changes in angle of attack.*

Manufacturers of helicopter blades now build blades with both symmetrical and non-symmetrical shapes. Although the symmetrical shape has the advantage of a static center of pressure, it is not a good lift producer because its maximum lift coefficient (C_{Lmax}) is not high. The introduction of high-stress-resistant materials has resulted in the use of blades that are non-symmetrically shaped. Tail rotor blades, which are able to absorb more stress and twist forces, are often non-symmetrical.

The center of pressure in non-symmetrical airfoils moves forward as the angle of attack increases and it moves rearward as the angle of attack decreases as shown in Figure 3-8. Both movements are along the chord line, which is the straight line connection between the leading edge and trailing edge of the airfoil. By convention, a forward movement of the center of pressure is referred to as an *unstable movement*, while a rearward movement is referred to as a *stable movement*.

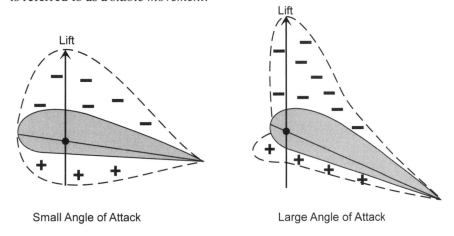

Small Angle of Attack   Large Angle of Attack

Figure 3-8. *Non-symmetrical airfoils can experience large movements of the center of pressure with changes in angle of attack.*

Aerodynamic Center

Imagine a rotor blade designed to pivot around a point in the center, with the total reaction acting through it, (Figure 3-9 A). Ignore for now the fixed position of the center of pressure. If the angle of attack of this blade is increased and total reaction acts farther forward, then the pitch angle of the blade, as well as its angle of attack, would increase away from their original value because of a stronger moment force.

Consider then the blade with its pivot point (T) at the trailing edge as shown in Figure 3-9 B. Even with the total reaction acting in the original position (in the middle), the pitch up moment would be a lot stronger than in A, but if the angle of attack is increased and total reaction moves forward, the pitch up moment is strengthened even further.

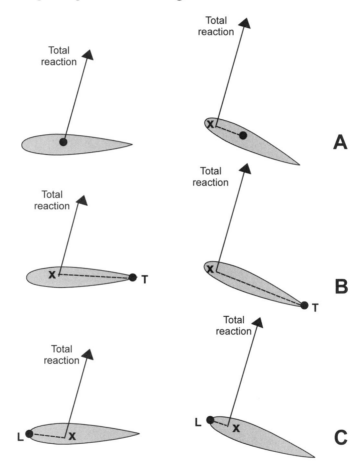

Figure 3-9. *Pitching moments and the aerodynamic center.*

Finally, consider the blade with its pivot point (L) at the leading edge as shown in Figure 3-9 C. With a small angle of attack and total reaction in the middle, the pitching moment is downward, that is, the blade wishes to decrease its pitch angle and its angle of attack. If the angle of attack is made to increase, this pitch down moment becomes stronger. Although this may appear somewhat contradictory because the center of pressure moves forward, this movement is relatively small and its effect is outweighed by the increased total reaction. In other words, moment "total reaction-X - pivot point L" is stronger because of the increased total reaction and in spite of the smaller lever arm.

Putting it all together then: if an increase in angle of attack produces increasing pitch-up tendencies about a point on the Trailing Edge (point T) and if progressive pitch-down tendencies are produced about a point on the Leading Edge (point L), then there must be a point somewhere in between where the pitching tendency is constant.

> **This point is referred to as the *aerodynamic center*, which can be defined as the point on the chord line about which no change in pitching moments is felt with changes in angle of attack.**

If a blade were built in such a way that its aerodynamic center was forward of the blade's feathering (pitch-changing) axis, then substantial stress and twist forces would occur as its angles of attack alter (a common occurrence). In Chapter 7 you'll see that the aerodynamic center and the more-or-less fixed center of pressure of a symmetrical blade are normally positioned on the feathering axis or close to it. The consequence is fewer stress-related problems within the blade.

Review 3

1. Blade angle is the angular difference between the _____ of the blade and the (plane of rotation/axis of rotation).

2. Feathering a blade means changing its _____ angle around the _____ axis.

3. When an airflow is deflected by an airfoil, the force acting more or less at right angle to the airfoil is called (total reaction/lift/drag).

4. The two components of total reaction are lift, acting (at right angles/parallel) to the relative airflow and drag, (at right angles/parallel) to the relative airflow.

5. When an airflow is made to speed up, the pressure within the flow (increases/decreases) provided the flow remains _____.

6. When a symmetrical airfoil is placed at 0° angle of attack to an aiflow, pressures are (different/the same) above and below the airfoil.

7. The lift coefficient of an airfoil is determined by its _____ and _____.

8. The peak of the C_L curve represents (C_{Lmax}/ C_{Lmin}) , the associated angle of attack is called the _____ angle.

9. The center of pressure is the point on the _____ line through which all _____ are said to act.

10. The center of pressure of a symmetrical airfoil (moves forward/moves aft/ remains steady) with changes in angle of attack.

11. The point on the chord line about which no change in pitching moments is felt with changes in angle of attack is called the (center of pressure/aerodynamic center).

The Drag Formula

Drag, in the broadest sense, is resistance to motion. It is formulated as:

$$Drag = C_D \; \tfrac{1}{2} \; \rho \; V^2 \; S$$

This formula looks less complex than the lift formula did at first glance because most of its components should be familiar by now.

C_D represents the *drag coefficient* that, simply stated, means the potential of an object to interfere with a flow of fluid (gas or liquid). For example, consider a cube. It has many sharp right angles and when placed in an airflow, causes the air to burble around it. The impact of the air onto the frontal surface and the eddying around the sides and rear of the cube interferes with the smoothness of the flow.

Compare the cube now to a ball that has air flowing over it. The roundness of its curved shape eliminates the eddies of air found around the sharp edges of the cube. The same roundness lessens frontal disturbance.

The interference of the cube and the ball on a smooth flow was caused by their shapes, but not their size. Whether a cube or ball is large or small, the shape factor of the drag coefficient determines the potential to interfere with the smoothness of flow.

The angle at which an object is presented to an airflow will also determine its drag coefficient. A thin book, placed at 0° angle of attack to a flow, has little effect on a smooth flow, but if the book is placed "broad-on," at a greater angle of attack, its interference is much greater.

Thus the drag coefficient describes the way in which an object can upset an airflow, and the amount of upset is determined by the object's *shape* and its *angle of attack*. You will recall that the lift coefficient also varies according to the same criteria.

Compared to the objects mentioned above, the airfoil has little potential to interfere with the smoothness of a passing airflow. Thus the drag coefficient of an airfoil is relatively small. That's not to say that the total drag of the airfoil is small because that depends also on the other components of the drag formula.

Like the lift coefficient curve in the previous chapter, it is possible to draw a drag coefficient curve representing the amount of drag coefficient for a given shape (say a helicopter symmetrical airfoil section) as its angle of attack alters. When the airfoil is at 0° angle of attack, its potential to interfere, (its drag coefficient) is lowest, and angles of attack either side of 0° show an increase in drag coefficient.

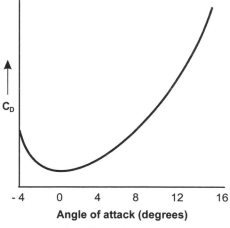

Figure 4-1. *Effect of angle of attack on C_D.*

$\frac{1}{2}\rho V^2$ again represents dynamic energy. Assuming all other factors remain constant, a decrease in ρ decreases dynamic energy, which means that with altitude, drag decreases as well. Alternatively, an increase in airspeed increases dynamic energy and therefore drag. Again, be aware of the square function; a four-fold increase in airspeed produces 16 times more drag. These examples assume that other factors of the drag formula remain constant, which is not always the case.

S again represents total surface area, which means that in principle, the larger the area, the greater the drag.

The drag formula, like the lift formula, indicates that drag is a combination of various factors that together produce the total drag of an object. By changing just one component of the formula you may not necessarily change total drag – it depends on what happens to the remaining factors of the formula as to how total drag responds.

Types of Drag

Drag, as formulated, is a combination of three types of drag, *parasite drag*, *profile drag* and *induced drag*. Textbooks vary somewhat in their subdivision of drag, but all are based on the same principles.

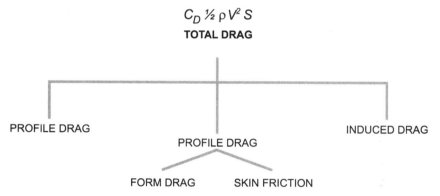

Parasite Drag

Aircraft parts are subdivided into two main categories, those that provide lift and that do not provide lift. In the case of helicopters, the rotor is in the first category while all other parts such as cabin, skids, and tail boom are in the second category. All components in the non-lifting category experience parasite drag. Some parts of a helicopter may contribute towards lift. For instance, the shape of the cabin may be such that lift is produced by it in forward flight, but the amount of lift obtained is so small that it may be ignored for the purpose of parasite drag.

The major consideration of parasite drag is that it varies with V^2, which means that the faster the aircraft flies the greater the parasite drag. Note again the squared function; a tripling of airspeed increases parasite drag nine times.

Since valuable engine power has to be used to overcome parasite drag, it is essential that parasite drag is kept to an absolute minimum. Such a lofty goal is normally achieved by shaping of all non-lifting components in such a way that their drag coefficient is as small as possible. Accordingly, by shaping the fuselage, skids, wheels, antennas and a host of other components as aerodynamically clean as possible, less power is wasted on this part of the aircraft's total drag.

Of interest here is the effect of slingloads. If, instead of carrying certain items inside the cabin, they are carried in a slingload, the aircraft maximum gross weight has not altered, but parasite drag certainly has. Power must be diverted to overcome the increased drag, the result being that the helicopter cannot perform to the same limit with a slingload as it can with the load inside the aircraft.

The rotor head, to which the blades are attached, is usually included as parasite drag even though the head is part of the rotor, the lift producer. Some manufacturers go to great lengths streamlining this part. A good example of this is the dome-shaped dish over the head of the Hughes 369 (500) helicopter.

If parasite drag includes all drags caused by non-lifting components of the helicopter, it follows that the other two drags, *profile* and *induced*, must be associated with the rotor system.

Profile Drag

Profile drag is made up of *form drag* and *skin friction*. Form drag is the resistance caused by frontal and rear areas of the rotor blades, while skin friction takes into consideration the slowdown of the airflow in close proximity to the skin of the blades, the *boundary layer*.

Form Drag

If a flat plate is presented flat-on to an airflow (Figure 4-2), a great deal of drag is caused by the flow's impact on the frontal surface, while a kind of suction occurs behind the plate. Drag so caused is called *form drag* and it may be reduced by *shaping*. Covering the frontal area with a rounded leading edge and attaching a wedge-shape trailing edge, as shown in Figure 4-2, substantially reduces form drag.

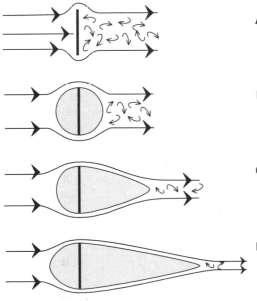

A. *Flat plate produces much impact drag at the front and substantial turbulence at the rear.*

B. *Ball shape reduces frontal impact and causes less turbulence at the rear. Form drag reduced to some 50% of the original.*

C. *Teardrop shape with a thickness/chord ratio of about 1 : 4 further reduces turbulence at the rear. Form drag now reduced to some 10% of the original.*

D. *Symmetrical airfoil shape produces large reduction in frontal impact drag and causes less turbulence at the rear. Form drag now reduced to about 5% of the original.*

Figure 4-2. *Effect of shaping on form drag produced by an object.*

Tests on helicopter blades have shown that a thickness to chord ratio (also referred to as fineness ratio) of approximately 1:7 (15 percent) produces relatively little form drag. The maximum thickness should be located about one-quarter the way back from the leading edge.

For a given shape, form drag produced is directly proportional to the V^2 of the airflow, so the higher the speed of the airflow the greater the form drag.

Skin Friction

When air flows past an object, air molecules closest to the skin are almost stationary with the skin. The next layers of molecules move at progressively faster rates until finally the outermost molecules move at the speed of the free relative airflow. Thus a layer of air is formed between the actual skin of the object and the relative airflow, called the *boundary layer*. Within this retarded layer, the motion of molecules produces friction, which is the cause of *skin friction drag*.

There are two types of boundary layer, the *laminar type* and the *turbulent type*. The laminar type can only be found in a region of decreasing air pressure, which means that a laminar boundary layer can begin at the leading edge of the airfoil, but cannot penetrate further than the point where the maximum deflection of the relative airflow occurs (and where minimum pressure is found).

The *laminar boundary layer* consists of very thin layers of air molecules sliding over each other. It is normally quite thin and produces little skin friction drag. It is extremely brittle, however, which means that even small specks of dust or ice on the airfoil surface can cause the layer to fracture into turbulence or even separate from the surface.

The *turbulent boundary layer* consists of revolving and disturbed air molecules. It is much thicker than its laminar counterpart and produces a great deal more skin friction drag. A good feature of the turbulent boundary layer, however, is its ability to adhere to the airfoil surface even if small obstructions such as dust are present.

The point where the laminar boundary layer changes into the turbulent boundary layer is called the *transition point*. Although the location of this point is partly governed by the pressure gradient within the relative airflow (it cannot be further back than the point where pressure is least), the major factor that determines the position of the transition point is the blade's airspeed. As airspeed is increased, the transition point moves forward due to an increase in the *Reynolds number* of the flow. (Reynolds number relates the inertial forces to the viscous forces in a flow and is affected, among other things, by airspeed.) As the result of the transition point moving forward with speed, a greater area of the blade becomes covered in the higher-drag turbulent boundary layer. Hence skin friction drag increases as airspeed increases, and vice versa.

The *separation point* is the point where the turbulent boundary layer thickens and separates from the airfoil and where the *wake* commences. The wake is similar to the disturbed water particles left behind a boat as it speeds through water.

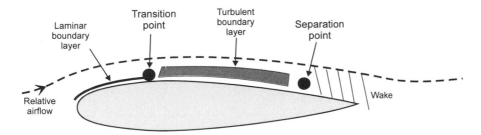

Figure 4-3. *Both types of boundary layer and the points delineating them. Note the "free" relative airflow passes over both boundary layers. For clarity the boundary layer below the airfoil has been omitted.*

There are three main factors that determine the amount of skin friction:

- **Surface Roughness**. The rougher the surface of an airfoil, the thicker the boundary layer and the greater the skin friction drag.

- **Shape of the Airfoil**. The further back the point of maximum thickness, the less the skin friction drag (ignoring airspeed).

- **Airspeed**. The higher the speed of air past a blade, the greater the skin friction drag.

Blade surfaces should be smooth and clean to reduce skin friction drag as much as possible. Skin friction drag is a serious hazard in helicopter operations because the engine power required to overcome it can be high. For instance, dust or spray from certain agricultural operations can accumulate on the blades to the extent that flight becomes impossible. Similarly, hoar frost on the blades can be totally incapacitating. The blades must be cleaned periodically during any operations where the surface of the blades becomes covered by impurities.

As mentioned earlier, form drag and skin friction combined produce profile drag, which is directly proportional to V (squared). Since V relates to the rotational velocity of blades (rotor rpm) and since this rotor rpm is more or less a constant, profile drag is essentially static (ignoring aircraft speed for the time being). By the same token, the local speed of a blade section near the rotor head is slower than that near the blade tip. Profile drag is then less further inboard and greater towards the tip of the blade sections.

Induced Drag

The previous chapter explained that lift production involves pressure differences between the air above the airfoil compared to that below because of deflection of air. Figure 3-1 in Chapter 3 supported the explanation that to produce net lift, there must be a positive deflection of air, which is assured when the downwash behind the airfoil is greater than the upwash in front. This downwash has a fundamental influence on induced drag, which is drag associated with lift production.

Imagine an airfoil at a certain angle of attack moving horizontally through air (Figure 4-4). Provided the velocity of the air remains subsonic (less than speed of sound), the downwash behind the trailing edge influences the manner in which the airflow approaches the leading edge. The greater the net deflection downward behind the trailing edge, the more the oncoming air approaches the leading edge from higher up.

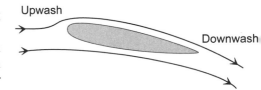

Figure 4-4. *Lift produced by greater downwash than upwash.*

The diagram of component forces in Figure 4-5 explains this behavior in simple terms. The net downwash (the actual downward movement of air after allowance has been made for the upwash at the blade's front) affects the oncoming horizontal unaffected relative airflow and causes it to approach the leading edge of the blade from above as the affected relative airflow. This reorientation depends on:

1. The *velocity of the relative airflow*, in that the faster the flow, the longer the unaffected relative airflow vector quantity and the smaller the effect of net downwash on the oncoming relative airflow.

2. The *amount of net downwash*, in that the stronger the downwash the greater the downward vector quantity and the greater its effect on the oncoming relative airflow.

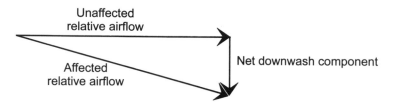

Figure 4-5. *Effect of downwash on unaffected relative airflow.*

The velocity of the relative airflow relates to rotor rpm (ignoring aircraft speed) and the effect of the relative airflow velocity in terms of induced drag is of minor concern, bearing in mind that rotor rpm is virtually a constant. The same cannot be said, however, for amount of downwash. The downwash created by a blade at a given rotational velocity is directly governed by angle of attack. The larger the angle of attack, the greater the resulting downwash is. In Chapter 3, Figure 3-5. we saw that the larger the angle of attack, the greater the lift coefficient and the smaller the angle of attack, the smaller the lift coefficient. Thus the downwash is directly proportional to lift coefficient.

A stronger downwash, produced by higher lift coefficient (angle of attack) values, provides a stronger induced flow. The reverse applies as well, the less the lift coefficient (angle of attack), the weaker the downwash and the less the induced flow. (Induced flow is essential for the production of the force that overcomes weight.)

Returning to Figure 4-5, one can see that downwash reorients the approaching (level, unaffected) relative airflow onto the leading edge of the blade. It causes it to come from higher up (producing the affected relative airflow). The greater the lift coefficient (the stronger the downwash) – the higher the direction from which the relative airflow strikes the airfoil.

Consider then the approaching relative airflow from two points of view, the unaffected airflow, which is level, and the *affected airflow*, which comes from higher up and which actually flows past the airfoil (Figure 4-6). The diagram exaggerates the distance ahead of the airfoil where the relative airflow reorients itself (this has been done to illustrate the point).

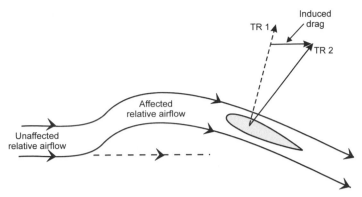

Figure 4-6. *Induced drag relates to the degree of reorientation of the unaffected relative airflow.*

TR 1 is the total reaction relative to the unaffected relative airflow, it is more vertical than TR 2, which is the total reaction resulting from the actual affected relative airflow. The vector quantity between these two total reactions, acting in the line of drag, represents induced drag. The induced drag so represented is totally determined by the degree of downwash behind the airfoil. If the downwash is stronger, TR 2 leans further aft and if the downwash is weaker, it leans closer to TR 1. Since the downwash is a consequence of lift production, it follows that the greater the amount of lift produced, the greater the induced drag experienced.

A blade airfoil, while in level flight, can generally alter its amount of lift (C_L ½ ρ V^2 S) only by altering its lift coefficient because V is more or less a constant (rotor rpm) and ½, ρ and S are similarly constants.

Thus an increase in the lift coefficient will increase induced drag and a decrease in lift coefficient will decrease induced drag.

Tip Vortices

In Chapter 3 we saw that lift production requires a pressure differential between the air above the airfoil and that below. Nature demands that whenever a pressure differential occurs, a pressure gradient will try to force air from the high pressure region to the low pressure region.

In the case of a helicopter blade there is a tendency for the higher pressure air below to move to the lower pressure air above. This can generally only take place around the blade tips. Figure 4-7 shows how this movement produces a circular motion of air around the tip, referred to as the tip vortex. The upward component of the vortex lies outside the span of the blade, it has no influence on the behavior of the relative airflow onto the blade. The downward component of the vortex occurs behind the blade, but within the span. Its effect is to increase the downwash. Thus tip vortex activity, by increasing the downwash behind the blade, must also increase the amount of induced drag.

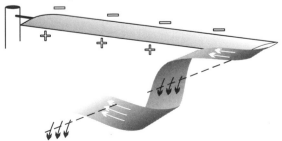

Figure 4-7. *Tip vortex produced by pressure gradient due to higher pressure below and lower pressure above the blade. Note downward component of the vortex is inside the blade span.*

The intensity of tip vortices responds to lift production. This means that the higher the angle of attack, the greater the lift coefficient, the stronger the effect of tip vortices and the greater the amount of induced drag. Tip vortices constitute a considerable portion of induced drag.

During the hover, tip vortices follow the travel of each blade tip and a spiral pattern of disturbed vortex air results. As the helicopter moves forward at increasing speeds, tip vortex activity becomes restricted to the lateral tip areas, and the disc behaves more like a solid form, shedding its vortices off the tips on the right and left, similar to fixed wing behavior.

Effect of Airspeed on Induced Drag

Since induced drag is proportional to induced flow, and since induced flow decreases as aircraft speed increases, it follows that induced drag reduces with airspeed. The reason for the decrease in induced flow with airspeed is discussed in detail in Chapter 6. For now, imagine the helicopter in a hover, where all the induced flow comes vertically down through the disc. If a strong wind were to blow, part of the downgoing induced flow would be blown horizontally "downwind," resulting in less air flowing through the disc vertically, and less induced flow. Forward speed has the same effect as the wind on induced flow. The faster the helicopter travels forward, the less the induced flow, and therefore, the less induced drag it experiences.

Effect of Aspect Ratio

Aspect ratio is the ratio of the blade's *span* to its *chord*. Typical ratios of light helicopter blades are roughly thirty to one (30:1). For example, a blade may have a length of 15 feet (450 cm) and a chord of 6 inches (15 cm). The aspect ratio of a blade determines to a large extent the amount of induced drag produced by the tip vortices.

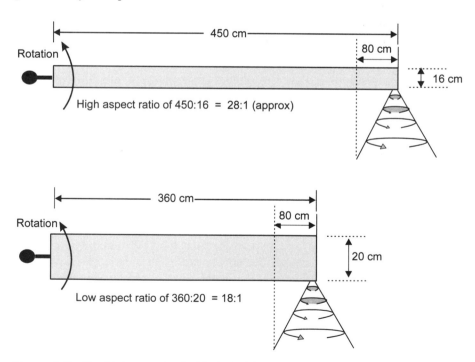

Figure 4-8. *The high aspect ratio blade had less area affected by tip vortices and as a result experiences less induced drag than the low aspect ratio blade which has a greater area affected by tip vortices.*

Figure 4-8 compares two blades of similar area. One has a larger span and smaller chord, thus a high aspect ratio, while the other has a smaller span and larger chord, and a low aspect ratio. The tip vortices produced by these blades are not greatly different in size since roughly the same amount of lift is produced by either blade. The high aspect ratio blade has less area affected by tip vortices, and as a result experiences less induced drag than the blade with a low aspect ratio, which has a greater area affected by tip vortices. Therefore:

The higher the aspect ratio of a blade - the smaller the amount of induced drag it produces.

To keep induced drag to an absolute minimum, blade designers try to build the longest blades possible (consistent with the expected role of the helicopter). In the past, material strength has limited designers in their quest to build high aspect ratio blades, but new, stronger, lighter metals and composite materials are beginning to whittle away at these design limitations.

Methods to Reduce Induced Drag

Wash-out

High angles of attack at a given rotor rpm produce high lift coefficient values, which result in large pressure differentials between the air above the blade and the air below the blade. Since a large portion of induced drag is produced near the blade tip regions through vortex action, reducing the lift coefficient in those regions should also reduce induced drag.

Wash-out is the structural design of a blade that reduces the lift coefficient at the blade tips. Wash-out is essentially the reduction in *blade angle* from the blade root toward the tip (built into the blade during construction). The effect of wash-out is a reduction in the angle of attack (and therefore reduction in C_L) of the blade sections near the tip compared to angles of attack near the blade root.

The wash-out design is also found in blades in order to distribute lift production as evenly as possible from root to tip. More detailed explanations of wash-out are found in Chapter 7.

Tip Design

Apart from wash-out, designers use various techniques to reduce the lift coefficient towards the tip by reducing the blade's camber and/or chord by using a taper in thickness or plan (ie, "pointing" the tip when viewed from above).

Total Drag Curve

When the three types of drag are plotted against indicated airspeed you obtain a curve that shows total drag (Figure 4-9).

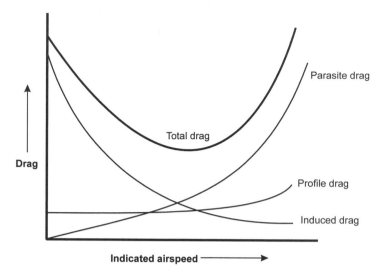

Figure 4-9. *Parasite, profile and inducted drag combine into total drag.*

Parasite drag is considered to be nil at zero airspeed. This ignores the possible drag caused by the downwash from the rotor onto the top of the fuselage while hovering, since such drag is considered insignificant. As airspeed increases, parasite drag increases with the square of velocity. The parasite drag curve therefore climbs rapidly as the aircraft speed increases.

Profile drag, relating to the blades, is essentially affected only by rotor rpm because that determines the speed of the flow past the blade.

Although airspeed in forward flight adds to the velocity of the advancing blade, the opposite happens to the velocity of the retreating blade. The effect is that at low airspeeds the gain on one blade cancels the loss on the other. However, the V^2 factor becomes considerably more effective on the advancing blade at higher airspeeds and therefore profile drag increases as these higher airspeeds are attained.

The profile drag curve is therefore more or less horizontal initially, but climbs as medium speed values are reached and exceeded.

Induced drag reduces as aircraft speed increases, so this curve starts high at the hover and lowers as speed increases. Since some lift production is essential at any speed, the induced drag curve will never reduce to zero.

Total drag is the sum total of the three drags plotted on the graph. Note that the total drag curve is U-shaped, indicating a high value of total drag at low as well as at high airspeeds. The minimum total drag is therefore found at an in-between speed, directly below the bottom of the U-shaped curve.

Because of the shape of the total drag curve, it is impossible to determine how total drag behaves with changes in airspeed unless a range of airspeeds is stipulated. For instance, one can only predict a decrease in total drag if the airspeed is from low to medium, which corresponds to the speed range where the U-shaped curve descends.

The bottom of the total drag curve is not the same as the bottom of the drag coefficient curve. This highlights the fact that drag coefficient is only part of total drag.

Conclusion

The force of drag must be overcome to ensure that the rotor maintains a satisfactory rpm (overcoming profile and induced drag) and to ensure that the helicopter's forward speed, whatever that may be, is maintained (overcoming parasite drag). In normal powered flight, power from the engine is used to combat the effects of total drag. Chapter 13 explains these aspects of flight under the headings of parasite power, profile power and induced power.

Review 4

Drag

1. The drag coefficient of an airfoil is determined by its _____ and _____, its minimum value is found at (zero/four) degrees angle of attack.

2. The three types of drag experienced by a helicopter in forward flight are _____, _____ and _____.

3. When the speed of a helicopter increases from 20 knots to 60 knots, parasite drag increases by a factor of (three/four/six/nine).

4. Form drag can be reduced by _____.

5. Skin friction drag is caused by friction between molecules in the _____ layer which is a (retarded/accelerated) layer of air between the airfoil and the _____.

6. A laminar boundary layer is normally (thick/thin), it produces (much/little) skin friction drag and it (is/is not) readily subject to separation from the airfoil surface.

7. A turbulent boundary layer is normally (thick/thin), it produces (much/little) skin friction drag and it (is/is not) readily subject to separation from the airfoil surface.

8. The point where the laminar boundary layer changes into the turbulent boundary layer is called the (separation/transition) point.

9. With an increase in airspeed, skin friction drag (increases/decreases) because the transition point moves (forward/aft) and the boundary layer (thickens/thins).

10. Induced drag is the result of differences in ____ above and below the airfoil and is (directly/inversely) proportional to induced flow.

11. With an increase in airspeed, induced drag (increases/decreases) and parasite drag (increases/decreases).

12. An increase in aspect ratio tends to (increase/decrease) induced drag.

13. Wash-out is a structural design which (increases/ decreases) the (blade angle/angle of attack) from blade root to blade tip.

14. Total drag of a helicopter is (high/low) at zero airspeed, it (increases/decreases) with an increase in airspeed and beyond medium airspeed it (increases/decreases).

Lift/Drag Ratio

A number of principles in aerodynamics are fundamental to flight. The lift/drag ratio, especially as related to helicopter aerodynamics, is one of those principles. Previous chapters dealing with lift, drag and total reaction were a prelude to discussing the lift/drag ratio.

As explained, the total reaction has two component forces, lift and drag. In a reverse sense, the magnitude of these two components and their relationship determine the length of the total reaction and its orientation.

Consider Figure 5-1. A given total reaction will "lean" away from the vertical (from lift, Figure A) because of a certain amount of lift and drag. If lift is increased while drag is kept constant (as in B), the total reaction will lean closer to the vertical. If drag is reduced while lift is kept constant (as in C), the total reaction will also lean closer to the vertical. In both cases the greater the lift and/or the smaller the drag (improved lift/drag ratio), the more the total reaction leans to the vertical (to lift).

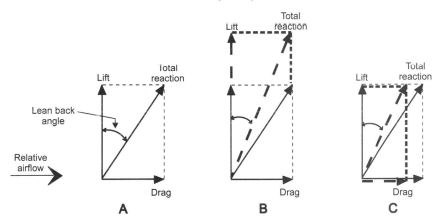

Figure 5-1. *Angular difference between lift and total reaction reduces when the L/D ratio is improved.*

For the sake of efficiency, a given total reaction should lean as close to lift as possible so that it provides the greatest amount of lift for the smallest amount of drag. It must be noted that drag will always be present to some extent. For that reason it is not possible for the total reaction to be in line with lift or for it to act at right angles to the relative airflow.

The angular difference between lift and total reaction (the lean-back angle of the total reaction away from lift) is determined by the relationship between lift and drag - the lift/drag ratio (L/D ratio). The common factors in the lift and drag formulas cancel out which permits us to define the L/D ratio as the lift coefficient/drag coefficient ratio (C_L/C_D ratio). In other words, lift relates to drag as the lift coefficient relates to the drag coefficient.

The lift coefficient and the drag coefficient are responsive to two factors only: *shape* and *angle of attack*. The lift/drag ratio of a given shape is therefore determined by the angle of attack and is a fundamental principle when considering L/D ratios.

Best (or Maximum) L/D Ratio

To determine the best L/D ratio (and therefore high efficiency), the lift coefficient and the drag coefficient are plotted against angle of attack on a single graph (Figure 5-2).

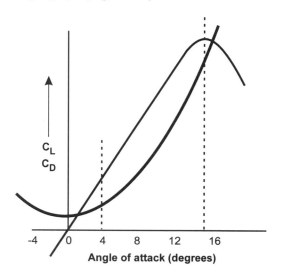

Figure 5-2. *Best L/D ratio is found at approximately 4° angle of attack. (Symmetrical airfoil.)*

The maximum lift coefficient occurs at the critical (stall) angle, which also has a high drag coefficient. Thus the ratio of lift coefficient to drag coefficient at high angles of attack is very poor and results in grossly inefficient performance. The minimum drag coefficient occurs at zero degree angle of attack (for the symmetrical shape) where the lift coefficient is zero. Aircraft performance is impossible at that angle of attack.

Thus the best L/D ratio lies somewhere between the two extremes just mentioned. It is found at the angle of attack where the greatest percentage surplus exists between the lift coefficient over the drag coefficient.

Figure 5-2 shows that the best L/D ratio for the airfoil under consideration is found at about 4° angle of attack. When the helicopter is flown so that the angle of attack on the blade is at or near this value, a high degree of efficiency is obtained. At that angle of attack, the production of lift is accompanied by the least amount of drag which permits us to say that flight at the best L/D ratio is flight at minimum drag (for the lift being produced).

Drag will be less if the rotor only is considered and it will be more for the entire helicopter. Thus the L/D ratio for the rotor only will be slightly better than for the entire helicopter and will usually be found at a smaller angle of attack. Figure 5-3 depicts typical angles of attack for the L/D ratios involving a particular rotor. Ratios for best L/D about 8:1 are not uncommon, the associated angle of attack is about 4°, varying by rotor type. When considering the entire aircraft, including slingloads, the L/D ratio is degraded.

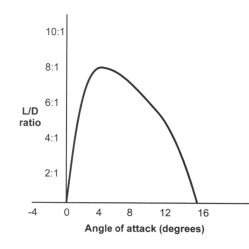

Figure 5-3. *Angle of attack giving the best L/D ratio of some 8:1 (for this symmetrical airfoil) is found at approximately +4°.*

A high L/D ratio does not mean that the blade's lift is at maximum production. Much more lift can be produced at higher angles of attack, improving the helicopter's performance. However, a reduced L/D ratio and more drag are the results. Since added drag demands more power, efficiency is lost.

Other Factors Influencing L/D Ratio

Apart from angle of attack and shape, any design that reduces drag without adversely affecting lift characteristics must produce a better L/D ratio.

Aspect ratio. For a given area (S), the higher the aspect ratio, the lower the drag for an almost unaffected lift, producing a better L/D ratio and more efficient blade performance.

Increasing the span of a constant-area blade and reducing the chord (thus improving aspect ratio) decreases induced drag, though profile drag remains the same. Since the total drag of the blade is the sum of profile drag and induced drag, it follows that by keeping the first-mentioned the same but reducing the latter, total drag must become less.

Rotor rpm. Rotor rpm (V) in the lift and drag formulas relates to the rotational speed of the rotor blades, that is, the rotor rpm. As a blade's profile drag varies in opposition to its induced drag with increased aircraft speed, the most favorable L/D ratios will be achieved in a specific rotor rpm range recommended by the designer.

Airspeed. Aircraft speed changes the induced flow through the rotor, which, in turn, alters the blade angle of attack and affects the L/D ratio. Most Flight Manuals recommend specific speeds for certain operations where maximum rotor efficiency is needed, such as during autorotation.

Conclusion

The orientation and size of the total reaction is determined by the lift and drag created by an airfoil. For any given amount of lift, the least amount of drag produces a total reaction nearest to lift, allowing the aircraft to fly close to its most efficient performance.

The three diagrams below indicate the common points where the best L/D ratio (minimum drag) is located. Four degrees angle of attack is approximate, some helicopters may have a best L/D ratio at higher or lower angles of attack.

Chapter 6, dealing with forces involved in helicopter flight, will refer to these diagrams repeatedly – you must understand the principles involved.

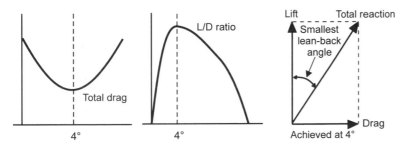

Figure 5-4. *All three diagrams depict flight under conditions of best L/D ratio, assumed to occur at approximately 4° angle of attack.*

Review 5

Lift/Drag Ratio

1. When an airfoil operates at its best lift/drag ratio, the angle between lift and total reaction is (zero/as small as possible).

2. The total reaction (can/cannot) act at right angles to the relative airflow.

3. If lift remains constant but drag is reduced, the lift/drag ratio (improves/gets worse) and the total reaction leans (closer/further away from) lift.

4. An airfoil's lift/drag ratio is determined by its _____ and _____ .

5. The best lift/drag ratio is normally found when an airfoil operates at a (large/small) angle of attack.

6. When operating at best lift/drag ratio, lift production (is/is not) at its maximum but drag is at its (minimum/maximum).

Aerodynamic Forces

Definitions

The following terms need to be understood before we proceed further. More definitions appear in the Glossary at the back of the book.

tip path.

The circular path described by the tips of rotor blades.

tip path plane.

The plane within which the tips of rotor blades travel. It is parallel to the plane of rotation which acts through the rotor head. A pilot may alter this plane through movement of the cyclic control.

axis of rotation.

The line through the rotor head at right angles to the plane of rotation (POR). The blades actually rotate around this axis.

shaft axis.

The line consistent with the rotor shaft (mast). Only when the plane of rotation is exactly perpendicular to the shaft axis will the axis of rotation coincide with the shaft axis.

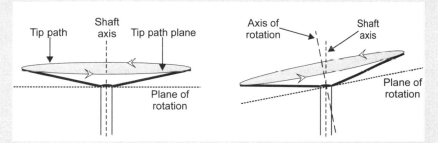

Tip path, tip path plane, shaft axis and plane of rotation. In the situation above, shaft axis and plane of rotation coincide.

Axis of rotation through the rotor head at right angles to the plane of rotation while the shaft axis remains in line with the rotor mast

disc area.

The area contained within the tip path plane. In flight, this area is not a constant since it is affected by the coning angle of the blades.

chord (line).

The straight line between the blade's leading edge and its trailing edge.

blade angle (also known as **pitch angle**).

The angular difference between the chord of the blade and the plane of rotation (POR). This angle may be altered by the pilot through movement of the collective lever or through the cyclic control.

> Most explanations in this book are based on counterclockwise rotating rotors viewed from above. But many helicopters have rotors that spin clockwise, which will affect the direction in which certain reactions work. In some instances, the text explains how this difference in rotation affects a particular situation, but in the absence of such text, you should determine the consequence of clockwise rotation yourself.

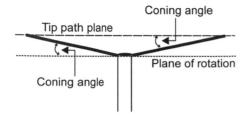

Coning angle

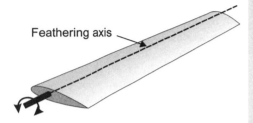

Blade angle can be altered by rotating the blade around the feathering axis

angle of attack.

The angular difference between the chord of the blade and the relative airflow (also known as relative wind).

coning angle.

The angular difference between the feathering axis and the plane of rotation. It may also be defined as the angular difference between the feathering axis and the tip path plane.

feathering axis.

The straight-line axis between the root of the blade and its tip about which the blade can alter its blade angle.

feathering.

The movement of the blade about its feathering axis (which results in pitch angle changes).

disc loading.

The gross weight of the helicopter divided by the disc area, expressed as lb/sq inch or kg/m^2. Since disc area is not a constant in flight, it follows that disc loading cannot be a constant.

blade loading.

The gross weight of the helicopter divided by the combined area of the helicopter blades, expressed as above. Since blade area does not alter, blade loading must be a constant in flight (ignoring weight and g changes).

solidity.

The ratio of total blade area to disc area. Solidity is a function of ability to absorb power from the engine and potential to provide rotor thrust.

flapping.

Movement of a blade in the vertical sense relative to the plane of rotation.

lead-lagging (dragging).

Movement of a blade forward or aft in the plane of rotation.

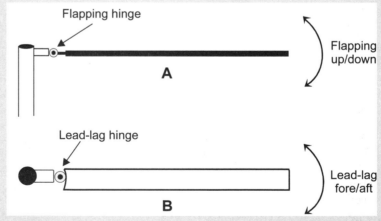

"A" shows a blade's ability to flap up/down around the **flapping hinge**.

"B" shows a blade's ability to move forward or aft around the **lead-lag hinge**.

Rotor Systems

fully articulated rotor.

This system allows blades to flap, feather and lead-lag (drag). Generally these movements are allowed through hinges or bearings. It is common for rotors with more than two blades to use the fully articulated principle.

semi-rigid rotor.

This system allows blade freedom to flap and feather but not to lead-lag. This rotor utilizes the "see-saw" principle where one blade flaps up while the other flaps down around a gimbal ring arrangement, also referred to as a *teetering hinge*. It is a common system used in two-bladed rotors.

Although lead-lag forces apply in this system just as they do in fully articulated rotors, lead-lag is usually absorbed within the blades themselves. Some semi-rigid systems utilize flexible units at the blade attachment point, and/or a flexible mast to absorb a degree of lead-lag forces.

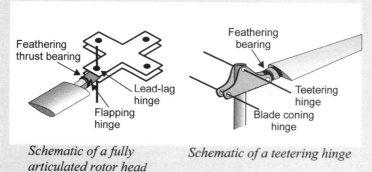

Schematic of a fully articulated rotor head   *Schematic of a teetering hinge*

rigid rotor.

This system allows the blade freedom to feather only, it does not allow for freedom to flap or lead-lag (drag). Control loads in this type of rotor are very high and stability is difficult to achieve. In advanced rigid-rotor systems, it is usual to incorporate computer systems to facilitate ease of control and stability.

Summary.

Modern technology has resulted in the production of rotor systems that use the combined principles of two or all of the above-described rotors. For instance, some manufacturers refer to their system as a "semi articulated rotor" while others combine the principle of the rigid hub with flexible blade root attachments.

Most rotor systems can be classified fundamentally as fully articulated, semi-rigid or rigid.

Introduction

Helicopters, unlike fixed-wing airplanes, obtain the required force to oppose weight from rotational movement of blades. Understanding how lift is produced by rotating blades is difficult to some because the airflow which ultimately passes each blade consists of a number of seemingly conflicting flows, produced by:

- rotation of the blades
- induced action, and
- airflow as a result of forward or sideways flight

Notwithstanding the difficulties, it is important that you understand the cause and effects of these flows, and their interaction.

Rotational Airflow (Vr)

As a blade rotates it creates a relative airflow onto its leading edge, called Vr (velocity as a result of rotation). At the rotor hub Vr is slower than that at the tip, where the airflow is quite fast. A vector quantity used to represent Vr per blade section for a given rotor rpm, (see Figure 6-1) shows a large vector (A-B) for flow near the tip in the left diagram and a small vector (A-B) for flow near the hub on the right.

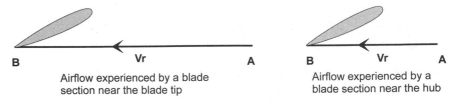

Airflow experienced by a blade
section near the blade tip

Airflow experienced by a
blade section near the hub

Figure 6-1. *Vector quantities of airflow experienced by different blade sections. Rotor rpm constant.*

The vector for Vr also changes with rotor rpm. If rotor rpm increases, the magnitude of Vr increases and if rotor rpm decreases, the magnitude of Vr decreases. In Figure 6-2, vector A-B represents Vr for a given blade section at high rotor rpm in the left-hand diagram and vector A-B represents Vr for the same blade section at low rotor rpm in the diagram on the right.

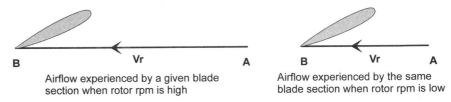

Airflow experienced by a given blade
section when rotor rpm is high

Airflow experienced by the same
blade section when rotor rpm is low

Figure 6-2. *Vector quantities of airflow experienced by a given blade section at high and low rotor rpm.*

Vr can be considered for any blade section and vectors will be longer or shorter depending on the section considered, as long as the rotor rpm is constant. Vr can also be discussed with respect to rotor rpm, in which case vectors will be shorter or longer depending on rotor rpm, as long as the blade section is at a constant position from the root or tip.

In summary, vectors A-B (Vr) can represent blade section or rotor rpm, but not both, as variable, at the same time.

Blade Angle and Angle of Attack

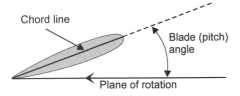

Figure 6-3. *Blade angle is the angular difference between chord line and the plane of rotation. In the absence of other airflows, blade angle is also angle of attack.*

The angle between the chord of the blade and the plane of rotation (Figure 6-3) is known as the *blade angle* or *pitch angle*, and is controlled through the collective pitch control. If the pilot pulls the collective lever up blade angle increases, and if the pilot pushes the collective lever down, the blade angle decreases. The airflow (vector A-B) is in the plane of rotation and as long as no other airflows interfere, the blade angle is also the angle of attack.

The blade angle does not affect the direction from which Vr occurs. Whether the plane of rotation is parallel to the ground or tilted, Vr will always be parallel to the plane of rotation.

Induced Flow

Newton's law of action and reaction supports the principle that during helicopter flight the rotor must force down a volume of air. This *induced flow* of air travels down through the rotor when the helicopter is in normal powered flight and is the result of lift that has deflected the airflow downward.

Induced flow is defined as the mass of air that is forced down by the rotor action.

Whereas most of the air molecules will pass through the rotor, those molecules enticed down from some height above the rotor disc may find that when they reach disc height, the helicopter has traveled forward so that they miss the rotor disc altogether. So induced flow can be defined as the total mass of air forced down by the action of the rotor, most of the air will pass through the rotor but a small part may miss it. Diagrams in the next few chapters displaying induced flow will refer only to what moves through the rotor.

If we take induced flow into consideration now, we see that the rotor blade experiences two airflows, one from straight ahead (vector A-B, Vr) caused by rotation and one from above (vector C-A) caused by induced flow. These two flows create a *resultant airflow* (vector C-B) onto the blade, and that *resultant airflow* (or *relative airflow*, RAF) is no longer parallel to the plane of rotation (see Figure 6-5).

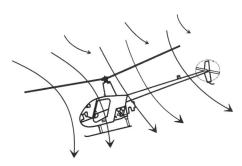

Figure 6-4. *Induced flow entails all air molecules forced down by rotor action; not all of these molecules go through the rotor.*

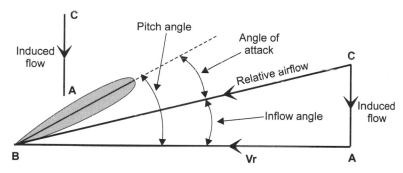

Figure 6-5. *Airflow due to rotation (A-B) and induced flow (C-A) combine to produce the relative airflow (C-B). Note the effect of induced flow on angle of attack.*

The resultant airflow presents a number of important variables (refer to Figure 6-5 as you read each of the following statements):

• The angle of attack decreases when induced flow becomes established, and is less than the blade angle. When the induced flow increases for a given blade section and rotor rpm, the angle of attack decreases, and when induced flow decreases, the angle of attack increases.

Angle of attack and induced flow are inversely proportional for a given blade section and rotor rpm.

• The inflow angle is the angle between the plane of rotation and the resultant airflow (RAF). For a given rotor rpm, the inflow angle increases as induced flow increases and decreases as induced flow decreases.

> **Inflow angle and the induced flow are directly proportional for a given Vr, rotor rpm.**

- When the rotor rpm (Vr) increases and the induced flow remains constant, the angle of attack increases and inflow angle decreases. A reduction in rotor rpm (Vr) will decrease the angle of attack and increase the inflow angle.

> **For a given induced flow, the inflow angle and rotor rpm are inversely proportional.**

Air Flow Caused by Aircraft Velocity

The resultant airflow from Vr and induced flow, (the relative airflow, explained above) is the airflow that affects the angle of attack only when the helicopter is stationary (hovering) in no-wind conditions. Whenever the aircraft is not stationary, or is stationary but affected by the wind, the aircraft velocity vector is introduced which influences the resultant airflow. This influence is discussed in the next chapter.

The Forces

Figure 6-6 shows lift drawn at right angles to the relative airflow and drag in line with the relative airflow. As explained in Chapter 5, lift and drag are components of the total reaction which responds to the lift/drag ratio as a vector in terms of length and in terms of orientation away (lean-back) from lift.

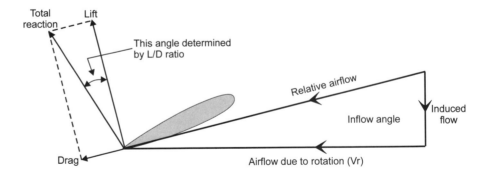

Figure 6-6. *Lift at right angles to the relative airflow and drag in line with the relative airflow are components of the total reaction.*

Total Rotor Thrust

The total reaction (TR) shown in Figure 6-7 is required to provide the opposing force to weight, but the diagram clearly shows that the TR does not act in line with weight; it "leans back" from the vertical. Thus a component of the total reaction must be vectored that *does act* in line with and opposite to weight. That component vector is called *rotor thrust* (RT), it is the force produced by each blade section to overcome part of the helicopter's weight. When the rotor thrusts of all the blade sections are combined, *total rotor thrust* (TRT) acting through the top of the mast provides the force (or component force) that overcomes the weight of the helicopter.

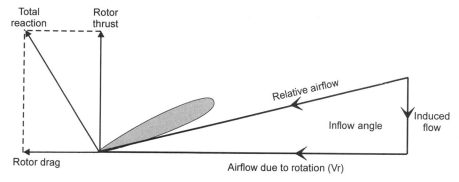

Figure 6-7. *Total reaction can be split up into two component forces: rotor thrust, acting against the gross weight of the helicopter; and rotor drag (torque), acting against rotation of the blade.*

Total rotor thrust acts in line with the axis of rotation at right angles to the plane of rotation. Its magnitude is equal to aircraft weight when the helicopter is hovering in no-wind conditions or in certain unaccelerated steady flight conditions, such as stabilized vertical climbs or descents.

Whenever the rotor disc is not parallel to the earth's surface (such as in forward flight), total rotor thrust is split into a vertical and a forward component. Under those conditions, the vertical component of total rotor thrust must overcome the gross weight of the helicopter (Figure 6-8).

Rotor Drag (Torque)

Rotor drag is the component of total reaction at right angles to rotor thrust (Figure 6-7). Rotor drag is in the plane of rotation, but in a direction opposite to that of blade travel. Many texts refer to rotor drag as torque and to accommodate that custom, our text will occasionally add that term (or the abbreviation TQ) in brackets after rotor drag. Do be careful not to confuse *rotor drag* (acting in the plane of rotation) with *aerodynamic drag* (acting in line with the relative airflow).

A helicopter in powered flight requires engine power to overcome rotor drag so that the rotor will maintain its rpm. During autorotative flight, rotor drag is overcome by an aerodynamic force.

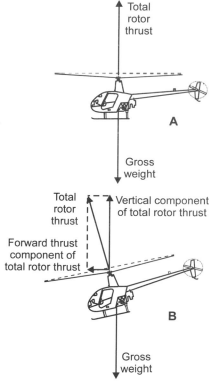

Figure 6-8. *In a calm hover (**A**), total rotor thrust is equal and opposite to the aircraft gross weight.*
*In forward flight (**B**), the vertical component of total rotor thrust is equal and opposite to the gross weight.*

Angle of Attack and the Rotor Thrust/Rotor Drag Ratio

Total rotor thrust (TRT) is the force that overcomes weight, but a penalty must be paid for the associated rotor drag (or torque) in terms of power, which is limited. For the sake of efficiency, there should be as much total rotor thrust (TRT) and as little rotor drag as possible, that is, the TRT/rotor drag ratio should be as high as possible.

In both diagrams of Figure 6-9 we can see once again that the total reaction determines the amounts of rotor thrust and rotor drag. If the TR leans further away from the axis of rotation, possibly due to a high angle of attack (as in the right hand diagram), the amount of rotor thrust reduces while rotor drag increases. Similarly, if the TR were to "stand up" more, possibly because of a small angle of attack (as in the left hand diagram), the amount of rotor thrust increases and rotor drag decreases. Thus the TRT/rotor drag ratio is entirely determined by the size and orientation of the total reaction (TR). Chapter 5 explained that the TR leans as close to lift (or axis of rotation here) when the L/D ratio is maximum.

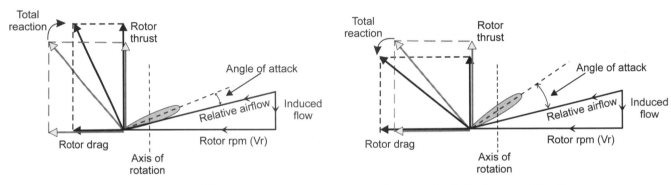

Small angle of attack - good L/D ratio. Total reaction orientated closer to the axis of rotation, a better ratio of rotor thrust/rotor drag is produced

Large angle of attack - poor L/D ratio. Total reaction orientated further away from the axis of rotation, a worse ratio of rotor thrust/rotor drag is produced

Figure 6-9. *Effect of changes in angle of attack on orientation of the total reaction. Total reaction closer to or further away from the axis of rotation influences the rotor thrust/rotor drag ratio.*

Therefore, if the TRT/rotor drag ratio is to be at its best, the total reaction should lean as close as possible to the axis of rotation, the blade should operate at the angle of attack for best L/D ratio, (minimum drag).

Induced Flow and the Rotor Thrust/Rotor Drag Ratio

Induced flow also influences the orientation of the total reaction (Figure 6-10). In the right-hand diagram you can see that if the induced flow decreases while rotor rpm stays the same, the inflow angle decreases and the angle of attack increases (if the blade angle is kept constant). To avoid an increased angle of attack the collective control lever is lowered by the pilot, which reduces the blade angle. The smaller inflow angle causes the total reaction to orient itself more to the vertical (towards the axis of rotation). As a result, rotor thrust increases, while rotor drag decreases.

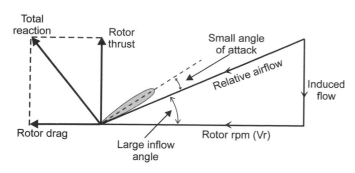
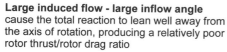
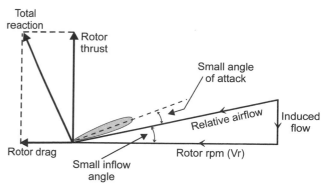

Large induced flow - large inflow angle
cause the total reaction to lean well away from
the axis of rotation, producing a relatively poor
rotor thrust/rotor drag ratio

Small induced flow - small inflow angle
cause the total reaction to lean closer to
the axis of rotation, a better
rotor thrust/rotor drag ratio results

Figure 6-10. *Effect of difference in induced flow and inflow angle on the rotor thrust/ rotor drag ratio. In both diagrams the angle of attack and Vr are the same. The lift and drag vectors have been omitted for clarity.*

In the left diagram of Figure 6-10, a larger inflow angle and a larger blade angle (high collective setting) can maintain a given angle of attack. However the orientation of the relative airflow and size of the inflow angle cause the total reaction to lean well away from the axis of rotation, resulting in a poor rotor thrust/rotor drag ratio.

Note from these explanations the relationship between induced flow and collective lever setting for a given rotor rpm and angle of attack.

Let us now consider the influence of both angle of attack and induced flow on the TRT/rotor drag ratio. It can be stated that:

> **Best efficiency is obtained (maximum TRT/rotor drag ratio) when the angle of attack on the blade produces the least amount of drag and when the collective lever is at the lowest position possible.**

Inflow Angle

Since Vr is more-or-less a constant and the range of angles of attack is relatively small, the inflow angle has a very strong influence on the total reaction, and hence the TRT/rotor drag ratio. *In generalized terms*, the higher the collective setting, the larger the inflow angle, the greater the amount of rotor drag and the greater the requirement for power. In contrast, the lower the collective setting, the smaller the inflow angle, the less the amount of rotor drag and the less the requirement for power.

The Force Opposing Weight

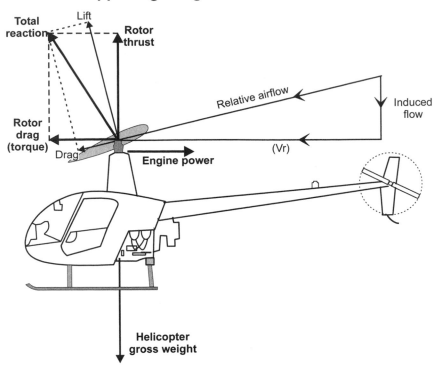

Figure 6-11. *Diagram showing all the forces acting on the blade and depicting rotor thrust as the force that assists in overcoming the gross weight of the helicopter.*

Figure 6-11 illustrates all the forces acting on the rotor blade in hover flight. These forces contribute to the production of total rotor thrust (acting through the rotor head), which overcomes the weight of the aircraft. If weight does not change, the requirement for total rotor thrust (or its component) does not change. This is highlighted in Figure 6-12 which shows two helicopters, identical in all respects, hovering at the same height, same rotor rpm and similar gross weight. Since their weights are the same it follows that their total rotor thrusts are the same.

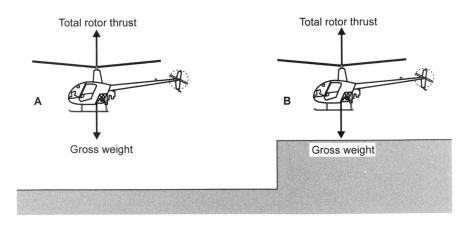

Figure 6-12. *Helicopters A and B have precisely the same total rotor thrust but B produces the total rotor thrust at a slightly smaller angle of attack, less lift and less power (and a slightly lower collective setting).*

Factors Influencing Rotor Thrust

The following four factors have a fundamental effect on rotor thrust production and/or the requirement for rotor thrust:

- air density
- rotor rpm
- blade (pitch) angle
- disc area

Air Density

Rotor thrust is dependent on lift production. Chapter 3 explained that density of air has a strong influence on lift produced and to understand how this influence affects rotor thrust we must examine the lift formula.

$$Lift = C_L \; \tfrac{1}{2} \, \rho \, V^2 \, S$$

$\tfrac{1}{2}$ and S (surface area of blades) are constants while V can be considered essentially a constant since it relates largely to rotor rpm (Vr) which does not alter greatly in practice (ignoring aircraft speed). Thus the two remaining items in the formula which are able to be changed are C_L and ρ. This means that for a constant lift, a reduction in ρ must involve a corresponding increase in C_L. We learned in Chapter 3 that C_L is directly proportional to angle of attack and therefore an increase in C_L is achieved by increasing the angle of attack which, invariably, involves a higher collective setting.

There are a number of items that reduce air density: low atmospheric pressure, increased altitude, hot and humid conditions. In contrast, high pressure, low altitude, cold and dry conditions increase density. Each combination is associated with a specific angle of attack.

To illustrate this practically, when a helicopter flies level at increasing altitudes where ρ becomes less, the blades must operate at progressively greater angles of attack (involving greater blade angles and inflow angles) to generate enough rotor thrust for flight. The greater the inflow angle, the worse the TRT/rotor drag ratio and the greater the demand for power.

Since power is finite it follows that there must come an altitude where the available power is insufficient for sustained level flight. Alternatively, there must come an altitude where the blades reach their maximum useable angle of attack, C_{Lmax}. Thus ρ ultimately determines how high a helicopter can fly, whether it can hover at a given altitude or whether it can carry out maneuvers, such as turning.

In summary, reduced air density causes the helicopter pilot to struggle with:

- a requirement for larger angles of attack
- a worsening TRT/rotor drag ratio
- a requirement for more power

The helicopter's maximum operating altitude and maneuverability are therefore directly related to these limiting factors.

Rotor rpm

In general, an increase in rotor rpm increases rotor thrust, and a decrease in rotor rpm decreases rotor thrust.

Blade Angle

In general, an increase in blade angle increases total rotor thrust while a decrease in blade angle decreases total rotor thrust.

Disc Area

Generally speaking, the larger the rotor disc the greater the total rotor thrust produced. Although the diameter of a given rotor disc ought to be determined by blade length (a fixed value), the influence of the coning angle is to reduce the size of the disc to some degree. The coning angle is dictated by two forces, the combined rotor thrust of the blade and centrifugal force.

In Figure 6-13 you see that the combined rotor thrust of the blade, acting at right angles to the feather axis, tries to increase the coning angle. Centrifugal force, determined by rotor rpm, acts in line with the plane of rotation and tries to reduce the coning angle. (For a constant radius, centrifugal force is equal to centripetal force.)

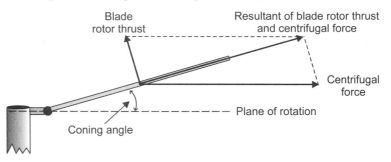

Figure 6-13. *Coning angle, governed by the resultant of combined rotor thrust of the blade, and centrifugal force acting through the blade's centre of gravity.*

Thus the resultant of a blade's total rotor thrust and centrifugal force determines the coning angle. If the rotor thrust increases and centrifugal force remains the same, the coning angle increases and disc area becomes smaller. Similarly, if the centrifugal force increases (when rotor rpm increases) while rotor thrust remains the same, the coning angle decreases and disc area becomes larger.

Without centrifugal force, coning angles would continue to increase until the blades finally meet directly above the mast, the result would be most unfortunate. It is therefore very important that you never exceed rotor rpm limits, especially the low limit, determined by the manufacturer.

Centrifugal force is formulated as: $\dfrac{m \ x \ V^2}{r}$

With V (rotor rpm) practically a constant, if mass increases then centrifugal force increases and, for a given rotor thrust produced by the blade, the coning angle decreases. Thus by adding mass to a rotor blade, centrifugal force increases with beneficial results for the coning angle. This technique is used in some "high inertia blades" when a few ounces of lead are placed inside the blade tips, which travel at considerable speed.

The addition of mass at the tips increases the moment of inertia of blades (which increases angular momentum) so that for the same rotor rpm, the blades operate at a smaller coning angle compared to blades without weights at their tips.

Significant aspects of high-inertia blades are:

1. Rotor rpm tends to fluctuate less. A number of factors causes blades to speed up or slow down as they rotate. A high-inertia blade acts like a flywheel, resisting rpm changes, and therefore, rotor rpm is more stable.

2. Once operational, maintaining rotor rpm requires less power. A blade with a huge coning angle has its rotor thrust pointing inward and therefore the rotor thrust, needed for the vertical component that opposes the aircraft weight, has to be large (Figure 6-14, A). Reducing the coning angle creates a more vertical rotor thrust which decreases the total requirement for rotor thrust (Figure 6-14, B). As a consequence, a rotor which operates with a small coning angle requires less rotor thrust compared to a rotor with a large coning angle (while at similar rotor rpm). This allows the helicopter to operate at a smaller angle of attack, with less rotor drag and less power.

3. The helicopter's landing flare is easier to execute. Low-inertia rotors tend to lose rotor rpm quickly towards the end of the flare, leaving little time to maneuver the aircraft. High-inertia rotors maintain rotor rpm better and in some helicopters the pilot can flare at the end of an autorotation, turn the aircraft around and land it.

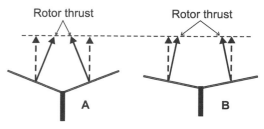

Figure 6-14. *Effect of coning angle on rotor thrust required to provide the opposing force to weight.*

Although high-inertia blades have great advantages, design problems and operational requirements still result in some helicopters being produced with low-inertia blades. Light helicopters, especially those with internal combustion engines, cannot be fitted with the rotor head strength required for high inertia systems. If high inertia blades were fitted, the required strength and associated weight might well be unacceptably high.

From an operational point of view, low inertia rotors allow for considerable ease of disc attitude control, they are more maneuverable but staying within rotor rpm limits requires more vigilance in turbulence. Should rotor rpm fall to low values as the result of poor piloting techniques, regaining rotor rpm is quicker in the low inertia system. This point is worth noting by pilots who are accustomed to flying low inertia rotor helicopters and then change to a high inertia rotor helicopter.

Conclusion

A most important matter to remember from this chapter is the association between total rotor thrust (TRT) and rotor rpm. If the rotor rpm reduces by 10%, the TRT (not lift) reduces by 20%, etc. This means that a small reduction in rotor rpm has a dramatic effect on TRT. It once again underlines the necessity, throughout flight, to maintain rotor rpm within the limits set by the manufacturer.

Review 6

Aerodynamic Forces

1. The axis of rotation passes through the _____ and is always at right angles/parallel) to the plane of rotation.

2. The disc area is the area contained with the _____ and in flight, the area (is/is not) constant because it is affected by the ____ angle.

3. Disc loading means the _____ of the helicopter divided by the _____.

4. Flapping means the movement of blades in the (vertical/horizontal) sense relative to the plane of rotation/tip path plane).

5. Lead-lagging means movement of the blade (forward-aft/up-down) in (the plane of rotation/line with the shaft axis).

6. The difference between a fully-articulated rotor and a semi-rigid rotor is that the latter (does/does not) allow for (feathering/lead-lagging) through hinges.

7. The semi-rigid rotor system is common with (two/more than two) bladed rotors and (lead-lagging/flapping) is generally taken up within the blades or in the blade attachment components.

8. The relative (or resulting) airflow that influences the rotor blade in forward flight is a combination of airflows due to _____, _____ and _____.

9. Airflow due to rotation (Vr) is (always/ sometimes) in the (tip path plane/plane of rotation).

10. Induced flow means the airflow forced down by rotor action (all of which/most of which) passes through the rotor.

11. When the induced flow increases, the inflow angle (increases/decreases) and for a given blade angle and rotor rpm, the angle of attack will (increase/decrease).

12. Rotor thrust is a (resultant/component) of the total reaction which (can/cannot) be perpendicular to the relative airflow.

13. Total rotor thrust always acts at (right angles to/in line with) the (shaft axis/axis of rotation).

14. The force that overcomes the gross weight of the helicopter is _____ or a component of that force.

15. Rotor drag is a force which acts in the (plane of rotation/relative airflow) and it acts to (increase/decrease) rotor rpm.

16. Assuming constant rotor rpm, when the inflow angle decreases and collective is lowered proportionally, the total rotor thrust/rotor drag ratio (improves/ worsens) so that (more/less) power is required to maintain rotor rpm.

17. A rotor operates at its most efficient when the total rotor thrust/rotor drag ratio is at its (best/worst) and the collective lever is as (high/low) as practically possible.

18. Compared to a cool dry day, on a hot and humid day the blade's angle of attack needs to be (greater/smaller/the same) and the total rotor thrust/rotor drag ratio is (better/worse).

19. With a constant rotor rpm, raising of collective will (increase/decrease) the coning angle, rotor drag will (increase/decrease) and the requirement for _____ goes up.

20. The advantage of the high inertia rotor over the low inertia rotor is that rotor rpm tends to fluctuate (more/less) and the flare is (easier/more difficult) to execute but recovery from low rotor rpm is achieved (quicker/less quickly).

Rotor Blade Airfoils 7

As the rotor turns, helicopter blades are subjected to substantial drag forces and twisting moments. To withstand these forces, designers create blades that meet stringent strength and weight-bearing requirements while still being comparatively long and light.

Drag Factors

The main drag factors are parasite drag, profile drag and induced drag. Parasite drag includes drag generated by all aircraft components that do not contribute to lift. Profile drag and induced drag relate to those parts of the helicopter that do produce lift, namely the rotor.

Profile drag consists of *form drag* and *skin friction*. To reduce profile drag, one must shape the airfoil such that the *fineness ratio* (the thickness of the airfoil as a percentage of the chord length) produces the least possible interference to airflow. An airfoil with a maximum camber approximately a quarter of the way back from the leading edge and a fineness ratio of about 15% experiences relatively little profile drag. To reduce skin friction, the boundary layer around the blade (described in Chapter 4) needs to be as thin as possible which can be facilitated by using high quality materials that allow for smooth surfaces which minimize the development of thick boundary layers.

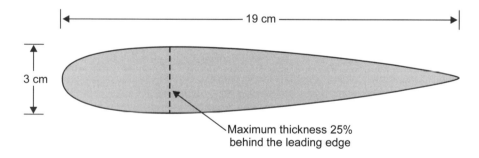

Figure 7-1. *Maximum thickness of 3 cm 25% aft of the leading edge and chord of 19 cm produce a fineness ratio of 3 : 19 = 15% approximately.*

Correcting airfoil characteristics that encourage tip vortices can significantly cut down on the amount of induced drag experienced by rotor blades. A high aspect ratio (large span to small chord), wash-out and reduced camber and chord towards the tips all combine to ensure the lowest possible induced drag.

Reducing drag often clashes with the objective to increase lift. To produce the best possible lift, the C_{Lmax} of a blade should be as high as possible, the mean camber line should be strongly curved and the total area should be as large as possible. The ultimate design of a helicopter blade is therefore a compromise, at best, between the highest possible lift for the least possible drag. In the final analysis blades must reflect the role for which the aircraft has been built. Most light helicopters, particularly those equipped with piston engines, must have blades that produce a reasonable amount of lift with little drag penalty, because their available engine power is generally low.

Stress Factors

Twisting moments generally result from a shift in the center of pressure relative to the feathering axis when angles of attack change. If the aerodynamic center is in front of or behind the blade's feathering axis twisting results. Twisting also occurs if the blade's center of gravity is away from the feather axis.

Symmetrically shaped blades minimize twisting moments largely due to their unique characteristic that ensures a *fixed* center of pressure position with changes in angle of attack. The blades are constructed so that the center of pressure and the aerodynamic center are located on the blade's feather axis and the center of gravity is as close as possible to that axis as well (Figure 7-2). The result is that symmetrical blades can be built from lightweight materials with minimal internal bracing and with shallow spars.

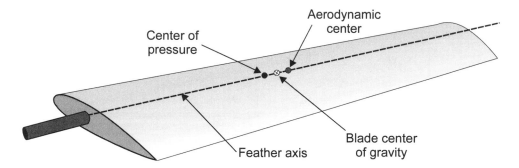

Figure 7-2. *Center of pressure, aerodynamic center and blade center of gravity located on or near the blade's feather axis minimizes stress forces on the blade.*

Most light helicopter blades use a type of D-Spar arrangement for root-to-tip strength and light hollow alloy construction behind the spar, as shown in Figure 7-3.

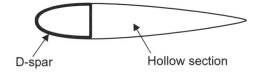

Figure 7-3. *D-spar at the front and hollow section at the rear which may be filled with honeycomb-like material.*

Although the symmetrical shape is advantageous from the drag point of view, its lift coefficient (and lift potential) is limited and the relatively sharp leading edge associated with the design does not usually permit a large critical angle (stall angle).

Effect of Local Air Velocity on Blade Design

Airflow speed at the blade root is much less than that near the blade tip. As a result, the blade produces increasing amounts of lift from root to tip as the local V factor increases.

Increased lift at the tip imposes strong bending forces on the blades. To reduce this problem, most helicopter blades incorporate *wash-out* – a design that decreases the *blade angle* from root to tip maintaining the associated angle of attack or, in many cases, reducing it. Thus wash-out controls the lift coefficient from root to tip to ensure even, or controlled, lift production throughout the blade.

In addition to wash-out, designers can compensate for the high V factor near the tip by reducing the camber and/or the chord of the blade towards the tip (taper in plan and thickness, "pointing" it), which also reduces the lift coefficient.

The concentration of lift forces within those areas of the blades where large forces can be tolerated, is achieved by design features that reduce the lift coefficient from root to tip. Figure 7-4 shows three situations where the required design features have been either omitted or underdone, overdone or correctly done. Ideally, the blade lift envelope should show an oblong pattern that produces lift as evenly as possible along the blade. In the case of many blade designs, however, the envelope is curved as shown.

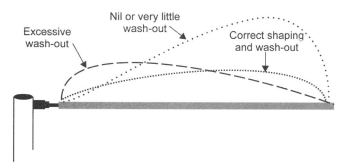

Figure 7-4. *Lift envelopes indicating varying degrees of shaping and wash-out.*

Blade Tip Speeds

The local V factor near the blade tip can, in some cases, be such that sonic (speed of sound) problems are encountered. One of the major consequences of sonic velocity is greatly increased drag as shock waves develop. Left unattended, this sharply increased drag causes unacceptably high vibrations that are felt throughout the aircraft.

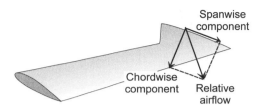

Spanwise component

Chordwise component

Relative airflow

Figure 7-5. *Sweepback produces a smaller chordwise component of the relative airflow past the affected blade section, allowing for higher tip speeds.*

Tip speeds are determined not only by rotor rpm and blade length but also by the aircraft's forward speed. As the helicopter flies faster, the advancing blade experiences an increasing V factor that, at the tip, may become supersonic. Rotors of relatively small diameter and/or operating at fairly low rotor rpm are less susceptible to the problem than large diameter rotors and/or rotors at high rotor rpm. Higher rotor and aircraft speeds and improved stall behavior are achieved by incorporating a sweep-back design near the blade tip (Figure 7-5). This design reduces the chord-wise speed of the airflow over the blade tip section. By positioning the sweep-back area forward from the leading edge of the inner part of the blade, the blade's center of gravity is retained on the feather axis in the affected tip area.

Developments In Blade Design

The lack of suitable materials that can withstand massive twist, stress and load factors while being light and reasonably priced limited blade construction in the past. Recent development and availability of materials that can accept high loads and large pitching moments have allowed blade designers to use asymmetrical rotor blade shapes. Asymmetrical blades incorporate airfoil sections that provide improved lift coefficient values without a weight penalty. Unusual features have been added to blades to control and minimize flutter and to allow higher local speeds.

Review 7

1. A high aspect ratio rotor blade has a (larger/smaller) span and a (larger/smaller) chord than a low aspect ratio blade.

2. Blade twisting forces can be kept to a minimum by using the _____ airfoil shape and ensuring that the blade's center of gravity, center of pressure and aerodynamic center are (on/away from) the blade's _____ axis.

3. Many rotor blades have (wash-in/wash-out) which means that blade angles (increase/decrease) from root to tip.

Rotor Blade Airfoils

4. The main purpose of helicopter blade (wash-in/wash-out) is to control the amount of (lift/drag) production from root to tip.

5. The worst combination of blade length and rotor rpm in producing tip speed sonic problems is the (long/short) blade rotating at (high/low) rpm.

6. Using the sweep-back design near the blade tip permits (lower/higher) tip speed and _____ forward speed.

Rotor Drag (Torque)

In powered flight the resistance to rotor rpm is constantly present because of the orientation of the total reaction, which is governed by the following factors:

1. The *lift/drag* (*L/D*) *ratio*, which varies with angle of attack. The greater the angle of attack beyond that for the best L/D ratio, the worse the ratio and the further the total reaction will lean away from the axis of rotation.

2. The *induced flow* and the *inflow angle experienced*. The larger the induced flow (for a given angle of attack) and the larger the inflow angle, the further the total reaction will orient away from the axis of rotation.

Thus large angles of attack, with their associated poor L/D ratios and large inflow angles, cause the total reaction to lean away from the axis of rotation, increasing rotor drag, which must be overcome by higher power settings (refer to Figures 6-9 and 6-10 in Chapter 6). The following factors determine the magnitude of rotor drag as the result of changes in angle of attack:

- changes in disc loading (as during maneuvers)
- changes in gross weight
- changes in altitude
- changes in configuration (such as sling load operations)
- ground effect
- translational lift

Disc Loading Changes

Carrying out maneuvers, such as turning or recovering from descents, involves an increase in disc loading which goes hand in hand with a requirement for more total rotor thrust (TRT). This often entails a requirement for more lift. Since lift can be altered by changing the lift coefficient (C_L) and V (shown as V^2 in the formula), and since V is largely determined by rotor rpm (generally a constant), extra lift can essentially be obtained only through an increase in C_L. This increase is affected through an increase in the angle of attack which causes the orientation of the total reaction to deviate further away from the axis of rotation. The resulting reduction in the TRT/rotor drag ratio demands more power.

It is important to note that under certain conditions, such as during a flare, the effect of increased disc loading can move the total reaction closer to the axis of rotation and decrease rotor drag. This will be further discussed in Chapter 16.

Whichever factor predominates, increases in disc loading may cause an increase in rotor drag, which requires more power. And as explained previously power is finite, which means that a helicopter's maneuvering ability is limited.

Changes in Gross Weight

An increase in gross weight requires more total rotor thrust, which demands a larger total reaction. The angle of attack must be increased, inflow angles will increase, and the total reaction will deviate further from the axis of rotation. The result is an increase in rotor drag, which requires more power. Again, the limitation of power has a strong influence on the amount of weight that the helicopter can carry.

Changes in Altitude

The decrease in air density with altitude needs to be compensated by an increase in angle of attack. As in the previous paragraphs, the resulting increase in rotor drag demands greater power. Once more, power available is the limiting factor that determines the highest altitude at which a helicopter can fly.

Changes in Configuration

Carrying slingloads, flying with doors removed or using floatation gear increases parasite drag which increases the demand for total rotor thrust (for reasons to be explained in Chapter 12). The angle of attack must be increased to keep flying. As a consequence, any item that adds to the helicopter's parasite drag causes an ultimate increase in rotor drag, which, again, points to power as being a limiting factor.

Ground Effect

When flying a helicopter near the earth's surface, the rotor downwash is unable to escape as readily as it can when flying higher and creates a ground effect.

> On reaching the surface, the induced flow downwash ceases its vertical velocity *which has the effect of reducing the induced flow at the rotor disc.*

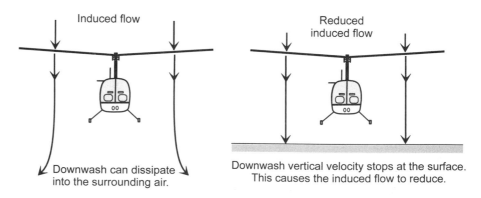

Induced flow

Downwash can dissipate into the surrounding air.

Reduced induced flow

Downwash vertical velocity stops at the surface. This causes the induced flow to reduce.

Figure 8-1. *Influence of ground effect on induced flow.*

A smaller induced flow for a constant rotor rpm and blade angle increases the blade's angle of attack. Figure 8-2 shows the effects of this on the power required to hover. The figures used in each situation are totally arbitrary and only serve to provide simplicity of explanation.

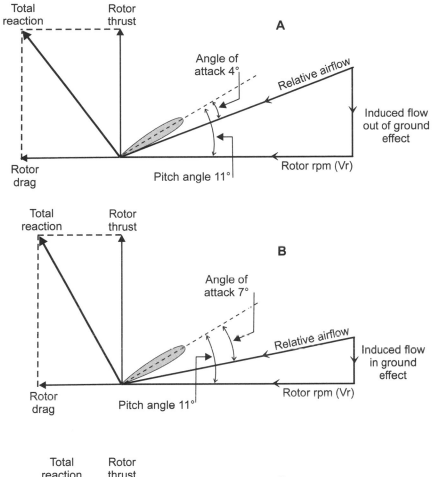

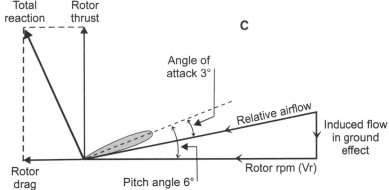

Figure 8-2. *Influence of ground effect on rotor drag.*

In Figure 8-2A, the helicopter is hovering *out of ground effect* (*OGE*), total rotor thrust opposes the aircraft weight. Assume the pitch angle is 11° and angle of attack is 4°. In Figure 8-2B, the helicopter descends *in ground effect* (*IGE*) and as stated above, the induced flow decreases. If the pitch angle remains at 11°, the angle of attack must increase to, say, 7°. The larger angle of attack, increased lift, larger total reaction and more rotor thrust, cause the aircraft to climb.

If the hover height in ground effect must be maintained, as in Figure 8-2C, the aircraft can only be kept at one height by reducing the angle of attack so that the total reaction produces a rotor thrust exactly equal and opposite to weight. The collective lever must be lowered until the pitch angle (say 6°) produces the required angle of attack (3° in this example). Note that the total reaction leans closer to the axis of rotation (better L/D ratio and smaller inflow angle) which results in less rotor drag for a given total rotor thrust requirement.

Chapter 6 explained that rotor efficiency increases when a blade operates at or near its best L/D ratio and when the collective is at its lowest position possible. Hovering in ground effect is an excellent example of this principle. While producing the same total rotor thrust (because the gross weight has not changed), a lower collective setting and less power can be used for level flight (hovering in ground effect) as compared to flight out of ground effect because less rotor drag (or torque) is encountered.

The angle of attack in Figure 8-2A (hover out of ground effect) was assumed to be 4°, while the angle of attack in Figure 8-2C (hover in ground effect), is 3°. The reason for this small reduction in angle of attack is that when out of ground effect, the total reaction leans a given distance away from the axis of rotation and it must be of a certain length to produce the total rotor thrust required to overcome weight. When in ground effect, the combination of a lower relative airflow, a smaller inflow angle and improved L/D ratio reduces the angle between the total reaction and the axis of rotation. Thus a smaller total reaction, but leaning closer to the axis of rotation, will provide the required rotor thrust to overcome weight.

A smaller total reaction (closer to the axis of rotation) can only be produced when lift is reduced. At a constant rotor rpm this reduction can only be attained by decreasing the angle of attack. Thus when hovering in ground effect, the angle of attack is slightly less than when hovering out of ground effect, provided the rotor rpm is the same in both cases.

Summarizing, when hovering in ground effect the angle of attack is slightly less, the amount of total rotor thrust is the same as the gross weight, the blade angle is smaller, the power required to overcome the reduced rotor drag (or torque) is less and the collective control lever is lower than when hovering out of ground effect. This conclusion applies equally to flight in ground effect other than the hover, but the effect is not as great.

Translational Lift

When hovering in calm conditions, a given induced flow passes at right angles through the rotor disc. If a 30 knot wind were now to blow, part of the induced flow would be blown "down-wind", parallel to the disc, so that a reduced amount will pass through the disc. Thus the wind, in this example, has reduced the induced flow, as shown in Figure 8-3.

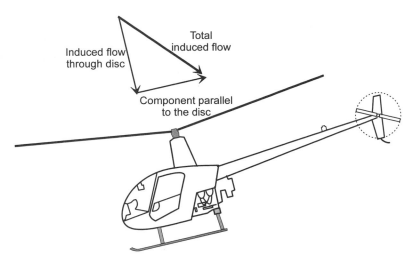

Figure 8-3. *Part of the total induced flow travels parallel to the disc, causing the induced flow perpendicular to the disc to become smaller.*

Whether a helicopter is hovering in a wind or flying at a certain airspeed, the same effect takes place. As airspeed is increased, the increasing component of the induced flow parallel to the disc causes a proportional decrease in the induced flow through the disc and smaller inflow angles result. For a given blade angle, the angle of attack must then increase which produces increased total rotor thrust and the aircraft will climb. To prevent climbing, the increase in angle of attack must be avoided by lowering the collective lever which reduces the blade angle.

The reduction in inflow angle causes the total reaction to lean closer to the axis of rotation and, like in ground effect, for a given rotor thrust requirement the amount of rotor drag experienced will be less. Therefore, translational lift permits the production of total rotor thrust *for less power* (if flight remains level). Alternatively, if power is not reduced by lowering the collective when translational lift sets in, translational lift can then be defined as the *gain in height for no increase in power*.

The effect of translational lift becomes noticeable as the aircraft accelerates through about 12 to 14 knots, maximizing around 50 knots. Beyond that speed its benefit decreases, mainly because the influence of a rapidly increasing parasite drag demands a greater (tilted) total rotor thrust. Airspeed figures vary, depending on helicopter make and type.

Summary

The amount and orientation of the total reaction determine the relationship between rotor thrust and rotor drag. Reductions in induced flow (which invariably reduce the inflow angle) and/or favorable angles of attack cause the total reaction to lean more towards the axis of rotation, with less rotor drag accompanying total rotor thrust and requiring less power. This is what helicopter operating efficiency is all about.

Review 8

1. When the disc loading is increased, total rotor thrust must be (increased/decreased) and since this involves (increase/decrease) in angle of attack it follows that there will be a (deterioration/improvement) in the total rotor thrust/rotor drag ratio.

2. When the total rotor thrust/rotor drag ratio gets worse, there is a requirement for _____ power.

3. When the gross weight of a helicopter decreases there is a requirement for (larger/ smaller) pitch angles which produce (larger/ smaller) inflow angles and power can be (increased/decreased).

Rotor Drag (Torque)

4. When a helicopter descends into ground effect, the induced flow (increases/ decreases) which results in an _____ in angle of attack if collective is not raised or lowered. The helicopter will then (maintain height/climb/descend).

5. Compared to hovering out of ground effect, when hovering in ground effect the requirement for total rotor thrust is (more/ the same/less), blade angles are (larger/ the same/smaller) and power required is (more/ the same/less).

6. When translational lift becomes effective on initial climb-out, (angles of attack/blade angles) increase and if collective is neither lowered or raised the rate of climb will initially (increase/decrease).

The Anti-Torque Rotor 9

When in powered flight in a single-rotor helicopter, the main rotor tries to remain stationary while the fuselage is subjected to a torque couple trying to rotate it in a direction opposite to that of main rotor rotation.

Figure 9-1 shows how, under the influence of the main rotor torque couple, the nose of the helicopter is encouraged to yaw to the right. (In the case of helicopters that have the rotor rotating in a clockwise fashion, looking from above, there is a tendency for the nose of the aircraft to yaw to the left.) The tendency to yaw occurs when the rotor is driven from a central point (such as from the mast) and the degree of yaw is determined by the amount of power used.

The greater the power output, the stronger the tendency to yaw.

Since potential yaw is caused by a torque couple it is logical that an opposing couple should be used to counteract it; when equal and opposite, the nose of the aircraft would not yaw left or right. The use of an opposing couple, however, poses considerable construction problems and for that reason the torque couple is opposed by a moment produced by the thrust of the anti-torque rotor (tail rotor) positioned at the tail.

The magnitude of a moment is determined by the force applied over a given distance. Thus the tail rotor, producing thrust to the right, provides the force required while the position of the tail rotor well behind the mast (upon which the torque couple is centered) gives the required distance. If this distance is increased, the anti-torque moment produced by the tail rotor thrust is more powerful.

Thrust from the anti-torque rotor is produced on the same principle as thrust from the main rotor. The tail rotor draws air from one side (the right in this case) and accelerates it rapidly to the other side (to the left). The action-reaction principle then ensures that the accelerated air to the left encourages the tail rotor to go to the right which is the basis of tail rotor thrust (to the right). Figure 9-2 shows that the correct amount of tail rotor thrust will produce the required moment (anti-torque) to oppose the torque couple.

Anti-Torque Functions

The main purpose for the anti-torque rotor is to provide the required thrust to overcome main rotor torque.

The anti-torque rotor also enables the helicopter to have hover turn capability and balanced forward flight.

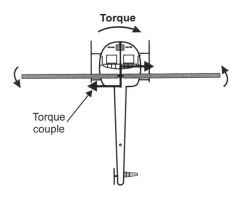

Figure 9-1. *Counterclockwise blade rotation causes the torque couple to attempt to rotate the fuselage clockwise around the rotor mast.*

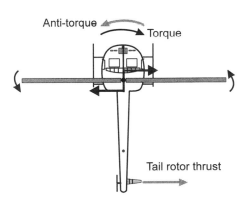

Figure 9-2. *The anti-torque (tail) rotor produces the thrust required to oppose torque.*

Mechanical Considerations

The tail rotor is driven by a shaft originating from the main rotor gear box. If the engine fails, continued main rotor rpm will maintain tail rotor rotation. Tail rotor rpm cannot be adjusted or altered independently; it can only be adjusted through the main rotor rpm.

To adjust the tail rotor thrust to meet varying anti-torque requirements, the tail rotor blade angle is altered. If more anti-torque is required, the tail rotor blade angles must increase and, when less anti-torque is required, the blade angles must decrease.

The blade angle control mechanism on or near the tail rotor shaft is activated by pilot inputs through the anti-torque pedals. Moving the left pedal forward produces more anti-torque and yaws the helicopter nose to the left. Right pedal produces less anti-torque and yaws the nose to the right. Since a pilot-induced left yaw involves tail rotor thrust greater than that required to keep the nose stationary, increasing left pedal increases the tail rotor blade angles and right pedal decreases them. (In clockwise main rotor rotating helicopters these directions are reversed, right pedal more anti-torque, left pedal less anti-torque.)

As stated in a previous paragraph, the degree of torque from the main rotor depends largely on the power being used. In the hover, which involves high power use, substantial anti-torque is required, the left pedal is forward. Under high gross weight, high altitude and high density altitude conditions, which associate with large inflow angles on the main rotor blades and very high power requirements, anti-torque needs to be larger, thus the left pedal is well forward.

Sometimes gross weight is so great and/or the altitude so high, that all available anti-torque (full left pedal) may not stop the nose from yawing to the right. In those circumstances it is advisable to make the helicopter "light on the skids" (maintain ground contact) initially and if yaw cannot be eliminated with the available left pedal, the pilot should use specific lift-off techniques or abandon the lift-off altogether.

Anti-Torque and Demand for Power

When operations demand anti-torque, the main rotor rpm tends to decrease because of the connection between the main rotor drive and the tail rotor, which experiences drag. Put simply, anti-torque "bleeds off" power. Slightly more power must therefore be provided to stop the main rotor from losing rotor rpm. Coordinated use of the throttle twist grip and/or collective is required to retain main rotor rpm while anti-torque demands are being met.

When turning to the left in a hover (which increases the demand for anti-torque and needs more power), the helicopter tends to decrease height if extra power is not supplied. When turning to the right in a hover, height will increase if power is not reduced by the correct amount (assuming counter-clockwise main rotor rotation).

Effect of the Wind

The wind only affects the airflow onto a helicopter when it is being flown relative to a ground feature, for example, when positioning for an approach to a landing site. Similarly, when hovering over a spot the wind has an effect. The following explanations are based on flight relative to a ground feature.

When the wind strikes the aircraft from certain sectors a sudden reduction in tail rotor efficiency, resulting in an unintended yaw to the right, may occur called *loss of tail rotor effectiveness* (*LTE*). (In the case of clockwise rotating rotors the unintended yaw will be to the left.)

With the wind blowing directly onto the nose of the helicopter, the fuselage and empennage tend to behave like a weathervane (directional stability), holding the nose of the aircraft into the wind and reducing the requirement for anti-torque from the tail rotor. When the wind blows from the side and the aircraft is at an airspeed of less than 30 knots, however, three basic problem areas can be identified:

1. Winds from 120° to 240° relative give rise to weathercock action.

2. Winds from 210° to 330° relative encourage the tail rotor into the vortex ring state condition.

3. Winds from 285° to 315° relative encourage main rotor disc vortex interference on the tail rotor.

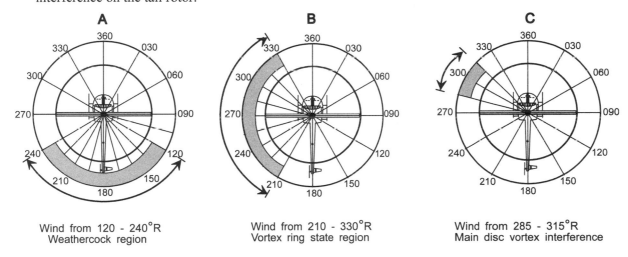

A
Wind from 120 - 240°R
Weathercock region

B
Wind from 210 - 330°R
Vortex ring state region

C
Wind from 285 - 315°R
Main disc vortex interference

Figure 9-3. *Effect of the wind on tail rotor thrust.*

These wind regimes are shown in Figure 9-3. In Figure 9-3A, the wind on the helicopter's tail tries to yaw the nose left or right depending on its actual approach angle. If the aircraft is allowed to rotate through the regions identified in Figure 9-3B and 9-3C, the rate of turn may accelerate. Timely corrections must be made by the pilot to prevent the development of unwanted yaw when operating in tail wind conditions.

In Figure 9-3B, the wind from the left quadrant interferes with the accelerating flow through the tail rotor disc from right to left (which provides tail rotor thrust). This may produce a vortex ring state situation (to be discussed fully in Chapter 19), which can seriously affect tail rotor thrust in terms of erratic pedal requirements, which is accentuated if the wind is strong and gusting.

In Figure 9-3C, the wind is likely to blow the main rotor disc vortex (as discussed in Chapter 4) onto the tail rotor, which produces alternating requirements for right and left pedal.

All of these factors are aggravated under high power use, such as when the aircraft is heavily loaded, flying at high altitudes or, as stated at the beginning of this section, flying at low airspeeds. Reducing airspeed below 30 knots demands a power increase to compensate for the associated reduction in translational lift. Therefore, the risk of loss of tail rotor effectiveness increases when translational lift is absent or reduced. Under these circumstances, wind from any direction may produce unwanted yaw.

In terms of crosswind effect on *power required to hover*, wind from the left or right may increase the need for power in a hover, especially if the helicopter side areas are flat and the wind is strong and gusting. Under these conditions, the main disc may need to be tilted substantially to counteract the crosswind and more power will be required as a consequence, notwithstanding the possible benefit from translational lift.

In general, helicopters can be flown in most wind conditions. Nevertheless, any tendency towards unwanted yaw must be arrested without delay. This emphasizes the fact that flying in gusting and turbulent conditions increases the pilot's work load.

Translating Tendency (Tail Rotor Drift)

You can see in Figure 9-4 that one part of the main rotor torque couple (the forward part) points to the right and the tail rotor thrust points to the right as well. The other part of the main rotor torque couple (the part behind the mast) points to the left.

As soon as the helicopter lifts off, there is a tendency for the aircraft to drift to its right under the influence of these uneven forces (two to the right and one to the left). This movement is known as *translating tendency*, also referred to as *tail rotor drift*. Translating tendency must be corrected by moving the cyclic to the left so that the disc tilts slightly left and stops the drift to the right.

Some designers incorporate methods that automatically correct for tail rotor drift. The most common ones are:

1. Construction of the main rotor mast so that it tilts slightly to the left and the rotor disc is automatically oriented to the left.

2. The use of a "bias" in the cyclic control mechanism. This involves an arrangement in the cyclic control linkage which holds the cyclic stick slightly to the left, so that the pilot does not have to place it there.

Translating tendency occurs anytime in flight when power is in use, it must be corrected. In forward flight and especially at speeds approaching cruise speed or higher, the directional stability of the aircraft reduces the requirement for anti-torque so that tail rotor drift becomes less significant.

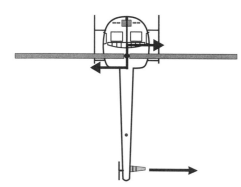

Figure 9-4. *The front component of the torque couple and tail rotor thrust (two forces) cause the helicopter to drift to the right.*

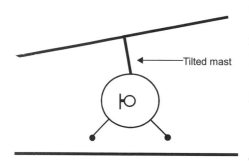

Figure 9-5. *Tilted mast viewed from the rear. The amount of tilt exaggerated for clarity.*

During a maximum performance takeoff from a confined area, however, where the power use is high and the airspeed is low, if tail rotor drift is not corrected properly, the aircraft tends to drift to its right. The reverse applies when a large amount of tail rotor thrust is used to maintain a constant heading in a hover and the throttle is closed rapidly (to simulate engine failure). A rather abrupt drift to the left then occurs if the disc is not leveled (with right cyclic) as the power is reduced.

Rolling Tendency

After translating tendency has been corrected for by slightly tilting the disc to the left, the horizontal component of total rotor thrust points left while tail rotor thrust points right. These two vectors form a couple tending to roll the helicopter to its left (Figure 9-6).

A number of design features and procedures can reduce this tendency:

1. **Reducing the couple lever arm**. By placing the tail rotor on a pylon, the vertical distance between the horizontal component of the total rotor thrust and tail rotor thrust is smaller, and the couple strength is reduced. A similar result is obtained by slanting the tail boom upward, as seen on a number of helicopters.

2. **Offsetting the mast to the left**. This causes the lateral center of gravity of the aircraft to be to the right of the mast, which tends to oppose the rolling tendency.

3. **Correct loading**. Flying the aircraft from the right seat when solo or placing heavier passengers on the right will ensure that the lateral center of gravity is on the right of the butt line. Take particular note, however, weight and balance limits must not be exceeded and the Flight Manual instructions regarding pilot-in-command position must be obeyed.

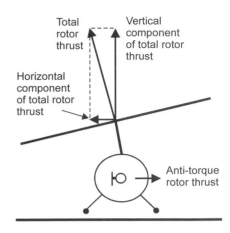

Figure 9-6. *A couple is produced by the horizontal component of total rotor thrust and tail rotor thrust causing a rolling tendency to the left.*

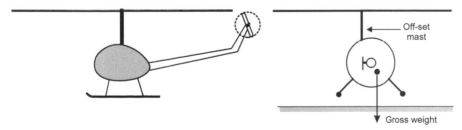

Figure 9-7. *The vertical lever arm between the rotor hub and tail rotor is reduced by placing the tail rotor on a pylon. Rolling tendency is reduced.*

Figure 9-8. *Offset mast viewed from the rear. The amount of offset is exaggerated for clarity.*

Tail Rotor Flapping

In forward flight, the advancing blade of the tail rotor experiences a higher velocity than the retreating blade and asymmetry of lift occurs, which must be corrected through flapping. Thus the tail rotor must have "flapping ability," and various mechanical designs are available that allow tail rotor blades to flap. Although some forces on the tail rotor blades may cause lead-lag tendencies, most designs do not incorporate lead-lag hinges, therefore, most, but not all, tail rotors can only flap and feather.

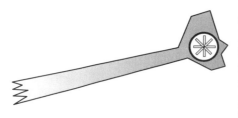

Figure 9-9. *Fenestron anti-torque rotor.*

Shrouded Tail Rotors

Conventional (exposed) tail rotors operate in difficult airflow conditions. Main rotor downwash, disturbances from the fuselage and other sources tend to subject the tail rotor to confused airflows. The position of the tail rotor at the end of the tail boom subjects it to vibration. The risk of damage from foreign objects striking the tail rotor and the potential threat of injury to persons from the exposed blades favor a protected environment for the tail rotor.

The shrouded tail rotor, also known as a *Fenestron*, provides that protection. It consists of a number of small blades rotating within a protective shroud. Because asymmetry of lift is eliminated there is no requirement for the blades to have flapping ability, they only need freedom to feather. A servo unit is needed to facilitate pitch control and a structural problem occurs fitting the shroud in the tail boom assembly. Comparing tail rotor designs we can say that the conventional tail rotor is simpler to build and install, but the shrouded Fenestron eliminates most of the confused airflows onto the blades and protects the rotor and ground personnel from damage. Finally, the Fenestron is more effective compared to conventional tail rotors of similar diameter.

Tail Rotor Blade Design

To produce the greatest amount of anti-torque thrust for the smallest rotor diameter and rpm, blades possessing high values of maximum lift coefficient, high C_{Lmax}, (typically asymmetrical in shape) are desirable. While the same requirement applies to main rotor blades, the stresses imposed through shifting centers of pressure with angle of attack changes are unacceptably high in most helicopters, necessitating symmetrical main rotor blades.

Tail rotor blades, being much shorter than main rotor blades, can be built strongly without excessive weight penalties, so non-symmetrical airfoils can be used. In some cases, considerable curving of the camber line indicates the presence of a high built-in lift coefficient. The stall angle of the asymmetrical shape can also be relatively high, allowing for a large range of angles of attack.

Other Methods of Anti-Torque Control

While the conventional tail rotor produces the simplest remedy to main rotor torque, the following alternative designs are available:

- The main rotor is driven from the tips rather than the center using tip-jets (as in fireworks rotation). Although the principle has merit, it presents a plethora of construction problems.

- Twin rotor design (as in the Chinook).

- Counter-rotating designs (where one disc operates clockwise above another, which rotates counterclockwise).

- Sideways tail propulsion through high velocity jet flows from adjustable nozzles. This principle is incorporated in the NOTAR design. (More on this design in Chapter 20.)

Strakes and Anti-Torque

The near-vertical downwash from the main rotor passing the tail boom can be utilized for anti-torque purposes by "spoiling" the downward airflow on the left-hand side of the tail boom (viewed from the rear). A simple means of achieving this is by using a "strake", a flat metal strip attached lengthwise more or less at right angles to the tail boom. It has been shown that the best results are achieved when the strake is attached above the midway line of the tail boom.

In Chapter 3 it was explained that when an airflow is forced to curve, its velocity increases and pressure reduces, resulting in a lift force at a right angle to the airflow. In similar fashion as an airflow passing an airfoil, this lift process also occurs when the main rotor downwash passes the tail boom. When the downwash is vertically down, the curving around the tail boom on the left is identical to that on the right and the lift forces to either side would cancel out. However, if the airflow on one side is deliberately made turbulent, then the lift force on that side reduces sharply while the lift force on the other side is retained.

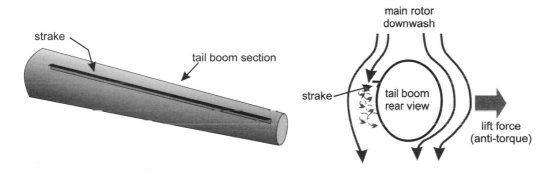

Figure 9-10. *The effect of strakes on the main rotor downwash over the tail boom.*

Figure 9-10 shows the effect of the strake on the airflow around the tail boom, commonly referred to as the "*Coanda Effect*". It can be seen that the remaining lift force to the right results in the tail boom moving to the right, in the same direction as the required anti-torque. As a consequence, the thrust provided by the tail rotor can be reduced; – tail rotor blade pitch angles will be smaller which means that the problem associated with left pedal limits is eased. There is also a significant reduction in power required, and this has particular importance for improved anti-torque capability at higher weights, higher altitudes etc.

The coanda effect is at a maximum when the helicopter is in the hover in nil wind conditions when the main rotor downwash is as near to the vertical as possible. As forward speed increases, or when there is a wind blowing, the main rotor downwash develops a horizontal component which lessens the benefit of the strake. But this loss is somewhat compensated in forward flight by an increase in directional stability when the fuselage tends to align itself with the direction of flight.

A secondary benefit of the strake is an improvement in maintaining heading when flying sideways to the right, or when experiencing a crosswind from the right because more left pedal is available. However, as sideways speed increases and a smaller percentage of the main rotor downwash passes the tail boom, the benefit decreases. This is aggravated by the increasing pressure build-up on the right of the fuselage and tail boom as sideways speed increases, this factor varies greatly between between different helicopter designs.

A disadvantage of the strake is its exposure to downward pressure from the main rotor downwash, and to some extent, its weight. The additional total rotor thrust required to overcome these factors depends largely on the strake design.

Tail Rotor Failure

Single-rotor helicopters lose their anti-torque capability when the tail rotor fails. If failure occurs in powered flight, the immediate reaction is a yaw to the right, the degree depending on airspeed and amount of power in use. With clockwise rotating rotors the yaw will be to the left. If the power in use is high it is possible that directional control may be lost. If the forward speed of the aircraft provides adequate directional stability, loss of anti-torque capability is not immediately threatening, but the helicopter probably cannot land at that speed. As speed is reduced, the need for anti-torque increases and directional control is jeopardized.

Since power output is one of the major factors that determine the anti-torque requirement, if directional control cannot be maintained following tail rotor failure, power must be reduced by lowering the collective. In extreme cases it may be necessary to enter autorotation using no power, which may create a small tendency to yaw to the left (right with clockwise rotating rotors).

A potentially damaging situation exists when total tail rotor loss occurs unexpectedly at lower than cruising speeds. The fuselage will begin to rotate immediately and it will be difficult to regain directional control. At cruising speeds the effect of tail rotor failure will not be as serious, but a directional problem will occur when speed is reduced. In slow-speed forward flight, some anti-torque can be produced by carrying out a slipping maneuver to the left. The subsequent yaw to the left will act against torque, enabling more power to be used which may produce a reduction in the rate of descent.

Tail rotor failure or limitation (other than through a break in the drive mechanism) can occur when a pedal is stuck or obstructed. If a small amount of left pedal is stuck forward, use of power should enable the pilot to maintain directional control to the end of a landing. Right pedal stuck forward however, may be more difficult because such a configuration discourages the use of power. Either pedal, stuck well forward, presents a serious situation from which a safe landing may not be possible.

Review 9

1. The rotor thrust required from an anti-torque rotor is (directly/inversely) proportional to power in use.

2. A helicopter fitted with the main rotor rotating clockwise viewed from above tends to _____ to the (right/left) when power is applied and to counteract the yaw the tail rotor blade angles must be (increased/decreased) which is achieved by applying sufficient (left/right) pedal.

3. Viewed from behind, tail rotor thrust of a helicopter with a counterclockwise rotating main rotor acts to the (left/right) and it does so by drawing air from the (left/right) and accelerating it to the (left/right).

4. Tail rotor rpm is controlled by the (main rotor/foot pedals).

5. When lowering collective, the (increased/decreased) demand for anti-torque requires (less/more) left pedal.

6. As you commence a left-hand hover turn you do not raise or lower the collective lever. As the turn progresses, your height will (increase/ decrease) because there is a (increased/ decreased) requirement for anti-torque.

7. When you hover out of ground effect you require a certain amount of ____ pedal to maintain heading. If you then descend into ground effect without changing pedal position, the helicopter will yaw (right/left) as you maintain your new height.

8. Factors that cause loss of tail rotor effectiveness are aggravated when the wind is (weak/strong), the helicopter's gross weight is (high/low) and the airspeed is (low/high).

9. A method to counteract translating tendency (tail rotor drift) automatically is a (tilted/ offset/) mast to the (left/right).

10. A tail rotor placed on a pylon assists in (increasing/decreasing) the degree of (tail rotor drift/rolling tendency).

11. Given the same size and similar rpm as an exposed tail rotor, the shrouded (Fenestron) tail rotor is (more/less) effective, is (easier/more difficult) to install and (does/ does not) need freedom to flap.

12. When the tail rotor drive shaft breaks while in cruise flight, the helicopter will ____ to the (left/right) and as speed is reduced it is necessary to (increase/ decrease) power to maintain directional control.

Controls and Their Effects 10

Having discussed the anti-torque control in Chapter 9 we must now consider the collective control and cyclic control. Both controls perform their functions via a *swashplate* arrangement (also known as the *control orbit*) that varies in design from one helicopter to another. The following are principles common to most swashplates.

The swashplate arrangement consists of two circular or angular plates (or *stars*) fitted horizontally one above the other and positioned on top of, or near the top of, the mast. A ball bearing arrangement separates the two plates and allows horizontal (circular) movement between them. The lower plate is fixed in terms of rotation, but has the ability to move up and down and/or tilt in any given direction. It is referred to as the *stationary* or *non-rotating plate* (or *star*). Pilot inputs alter the vertical position of the plate through the *collective control* and the tilt of the plate through the *cyclic control*.

Above the stationary plate is the *rotating plate* which, as the name implies, has freedom to rotate. Since the rotating plate always follows the orientation of the stationary plate, any pilot input to the stationary plate is passed on to the rotating plate above it. The rotating plate is connected to each individual blade via *pitch links* to *pitch horns* fitted either to the leading or trailing edge of each blade. Thus the rotating plate can alter the blade angle of each blade.

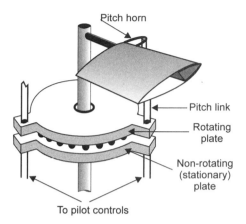

Figure 10-1. *Principles of a swashplate system.*

Collective Control

Pulling the collective lever up moves the swashplate vertically so that *all blades* obtain the same increase in blade angle. Similarly, pushing the collective down decreases the blade angle to all blades. Variations in blade angle change the amount of total rotor thrust produced. Accordingly, changes in collective cause changes in total rotor thrust (but they do not alter total rotor thrust orientation).

The actual vertical movement of the swashplate associated with up collective depends on where the pitch horn is attached to the blade. For example, when the pitch horn is attached to the leading edge of the blade (as shown in Figure 10-1), the swashplate must move up to increase blade angle. If the attachment point was at the trailing edge of the blade the swashplate must move down to increase blade angle. Pitch horn location varies from aircraft to aircraft.

An increase in all blade angles (up collective), under most conditions, increases rotor drag and may decrease rotor rpm. To facilitate maintenance of rotor rpm, a correlating unit (a cam-link arrangement) is fitted between the collective control and the throttle butterfly, increasing power automatically and avoiding a loss of rotor rpm whenever collective is pulled up. The correlating unit decreases power when collective is pushed down.

The twist-grip type throttle at the end of the collective is, in many helicopters, predominantly an engine rpm *fine tune control*, even though its use has some influence on manifold pressure. In most modern helicopters a *governor* is fitted to automatically maintain the required engine rpm and therefore rotor rpm. Technical details relating to the governor are included in Chapter 20.

Cyclic Control

Moving the cyclic control left/right, fore/aft or any combination thereof tilts the swashplate, which changes the blade angle of individual blades. For instance, in a two-bladed rotor, moving the cyclic forward decreases the blade angle on the right blade and increases the blade angle on the left blade.

Although moving cyclic alters the *tilt* of the total rotor thrust, the *amount* of total rotor thrust *is not affected*. Cyclic merely points the total rotor thrust in any required direction, it doesn't increase or decrease it.

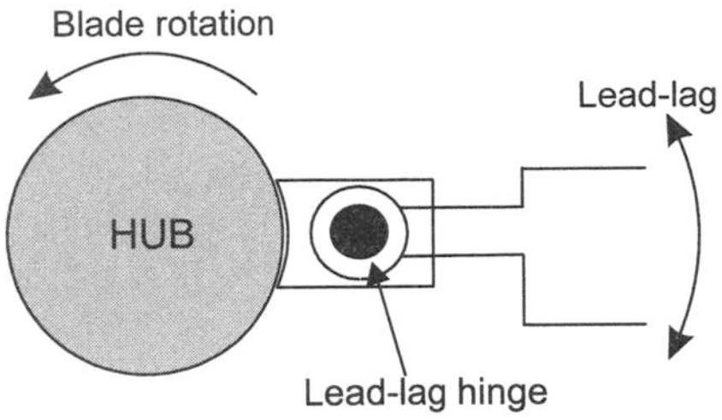

Effect of Controls on Blade Lead-Lag Behavior (in fully articulated rotor systems)

Using any control inevitably changes the amount of rotor drag experienced by the blades, which affects the position of blades on their lead-lag hinge.

Rotor systems that do not incorporate hinges that would allow blades to lead-lag, still experience increases and decreases in rotor drag but in most cases the associated resistance in the plane of rotation is taken up in the blades themselves or in the blade-root attachment. So the blades or attachments must be strong and resilient to absorb these stress forces.

Mean Lag Position

If the blades are able to move forward or back on their lead-lag hinge there must be a "neutral" position about which lead-lag takes place.

When a rotor operates in a vacuum all the blades are neutral on their lead-lag hinges because there is no drag. If a full atmosphere is suddenly introduced, all the blades move aft on their lead-lag hinge, placing themselves at their *mean lag position*. Under normal powered flight conditions the blades of rotor systems that permit lead-lag, move forward or aft relative to the mean lag position, which is almost always behind the neutral position.

The Four Main Causes of Movement About the Lead-Lag Hinge

Conservation of Angular Momentum (Coriolis Effect)

Conservation of angular momentum (Coriolis effect) influences the rotational velocity of a blade when it flaps up or down. Any section of a blade travels on a given radius at a given velocity and because of this, each section (and ultimately the entire rotor blade) has a certain angular momentum that tends to be retained.

When the radius on which the center of gravity of the blade travels is reduced, such as when the blade flaps up or cones upward, the center of gravity moves in towards the axis of rotation (circumference A changes to B in Figure 10-4), the blade travels in a smaller circle. The blade will then increase its rotational velocity to conserve angular momentum (in this smaller circle). When a blade flaps down its center of gravity moves out from the axis of rotation onto a larger radius and its velocity slows down.

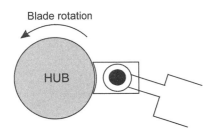

Figure 10.2. *Simplified presentation of a lead-lag hinge arrangement.*

Figure 10-3. *Mean lag position.*

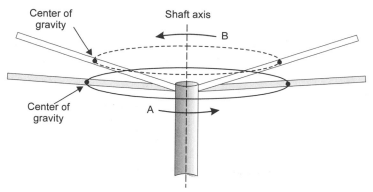

Figure 10-4. *Blade center of gravity travels on a smaller circle when the blade has flapped up.*

Conservation of angular momentum therefore influences the position of a blade on its lead-lag hinge. Flapping up moves the blade forward on the hinge as the blade speeds up and flapping down moves it aft as the blade slows down.

Hookes Joint Effect

In (I) and (II) of Figure 10-5 the aircraft is hovering in calm conditions, the tip path plane is horizontal and the axis of rotation and the shaft axis are in line. In (III) and (IV) however, forward cyclic has tilted the disc forward, but the shaft axis is still vertical. From overhead we see the tip path plane has moved forward (as shown by the dotted circle), and the blade tips retain their respective opposite positions on the tip path circumference and their velocity remains constant. To achieve this, the advancing blade (A) must move forward on its lead-lag hinge and the retreating blade (C) must move aft, a phenomenon known as *Hookes joint effect*.

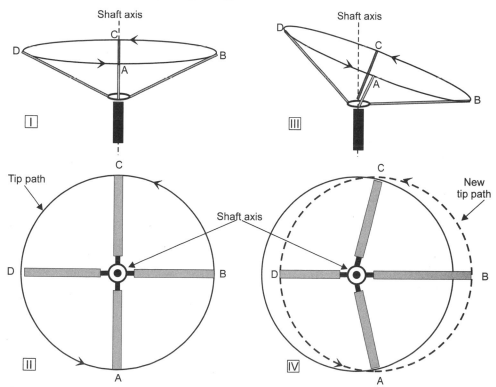

Figure 10-5. *Hooke's joint effect.*

Hookes joint effect demonstrates itself whenever the axis of rotation and the shaft axis are not in line. Although Hookes joint effect causes movement on the lead-lag hinge almost continuously during a blade's rotation, most of the effect occurs as the blade passes the axis of disc tilt, that is, the middle of the advancing and retreating sides.

Periodic Drag Changes

Flight at other than the calm hover causes rotor blades to flap up and down continually during each revolution, constantly altering the angles of attack of the blades. The drag of each individual blade is therefore different at any given position and as a result, blades move forward or aft on their lead-lag hinges. Since advancing blades decrease their angles of attack and retreating blades increase their angles of attack it follows that maximum lead-lag changes occur in the middle of the advancing and retreating side.

Random Changes

Blades experience random drag changes in flight when angles of attack alter because of outside influences, such as turbulence. These changes produce blade movement on the lead-lag hinge to no set pattern.

Review 10

1. When the pitch horn is attached to the trailing edge of the blade, raising of collective will cause the swash plate to (rise/fall) so that the blade angle (increases/decreases).

2. Using collective (will/will not) affect the amount of total rotor thrust and it (will/will not) change the orientation of total rotor thrust.

3. Moving the cyclic control (will/will not) raise or lower the swash plate but it will _____ the swash plate so that (all blades together/ individual blades) obtain changes to their (blade angle/angle of attack).

4. Cyclic and collective controls activate the _____ plate (or star) of the swashplate and control inputs are transferred to the blades via the _____ plate (or star).

Controls and Their Effects

5. The function of a correlator unit is to (increase/decrease) engine power as collective is raised. As altitude is gained the correlator unit becomes (more/less) effective.

6. When a blade flaps up, its center of gravity moves (in towards/out from) the axis of rotation and as the blade (increases/ decreases) its speed it will move (forward/rearward) on its lead-lag hinge. This is known as _____ effect.

7. Periodic drag changes occur in forward flight when (blade angles/angles of attack) change because of blade flapping.

The Hover 11

A helicopter hovers when the following four elements remain constant:

- position over the surface
- height above the surface
- rotor rpm
- heading

Since no acceleration takes place during the hover the aircraft is in equilibrium. Total rotor thrust must equal the gross weight of the aircraft except in wind conditions where the vertical component of an enlarged total rotor thrust performs this function.

Many takeoffs and landings are carried out via the hover, which identifies it as a maneuver normally carried out close to the surface. The amount of hover power required to maintain the rotor rpm needed to produce the necessary total rotor thrust varies depending on a number of factors, height above the surface is of major importance.

Hover Out-of-Ground Effect (OGE) and In-Ground Effect (IGE)

For the rotor to produce the aerodynamic force required to sustain the helicopter in flight at a constant height, it must exert an equal and opposite force on air. In other words, the net rotor thrust upward must be equal to the net downwash. Air is drawn down from a state of rest above the disc and accelerated through the disc, reaching its final downwash velocity about two rotor diameters below the disc (in free air conditions).

The final downwash velocity is approximately twice the induced velocity. Its magnitude depends on:

- disc loading
- air density

The higher the disc loading, the higher the downwash velocity. Since, in the hover, disc loading is proportional to gross weight and total rotor thrust it follows that the heavier the helicopter, the greater the downwash velocity.

The less dense the air, the higher the downwash velocity. Hover flight at high altitude or under conditions of high density altitude involves greater downwash velocities.

When hovering more than one disc diameter above the ground and out-of-ground effect, the downwash beneath the disc dissipates into the surrounding air without appreciable surface interference. When the pilot lowers the aircraft to within about three-quarters disc diameter of the ground (in-ground effect), however, the downwash cannot escape as readily.

In Chapter 8 we saw that the downwash cannot continue downward on reaching the surface. When its vertical velocity ceases, the effect is felt at the rotor disc. The situation is similar to the effect of downwash behind the blade on the oncoming relative airflow (relating to induced drag) as explained in Chapter 4, Figure 4-6. The result of ground interference (on the airflow approaching the disc from above) is to reduce the induced flow.

If blade angle and rotor rpm remain the same, angles of attack on all the blades increase as the induced flow reduces. Lift increases in magnitude and becomes more vertical because it retains its perpendicular position to the relative airflow, which now comes from lower down. Total reaction increases and orients more closely to the axis of rotation which causes total rotor thrust to increase and the aircraft to rise. When it reaches an altitude where surface interference is negligible, the aircraft ceases to climb.

To enter the hover in-ground effect and maintain a steady height above the ground, you must avoid increasing angles of attack – reduce the blade angles by lowering the collective. Because a lower collective setting involves reduced power output, it follows that a hover in-ground effect produces the required total rotor thrust with less power (see Figure 8-2 in Chapter 8).

Factors Affecting Ground Effect

Helicopter Height Above Ground Level (AGL)

Generally, the maximum hover height in-ground effect is approximately equal to three-quarters the helicopter's disc diameter. Technically this height relates to disc height but many performance graphs refer to it by skid height.

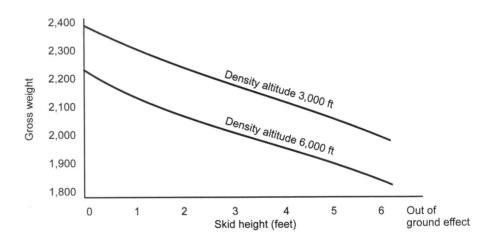

Figure 11-1. *Effect of density altitude and gross weight on hover height.*

Density Altitude and Gross Weight

For a given power limitation, the greater the gross weight, the lower the maximum height for hover in-ground effect. The graph in Figure 11-1 shows that the maximum hover height lowers with higher gross weight, and/or when operating at higher density altitudes.

Gross Weight and Power Required

Figure 11-2 shows that for any given weight, the hover horsepower required (HPR) increases as hover height in-ground effect increases.

The horsepower available (HPA) must meet the horsepower required. Since horsepower available decreases with altitude, there must come an altitude above which a hover in-ground effect is impossible for that particular weight.

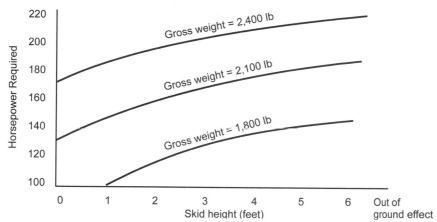

Figure 11-2. *Effect of aircraft gross weight on hover height and hover power required.*

Figures 11-1 and 11-2 therefore show that the maximum height for hovering in-ground effect lowers when:

- gross weight increases
- altitude increases
- density altitude increases
- available power decreases

Nature of the Surface

Any surface that absorbs downwash energy and causes molecular movement reduces the benefit of ground effect. For example, hovering over water causes surface ripples which absorb energy, taking away from the potential energy contained within the rotor downwash. Similarly, hovering over tall grass, dry sand, or snow lowers the hover in-ground effect ceiling. As a side effect, loose dirt or snow can cause a brownout or whiteout, respectively. If you intend to rely on ground effect when operating at altitude and/or at high gross weight it is important to remember that surface disturbances can seriously reduce the benefits of ground effect.

Slope

Hovering over a slope allows the down-slope downwash to escape, lessening the effect on induced flow and lowering the in-ground effect ceiling. Keep this in mind when hovering at landing spots adjacent to steep down-sloping terrain, such as at the top of a steep rise. While a large part of the disc is over the landing area surface, the remaining part is over the steep terrain, resulting in a rather unwelcome pitch or roll caused by the non-symmetrical rotor thrust production over the entire disc.

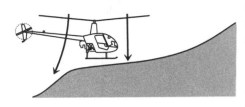

Figure 11-3. *The rear of the disc does not benefit from ground effect.*

Only the front half of the disc in Figure 11-3 experiences ground effect and more rotor thrust is produced at the front than the rear. With counterclockwise rotor rotation this aircraft is likely to roll right.

Wind Effect

Wind has the same effect as slope on a helicopter hovering in-ground effect because the disc must be tilted into the wind to maintain the aircraft's position. Part of the downwash escapes, and the in-ground effect ceiling lowers. Wind benefits in terms of translational lift, however, may be greater than the loss of ground effect in some circumstances.

Confined Areas - Recirculation

As rotor downwash strikes the surface it splits, and a large part diffuses horizontally. If obstructions such as buildings or trees interfere with the escaping airflow, it moves vertically up the obstruction and re-enters the disc from above, increasing the induced flow. The speed at which this recirculation takes place increases over time, progressively strengthening the induced flow. For a given rotor rpm and blade angle, the increased induced flow reduces the angle of attack and reduces total rotor thrust. The result is that the hover height lowers. To avoid losing altitude, the pilot must raise the collective, but this, in turn, increases induced flow, necessitating more up collective.

When collective reaches full up, nothing the pilot does can keep the helicopter from sinking towards the surface.

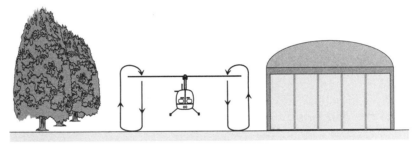

Figure 11-4. *Obstructions have the potential to cause recirculation.*

Factors Determining the Degree of Recirculation

Gross Weight. The greater the gross weight, the stronger the downwash and the greater the degree of recirculation.

Hover Height. The lower the hover height, the stronger the outbound flow and the greater the degree of recirculation.

Type of Obstruction. The more solid the obstruction, the greater the recirculation. Hovering close to large buildings (such as hangars) creates more recirculation than hovering near trees.

Distance from Obstructions. The highest velocity of horizontal outflow escaping from beneath the helicopter occurs at a distance that is roughly 30 percent of the disc diameter beyond the disc tip. For example, with a 30-foot disc the highest velocity occurs about 10 feet away from the tips. Although the velocity beyond that distance decreases sharply, substantial horizontal velocity values can still be encountered.

Thus recirculation can occur when obstructions are reasonably far away from the disc tip, but in general, the shorter the distance, the greater the risk of recirculation.

Recirculation is clearly a distinct possibility when operating in confined areas. An approach into such an area should involve the shortest possible hover prior to touchdown. For takeoff, the same rule applies.

Not always is the entire disc involved in recirculation. For instance, when hovering close to a building, only half the disc may be affected by recirculation and a roll or pitch movement may develop, depending on the aircraft's heading. In all likelihood, however, the air hitting the building will surge out in all directions, disturbing the entire airflow through the disc, resulting in random roll, pitch and yaw.

In the same context, when hovering close to buildings and other obstructions in windy and/or gusty conditions, a recirculation effect may occur on the leeward side. A descending wind flow over the top of the obstruction has the same effect, increasing induced flow (thereby reducing angles of attack and total rotor thrust).

Over-Pitching

Over-pitching is different from recirculation even though the symptoms have similarity. While over-pitching can occur at any altitude and at various stages of flight, it is more likely to occur when approaching a hover or during a hover.

If the rotor rpm decreases during those phases (for whatever reason), total rotor thrust reduces and an unwary pilot might attempt to restore the rotor thrust by pulling up collective. Chapter 6 explained that this action invariably tilts the total reaction away from the axis of rotation, worsening the total rotor thrust/rotor drag ratio. Thus up collective will only result in further decay in rotor rpm.

Decaying rotor rpm also causes the helicopter blades' coning angles to increase. The consequence of this is that, firstly, the disc becomes smaller so that total rotor thrust falls off. Secondly, large coning angles cause rotor thrust to point inward so that smaller vertical components become available to overcome the helicopter's weight, see Figure 11-5.

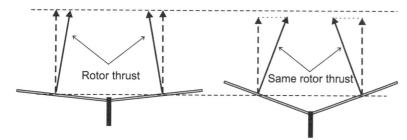

Figure 11-5. *With a constant rotor thrust, greater coning angles result in not enough component force to oppose gross weight.*

There comes a stage where the rotor rpm is so low that even full power can no longer restore it, this is the beginning of over-pitching. Any further raising of collective creates more rotor drag and rotor rpm decays even further.

The only recovery action from over-pitching and restore rotor rpm is to roll on throttle and simultaneously lower the collective lever. This will invariably cause the helicopter to lose some height.

Over-pitching may occur when approaching a high altitude landing site if the power required to hover is not available. As airspeed decreases and the need for power increases, the helicopter's descent rate builds when the engine cannot supply the power required. Pilots who then instinctively pull up collective to arrest the sink rate are in trouble. The high inflow angles and associated rotor drag quickly decay the rotor rpm and the stage is set for over-pitching. The best scenario ends in a hard landing, while the worst scenario ends in a full rotor stall, at which point the helicopter virtually falls out of the sky.

Mechanical factors that underline the need to avoid over-pitching are the risk of over-boosting and damage to transmission components.

Review 11   The Hover

1. The downwash velocity during the hover is increased when gross weight is (greater/smaller) and density altitude is (higher/lower).

2. When hovering in ground effect, rotor drag is _____ than when hovering out of ground effect but total rotor thrust required is (more/the same/less).

3. For a given power limitation, the less the gross weight of a helicopter, the _____ the maximum skid height during hover in ground effect.

4. Maximum skid height for hover in ground effect is _____ when power available is less.

5. When, during the hover, the front of the disc is in ground effect and the rear is not, the helicopter tends to (pitch/yaw/roll) (down/to the right/to the left).

6. When you hover close to obstructions, recirculation becomes evident when you require (higher/lower) collective settings to maintain hover height and (the higher/the lower) the hover height the less the degree of recirculation.

7. During the approach to a high altitude landing site you note the rotor rpm is near the bottom of the green range. If you do not (increase/decrease) rotor rpm at this stage, the rate of descent will _____ as you reduce your airspeed and rotor rpm is likely to (reduce/increase) further.

8. Your collective lever is close to full up as you approach a landing site at maximum gross weight. As airspeed decreases, reserve power available becomes (more/less) and the rate of descent _____. If the rotor rpm continues to reduce your best course of action is to maintain at least _____ speed and _____ the approach.

Forward Flight **12**

One of the main differences between hovering and forward flight is parasite drag: there is essentially no parasite drag when hovering. Chapter 4 explained that parasite drag increases with the square of the speed increase which means that the force required to overcome parasite drag must become progressively greater as airspeed increases. The force which overcomes parasite drag is provided by total rotor thrust because, when tilted forward and appropriately increased, it will produce:

- a vertical component equal and opposite to weight
- thrust, in the direction of flight, to deal with parasite drag

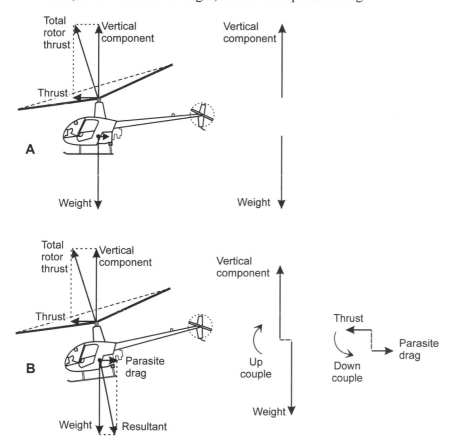

Figure 12-1. *Helicopter accelerates from the hover into forward flight.*

When the disc is made to tilt forward initially with forward cyclic, the fuselage attitude remains the same briefly. The forces are then as shown in Figure 12-1A. Parasite drag has not yet formed or is still insignificant. The slightly increased total rotor thrust (from a touch of up collective) is inclined forward and produces a nose-down moment around the aircraft center of gravity.

At the same time, the vertical component of total rotor thrust is precisely equal and opposite the helicopter's weight, so that the aircraft's height stays constant. As the helicopter's speed increases, the forward thrust and slowly increasing parasite drag produce a couple arrangement that causes the fuselage to pitch nose down (Fig. 12-1B). Because of this nose-down pitch, the aircraft's center of gravity swings slightly aft relative to the rotor hub (through which the vertical component of total rotor thrust acts). A nose-up couple is then produced (a combination of the vertical component of the total rotor thrust and aircraft weight) that opposes the thrust/parasite drag nose-down couple.

The amount of parasite drag increases with increasing airspeed, so that the thrust/parasite drag (nose-down) couple becomes stronger. Eventually the nose-up couple formed by the vertical component (of TRT) and weight is equal and opposite to the nose-down couple produced by thrust/parasite drag. At this stage, the resultant of weight and parasite drag is opposite, in line with and equal to total rotor thrust. Both resultant vector quantities pass directly through the aircraft's center of gravity (Figure 12-2) which confirms that the center of gravity position basically determines the fuselage attitude in straight and level flight. Factors such as fuselage shape and horizontal stabilizer loading, however, do have some influence.

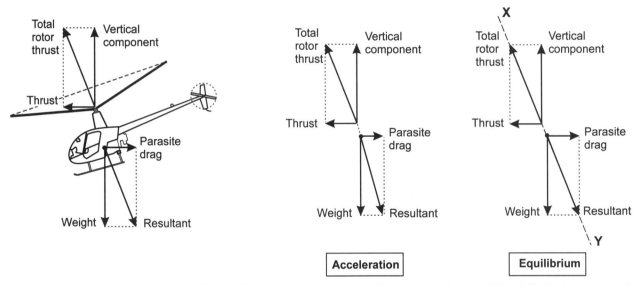

Figure 12-2. *Helicopter in equilibrium in straight and level flight at a constant airspeed.*

During the accelerating phase, prior to achieving equilibrium (Fig. 12-2), total rotor thrust and the resultant are not in line or acting through the aircraft center of gravity. Any increase in forward speed must be accompanied by a change in disc attitude so that increased total rotor thrust (oriented forward) continues to oppose the increased resultant of weight (a constant) and parasite drag (an increasing variable). The fuselage attitude also changes so that ultimately total rotor thrust and the weight/parasite drag resultant continue to act through the helicopter's center of gravity (as shown by the line X-Y).

Three Basic Aspects of Horizontal Flight

Three basic aspects involved in horizontal flight are:

- factors involved in changing disc attitude, (use of cyclic)
- consequences of changing disc attitude as it relates to dissymmetry of lift
- factors involved in eliminating dissymmetry of lift

Tilting the Disc With Cyclic

Cyclic alters the plane of the stationary plate of the swashplate so that the rotating plate, which orients itself in the same plane, changes the blade angles of a blade continually as it completes each revolution.

When cyclic is moved forward, the stationary plate tilts forward (to keep things simple just now) and stays like that until the cyclic is repositioned. As a consequence, the rotating plate increases a given blade's pitch angles for 180° and decreases them for the next 180°, repeating the cycle as long as the cyclic remains in one position.

The following explains how the cyclic control alters the plane of rotation of the rotor disc. The explanation ignores, for the time being, the effect of airflow resulting from forward speed. The explanation simply examines the way cyclic works in total isolation.

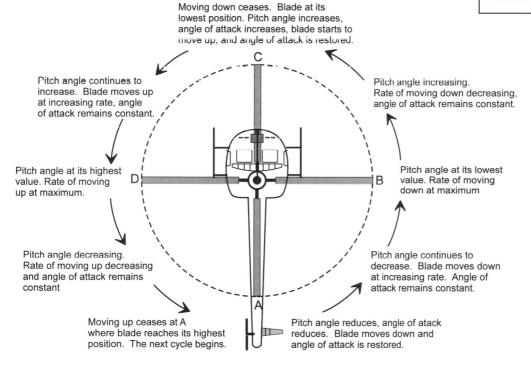

Moving down ceases. Blade at its lowest position. Pitch angle increases, angle of attack increases, blade starts to move up, and angle of attack is restored.

Pitch angle continues to increase. Blade moves up at increasing rate, angle of attack remains constant.

Pitch angle increasing. Rate of moving down decreasing, angle of attack remains constant.

Pitch angle at its highest value. Rate of moving up at maximum.

Pitch angle at its lowest value. Rate of moving down at maximum

Pitch angle decreasing. Rate of moving up decreasing and angle of attack remains constant

Pitch angle continues to decrease. Blade moves down at increasing rate. Angle of attack remains constant.

Moving up ceases at A where blade reaches its highest position. The next cycle begins.

Pitch angle reduces, angle of atack reduces. Blade moves down and angle of attack is restored.

Figure 12-3. *Principle of operation of the cyclic control.*

A counterclockwise rotor in a hover, such as that in Figure 12-3, experiences forward cyclic at position A, causing the blade over the tail to reduce its pitch angle. This action is simply the result of the swashplate position which feeds the cyclic input through to the blade in question. The angle of attack of that blade lessens and the blade starts to descend. When descending, airflow created by the descent causes the relative airflow onto the blade to come from lower down. This results in the angle of attack returning to its original value, the blade has *flapped to equality*.

As the blade progresses on its circular path, blade angles decrease (due to swashplate orientation) so that the rate at which the blade descends increases while the angle of attack continuously flaps to equality. Thus the angle of attack essentially does not change.

When at position B the blade angle reaches its minimum value and starts to increase. This is to ensure that the rate of going down is reduced so that the rate becomes zero when the blade is over the nose at position C. (If the blade angle were allowed to decrease beyond B, the blade would not stop its descent over the nose of the aircraft.) Thus at position B the rate of downward movement is maximum, and lessens as the blade approaches the front.

At position C the rate at which the blade moves down becomes zero and the disc has reached its lowest point over the nose of the aircraft. The blade angle increases here (due to the orientation of the swashplate). As a consequence, the blade's angle of attack briefly increases, the relative airflow comes from higher up (because of the blade's ensuing climb) and the angle of attack returns to its original value as it flaps to equality. The blade angle continues its increase so that the rate of the blade's upward movement increases.

At position D the blade reaches maximum blade angle and the rate of upward movement is also maximum. From here on, the blade angle decreases so that the rate of upward movement decreases.

Returning to position A the rate of upward movement becomes zero, the blade reaches its high point over the tail, and the next sequence starts.

Thus we can summarize at this stage:

> **Forward cyclic causes the plane of rotation to tilt forward under the influence of changes in blade angle while angles of attack remain essentially constant. The rate at which blades move down and up will be greatest when blade angles are smallest and largest, respectively.**

Having established the sequence for forward flight, the same principles apply for movement in any other direction.

We referred in the foregoing explanations to blades "moving up" and "moving down" so as to avoid confusion with the term "flapping" up and down which will be covered shortly. When the overall picture is understood, the term flapping should not cause confusion for vertical blade movement due to any action.

Remember: the explanation so far dealt with cyclic action only, we ignored the influence of airflow resulting from airspeed.

An Alternate Explanation of Cyclic Action

If a horizontally rotating rotor disc reorients itself so that its low point is over the nose of the helicopter, then the greatest input for downward movement must be made 90° beforehand in accordance with the principle of gyroscopic precession. Thus the blade angle must be least on the right-hand side of the helicopter, where the rate of downward movement must be greatest, and beyond which the downward velocity decreases. If the disc shall have its high point over the tail, the greatest input for upward movement must be made 90° beforehand, on the left-hand side. That is where the blade angle must be greatest and beyond which the rate of upward movement decreases.

> The principles of gyroscopic precession simplifies the detailed explanation of aerodynamic factors involved when the cyclic is moved. The end result of either explanation is exactly the same.

Dissymmetry of Lift

Dissymmetry of lift results after a cyclic input changes the plane of rotation (forward in this case) and forward movement has begun. (For the moment we will not consider the changes in blade angle that continue taking place as long as the cyclic stick is held in a steady forward position.). The term *dissymmetry of lift* is unfortunate. It is the uneven production of rotor thrust that causes real problems.

Once the rotor disc tilts forward, the aircraft moves away from the hover and goes through transition (movement from the hover to forward flight and forward flight back to the hover).

Because one rotor blade moves forward and the other blade moves back relative to the helicopter as forward airspeed is gained, the advancing blade operates at its rotational velocity plus the airflow created by forward airspeed, while the retreating blade operates at its rotational velocity minus the airflow created by forward airspeed.

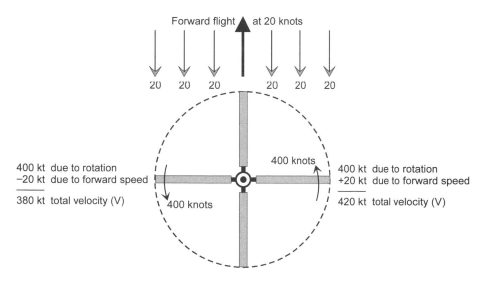

Figure 12-4. *Advancing blade experiences a greater velocity (V) than the retreating blade which will cause dissymmetry of lift (rotor thrust).*

Figure 12-4 shows a counterclockwise rotor flying towards the top of the page. It assumes that the velocity caused by rotation of the blade section is 400 knots and the aircraft forward speed is 20 knots. The forward speed creates an airflow that moves onto the entire helicopter at a speed equal to the forward velocity. In Figure 12-4 this movement is represented by six arrows of 20 knots each.

The advancing blade section on the right experiences 400 knots from rotor rpm plus the 20 knots created by forward airspeed, an effective relative airflow of 420 knots. The retreating blade on the left experiences an airflow caused by rotation minus the airflow from forward speed: 400 knots minus the 20 knots caused by forward velocity, producing an effective relative airflow of 380 knots.

Lift production is the result of a given angle of attack (the lift coefficient) and velocity (V). At this stage let us consider the lift coefficient to be the same on both blades. A higher V (at the square function) on the advancing blade produces more lift than the reduced V on the retreating blade. Consequently, the total rotor thrust produced on the advancing half of the disc is greater than that produced on the retreating half and the helicopter rolls to the retreating side, which is *dissymmetry of lift*.

Thus dissymmetry of lift is caused by the airflow created by aircraft airspeed, or caused by the wind when the helicopter is stationary such as when hovering. If the speed of the helicopter increases, say to 50 knots, or if the wind is stronger, dissymmetry of lift increases.

Eliminating Dissymmetry of Lift

The fundamental problem with dissymmetry of lift is that lift (and rotor thrust in the final analysis) on one side of the disc is greater than that on the other side. The remedy lies in an action that automatically counters the effect of different velocities so that lift is the same on both sides.

To solve the velocity problem we must examine the lift formula, $C_L \frac{1}{2} \rho V^2 S$. At any given position and altitude, ρ (air density), $\frac{1}{2}$ and S (blade area) are constants. The only other factor that contributes towards lift and that is not a constant is the lift coefficient, C_L, which relates directly to angle of attack. Our problem is solved if we can find a means whereby blades' angles of attack automatically change to oppose the effects of changes in blade velocity so that total lift does not alter. *Flapping* constitutes that means.

Watch what happens to an airfoil's angle of attack when the airfoil is moved up or down. When flying level, the relative airflow approaches the blade from within the horizontal plane and a given angle of attack results. If the blade flaps vertically up without forward speed, the relative airflow strikes the top of the blade so that the angle of attack is −90°. If the two movements are now combined so that the blade moves forward as well as up, the resultant relative airflow arrives from between horizontal and vertical. Since the horizontal velocity component is much stronger than the vertical one, the relative airflow approaches from slightly higher than the horizontal and a reduction in the angle of attack occurs. If the rate of upward flapping increases, the reduction in the angle of attack is more marked.

The same phenomenon applies to a blade flapping down. The combined relative airflow resulting from forward and downward velocity comes from slightly below the horizontal and the angle of attack (and lift coefficient) increases. Again, an increase in the blade's rate of downward flapping causes the increase in the lift coefficient to be more marked.

Applying the foregoing to dissymmetry of lift, when the blade flaps up (reducing the lift coefficient) as V increases, and flaps down (increasing the lift coefficient) as V decreases, the effect of different V values is eliminated. In the fully articulated rotor system this freedom is provided by flapping hinges fitted between the rotor hub (mast) and blade attachment points. In the semi-rigid system, it is provided by the action of the teetering (or flapping) hinge.

The amount of lift coefficient compensation for different V values is always exactly that required and is automatically provided by a freely flapping blade.

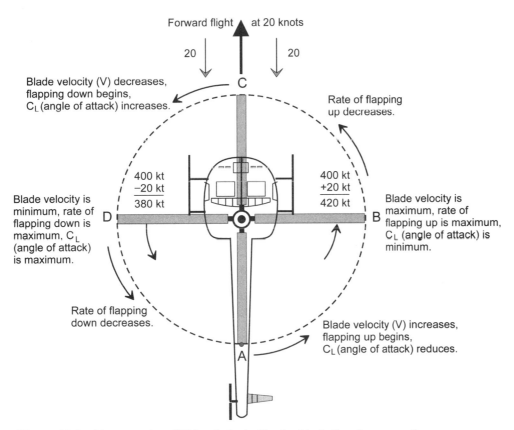

Figure 12-5. *Dissymmetry of lift is eliminated by the blade flapping up on the advancing side and flapping down on the retreating side.*

Figure 12-5 explains the effect of flapping. Assume that the pilot moved cyclic forward initially to gain airspeed, and that beyond that first movement, the stick was held still. When the blade leaves the tail position A and progresses on the advancing side, the increasing V strengthens the lift force so that the blade starts to flap up, through the action of the flapping hinge. Upward flapping reduces the angle of attack.

As the blade reaches the middle of the advancing side B, the influence of forward speed on increasing V is highest, and the rate of flapping up is at its maximum and the angle of attack is at its minimum. From B forward, the influence of aircraft forward speed on the blade's V decreases and the rate of flapping up diminishes. The angle of attack starts to increase again and when the blade reaches the nose position C, flapping up ceases.

As the blade moves onto the retreating side, V reduces, lift reduces and the action of the flapping hinge allows the blade to flap down. The flapping down action causes an increase in the blade's angle of attack and an increase in the lift coefficient that is proportional to the reduction in V. At the midway point D on the retreating side, the V value is least, and the rate of flapping down is greatest, so that the angle of attack (and the lift coefficient) is at its maximum. From here on towards the tail position, the effect of aircraft speed on V reduces, the rate of flapping down diminishes and when the blade arrives at the tail position, flapping down ceases.

Summarizing, if the blade is allowed to flap freely:

- as V increases, the lift coefficient decreases
- as V decreases, the lift coefficient increases

The dissymmetry of lift (or better, dissymmetry of rotor thrust) problem is solved. Do take particular note that dissymmetry of lift is eliminated through flapping which acts on angles of attack. This is in sharp contrast to cyclic control which acts on blade (pitch) angles.

Blow-Back (Flap-Back)

When the cyclic is pushed far enough forward to produce forward flight and held there, the swashplate orientation is constant.

Figure 12-5 shows that as the blade flaps up on the advancing side and flaps down on the retreating side (to prevent the changing V values from altering total lift), the attitude of the disc is affected. It reaches a high point over the nose and a low point over the tail. This reaction to dissymmetry of lift and flapping is known as *blow-back* or *flap-back*.

Figure 12-6 shows how the disc was originally oriented front-down following the initial cyclic input, but as airspeed was gained and flapping eliminated dissymmetry of lift, the front of the disc went up and the back went down. This reorientation of the rotor disc changes the direction in which total rotor thrust acts so that the helicopter's forward speed slows, and, in some cases, the aircraft may come to a complete stop. When airspeed reduces, pendulum action brings the nose of the helicopter up and the tail down.

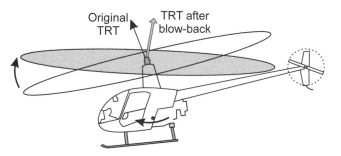

Figure 12-6. *Blow-back (flap)-back*.

Thus while flapping acts to eliminate the problem of dissymmetry of lift, it introduces an undesirable blow-back reaction that interferes with the helicopter's airspeed.

As soon as the disc experiences blow-back, the cyclic must be moved forward yet again to overcome the problem. As airspeed becomes progressively higher, blow-back becomes stronger and further forward movement of cyclic is called for. Strictly speaking, there comes a speed where the cyclic stick is on its forward limit and the helicopter cannot fly any faster.

Blow-back limits the helicopter's forward speed.

Blow-Back(Flap-Back) When Using Collective

When you raise the collective lever while in unaccelerated forward flight, blow-back is experienced and the opposite effect takes place (blow-forward) when you lower the collective lever. The reason for this is that when the same increase or decrease in angle of attack is applied simultaneously to both blades through collective action, a difference is caused in the amount of lift generated by the advancing and retreating blades.

It will be recalled that in the lift formula ($C_L \frac{1}{2}\rho V^2 S$), $\frac{1}{2}\rho V^2$ represents dynamic pressure (read again Indicated Airspeed/True Airspeed in Chapter 3). Considering the blade area (S) is a constant we can ignore that item in the formula. Thus lift is essentially the product of C_L and dynamic pressure (or dynamic energy if you like).

When you consider Figure 12-7 which shows the dynamic pressure on the blades during forward flight, you can see that the rotational velocity (Vr) plus the airflow due to forward flight on the advancing blade is greater than Vr minus airflow due to forward flight on the retreating blade. Therefore the dynamic pressure on the advancing blade is higher than that on the retreating blade.

When the collective lever is raised and both blades experience a similar increase in their angles of attack (C_L), the product of an increased C_L x higher dynamic pressure is greater than the product of the same increased C_L x a lower dynamic pressure. Thus the lift produced when raising collective is greater on the advancing blade than on the retreating blade. Through precession this results in the disc being higher at the front and lower at the rear – blow back has resulted. In similar fashion, blow forward will result when the collective lever is lowered (and C_L is evenly reduced), often experienced when lowering the lever firmly at the start of an autorotation.

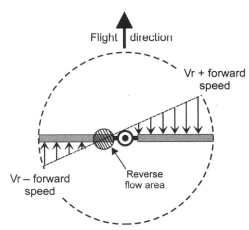

Fig. 12-7. *The combination of Vr and aircraft speed causes the dynamic pressure to be greater on the advancing blade than on the retreating blade. (Reverse flow is explained shortly.)*

Summary

The helicopter flies forward because of many interacting factors. Forward flight (or any flight involving airspeed, for that matter) always introduces dissymmetry of lift, which is instantly (and without pilot input) prevented from developing through flapping. The associated blow-back (flap-back) in forward flight, however, must be overcome through cyclic feathering if flight at speed is to continue. Should the pilot change the cyclic position at some stage and increase the helicopter's speed, the degree of blow-back will increase and the pilot must correct for it with further forward cyclic. The same sequence then repeats. If the pilot slows the helicopter down, the disc flaps forward, which must similarly be corrected, with (aft) cyclic.

In non-hover flight the lowest blade angle is midway on the advancing side (to provide disc attitude control, cyclic and swashplate position) where the angle of attack is at its minimum value (to eliminate dissymmetry of lift, flapping). The blade angle is greatest midway on the retreating side, where the angle of attack is at its maximum value. Thus blade (pitch) angle and angle of attack changes are superimposed on one another throughout each blade revolution.

Designs that Reduce Flapping Amplitude

When the degree of flapping must be reduced as much as possible (as with many tail rotors, for instance), two basic design features, Delta-3 hinges and offset pitch horns are often used.

Delta-3 Hinges

Delta-3 hinges are set relative to the feathering axis at an angle other than 90° (Figure 12-8). When the blade flaps up, its pitch angle reduces automatically. A hinge at 90° to the feather axis, in contrast, does not cause any difference to the pitch angle when flapping.

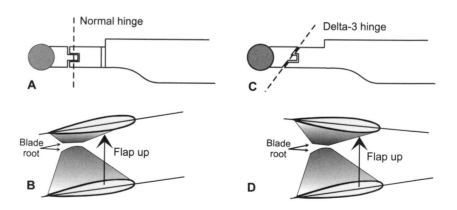

Figure 12-8. *The Delta-3 hinge. In A and C the blade flaps up out of the page towards the reader.*

In Figure 12-8 (A and B) the blade attaches to the rotor hub with right-angle flapping hinges. B shows that flapping up and down has no influence on the pitch angle of the blade. Thus any alteration in the lift coefficient to eliminate dissymmetry of lift happens solely by flapping up or down.

In Figures 12-8 C and D, the flapping hinge is at an angle other than 90°. If the blade flaps up out of the page towards the reader (in C), the trailing edge rises more than the leading edge because of the geometry of the hinge. This is shown clearly in Figure 12-8 D, where flapping up (to decrease the lift coefficient) is associated with a decrease in pitch angle. This decrease helps reduce the lift coefficient, so the blade flaps less to achieve the same result.

Offset Pitch Horns

Offset pitch horns are alternatives to Delta-3 hinges (Figure 12-9). Consider point A is fixed and the blade flaps up in response to an increasing V on the advancing side. When the blade flaps up, the attachment of the pitch horn to the leading edge of the blade arrests that part of the blade and the blade angle reduces. The reverse holds true when the blade flaps down.

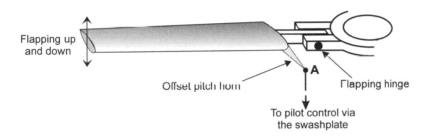

Figure 12-9. *Offset pitch horn producing Delta-3 effect. Point A is fixed unless activated by the pilot.*

In summary, Delta-3 hinges and offset pitch horns reduce the degree of flapping without affecting the required amount of C_L increase/decrease to eliminate dissymmetry of lift. While the designs may have some advantages in main rotor systems, they are favored in anti-torque (tail) rotors primarily because tail rotors are highly exposed and vibration-prone pieces of equipment. Delta-3 hinges allow the tail rotor location to be closer to the tail boom. Helicopter drive shafts and linkages are then shorter and stronger, and the reduced flapping amplitude gets rid of some of the vibration.

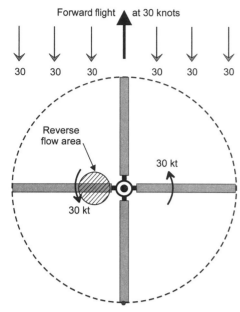

Forward flight at 30 knots

30 30 30 30 30 30

Reverse flow area

30 kt

30 kt

Figure 12-10. *Reverse flow. Within the striped reverse flow area, the airflow past the airfoil due to aircraft speed is higher than the speed due to blade rotation.*

Reverse Flow

The local velocity of blade sections is faster near the tips and slower near the rotor head.

Figure 12-10 assumes that the local velocity of a blade section near the mast is 30 knots, which means that between that section and the mast itself, the local velocity must be less than 30 knots. As the aircraft forward speed increases to 30 knots and more, the retreating blade sections in question produce a 30 knot or less relative airflow onto the leading edge because of rotation. However, they have a greater speed of air going *from trailing edge to leading edge* due to the higher aircraft forward speed. Consequently, these sections of the blade experience *reverse flow*. As the helicopter speed increases, the size of the blade area affected increases.

Reverse flow does not produce effective rotor thrust which means that the retreating blade loses part of its working area. To prevent the differences in total rotor thrust on the advancing and retreating side from pitching and/or rolling the aircraft, the unaffected part of the retreating blade outside the reverse flow circle must increase its work to compensate for the reverse-flow section.

The only way the unaffected part of the retreating blade can increase its rotor thrust is through increased angles of attack, which require more flapping. Thus the amplitude of down flapping is higher when the reverse flow area increases, and vice versa. Since there is a limit to the angle of attack available, there is a forward speed where the retreating blade reaches its maximum angle of attack and the blade stalls. This is known as *retreating blade stall*, discussed more fully in Chapter 17.

Note the following characteristics of reverse flow:

1. Blade sections within the reverse flow area are not stalled. The blade sections simply experience a flow from the trailing edge to the leading edge, and this flow is not necessarily turbulent. Furthermore, these blade sections are not operating beyond their maximum lift coefficient value.

2. Reverse flow areas only exist on the retreating side, they can never be centered on the mast.

3. Reverse flow deflects around the trailing edge and the leading edge in such a way as to encourage a blade pitch-up moment, subjecting the blades to unwanted twisting forces.

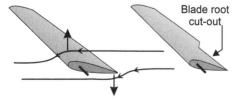

Blade root cut-out

Figure 12-11. *Reverse flow causing stress forces at the blade root. Cut-out design can decrease the effect.*

Figure 12-11 shows the relative airflow deflecting around the trailing edge and leading edge. The associated increase in velocity within those areas produces reduced air pressures (venturi effect). Some blades are manufactured with cut-out sections at their trailing edge for some distance from the blade root to lessen this undesired effect.

Although aircraft speed determines the size of the reverse flow area for the most part, changes in rotor rpm also have their effect. Increased rotor rpm produces higher local speed values per blade section and the reverse flow area will be smaller. However, the small tolerance in limits of rotor rpm reduces the influence of rotor rpm changes on reverse flow.

Translational Lift

Chapter 8 touched on translational lift when it stated that flight other than the "calm" hover causes part of the induced flow to travel horizontally across the disc instead of at right angles through it, reducing induced flow. This was illustrated in Figure 8-3.

The amount of horizontal flow compared to perpendicular flow depends on the inclination of the disc and the speed of the aircraft. At slow speeds the perpendicular flow is substantial, but as airspeed increases it lessens while the horizontal component increases. At high speeds, the horizontal flow component is very large and would only reduce if the disc inclination becomes greater (Figure 12-12).

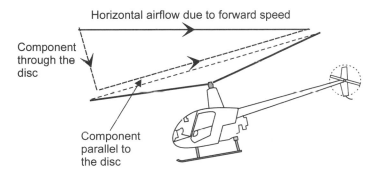

Figure 12-12. *Horizontal flow has two components: one at right angles and the other parallel to the disc.*

If the inclination were 90°, there would be no horizontal flow at all. The horizontal component resulting from forward speed would only be parallel to the disc if the rotor were truly horizontal, that is, in line with the path of horizontal travel. This cannot happen because the disc must be tilted somewhat to provide the forward component (thrust) of total rotor thrust.

Thus the horizontal flow (resulting from airspeed) passing over the disc and effectively reducing the induced flow has a component going through the disc whose size depends on disc tilt. The greater the tilt, the larger the component adding to induced flow.

The inclination angle of the disc to line of flight in cruise configurations is fairly small. If increasing airspeeds involve large disc inclinations, however, the effective induced flow will increase again beyond a given airspeed.

The main consideration with horizontal flow across the disc is its influence on induced flow, which it decreases (so that inflow angles reduce). This ignores the small vertical component because of forward speed. As a result, for a given rotor rpm and collective setting, the angle of attack increases.

As with ground effect, the larger angle of attack and the more-vertical orientation of the total reaction (as the relative airflow comes from lower down from smaller inflow angles), increases the total rotor thrust and the helicopter climbs.

> Since the collective has not changed, power output has not changed. We can therefore say that *translational lift describes a gain of altitude not caused by an increase in power.*
>
> If the collective is lowered (less power) to prevent a height gain when translational lift is encountered, *translational lift* can be defined as *the production of total rotor thrust for less power.*

In either definition, the term *lift* is somewhat misleading. The phenomenon has nothing to do with lift other than causing it to become more vertical. During the accelerating stage, when the disc is often inclined more than in cruise flight and the requirement for total rotor thrust is large, more lift is needed. At cruise airspeeds, or when in non-accelerating conditions, however, the actual requirement for lift is impossible to establish because of the number of variables.

Translational lift occurs at any time in flight other than a calm hover, but at very low speeds it is practically impossible to detect. Translational lift becomes noticeable in most helicopters as the aircraft moves through 12 to 15 knots, and is manifested as a vibration or shudder.

> As airspeed increases, translational lift increases.

Increasing parasite drag at 50 to 60 knots airspeed and higher overshadows the benefit of translational lift. Thus when accelerating beyond 12 knots in level flight, the pilot lowers collective progressively and power output reduces. Beyond 50 knots the pilot raises collective and power output increases.

The benefits of translational lift are :
- more weight can be carried
- flight at greater altitudes is possible
- flight in higher density altitudes is possible
- less power is required

Translational lift is present in a hover when the wind is greater than 12 to 15 knots. Indeed, the effect of a strong (smooth) wind is a prominent feature in reducing power requirements through translational lift. When the helicopter is in ground effect and accelerating, translational lift may compensate for the loss of ground effect. The wind does not have to be on the nose and the flight path does not have to be forward for translational lift to occur.

When in flight without reference to a ground feature, the amount of translational lift is dependent on the airspeed and not the groundspeed. For example, in unaccelerated flight at an indicated airspeed of 5 knots in a 30 knot tailwind, there is no noticeable benefit of translational lift.

Transverse Flow Effect (Inflow Roll)

With increasing airspeed the front of the disc enters air that has not had a great deal of warning of the approaching disc, whereas the air above the disc and particularly towards the back of the disc has already experienced the influence of induced flow (Figure 12-13).

As a consequence, the perpendicular flow through the disc is more pronounced at the rear of the disc than at the front. Thus rotor thrust is less at the rear because the induced flow is stronger, and because of that, the angle of attack of the blade in that region is smaller. The rear of the disc wants to descend, but because of precession, the effect occurs 90° further on in the direction of rotation and the helicopter will roll right (left for clockwise rotating rotors). This phenomenon is known as *transverse flow effect* or *inflow roll*. Transverse flow effect is more pronounced in the lower speed range just above translational lift speed (12 to 15 knots).

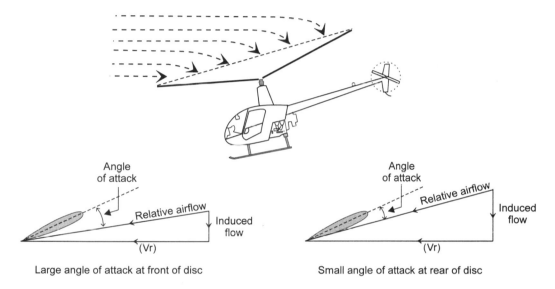

Large angle of attack at front of disc

Small angle of attack at rear of disc

Figure 12-13. *Inflow roll is caused by less rotor thrust produced at the rear of the rotor disc than at the front which results in a roll to the advancing side.*

Review 12

1. During straight and level flight the two components of total rotor thrust are the forward _____ component to overcome (weight/parasite drag) and the _____ component to overcome (weight/parasite drag).

2. In stabilized straight and level flight, the fuselage attitude is determined by the resultant of _____ and _____ passing through the center of (pressure/gravity) of the aircraft.

3. When moving cyclic forward, the pitch angle is (greatest/smallest) on the advancing side of the disc and angles of attack, as a direct result of cyclic, (do/do not) change.

4. When moving cyclic to the right in a helicopter fitted with a clockwise rotating rotor, the pitch angle is greatest when the blade is over the (nose/tail/left side/right side) of the aircraft.

5. Dissymmetry of lift is caused by _____ airspeed affecting the advancing blade and _____ airspeed affecting the _____ blade.

6. Dissymmetry of lift is corrected by blade (coning/flapping) which (increases/ decreases) the (angle of attack/blade angle) of the advancing blade.

7. When flying horizontally to your left, the blade angle of the blade over the nose is at its (greatest/smallest) and the angle of attack is at its (greatest/smallest).

8. Blow-back (or flap-back) is caused by (coning/flapping) of the blades to eliminate _____.

9. When airspeed increases, a reverse flow area develops on the _____ side of the disc. In this area, blade sections (are/are not) stalled.

10. As you accelerate through 12 - 15 knots you do not move the collective up or down. The helicopter will then (climb/remain level/ descend) under the influence of _____.

11. Transverse flow effect (or inflow roll) is more pronounced at (high/low) airspeed and is caused by (greater/smaller) induced flow being experienced at the rear of the disc than at the front. The helicopter tends to (yaw/roll) to the (advancing side/retreating side).

Power, Range and Endurance 13

Range and endurance flying involves techniques that require precise engine handling. To assist understanding we will first examine the power involved in straight and level flight.

Power

A helicopter in flight experiences various types of drag which must be overcome by engine power so that the aircraft can fly at any airspeed and configuration. Four power requirements are identified to:

1. Drive ancillaries such as generators, hydraulics and tail rotor.

2. Overcome blade profile drag (form drag and skin friction) so that rotor rpm can be maintained at any required value.

3. Overcome the portion of rotor drag that is associated with total rotor thrust in its function of supporting weight.

4. Overcome parasite drag in flight that manifests itself in the form of additional rotor drag due to disc tilt.

Ancillary Power

The power required to drive ancillaries is not affected by the helicopter's airspeed, it is a constant. The power required to drive the tail rotor, however, reduces with airspeed because:

1. The tail rotor benefits from its own translational lift.

2. Less anti-torque is needed when power requirement is reduced as translational lift is gained with forward speed.

3. Increasing airspeed improves directional stability (e.g. improved vertical stabilizer effect).

4. The tail rotor blows (or flaps) back and experiences a continuous flare effect that reduces tail rotor drag.

These effects taper off towards the higher speed range when increasing parasite drag demands high power delivery to the main rotor.

Profile Power

Profile drag varies with the square of the velocity (V^2) of a rotor blade when it is at its minimum pitch angle and minimum drag coefficient. Velocity (V) is greater on the advancing blade and less on the retreating blade. When the helicopter is operating at low speeds, the gain on one and the loss on the other more or less cancel out. However, at higher airspeeds the squared relationship causes the profile drag on the advancing blade to exceed that on the retreating side, so that profile drag overall increases towards the higher speed range.

> **Combining ancillary with profile power, total rotor profile power is defined as the power required to maintain a given rotor rpm when the collective is at its minimum setting and to overcome the drag associated with ancillary equipment.**

The plotted curve (Figure 13-1) commences at a certain power required value while the helicopter is at zero airspeed (where it constitutes about 40 percent of the total power required to hover) and remains relatively level until the helicopter reaches higher speeds. From that stage on, the curve starts its climb.

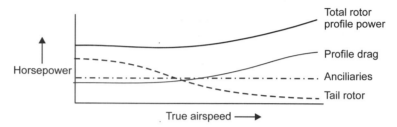

Figure 13-1. *Components of total rotor profile power.*

Induced Power

The induced power required to drive the main rotor (when sufficient total rotor thrust must be provided to overcome weight) reduces with airspeed. This is because translational lift reduces inflow angles which causes the total reaction to move more vertical so that rotor drag reduces. The effect is relatively rapid beyond the 12 to 15 knot speed range and tapers off at higher speeds, but, as mentioned earlier, translational lift continues to show benefits as speed increases.

When collective settings and drag coefficient are at their minimum, little rotor thrust is being provided to sustain level flight. Thus if total rotor thrust is to equal the weight, pitch (blade) angles must be increased, which leads to an increase in drag coefficient and an increase in the induced flow. Both of these cause an increase in rotor drag and more power must be supplied to maintain rotor rpm. This extra power is known as *induced power*.

It is important to differentiate between rotor profile power and induced power. Induced power is highest when the induced flow is maximum. Because the induced flow (and inflow angles) reduce as airspeed increases, as explained above, induced power is maximum at zero airspeed (where it accounts for about 60% of the power required to hover) and reduces with forward speed. On the power-required graph the induced power curve starts high, at zero airspeed, and lowers progressively. Since there must always be some induced flow in powered flight, induced power can never be zero.

Parasite Power

Parasite drag from the fuselage and its components increases in proportion to the square of the velocity (V^2) of the helicopter. As this occurs, the disc must be tilted in such a way that:

- a force is produced to equal the weight (as accounted for in induced power)

- a force is supplied to overcome the increasing parasite drag

The effect of disc tilt produces a component of the horizontal airflow passing perpendicular through the disc (see Chapter 12, Figure 12-12). The larger the tilt, the greater this component, which effectively adds to the induced flow. The consequence of this is that:

1. the inflow angle increases, which, in turn, causes the total reaction to tilt aft so that rotor drag increases

2. the increased inflow angle also reduces the angle of attack and through that, the total rotor thrust required to sustain level flight

(These effects must not be confused with translational lift, which always causes the inflow angle to reduce as airspeed increases.) The pitch angle must be increased to provide a total rotor thrust large enough to produce the two required component forces: the force opposing weight and forward thrust. As a consequence, the helicopter's power requirement increases.

We can therefore conclude that induced power *reduces* with forward speed (because induced flow and inflow angles reduce) whereas parasite power increases with forward speed partly because of increasing fuselage drag and partly because of disc tilt (which causes an increase in inflow angles and rotor drag).

In the power required graph, the parasite power curve starts at zero in a calm hover and climbs progressively steeper as airspeed increases. This context ignores rotor downwash onto the fuselage in a hover but this cannot be done for hover flight with a slingload attached (see Chapter 22).

Figure 13-2 identifies induced, profile and parasite power.

- **Induced power** relates to the force opposing weight, including any change to induced flow (and the lift coefficient) that comes into play with changes in altitude, density altitude and load factors.

- **Profile power** relates to the maintenance of rotor rpm, excluding factors associated with induced flow and lift coefficient changes accounted for by induced power. The power required to drive the tail rotor and ancillaries is also in this category.

- **Parasite power** deals with the forward thrust component of total rotor thrust proportional to disc tilt and airspeed. It attends to all the parasite drag produced by the aircraft because the fundamental reason for disc tilt is parasite drag.

The Total Horsepower Required Curve (the HPR)

When the power requirements are combined a total horsepower required curve for straight and level flight forms. The curve in Figure 13-3 shows that lots of power is needed for level flight at low speeds, under the influence of high induced power, and at high speeds, under the influence of parasite and increasing profile power. The curve is U-shaped, preventing us from applying a general rule of total power requirements with increasing or decreasing airspeeds. For instance, an increasing airspeed only relates to less power required provided a given speed (below the bottom of the curve) is not exceeded.

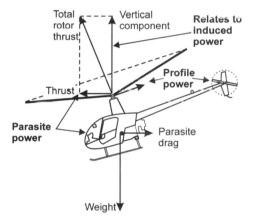

Figure 13-2. *Simplified presentation of induced, profile and parasite power.*

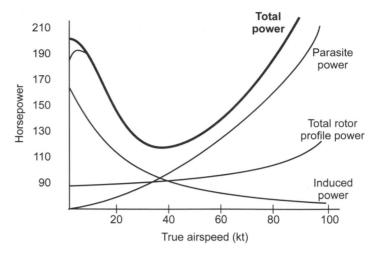

Figure 13-3. *The horsepower required curve (HPR).*

The curve depicts the power required to fly a helicopter in straight and level configuration. This speed must be true airspeed (TAS) because power, which is the rate of doing work (force x distance moved), can only be plotted against a speed that depicts the actual distance traveled through the airmass, that is, TAS.

The shape of the curve at zero airspeed is interesting. Remember that hovering in-ground effect requires less power than hovering out-of-ground effect for the same aircraft weight and environment conditions. As airspeed starts to build up, the benefit of ground effect reduces while translational lift has not yet started to produce its benefits. Once translational lift sets in, however, the requirement for power rapidly decreases.

The following factors influence the position of the horsepower required curve (HPR) both horizontally and vertically:

- altitude
- weight
- slingloads and parasite drag

Altitude

For a given IAS (indicated airspeed), the amount of parasite drag and parasite power is unaltered with changes in altitude. But decreased density with an increase in altitude does affect:

1. **Induced Power.** Less density requires a higher induced flow to maintain mass flow. Pitch angles, angles of attack and inflow angles must be greater, resulting in a poorer total rotor thrust/rotor drag ratio, which causes the induced power curve to rise.

2. **Profile Power.** The maintenance of rotor rpm is influenced by the measure of TAS that affects the rotor, especially as speed increases. Additionally, the higher power required due to induced flow (mentioned in the preceding paragraph) requires more anti-torque (tail rotor) thrust, which adds to profile power requirements, and the profile power curve rises.

Because the induced power effect is predominant and is augmented by more profile power at higher speeds, the horsepower required curve moves up and to the right with increased altitude and down and to the left with decreased altitude (Figure 13-4).

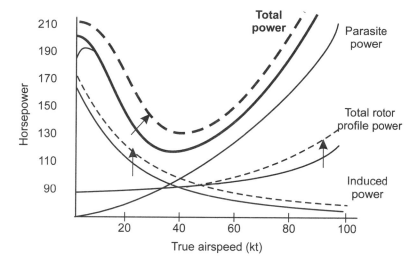

Figure 13-4. *Increased altitude and gross weight move the horsepower required curve up and to the right, and vice versa.*

Weight

An increase in the gross weight of an aircraft requires a larger total rotor thrust (with increasing airspeed) so that its vertical component balances the new weight. The induced flow and induced power must increase. Accordingly, the horsepower required curve moves up and slightly to the right. Extra power demands more anti-torque (tail rotor) thrust, affecting profile power. A further slight rise of the horsepower required is manifest.

> **An increase in altitude and gross weight causes the horsepower required curve to move up and to the right while a decrease in altitude and gross weight causes it to move down and to the left (Figure 13-4).**

Slingloads and Parasite Drag Items

For a similar weight and altitude, slingloads and other parasite drag items have little influence on the horsepower-required curve at low airspeeds, but as the helicopter's speed increases the associated parasite drag responds by the square of the increase. This causes the parasite power curve (and therefore the total power curve) to move progressively further up on the right.

The speed at which slingloads should be flown depends more on the nature and shape of the load than on the behavior of the horsepower required curve. In the hover, however, the downwash from the main rotor onto the slingload adds a downward force to the load, making it seem heavier. More induced power is needed under those conditions. The effect generally disappears as airspeed is increased and the downwash passes behind the slingload. Use of a long strap or long cable lessens the effect.

Flying the Helicopter for Range

Range flying means traveling the maximum *number of air nautical miles on the fuel carried*. Although the wind obviously has an effect on distance covered, for now we'll leave it out.

Fuel transfers the heat energy within itself into power so that the engine can do work in overcoming the various types of drag. Thus:

Fuel = Power

The *fuel* carried must provide the power required to overcome *drag* at any given altitude at a given *airspeed (fuel = power = drag x airspeed)*. But which airspeed applies, the airspeed indicated on the aircraft's airspeed indicator or TAS ? To find the answer we must examine the term "power".

Power is the rate of doing work, – force x distance over time. Since the only airspeed depicting the actual distance covered through the air over time is TAS, the airspeed to be used for power must be TAS, not the airspeed indicated on the airspeed indicator. Therefore:

Fuel = Power = Drag x TAS

Depending on the amount of fuel carried in the fuel tanks, power will be available for a certain *time* during which d*rag x TAS* can be overcome. Therefore, multiplying each side of the above formula by time:

Power x Time = Drag x TAS x Time

But, *TAS x Time = Distance*. For example, traveling at 100 knots for 2 hours means covering 200 nautical miles in that time. By replacing *TAS x Time* with *distance* we can say:

Power x Time = Drag x Distance

For a given quantity of fuel carried, power is available for a certain time. At any stage of flight the quantity of fuel carried is a fixed value at that instant in time. Therefore, if the fuel available is proportional to *drag x distance* and if the distance is to be as great as possible then the *drag should be minimum*, ie, the aircraft should be flown at the speed that equates to the least amount of drag. Thus we can conclude:

Flying for Range = Flying at Minimum Drag

The bottom of the drag curve (Chapter 4, Fig. 4-9) marks the indicated airspeed (IAS) for minimum drag. But range is determined by TAS, which makes the drag curve unsuitable. The *horsepower-required curve* (the *HPR*) is used instead, which indicates the horsepower required to fly the helicopter straight and level at any TAS (Fig. 13-5).

Minimum drag is *not found* at the bottom of the HPR curve because, although the total drag and the horsepower required curves look similar, they are not the same since, firstly, drag is plotted against IAS while power is plotted against TAS. Secondly, power is not drag, which is clearly shown by re-stating that:

Power = Drag x TAS

If drag were the same as power then the formula only applies if the TAS is one knot!

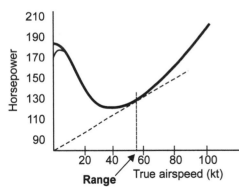

Figure 13-5. *The tangent to the horsepower required curve establishes range speed.*

The question then arises, where can we find minimum drag on the horsepower required curve? Rearrange the power formula and we can see that:

$$Drag = \frac{Power}{TAS}$$

The ratio of power to TAS must show the least amount of power for the greatest amount of TAS to minimize drag. On the power curve this can be found by drawing the tangent to the HPR curve (Figure 13-5). Thus the minimum drag (indicated airspeed) on the total drag curve can be found on the horsepower-required curve (HPR) directly below the point where the tangent strikes the curve (approximately 56 knots in this example).

If factors that influence the horsepower-required curve are taken into account we see that the TAS (beneath the point where the tangent strikes the HPR) varies, depending on the lateral position of the curve. For instance, an increase in gross weight moves the horsepower required curve up and to the right. Consequently, the TAS for maximum range increases with a greater gross weight, and vice versa.

Effect of the Wind

The effect of the wind on range is significant in a helicopter because it flies at relatively slow speeds.

If the aircraft flies at 30 knots TAS into a 30 knot headwind it is going nowhere. Even if the helicopter is subsequently flown at the recommended range speed for no-wind conditions (56 knots, speed A in Figure 13-6.) range is still not the best we can expect.

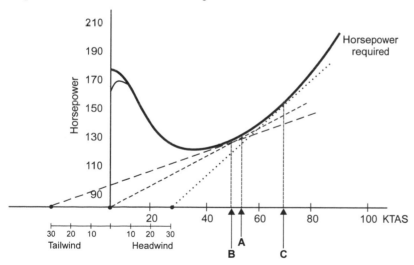

Figure 13-6. *Effect of headwind and tailwind on the TAS for range.*

To establish range in windy conditions the tangent to the horsepower required must commence at zero groundspeed for a headwind and the equivalent value to the left of the vertical graph leg for a tailwind. For instance, in a 30 knot headwind, the zero groundspeed value is found at 30 knots TAS.

The influence of a tailwind on adjusted TAS for range (speed B) is small, and involves only a few knots because the tangent, from its new source to the left, still strikes the horsepower-required curve fairly close to the zero-wind tangent, speed A in Figure 13-6. The influence of a headwind is more pronounced, however. The tangent, from its new source to the right, lies almost flat to the horsepower required curve and a band of speeds (centered on speed C in Figure 13-6) is now produced for range, with greater power required. By flying faster within the available band, up to about 80 knots, time in the air and exposure to the headwind is less, so range is only minimally affected

Engine Considerations

The more or less constant engine rpm in piston-engine helicopters when flying for range at the various airspeeds keeps the *specific fuel consumption* (SFC = lb/BHP/hr) from varying a great deal with changes in power requirements. Thus the horsepower-required curve can be used without having to pay much attention to different specific fuel consumption at varying speeds.

The same cannot be said for turbine-engine helicopters. Turbine engines do not operate at constant rpm settings and produce their best specific fuel consumption over a narrow band of rpm near their (high) design optimum. Accordingly, better efficiency is generally found at high power in turbine engines. Flying at an airspeed for range as dictated by aerodynamic considerations would place the engine at a lower rpm value, which wastes fuel. The higher engine efficiency gained by flying faster more than compensates for the aerodynamic loss. As a result, turbine-engine helicopters usually have higher range speeds than their piston-engine equivalents. Turbine-engine helicopter best speeds for range are also higher than the horsepower-required curve implies.

Range Summary

* The effect of altitude on range is, in principle: the higher the altitude the greater the range. This is mainly because of engine considerations, but a number of factors go against the principle, such as the high fuel consumption associated with a lengthy climb. The wind is often the deciding factor as to what altitude to fly for range.

Item	Required TAS	Effect on Range
Increased Altitude	Higher	Increased*
Decreased Altitude	Lower	Decreased*
Increased Gross Weight	Higher	Decreased
Decreased Gross Weight	Lower	Increased
High Density Altitude	Higher	Decreased
Low Density Altitude	Lower	Increased
Headwind	Higher	Decreased
Tailwind	Lower	Increased
Slingload	Optional	Decreased

Flying the Helicopter for Endurance

Endurance means keeping the helicopter airborne as long as possible. The aim is to stay in the air for the maximum amount of time on the fuel available – distance or the wind is of no concern. When flying for endurance the helicopter should be maintained in level flight using the least amount of power.

The horsepower-required curve shows that the TAS for least amount of power, while maintaining straight and level flight, is found directly beneath the bottom of the curve (42 kt in Figure 13-7). The maximum endurance point on the chart does not, interestingly enough, coincide with the minimum drag point because that is found by drawing the tangent to the horsepower-required curve.

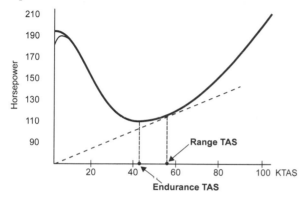

Figure 13-7. *Endurance speed is found below the bottom of the horsepower required curve.*

Therefore, when flying for range, a little more power than minimum is used, but the aircraft operates with the least rotor drag. When flying for endurance, the least amount of power is used, but the aircraft experiences a little more rotor drag.

> **Thus range and endurance can never be achieved at one airspeed. Endurance speed is always slower than the maximum range speed.**

Endurance Summary

Item	Required TAS	Effect on Endurance
Increased Altitude	Increased	Decreased*
Decreased Altitude	Decreased	Increased*
Increased Gross Weight	Increased	Decreased
Decreased Gross Weight	Decreased	Increased
High Density Altitude	Increased	Decreased
Low Density Altitude	Decreased	Increased
Headwind	No effect	No effect
Tailwind	No effect	No effect
Slingload	Optional	Decreased

* The indicated airspeed/TAS relationship dictates that endurance is increased when flying at the lowest possible altitude where indicated airspeed equals TAS, usually sea level. If the aircraft is already at altitude, however, endurance can be improved by using slightly less than minimum power and adopting a small rate of descent.

Review 13

Power, Range and Endurance

1. Total rotor profile power is the power required to drive the rotor when the collective lever is at the _____ setting and (includes/excludes) the power required to drive the tail rotor.

2. Induced power is the power required to drive the rotor when it operates at (increasing/ decreasing) blade angles to support the _____ of the helicopter in flight.

3. Parasite power is the power required to overcome _____ drag.

4. With an increase in airspeed from about 40 knots to Vne, induced power (increases/ decreases), profile power (increases/ decreases/remains steady) and parasite power (increases/decreases).

5. The power required to maintain straight and level flight (increases/decreases) with an increase in altitude and the TAS for minimum power goes (up/down).

6. When flying for maximum range you must fly at a TAS which produces minimum _____. This speed can be found on the power required curve by drawing the _____ to the curve.

7. When your gross weight is greater, the required TAS for maximum range is (higher/lower) and range is (improved/ reduced).

8. When flying for range in a headwind, range is (improved/reduced) and the TAS should be (increased/decreased).

9. When flying for maximum endurance, drag (is/is not) at its minimum and the associated TAS can be found below the _____ of the power required curve.

10. A headwind (does/does not) affect endurance and the TAS (should/should not) be adjusted to allow for this wind.

11. Flying for range requires minimum (power/drag) whereas flying for endurance requires minimum (power/drag).

Climbing and Descending **14**

Climbing

When a helicopter is hovering in calm conditions a few inches off the ground, its total rotor thrust is exactly equal and opposite to its gross weight. If the pilot raises the collective and increases the total rotor thrust, the aircraft begins a vertical climb at a slowly increasing rate of climb (ROC).

An airflow from above, caused by the rate of climb, effectively adds to the induced flow, increasing inflow angles and reducing angles of attack. To sustain the climb the pilot must raise the collective further. This action affects the relationship between total rotor thrust and rotor drag because the total reaction leans further away from the axis of rotation as inflow angles increase. Accordingly, total rotor thrust decreases while rotor drag increases.

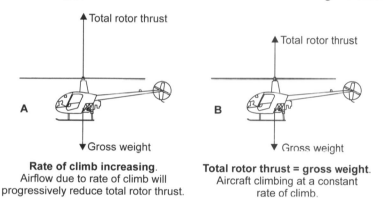

Figure 14-1. *Helicopter in a vertical climb.*

At the start of the vertical climb the total rotor thrust was larger than the gross weight and an increasing rate of climb resulted (Figure 14-1 A). Eventually, however, the total rotor thrust becomes equal to the gross weight (Figure 14-1 B). Provided that enough power is available and used, the helicopter continues a stable vertical climb at *a constant rate*.

Since direction and vertical velocity are now constant in this example, the helicopter must be in a state of equilibrium. Total rotor thrust and gross weight must be equal and opposite in such a climb, if not, the helicopter's rate of climb would alter. Although this is perhaps difficult to accept, you must realize that the power in use to sustain this vertical climb at a constant rate is in excess of the power required to hover. In essence, the extra energy or work done by the engine is changed into potential energy in terms of increased altitude.

Thus the ability to climb is determined by availability of surplus power over and above that required to maintain an altitude, in the hover or in straight and level flight. Consequently, if the power required to maintain straight and level flight can be calculated and if the amount of power available is able to be established from manufacturer's information, then a rate of climb can be determined from the surplus power available.

The horsepower-required curve (HPR, see Chapter 13) indicated the power required to fly straight and level at any desired TAS. If the horsepower-available curve is superimposed on the horsepower-required curve, the helicopter's ability to climb can be assessed by comparing the "gap" between the two curves.

The Horsepower-Available Curve (the HPA)

Unlike airplanes, which rely on thrust horsepower to drive the propeller, helicopters rely on shaft horsepower, which is unaffected by aircraft speed. Consequently, a constant amount of power is available at any speed after allowance has been made for the inevitable loss within the engine itself, since 100% efficiency is not possible. When plotted on the horsepower graph, the horsepower available curve (HPA) is a straight horizontal line that always has its highest position slightly lower than the maximum certificated power value. The power involved in driving the tail rotor and ancillaries has already been allowed for in the horsepower required curve under profile power, reinforcing the fact that the horsepower-available curve is a straight line. The horsepower-available curve shown in Figure 14-2 assumes full power is being delivered by the 210 hp engine when the helicopter starts its climb from sea level.

Note the significance of 108 knots, the point on the graph where the horsepower required and horsepower available curves intersect. This is the maximum straight and level speed for this power setting, altitude and gross weight. Flight beyond this speed results in a descent and flight at less than 108 knots results in a climb.

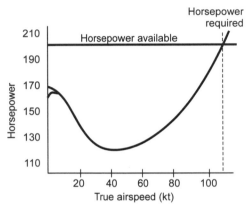

Figure 14-2. *The horsepower available curve added to the horsepower required curve.*

Factors Affecting the Horsepower Available Curve

Altitude

The density of air decreases with altitude, decreasing horsepower available, but the type of engine determines at what altitude the loss of horsepower begins. A non-supercharged piston engine loses horsepower from sea level up, whereas a turbine engine that has been de-rated from 600 shp to 450 shp, for example, maintains its power output up into the higher altitudes. Nevertheless, all engines eventually reach a ceiling above which they decrease their power output with altitude.

In the end, horsepower available decreases with altitude, this has a negative effect on helicopter performance.

Density Altitude

A reduced air density resulting from low pressure, high temperatures and/or high humidity has the same effect as altitude. A high density altitude causes the horsepower available to decrease, while a low density altitude causes the horsepower available to go up.

Leaning the Mixture

Correct leaning (as detailed in the aircraft Flight Manual) improves power output from the engine, and horsepower available increases. Most piston-engined helicopters are equipped with an automatic mixture control (AMC).

Collective Setting

The collective lever directly determines the throttle butterfly position (or fuel flow in most turbine engines). The control is therefore a "limiter" of power output, so lowering the collective lowers the horsepower available curve while raising the collective raises the horsepower available. Movement of the throttle relative to the collective is accomplished with a correlator. The two can be operated independently of each other, as well.

Although the twist grip throttle is mainly a rotor rpm fine-tuner, it does have some influence on manifold pressure because of the correlator, and in general, may be seen in the same light as the collective.

Rate of Climb

> **Rate of climb is the gain of altitude per time and is normally expressed in feet per minute.**

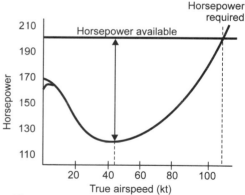

Figure 14-3. *Maximum rate of climb is found where the greatest surplus power occurs.*

When the horsepower available curve is compared to the horsepower required curve, the rate of climb is maximum for a given gross weight, power setting and altitude where the vertical gap between the two curves is greatest (Fig.14-3). The TAS directly beneath the largest vertical gap is the speed for maximum rate of climb, 42 knots in this example. Climbing at speeds faster or slower than 42 knots produces a reduced rate of climb.

When the behavior of the horsepower-required and horsepower-available curves is taken into account, the rate of climb can be predicted. For instance, an increase in altitude lowers the horsepower available while the horsepower required moves up and to the right. Consequently, the gap between the curves is smaller, causing the rate of climb to decrease. The widest gap shifts to the right showing that the associated TAS for the best rate of climb is higher.

Or, a reduced gross weight does not affect the horsepower available, but it does move the horsepower required down and to the left. The rate of climb then is greater (because the gap between the HPR and HPA becomes larger), while the associated TAS for the best rate of climb is slower.

Understanding the movement of the curves makes understanding the rate of climb and associated TAS simple.

Angle of Climb

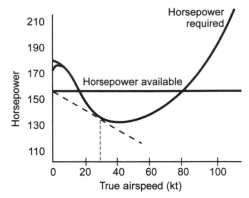

Figure 14-4. *When power available is insufficient to hover, best angle of climb speed can be found by drawing the tangent to the horsepower required curve.*

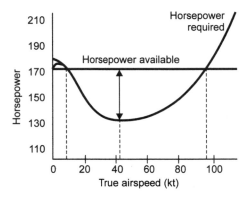

Figure 14-5. *Effect of reduced horsepower available.*

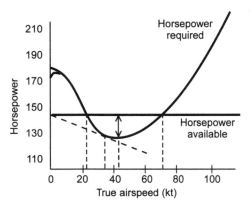

Figure 14-6. *Effect of further lowering of the horsepower available.*

> **The angle of climb is a function of height gained per forward speed, which means that the slower the forward speed with a gain in altitude, the steeper the climb angle. The faster the forward speed per gain in height, the shallower the climb angle.**

The horsepower available and horsepower required curves in Figure 14-3 indicate that at zero airspeed, in the hover, surplus power is available for climbing. The gap between the curves is relatively small, indicating that rate of climb will be low, but climbing at zero forward speed does mean that the angle of climb is vertical.

Whenever there is surplus power at zero airspeed, the angle of climb can be 90°, which implies that when surplus power is not available at that speed (such as at high altitude), it is impossible to climb vertically (ignoring the wind factor).

When there is no surplus power at zero airspeed, climbing out at various speeds produces differing angles of climb. To establish the TAS for the *steepest angle of climb*, draw the tangent to the horsepower-required curve commencing where the horsepower *available* intersects the vertical graph axis (the Y-leg) as shown in Figure 14-4. In this example, 28 knots produces the steepest possible angle of climb.

Effect of a Lowering Horsepower Available Curve

The following sequence of graphs shows the effect on helicopter climb performance when the horsepower available reduces, such as when the collective is lowered or when altitude is gained. For the sake of simplicity, the effects of gross weight and altitude on the horsepower required curve are ignored, which in no way detracts from the principles involved.

In Figure 14-5, the horsepower available just satisfies the horsepower required at the hover in-ground effect, and a vertical climb is not possible. Below 8 knots the aircraft cannot fly level because the horsepower available does not meet the horsepower required. A running takeoff or a wind increase to at least 8 knots is necessary before flight can commence. Should the aircraft be in flight already, then slowing airspeed below 8 knots will incur a descent.

In this example, 8 knots is the minimum straight and level speed while the maximum straight and level speed has reduced from 108 knots (in Fig. 14-2) to 96 knots. The best rate of climb speed remains at 42 knots, but the actual rate in feet per minute has declined (compared to that in Fig.14-3).

Figure 14-6 shows that straight and level flight below 22 knots is not possible. Twenty-two knots becomes the minimum straight and level airspeed, while the maximum straight and level speed reduces to 72 knots. The best rate of climb speed remains at 42 knots and the actual rate of climb becomes smaller again. The tangent to the horsepower-required curve indicates that 38 knots is the TAS for the best angle of climb. (Although the tangent also applied to the previous diagram, it was left out for the sake of clarity.)

Figure 14-7 shows that the horsepower available has dropped to the stage where a climb is not possible. Indeed, the aircraft can only fly level at one TAS, 42 knots. Should the helicopter fly faster or slower than 42 knots, a descent will result. This graph shows the power output for endurance flight, as we saw in the previous chapter, because the horsepower available touches the horsepower required at minimum power.

Figure 14-8 shows that the horsepower available has fallen below the horsepower required curve so that straight and level flight is not possible at any speed. The greater the shortfall in power, the greater the rate at which the aircraft descends. The actual rate of descent is also influenced by the speed at which the aircraft is flown. If the pilot deviates the airspeed to either side of 42 knots, a higher rate of descent is created.

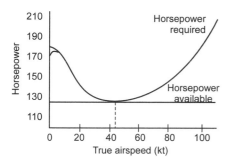

Figure 14-7. *Helicopter cannot climb at all and only one straight and level speed is possible.*

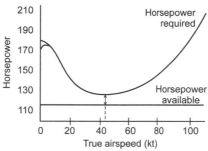

Figure 14-8. *Climb and straight and level not possible, helicopter will descend.*

Summary

When surplus power is available and used, a climb results. If a climb is not required, the horsepower available curve must intersect the horsepower required curve precisely above the desired speed so that no power surplus occurs at that speed. If the horsepower available falls below the horsepower required, a descent follows.

Figure 14-9 shows that if the aircraft is to be flown straight and level at 20 knots TAS, the horsepower available must intersect the horsepower required directly above that TAS. By computing altitude against temperature it is then possible to determine the associated calibrated airspeed. Interestingly, if the collective is held constant but the cyclic is moved forward so that the airspeed increases, the helicopter will climb and it will continue to do so until the TAS is 80 knots. At that speed, the aircraft will resume level flight. Under these conditions, one power setting (collective position) provides the pilot with the choice of two straight and level speeds (20 knots and 80 knots).

Effect of the Wind

Since rate of climb is a function of surplus power available over power required, it follows that the wind (provided it is steady) has no influence at all on the aircraft's rate of climb.

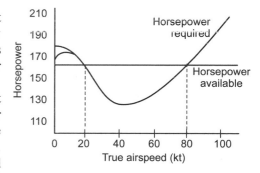

Figure 14-9. *To fly straight and level, the horsepower available curve must intersect the horsepower required curve directly above the required TAS.*

For angle of climb, however, the slower the groundspeed the steeper the angle in a steady headwind. Climbing at 30 knots into a 30 knot steady wind produces a vertical climb (but again note that the rate of climb may be less than it might have been at a higher airspeed). Gusty winds may produce short-term changes to both rate and angle of climb.

Climb Performance Summary

Bearing in mind the behavior of the horsepower required and horsepower available curves, the following tabulation summarizes the helicopter's climb performance:

Item	Rate of climb	Angle of climb	Required TAS
Increasing altitude	Decrease	Shallower ultimately	Increase
Increasing gross weight	Decrease	Shallower ultimately	Increase
Slingload	Decrease	Shallower ultimately	Optional
Headwind	No effect	Steeper	No effect
Tailwind	No effect	Shallower	No effect

Descending

When a helicopter is hovering at altitude in calm conditions, its total rotor thrust equals its gross weight. If the collective is lowered slightly, the total rotor thrust reduces, and as it becomes less than the gross weight, the aircraft commences a descent at an increasing rate of descent (see left-hand diagram, Figure 14-10).

The airflow resulting from the rate of descent (from below) reduces the induced flow so that inflow angles decrease and angles of attack increase and, as a consequence, the total rotor thrust increases. There comes a point at which the aircraft comes into equilibrium – when total rotor thrust equals the gross weight – and the rate of descent stabilizes at a constant value, say 500 ft/min (right-hand diagram of Figure 14-10). Although total rotor thrust and gross weight are equal and opposite now, the power in use is less than that required for a hover at a given altitude and so a descent is inevitable.

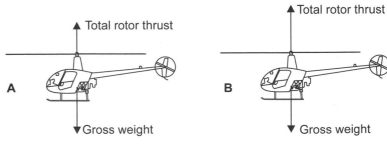

Figure 14-10. *Helicopter in a vertical descent.*

Rate of descent increasing.
Airflow due to rate of descent will progressively increase total rotor thrust.

Total rotor thrust = gross weight.
Aircraft descending at a constant rate of descent.

Two factors can now alter the rate of descent: changes in collective setting and in airspeed. Changing collective affects the horsepower available and through that affects the shortfall in power between power required for straight and level and power available. Similarly, changes in airspeed also affect the shortfall in power as shown in Figure 14-11. For example, a constant collective setting (horsepower-available position) produces an equal rate of descent at 22 knots and 72 knots, but produces an increased rate of descent at 88 knots.

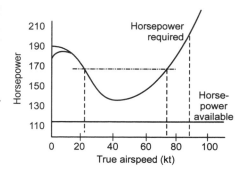

Figure 14-11. *Rate of descent is determined by the difference in horsepower available and horsepower required at any given TAS.*

Angle of Descent

Ignoring the wind for the time being, a descent at zero forward speed is obviously vertical to the surface, which implies that an increase in airspeed produces a shallower angle, so that a given distance is covered ("range"). This might give the impression that the faster the airspeed, the greater the range, but that is not the case.

The shallowest angle of descent (greatest distance covered – range) for a given power setting is achieved when the aircraft operates in its minimum rotor drag (best total rotor thrust/rotor drag ratio) configuration. (The associated speed is normally published in the helicopter's handbook.)

Figure 14-12 shows that at 58 knots TAS, forward distance will be greatest. Any other airspeed causes the descent slope to be steeper and distance covered to be less. The same does not apply to rate of descent, however, which is least at 46 knots. Although the left-hand diagram does not picture this, descent at 75 knots will likely produce a descent angle similar to that at 21 knots.

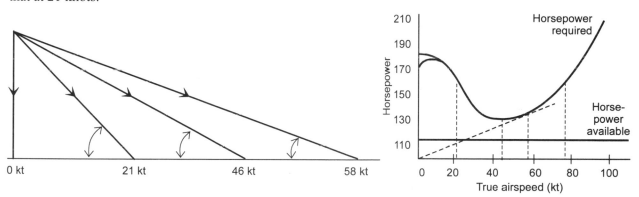

Figure 14-12. *Relationship between airspeed and angle of descent for a given power setting in zero-wind conditions.*

When the collective is "on the floor" and practically no power is being delivered (no horsepower available), the shallowest angle of descent relates to the TAS where the tangent strikes the horsepower-required curve (minimum rotor drag). If collective is now raised slowly (raising the horsepower available) and the airspeed maintained, the angle of descent becomes progressively shallower until the horsepower available intersects the horsepower required above the minimum drag speed. The aircraft then flies straight and level and the angle of descent is zero.

Admittedly straight and level could have been achieved sooner if the airspeed had been reduced to endurance speed, where the rising horsepower available first touches the horsepower-required curve.

> **The effect of increasing power on the angle of descent is that, provided a given speed is maintained, the angle becomes shallower. Since increasing power also reduces the shortfall in power, the rate of descent will similarly decrease until, upon regaining straight and level, it is zero.**

The influence of parasite drag produced by items such as slingloads, will cause the parasite power curve to rise (particularly on the right) so that the horsepower required moves up and to the left. Thus for a given airspeed, the rate of descent increases and the angle of descent steepens.

Effect of the Wind on Descents

A steady wind influences the angle of descent, but not the rate of descent. Neither the horsepower-required nor the horsepower-available curves are affected by the wind, so the gap between the two curves is unaffected.

A helicopter descending at 500 ft/min at its minimum drag speed of 50 knots into a 50 knot headwind has a forward groundspeed of zero, so its angle of descent must be 90°. By increasing the airspeed beyond the minimum drag value, some forward groundspeed is attained, which shallows out the angle of descent. This improves the helicopter's range by increasing the aircraft's ability to penetrate the headwind (even though the TAS may not be the correct one for best range).

The issue of headwind or tailwind on descending is exactly the same as that explained in "Flying for Range" (Chapter 13, Figure 13-6). The same graph (Figure 14-13) shows that in a 30 knot headwind, the adjusted tangent strikes the flat side of the horsepower-required curve and a number of speeds between approximately 65 knots and 80 knots are available for a range descent. The rate of descent is greater than would have been the case at 52 knots (zero-wind best-range speed) and is considerably greater at 80 knots.

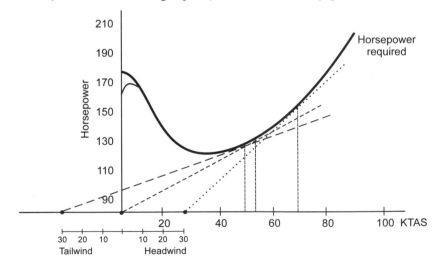

Figure 14-13. *Effect of headwind/tailwind on TAS for range in a descent. Horsepower available below the horsepower required has been deleted for clarity.*

In the case of a tailwind, the airspeed must be slightly reduced and the rate of descent decreases. The slower airspeed gives the helicopter more time in the air and the longer exposure to the tailwind further assists in making the descent angle shallower.

Descent Performance Summary

The following summary lists the various factors that affect descent performance:

Item	Rate of descent	Angle of descent	Required TAS
Decreasing altitude	Reduce	No change	Decrease
Increasing gross weight	Increase	Steeper*	Increase
Decreasing gross weight	Decrease	Shallower*	Decrease
Slingload	Increase	Steeper	Optional
Headwind	No effect	Steeper	No change**
Tailwind	No effect	Shallower	No change**

* Unlike fixed-wing aircraft, where changes in weight do not affect angle of descent provided airspeed is adjusted, in helicopters increasing weight increases the rate of descent to a small degree and decreases range, that is to say, the angle of descent is slightly steeper.

More weight produces a greater rate of descent, opposing the induced flow so that inflow angles reduce and angles of attack increase. This tends to increases total rotor thrust. The lower direction from which the relative airflow strikes the blade causes the total reaction to orient closer to the axis of rotation so that the total rotor thrust/rotor drag ratio improves when less rotor drag is suffered and higher collective settings are now required to maintain the rotor rpm at its given value. Combined, these factors tend to be self-correcting, as far as increasing rates of descent are concerned. However, the raised collective will tilt the total reaction aft, which means that rotor drag increases.

Factors increasing rotor drag outweigh those that decrease it, so that range is adversely affected with a higher gross weight. Changing rotor rpm, if done to maintain the angle of attack as close to optimum as possible, introduces changes to tail rotor and ancillaries requirements. Little, if anything is gained from the practice.

** This has not taken into consideration the option of altering the airspeed, as shown in Figure 14-13.

Review 14

Climbing and Descending

1. When you climb a helicopter vertically in calm conditions and at a constant rate of climb, total rotor thrust is (greater/smaller/the same as) the aircraft's gross weight.

2. During a sustained vertical climb, the requirement for anti-torque _____ .

3. When climbing at the speed for maximum angle of climb, the rate of climb (is/is not) maximum.

4. When you bank your helicopter during a climb, the rate of climb will _____ and the angle of climb become (steeper/shallower).

5. The TAS for maximum rate of climb (is/is not) the same as the TAS for maximum endurance and when climbing at this speed, the angle of climb (is/is not) steepest.

6. When the power available is less than the power required to hover, you (can/ cannot) climb vertically.

7. You climb your helicopter into a headwind. This (will/will not) affect the rate of climb but the angle of climb will be (steeper/shallower/not affected).

8. You are hovering at altitude and then you lower collective slightly. This causes the helicopter to descend at an (increasing/decreasing) rate of descent and when the rate of descent stabilizes, the total rotor thrust is (greater than/less than/equal to) the gross weight of the helicopter.

9. When descending for range in a tailwind, the TAS should be slightly (increased/ decreased) and the rate of descent will then (increase/decrease).

10. When descending in a headwind, the rate of descent (will/will not) be affected and the angle of descent will be (steeper/shallower/unaffected).

11. When descending for maximum range, increased gross weight (increases/ decreases) range and the rate of descent will be slightly (greater/smaller).

Maneuvers 15

Turning

An object traveling on a curve must have a force pulling it towards the center of the curve. That force is *centripetal force*. Chapter 1 explained the reason for CPF and formulated it as:

Centripetal Force (CPF) = $\dfrac{m \ x \ V^2}{r}$ or $\dfrac{w \ x \ V^2}{g \ x \ r}$

> where *m* represents mass, *V* true airspeed, *r* radius, *w* weight, and *g* earth's gravity.

The requirement for centripetal force in a turn is met by *total rotor thrust*, provided that it is *tilted* in the direction of the turn. Thus the helicopter must be banked to make a coordinated turn.

The tilted total rotor thrust in a banked turn provides two component forces:

1. The *vertical* component equal and opposite to weight, which ensures that the helicopter's altitude in the turn remains constant.

2. *Centripetal force*.

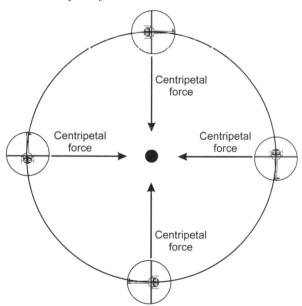

Figure 15-1. *Requirement for centripetal force at all stages of a 360° turn.*

Since total rotor thrust must perform an extra task in providing CPF, it follows that its amount must increase in a turn. This is achieved by increases in blade angles (up collective), which adversely affects the total rotor thrust/rotor drag ratio. As a result more power must be applied to maintain rotor rpm, especially at higher angles of bank (Figure 15-2).

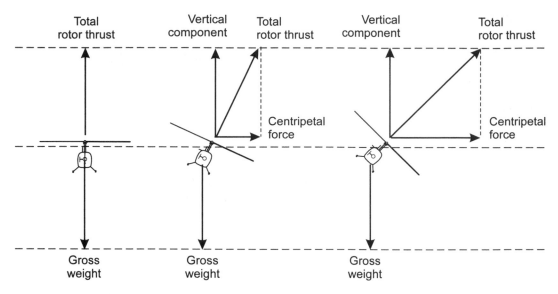

Figure 15-2. *Relationship between angle of bank and requirement for total rotor thrust to provide the vertical component and centripetal force.*

Rate of Turn

The number of degrees the nose passes around the horizon per unit of time is the helicopter's rate of turn.

Rates of turn are typically expressed as:

- *standard rate* (or *rate-1*): 3° per second, or180° per minute, or 360° per 2 minutes

- *double standard rate* (or *rate 2*): 6° per second, or 360° per minute

The squared velocity (V^2) factor in the centripetal force formula demands that the faster the aircraft flies, more centripetal force must be present to maintain a constant rate of turn. Since centripetal force is derived from the total rotor thrust, more total rotor thrust is needed (raised collective). But if the helicopter maintains a constant angle of bank when the total rotor thrust is increased, centripetal force increases, but so does the vertical component, and the helicopter climbs. Therefore, to increase centripetal force without climbing, the bank angle must be steepened as the total rotor thrust is increased. This confirms that there is a relationship between *angle of bank* and *airspeed* for a *given rate of turn*.

To calculate the angle of bank required to maintain a standard rate turn (rate-1) at varying airspeeds, remove the last digit from the aircraft's airspeed and add 7. For example, a helicopter flying at 60 knots is required to accomplish a standard rate (rate-1) turn. What shall be its angle of bank?

Take 60 and remove the last digit (0), which leaves 6. Add 7 to 6, which gives 13. At 60 knots, the aircraft requires 13° angle of bank for a standard rate (rate-1) level turn.

At a speed of 105 knots, the answer is:

Take 105 and remove the last digit (5), leaving 10. Add 7 to 10, which gives 17° for a standard rate (rate-1) level turn.

Radius of Turn

The same principle applies for radius of turn as for rate. The faster the aircraft travels, the greater the centripetal force must be (obtained from more total rotor thrust) and the larger the required angle of bank.

Rate and Radius Interaction

If the helicopter maintains a certain *radius of turn* and flies faster, then the nose passes the horizon at an increasing rate. Thus higher speeds increase the rate of turn, provided the angle of bank is increased and more (tilted) total rotor thrust is supplied. But if a certain *rate of turn* is to be maintained at increasing airspeeds, greater angles of bank and more centripetal force are required *and the resulting radius of the turn will be larger* . The reason for this is shown in Figure 15-3.

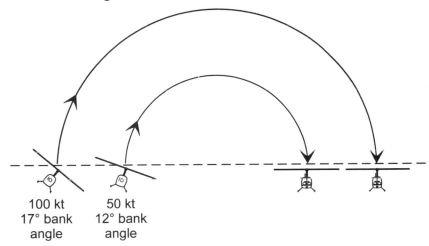

100 kt
17° bank
angle

50 kt
12° bank
angle

Figure 15-3. *The effect of different speeds on angle of bank and radius while rate of turn remains identical for both helicopters.*

Assume a helicopter does a 180° standard rate turn at 50 knots. The turn requires 12° angle of bank and results in a certain radius, say 3,000 ft. The same turn for a similar helicopter flying at 100 knots requires 17° angle of bank. The radius must be more than 3,000 ft, because both aircraft must finish on the same heading at the end of the turn. If not, one or the other has not maintained the correct rate of turn.

The Steep Turn

The steep turn involves angles of bank of 45° or more. Provided the turn is level at a given altitude, the increased angle of bank must be associated with a larger total rotor thrust so that the vertical component continues to equally oppose the aircraft weight. The associated centripetal force is then larger, meaning that the radius of the turn is smaller and the rate of turn is greater.

When an aircraft maintains a perfect constant-radius turn, the centripetal force inward must have an equally opposing force outward. There is much dispute about the name of this force but consistent with other texts, we call it *centrifugal force.*

Figure 15-4 shows two forces acting beneath the helicopter in a turn. Weight acts vertically to the center of the earth and centrifugal force acts horizontally in opposition to centripetal force. When these forces are added as vectors, a resultant force, *load factor*, is formed.

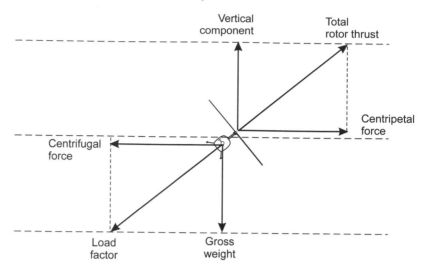

Figure 15-4. *Arrangement of forces in a steep turn.*

In a level, balanced turn, the load factor is equal and opposite to total rotor thrust and has a relationship to weight. The greater the angle of bank, the greater the load factor compared to weight as shown in the following table.

Angle of Bank	Load Factor
30°	1.2 (or 1.2 x the weight)
40°	1.4 (or 1.4 x the weight)
60°	2.0 (or twice the weight)
75°	4.0 (or four times the weight)

Power Requirement

As the angle of bank increases in a level steep turn, the increasing demand for total rotor thrust can be met only by increasing blade angles. Larger blade angles cause the total reaction to depart further from the axis of rotation, causing more rotor drag, which requires more power. The main reason for the added power requirement is the increasing induced drag as collective is raised. Remember, this type of drag is directly proportional to the lift coefficient and induced flow. Since raising collective increases these factors, induced drag increases.

> **The steeper the sustained level turn, the greater the total rotor thrust required, the higher the collective position and the greater the demand for power.**

Since power has a limit, the ultimate factor that decides the maximum steepness of a sustained, level and balanced steep turn is the *availability of surplus power*. Consistent with this, for maximum-rate (minimum radius) turns, pilots should use the speed that allows the greatest surplus in power, which is the *minimum straight and level (endurance) power speed*.

The Climbing Turn

No matter how steep or shallow the turn, there is a need for more total rotor thrust, which in the end always requires larger blade angles and more power. So the horsepower-required curve goes up, the degree depending on the steepness of the bank angle. For a given power available this means that the gap between the two curves (horsepower available and horsepower required) becomes smaller. The consequence is that the rate of climb decreases and the angle of climb becomes shallower.

> **The effect of increasing angles of bank while climbing is a decrease in the rate of climb and a shallower angle of climb. There is an angle of bank where climb performance is reduced to zero.**

The Descending Turn

The same effect applies in the descending turn. The increasing horsepower required causes a greater shortfall of power, which increases the rate of descent and the angle of descent becomes steeper. Do take particular note of this because performing steep descending turns close to the surface can result in unintended contact with the terrain.

Effect of Altitude on Rate of Turn and Radius of Turn

We saw in Chapter 3 that velocity (V in the formula) relates to TAS, not IAS. Thus centripetal force is proportional to TAS, which increases with a gain in altitude if a constant IAS is maintained.

Consider then a helicopter at a steady IAS (say 80 kt) doing a standard rate turn (rate-1) at sea level (angle of bank: 15°). If this angle of bank is maintained during a standard rate turn at a higher altitude and the IAS is held constant (at 80 kt), then the TAS is greater than the IAS and the angle of bank is insufficient to maintain standard rate (rate-1).

The radius of turn also responds to TAS, which means that even if the angle of bank is adjusted correctly for the higher TAS (as the standard rate turn is maintained at a higher airspeed), the resulting turn radius is still larger (refer again to Figure 15-3).

> **The effect of increasing altitude on turning is that the angle of bank required to maintain a rate of turn must be steeper and the radius will be larger. If the angle of bank is not corrected for the higher TAS, the rate of turn will decrease and radius will increase even further.**

Effect of Changes in Gross Weight on Rate and Radius

Changes in gross weight do not affect the angle of bank required for a given rate or radius of turn, rather, it is the speed at which the helicopter is flown under different gross weight conditions that determines the angle of bank required. If a helicopter at minimum gross weight flies at 80 kt, an angle of bank of 15° produces standard rate (rate-1) and a certain radius. If the aircraft is then flown at maximum gross weight at 80 kt, the same angle of bank of 15° again produces standard rate and the same radius. This is because when heavier, the helicopter produces more total rotor thrust and uses more power simply to fly straight and level. The greater centripetal force required by a greater weight is therefore automatically provided when the increased total rotor thrust is tilted as the aircraft banks.

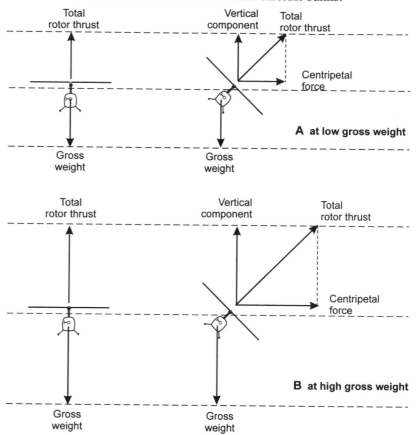

Figure 15-5. *Angle of bank is the same for both helicopters provided they fly at a common airspeed.*

Effect of the Wind on Rate and Radius

> **When a single angle of bank is maintained, the wind affects the radius of turn (with reference to the ground) but not the rate of turn.**

To maintain a constant-radius turn around a ground feature, however, the centripetal force must be adjusted to allow for the differences in groundspeed as the aircraft completes the turn. The higher the groundspeed, the larger the centripetal force required to maintain the radius.

Figure 15-6 shows that at position B the groundspeed is least and at D it is highest. Thus the angle of bank needs to be least at B and greatest at D to provide the correct amount of centripetal force for a constant-radius.

The angle of bank increases between B and C and decreases between D and A. The degree of angle of bank change must be such that the angle of bank is shallower at C than at A.

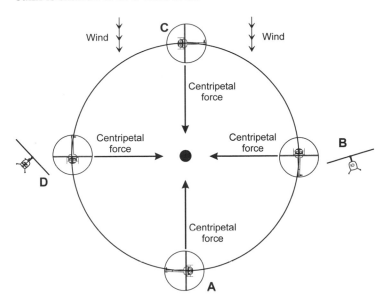

Figure 15-6. *Effect of the wind on angle of bank to maintain a constant radius around a ground feature.*

Effect of the Wind on Indicated Airspeed and Translational Lift

The wind is a much misunderstood phenomenon. It is simply the horizontal movement of air trying to flow from high to low atmospheric pressure. When an aircraft is part of that block of air, the pilot does not "feel" the wind. This is shown clearly in a manned balloon. Once the balloon takes off it becomes part of the migrating mass of air. If one lights a candle while in the basket beneath the balloon, the flame stands more or less straight up, regardless of the velocity of the wind. But if the balloon is tethered to the ground, the effect of the wind becomes instantly apparent and the candle flame tilts downwind. Therein lies the truth of wind effect.

The wind has no effect whatsoever (as in the case of the balloon) when flying a helicopter in a steady wind without reference to a ground feature. It is impossible to assess the wind velocity from the readings of the airspeed indicator. Completing a balanced 360° turn in a steady wind does not cause the airspeed indicator to change (ignoring effects from an increasing drag caused by higher collective settings). If we fly straight ahead into a headwind, then turn around and fly downwind, the airspeed indicator reads the same, provided we make no attempt to hold position relative to a ground feature. Under these conditions, the influence of the wind on translational lift is zero.

> **Translational lift only relates to the indicated airspeed at which the helicopter flies at any one time.**

When a turn is executed with reference to a ground feature, however, the wind has a varying influence on the aircraft, its airspeed, groundspeed and translational lift.

Imagine a helicopter flying downwind towards a landing area. On passing abeam it, the pilot commences a turn to position the helicopter for a short final approach into the wind. The reference is now a ground feature and, taking it to its extreme, if the helicopter is brought to an instant hover over a spot into the wind at that time, the disc will be tilted into the wind and the airspeed indicator will read the wind speed. In this example, the turn from downwind into the wind causes the wind to have a positive influence on airspeed, and translational lift is influenced similarly. The final result in terms of actual airspeed and translational lift acquired in the maneuver depends on what the pilot does to the attitude and collective setting of the helicopter.

The reverse holds true as well, and this is the basis of good advice from experienced helicopter pilots when they warn novices about turning downwind from an into the wind situation. If the turn is executed with reference to a ground feature, then the wind causes a reduction in indicated airspeed and, more importantly, reduces the benefit of translational lift as the helicopter turns downwind.

Flying a helicopter at less than 12 knots IAS in a 20 knot tailwind (an admittedly hazardous procedure), a pilot-induced reduction in airspeed to come to a halt over a ground feature theoretically improves translational lift. When the aircraft is brought to the hover over the spot, translational lift is caused by the full 20 knot tailwind (in this example). To reverse the situation and complete the transition from the downwind hover over a spot to an increasing IAS requires acceleration to a groundspeed equal to the strength of the tailwind (20 knot in our example), during which translational lift decreases. As the aircraft further accelerates and the IAS builds up, translational lift becomes evident again at the usual indicated airspeed value. This maneuver is risky because the need for power may be high when offsetting the temporary loss of translational lift. Heavily loaded aircraft at high altitude may not have enough power available to safely complete the maneuver, highlighting the hazardous nature of downwind maneuvers in general. When unavoidable, great care should be taken in assessing all the factors associated with a tailwind.

Effect Of Slingloads

The major effect of slingloads on turning is the associated increase in parasite drag. More total rotor thrust, power and collective is required to overcome this increase in straight flight, which means that less surplus power is available for other functions such as turning. Slingloads, apart from their other aerodynamic influences, reduce the turning capabilities of the helicopter. Helicopters operating with slingloads must, whenever possible, avoid downwind operations.

> **Operating downwind with a slingload could cause a vortex ring state condition (see Chapter 19).**

Effect Of Slipping And Skidding

Whenever a helicopter slips or skids, its presentation to the airflow produces greater parasite drag. To maintain a given airspeed, the total rotor thrust and power must be increased so that the thrust component increases to overcome the higher parasite drag.

If the helicopter slips or skids in a turn, the radius of turn is affected. Slipping into a turn reduces the radius. If the airspeed is maintained at a given value and the helicopter slips during a 360° turn, the turn's radius is smaller and (since the speed is unaltered), the rate of turn will increase.

Skidding during a turn produces a larger radius and, provided the original airspeed is maintained, the rate of turn decreases.

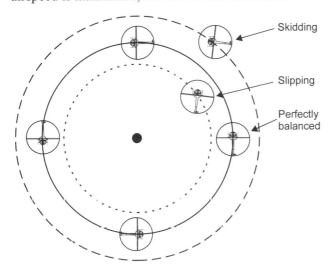

Figure 15-7. *The effect of slipping and skidding on radius and rate of turn.*

In a slipping or skidding turn it is almost impossible to verify airspeed because the intake of the pitot-tube is not facing the airflow correctly. When the helicopter is in coordinated flight, in a turn or whenever, the indicated airspeed reads correctly (ignoring instrument error). This applies even in wind conditions. As explained, there should be no change in IAS when stabilized in a turn into wind or downwind when the helicopter is in coordinated flight without reference to a ground feature.

Pull-Out From a Descent

Any maneuver involving circular movement requires centripetal force, which must be obtained from (more) total rotor thrust. The same factors discussed in turning apply to a recovery from a descent. The faster the airspeed, the greater the centripetal force required to obtain a given vertical radius. Since centripetal force is produced by total rotor thrust and since additional total rotor thrust is ultimately limited by blade angles, the higher the airspeed during recovery from a descent, the larger the radius of the pull-out will be once the collective has reached its up limits.

Thus great care is required when recovering from steep descents close to the surface. There is a speed beyond which it is impossible to maintain a radius that prevents the helicopter from colliding with the surface.

Any parasite drag, such as slingloads, makes matters worse. Operations in high density altitude conditions or at increased altitudes (the horsepower available decreases), are even more critical in terms of the height required to complete a safe recovery from a steep descent.

Helicopters exhibit a *flare effect* during a pull-out from a steep descent. By tilting the disc aft with cyclic, the forward speed causes a flow in opposition to induced flow that can significantly reduce inflow angles. The angles of attack and total rotor thrust increase while the more vertical total reaction decreases rotor drag so that less power is required. The effect is transient, however, since airspeed soon decays. The flare effect can be considerable, however, and increases with airspeed.

Review 15

Maneuvers

1. Centripetal force required to turn a helicopter is provided by (power/total rotor thrust) provided it is _____ in the direction of the turn.

2. During a standard rate (rate-1) turn the nose passes the horizon at (three/six) degrees per (second/minute).

3. If a helicopter maintains a certain radius but flies faster, the rate of turn will (increase/decrease) and the angle of bank required must be (shallower/steeper).

4. The angle of bank required to carry out a standard rate (rate-1) turn at an airspeed of 60 knots is _____ degrees.

5. When two identical helicopters at similar gross weight but different airspeed carry out a turn at the same rate of turn, the slower helicopter must bank (more/less) and the slower helicopter travels on (the same/a larger/a smaller) radius.

6. When two identical helicopters at similar gross weight but different speed carry out a turn on the same radius, the faster helicopter must bank (steeper/shallower/the same) and the faster helicopter will have a (greater/smaller/similar) rate of turn.

7. The load factor in a level turn is directly proportional to (weight/total rotor thrust) and (increases/decreases) with an increase in angle of bank.

8. When turning level at an angle of bank of 60°, the load factor is ____ times (greater/smaller) than (total rotor thrust/ weight).

9. The steeper the angle of bank in a level turn, the (greater/less) the requirement for ____ to overcome increased (profile/induced) drag.

10. Assuming a constant airspeed, when in a climbing turn, the rate of climb will be ___ than when in a straight climb and the angle of climb will be (steeper/ shallower).

11. Two helicopters are identical but one carries more weight than the other and both fly at the same airspeed. When turning on the same radius, the heavier helicopter must bank (more/less/the same) as the light one and its rate of turn will be (greater/the same/less).

12. To turn your helicopter at a constant radius around a ground feature in a wind, the angle of bank must be steepest when the wind is on the (nose/tail/left/right) of the aircraft and shallowest when the wind is on the (nose/tail/left/right).

The Flare 16

The helicopter's ability to finish flight onto a surface area not much larger than the circumference of its rotor is often only possible if the aircraft has the ability to hover briefly. Thus the aircraft's speed must be reduced from normal cruise to zero.

A hover does not always precede touchdown. Many landings are executed following an approach during which the airspeed is slowly bled off. In either case, however, the helicopter must lose airspeed, and the helicopter executes a flare to do so most of the time.

Initial Action

The flare is initiated by aft cyclic movement, which tilts the disc rearward so that:

1. Total rotor thrust leans back resulting in its horizontal component pointing rearward, which reduces the airspeed.

2. The vertical component of total rotor thrust can control height either by reducing the rate of descent or maintaining height.

If these two actions are successful the helicopter slows to zero speed at a given height above the surface.

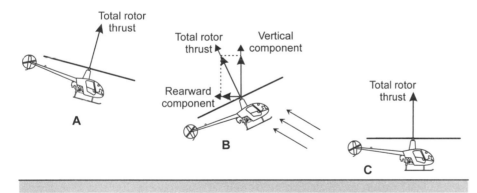

Figure 16-1. *The flare reorients and increases the total rotor thrust so that the rearward component slows the helicopters down while the vertical component controls the height of the helicopter.*

Flare Effects

Figure 16-1 shows a helicopter on a powered approach with the disc (and total rotor thrust) tilted forward (situation A). The disc has been tilted rearward by cyclic action in situation B.

Thrust Reversal

In Figure 16-1 (B) the rearward tilting disc causes total rotor thrust to act rearward. The horizontal component of total rotor thrust then acts in the same direction as parasite drag and the helicopter's speed slows. The rate of slowdown depends on the degree of rearward tilt. The fuselage responds to the deceleration by pitching up, first because reverse thrust is applied and second, because parasite drag lessens (remembering that parasite drag varies directly with V^2). The latter is governed to a large extent by the effect of the presentation of more fuselage area to the airflow.

Increasing Total Rotor Thrust

An added effect of the rearward disc tilt while the helicopter is still traveling forward is the introduction of an airflow from underneath the disc. The effect of this flow is essentially the same as ground effect – it reduces the induced flow and inflow angles so that the angles of attack and total rotor thrust increase.

The pilot must decide how to use the increased total rotor thrust. If the helicopter's rate of descent is to be reduced, the greater upward force will do that. On the other hand, if the helicopter is already in level flight, the pilot may have to lower collective to maintain height, or risk a climb.

Increasing Rotor rpm

There are three reasons why rotor rpm may rise during the flare.

1. *Lowering the collective if height gain is to be avoided.* Rotor rpm increases.

2. *Conservation of angular momentum (Coriolis effect).* The increasing total rotor thrust causes coning angles to increase. The center of gravity of each blade travels on a smaller radius around the axis of rotation and rotational velocity increases.

3. *Reduced rotor drag.* In spite of the fact that the higher angles of attack (caused by the reduced induced flow) attempt to add to blade drag and therefore reduce rotor rpm, the reorientation of the total reaction closer to the axis of rotation has a stronger effect, resulting in a higher rotor rpm.

Figure 16-2A shows the position of the total reaction in forward flight when the disc is still tilted forward, as indicated by the slanted plane of rotation. Notice the relative airflow. It approaches the blade from above the plane of rotation. Also, notice that the orientation of the total reaction is away from the axis of rotation.

In Figure 16-2B, the airflow from beneath the disc, after the rotor has been flared, causes the relative airflow to approach from below the plane of rotation. Thus the orientation of all forces is brought closer to the axis of rotation, which provides for a decrease in rotor drag.

As a result of the flare, the aircraft's airspeed slows and translational lift disappears. When the helicopter stops moving the power requirement increases to full hover power (Figure 16-1C).

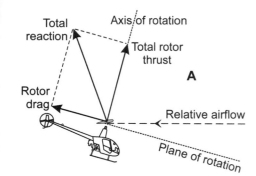

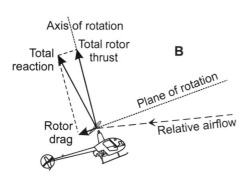

Figure 16-2. *Flare effect on rotor drag.*

Anti-torque needs change throughout the flare. The directional stability of the helicopter reduces sharply from cruise speed down to the hover. Collective position and throttle vary, and ground effect may influence power requirements in the ensuing hover. The coordinated use of the anti-torque pedals by the pilot ensures that directional control is maintained throughout the flare.

Management of Collective

The line of approach dictates how collective and throttle are used during the flare. If it is a descending approach and especially if the angle of descent is steep, the initial cyclic flare is followed shortly by pulling up collective, first to control rotor rpm and second to make maximum use of the increased total rotor thrust to reduce the rate of descent.

If the approach to the landing area is level, however, the initial flare is accompanied by the pilot lowering collective to prevent a climb (sometimes called ballooning). If the flare is executed without finesse in a level approach and rotor rpm exceeds its upper limit, there may be no alternative but for the pilot to raise collective briefly to maintain rotor rpm control. The pilot then has to cope with the resulting climb.

Flaring the helicopter downwind is risky. If the initial flare height is too low and the aircraft's groundspeed is high from the tailwind, there might not be sufficient altitude to execute a proper flare. A tailwind effects the aircraft's horizontal stabilizer, pushing the tail down (possibly into the ground on flare). The reduced aircraft speed, airflow from beneath the rotor, use of power and wind effect create conditions that may lead to a hazardous vortex ring state (see Chapter 19).

Review 16

1. When a helicopter flares prior to touch-down, one component of total rotor thrust acts (forward/rearward) while the other component acts (upward/ downward) to control (height/ airspeed).

2. During the flare, the induced flow (increases/ decreases) as the result of an airflow from (above/below) the rotor disc.

3. If the collective lever is kept unchanged during a level flare, the (greater/smaller) inflow angles cause total rotor thrust to (increase/decrease) and the aircraft tends to ____ .

4. Rotor rpm tends to _____ during a flare because the (greater/smaller) total rotor thrust causes (blade/coning) angles to increase which results in the blade's center of gravity moving (towards/away from) the axis of rotation. Coriolis effect then (increases/decreases) the rotational velocity of the blade.

5. When you initiate a level flare, collective must be (lowered/raised) and (right/left) pedal applied to maintain direction. As the helicopter slows down to the halt you must anticipate (raising/lowering) collective and applying (left/right) pedal to maintain direction.

6. If you allow rotor rpm to decay towards the end of the flare, forward movement of cyclic to level the disc (will/will not) assist in raising the rpm, it will further _____ the rpm.

Retreating Blade Stall 17

Chapter 12 explained how reverse flow affects the root part of the retreating blade as airspeed increases (refer to Figure 12-10). The affected area essentially ceases to produce rotor thrust and the remaining, unaffected part of the blade must compensate by operating at higher angles of attack. This is achieved through the blade's increased flapping down. As airspeed increases, the affected area becomes larger. Tests have shown that some helicopters at maximum forward speed have 40% of their retreating blade affected by reverse flow.

As airspeed increases there eventually comes a forward speed where the angles of attack of the non-affected retreating blade sections reach their maximum lift coefficient value (C_{Lmax}), and stall. Total rotor thrust reduces severely and the blade moves down.

While this dissymmetry of rotor thrust ought to cause a roll to the retreating side (left in the case of U.S. built helicopters), through precession, the effect is felt 90° in the direction of rotation, which is at the rear of the disc. Therefore the helicopter pitches its nose up and rolls to one side or the other. This condition is known as *retreating blade stall*.

The retreating blade stall places a limit on the maximum forward speed of a helicopter.

Effect of Increasing Airspeed on Stall Angle

The initial stall starts near the tip of the retreating blade as it passes approximately the ten-o'clock position. It intensifies at the nine o'clock position and fades completely by the seven o'clock position. This seems somewhat strange because the angle of attack is likely to be less outboard because of *wash-out* (or *blade twist*).

Whereas most airfoils have relatively large stall angles in the region of 12° to 20°, depending on shape of leading edge and curvature of the mean camber line, these angles are only achieved when the speed of the airflow is relatively low. As speed increases, the limiting useful angle of attack becomes smaller. In other words, with increasing airspeed maximum lift coefficient occurs at lower angles of attack.

The separation of air occurs more readily when flow velocity increases. The graph in Figure 17-1 shows the effect of faster airflows over an airfoil on its stalling angle of attack. The separation boundary involves a relatively large angle of attack at low airspeed, whereas the boundary is crossed at almost 0° angle of attack at high airspeeds.

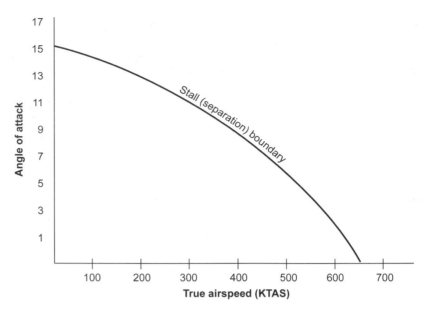

Figure 17-1. *Effect of increasing TAS on stall angle (sea level conditions).*

Even though the retreating blade has the aircraft forward speed deducted from its rotational velocity, its tip speeds are still in the 300 to 350 knot region. The stall angles of a blade with these kinds of tip speeds are small. This is one of the main reasons why the retreating blade stall originates at the tip and works inward towards the hub.

Factors Affecting the Advancing Blade

It is not only the retreating blade that limits a helicopter's forward airspeed, the advancing blade also plays an important part. Tip rotational speeds of 350 knots or more, combined with the aircraft's forward speed on the advancing side, invariably cause the blade section near the tip to move at, or close to, the speed of sound. When this happens, sharp rises in drag associated with shock waves produce a disturbed airflow over the affected airfoil sections. Vibrations are felt throughout the helicopter and may, under certain conditions, cause structural damage. Thus both blade stall on the retreating side and high-speed problems on the advancing side pose definite barriers to further increases in forward airspeed.

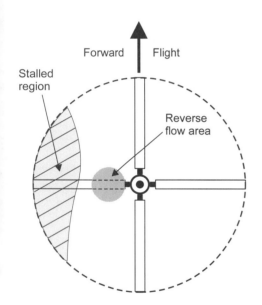

Figure 17-2. *Retreating blade stall.*

Symptoms of Retreating Blade Stall

Retreating blade stall is heralded by rotor roughness and vibration. As the stall develops on the retreating side, the nose pitches up and the helicopter may roll (helicopters equipped with semi-rigid rotor systems may not experience a pronounced nose-up movement). The direction of roll depends to a large degree on the helicopter's rotor rotation direction, but most often is to the left. Nonetheless, some helicopters do roll right.

Since high aircraft speed is the main contributor towards the problem and since the result is a pitch up of the nose, the nose-up pitch itself begins correcting the problem because it reduces the airspeed. During the period that the retreating blade is in the stalled condition the pilot may find the helicopter difficult, if not impossible to control. Pilots who do not recognize retreating blade stall and fail to begin corrective action immediately will have problems.

Years ago, in England, a hapless helicopter pilot and crew departed on a flight to test airspeed reductions with altitude. Subsequent investigations revealed that when at 11,000 feet and at an IAS of about 46 knots (associated with a much higher TAS of course) the helicopter was deeply in the retreating blade stall condition and totally out of control. The helicopter completed two barrel rolls so large that at the end of the second roll the aircraft collided with the ground. Miraculously the pilot and one crew member survived.

Recovery

Moving the cyclic aft when retreating blade stall occurs only worsens the stall. Aft cyclic produces a flare effect, reducing inflow angles and induced flow, and increasing angles of attack. Easing the cyclic forward when the nose pitches up also makes matters worse because forward cyclic produces blade angle changes with the greatest increase in blade angle on the retreating side. Since the stalled condition prevents flapping to equality (upwards), the greater blade angles place the blade into a deeper stall situation.

Any recovery from retreating blade stall must involve reducing the angles of attack through lowering the blade angles – you must lower collective. As soon as lowering collective has reduced angles of attack over the retreating blade, aft cyclic can be used to slow the aircraft down.

An increase in rotor rpm would, theoretically at least, constitute another means of recovery from retreating blade stall because it reduces the size of the reverse flow area and through that, enables the remaining blade sections to operate at smaller angles of attack. Unfortunately, the small latitude in rotor rpm limits makes this recovery academic.

Conditions likely to lead to retreating blade stall include:

* high aircraft forward speed
* maneuvers involving high load factors such as steep turns and pulling out from a high speed dive
* use of excessive or abrupt control movements
* flight in turbulence
* (as a contributing factor), high density altitude and/or high altitude

Since retreating blade stall is potentially serious, most manufacturers base the helicopter's V_{ne} (never-exceed speed) on its retreating blade stall speed (it is acknowledged that retreating blade stall is not the only reason for a V_{ne}). Most V_{ne} graphs in helicopter flight manuals indicate a decreasing V_{ne} with an increase in altitude. The main reason for this is that flight at a given indicated airspeed at increased altitudes uses larger angles of attack so that less surplus angles of attack are available.

Thus retreating blade stall will be encountered at a lower forward speed with altitude (Figure 17-3). This set of graphs gives the trend of retreating blade stall effect on V_{ne}, but is not related to a specific helicopter. Similarly, the graph in Figure 17-4, a commonly used graph, is used for trend purposes only. This graph shows the influence of a higher rotor rpm delaying retreating blade stall per altitude.

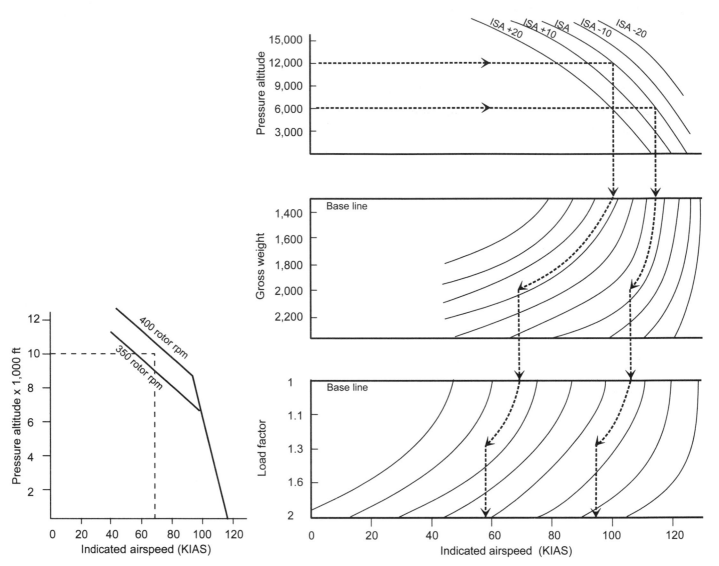

Figure 17-4. *The effect of different rotor rpm on the onset of retreating blade stall and on Vne.*

Figure 17-3. *Effect of temperature, pressure altitude, gross weight and load factor on indicated airspeed at which retreating blade stall (and Vne) can be expected.*

Factors Influencing V_{ne}

V_{ne} is primarily concerned with retreating blade stall that is associated with the retreating blade, and sonic (speed of sound) problems that occur with the high velocity of the advancing blade (especially the outboard section). Structural problems of V_{ne} are minor compared to control problems associated with V_{ne} speeds.

The main reasons for limitation of a helicopter's forward speed are:

- retreating blade stall, as explained above
- gross weight increases, which will reduce V_{ne} *
- increased density altitude reduces V_{ne}
- sonic problems on the advancing blade reduce V_{ne}
- external stores such as slingloads reduce V_{ne}
- rearward position of the aircraft's center of gravity reduce the amount of available forward movement of the cyclic thereby limiting V_{ne}
- use of stub wings relieves disc loading at higher aircraft speeds thereby increasing V_{ne}
- increase in number of blades produces less blade loading thereby increasing V_{ne}
- use of the *advancing blade concept* increases V_{ne}

> * Note: Placarding of V_{ne} information in helicopters normally assumes maximum gross weight loading.

The advancing blade concept involves one disc above the other, rotating in a different direction so that there is an advancing blade on each side. There are still two retreating blades however, which, combined with two high-speed advancing blades, cause unacceptably high vibrations at some high forward speed. A similar design incorporating two rotors rotating in opposite direction is the K-Max.

Conclusion

The theory of retreating blade stall has been under serious discussion of late. Tests have confirmed that the air's ability to separate from a blade section during the fraction of a second when the stall angle is exceeded is negligible. It is likely that the rapidly increasing drag coefficient experienced during the stalled condition is the only real contributor to retreating blade stall problems.

Review 17

Rotor Blade Airfoils

1. When airspeed increases and the reverse flow area on the (advancing/ retreating) side of the disc expands, the area of the blade not affected must operate at a (greater/smaller) angle of attack. It achieves this through (increased/ decreased) flapping (down/up).

2. When retreating blade stall begins, the sections of the retreating blade near the (root/tip) exceed their C_{Lmax}.

3. The symptoms of retreating blade stall in most helicopters are rotor _____ and _____ felt throughout the aircraft. As the stall develops, the helicopter pitches (up/down) and (rolls/yaws).

4. Using back-cyclic to recover from retreating blade stall (is/is not) recommended because the flare effect (reduces/increases) angles of attack.

5. Using forward cyclic when experiencing retreating blade stall (increases/ decreases) angles of attack on the advancing side and (increases/decreases) angles of attack on the retreating side which results in the stalled condition of the retreating blade becoming (worse/ better).

6. Conditions likely to lead to retreating blade stall include (high/low) airspeed, maneuvers involving (high/low) load factors and flight in _____ conditions.

7. The reason why V_{ne} (increases/decreases) with altitude is that retreating blade stall is experienced at (higher/lower) airspeeds because angles of attack for flight at increased altitude are generally (high/ low).

8. Flight at greater gross weight incurs a (higher/lower) V_{ne}

Autorotation

18

Autorotation is a condition of descending flight where, following engine failure or deliberate disengagement, the rotor blades are driven solely by aerodynamic forces resulting from rate of descent airflow through the rotor. The rate of descent airflow is determined mainly by airspeed.

When the helicopter's engine fails or the throttle is closed in flight, the rotor drag becomes unopposed. If no remedial action is taken the blades slow down, coning angles increase, total rotor thrust becomes grossly inadequate and a large rate of descent ensues. Clearly, there is an immediate need to maintain a satisfactory rotor rpm to ensure that the blades' coning angles stay within acceptable limits and that sufficient total rotor thrust is continually produced to control the rate of descent.

Anything that slows the rotor down, especially at the time the engine fails, must be eliminated or reduced. The engine must be disengaged from the rotor so that engine component resistance won't retard rotor rpm. Although the engine may be disconnected from the rotor, items such as the tail rotor, hydraulic systems and the like slow down the rotor rpm because they are driven by the main rotor shaft and cannot be disengaged.

The *freewheeling unit* disengages the rotor from the engine. The mechanism can be part of the main gear box or fitted as a separate unit somewhere in the transmission system. In general, as soon as engine rpm becomes less than rotor rpm, the unit automatically separates the rotor from the engine. There is no pilot input required.

If a high collective setting is in use when the engine fails, the associated high rotor drag tends to seriously retard rotor rpm. It is therefore vital that collective be lowered (except in a low height situation, to be discussed shortly). During the ensuing descent the pilot must maintain rotor rpm by manipulating the aerodynamic forces associated with specific regions of the rotor.

Initial Aircraft Reaction

There is some loss of airspeed, which causes the disc to flap forward. This is augmented by the act of lowering collective, which also causes the disc to flap forward (explained in Chapter 12 under Blow-back). The helicopter tends to yaw to the left when sudden removal of power cancels the need for left anti-torque pedal which is used to varying degrees in powered flight. A left roll is likely because some left cyclic is generally used to overcome the effects of transverse flow effect (inflow roll).

> **In all, when the engine fails there is a combined tendency for the helicopter to enter a left descending turn.**

The Lift/Drag Ratio and Forces Involved

A total engine failure involves a complete lack of horsepower available which must cause the aircraft to come down. Induced flow from above, produced by the engine-driven rotor, ceases, and is replaced by an airflow from underneath the aircraft resulting from the helicopter's rate of descent. The value of this rate of descent flow from underneath the helicopter is controlled by the aircraft's speed.

To clearly understand the forces involved, imagine the helicopter in a vertical autorotation. The force that drives the rotor is dependent on the retention of a satisfactory lift/drag ratio over a large part of each blade. The lift/drag ratio determines the orientation of the total reaction relative to the axis of rotation. During an autorotation, the total reaction's position is critical.

Figure 18-1 shows the rotor divided into three main regions, each playing its part in maintaining rotor rpm through different lift/drag ratios. The presence of these regions and their magnitude depend on the type of rotor and the aircraft's speed. (The airflow approaching the disc from below as the result of rate of descent – ROD - is referred to as *rate of descent flow* in following diagrams. Also, vector quantities are not to scale.)

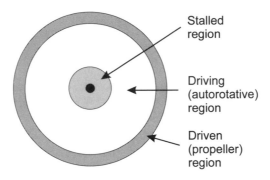

Figure 18-1. *The three regions of the rotor disc during vertical autorotation.*

The Stalled Region

Airflow caused by rotational velocity (Vr) on a small radius is relatively slow close to the hub of the rotor. When this airflow's vector is added to the airflow from the rate of descent, a resultant relative airflow is produced that comes from well below the disc (Figure 18-2).

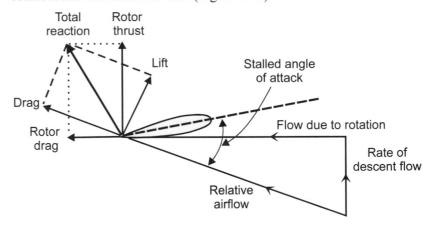

Figure 18-2. *The stalled region produces force against rotation – rotor drag.*

When this resultant relative airflow is such that the blade sections operate beyond their maximum lift coefficient, sections within the region are stalled. In, or near the stalled condition, the lift/drag ratio is exceedingly poor – the diagram of forces depicts that clearly. Relatively little lift at right angles to the relative airflow and large drag in line with the relative airflow produce a total reaction leaning well away from the axis of rotation.

The two components from the total reaction then produce rotor thrust, which acts to reduce the rate of descent and rotor drag, which attempts to slow the blade down. Thus the stalled region produces a component force, rotor drag, which acts in a direction opposite rotation. As such, its magnitude must be carefully controlled to maintain rotor rpm.

It should be noted that "rotor thrust" is still present during an autorotation even though no power and induced flow from above are present. This is because the only force at right angles to the plane of rotation is (by definition) rotor thrust; it is this force or its component that opposes the force of weight.

The Driven Region (Propeller Region)

The *driven region* involves the blade sections near the tip of the blade where the airflow component caused by rotational velocity (Vr) at a large radius is at its maximum (Figure 18-3).

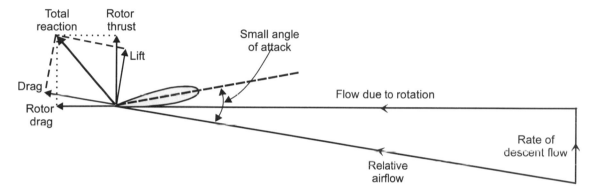

Figure 18-3. *The driven (propeller) region produces rotor drag opposing rotor rpm.*

Although the blade angle may be small as the result of wash-out and even though the relative airflow comes from not quite so low down, the lift/drag ratio is still not good because:

- induced drag is at its worst near the blade tips because of the presence of tip vortices

- profile drag is high because of the high local V^2 factor

Accordingly, the total reaction leans back from the axis of rotation so that its rotor drag component becomes a retarding force that works to slow the blade down.

> **The stalled and driven regions must be carefully controlled because they produce an anti-rotational force.**

The Driving Region (Autorotative Region)

In the *driving region* the combined airflows from rotation and rate of descent combine into a relative airflow that produces favorable lift/drag ratios.

Figure 18-4 shows that the total reaction leans forward relative to the axis of rotation, providing a component force in the plane of rotation that drives the blades as well as providing a substantial amount of rotor thrust to oppose the rate of descent.

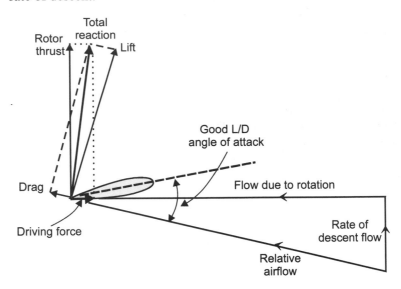

Figure 18-4. *The driving (autorotative) region produces the force in the direction of rotation.*

Combined Effect of All Regions

The two components of the total reaction in each region (rotor thrust and the force in the plane of rotation) must be examined so as to understand their functions clearly during a stabilized autorotation.

1. **Rotor Thrust**. The rotor thrusts from the three regions are added. When their combined total equals the aircraft's gross weight, the autorotation proceeds *at a steady, constant, rate of descent*. If the gross weight is greater than the combined rotor thrust from all three regions, the rate of descent increases, and if some action causes the combined rotor thrust to be larger than the gross weight, the rate of descent decreases briefly.

   On the boundaries between the three regions total rotor thrust is coincidental with the total reaction and in line with the axis of rotation. At those specific points there is no force influencing rotor rpm either way.

2. **Rotor Drag**. There are two regions that have rotor drag acting in the conventional direction, opposing rotor rpm, while the driving region has an autorotative component force in the direction of rotation. Provided the driving force in the autorotative region is equal and opposite to the sum of the rotor drags in the stalled and driven regions, the rotor rpm stabilizes. Should the rotor rpm need adjustment, the pilot need only raise or lower collective, as required, to alter the magnitude of each region's rotor drag or driving force and, through that, the helicopter's rotor rpm is controlled.

Figure 18-5 summarizes the manner in which the orientation of the total reaction determines the size and strength of the driving and opposing rotor rpm forces. The stalled condition in region A produces a large retarding force to rotor rpm while the rotor thrust value is rather limited. When autorotating in forward flight, the region is also affected by reverse flow on the retreating side, which further diminishes the amount of rotor thrust produced. At position B, the total reaction is in line with the axis of rotation and, as mentioned before, there is no force assisting or opposing rotor rpm at this location. The entire total reaction acts as rotor thrust. In region C the driving force attempts to accelerate the blade and a large proportion of rotor thrust originates from this region. At position D, the total reaction acts in similar fashion as at B and achieves the same functions. In region E the rearward acting total reaction produces a decelerating force to rotor rpm.

Provided that the accelerating forces in region C are equal to the combined decelerating forces in regions A and E, the helicopter's rotor rpm will stabilize at a required value.

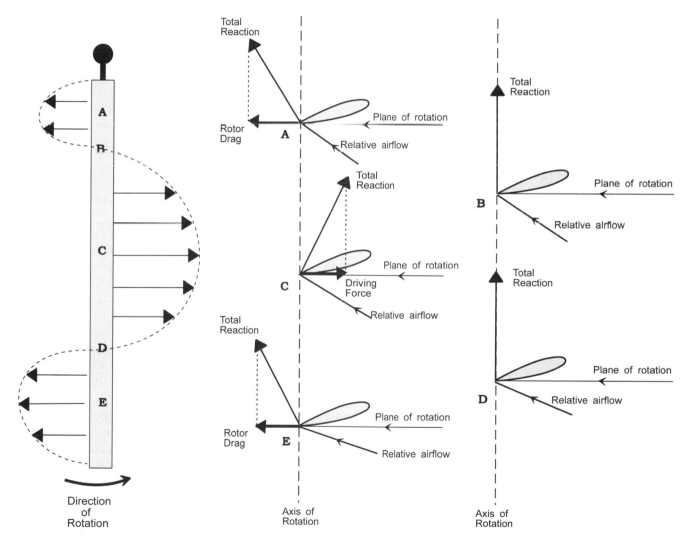

Figure 18-5. *Orientation of total reaction and autorotative forces in a vertical autorotation. (Angles and vectors not to scale.)*

Autorotation and Airspeed

So far we've considered the autorotation taking place in a vertical descent during which the combined rotor thrusts determine the rate at which the aircraft goes down. Since the stalled region does not contribute a great deal in the way of total rotor thrust (neither does the driven region) the helicopter's rate of descent is high in a vertical autorotative descent. Since power available is zero and power required is high at zero forward speed, the large shortfall in power during a vertical autorotation confirms that a high rate of descent will be experienced.

High rates of descent can be avoided and through that, more time made available during autorotation and final approach. The answer lies in how the blade angle of attack responds to airspeed.

There are three factors that influence the angle of attack as forward airspeed is gained, referred to here as *Factors X, Y and Z.*

1. **Factor X.** During a vertical autorotation, the airflow straight up towards the rotor does not pass through the rotor unimpeded; it is slowed down to some extent and "bunches up". While the rate of descent flow should be of a certain magnitude, the "bunching up" effect below the disc reduces the actual flow through the rotor. When the vertical descent is changed into forward flight, the rotor moves into air that has not been slowed down to the same extent. The result is that the up flow becomes larger and the inflow angle becomes greater (Figure 18-6). Since this increases the angle of attack on the blades, rotor thrust increases and so the effect of Factor X decreases the rate of descent.

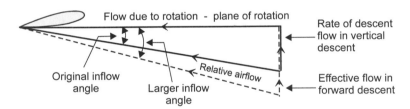

Figure 18-6. *Larger inflow angle due to forward flight.*

2. **Factor Y.** To change the vertical descent into part horizontal, the disc has to be tilted forward through forward cyclic. For a given rate of descent, this reduces the inflow angle and, through that, reduces the angle of attack. Another way of arriving at the same conclusion is to consider the effect on angle of attack when cyclic is moved back. This tilts the disc back and angles of attack increase. Moving the cyclic forward to tilt the disc forward must have the opposite effect on angle of attack (Figure 18-7). Decreasing the angle of attack ultimately reduces rotor thrust so that the effect of Factor Y is an increased rate of descent.

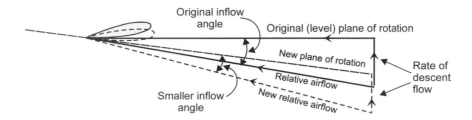

Figure 18-7. *Smaller inflow angle due to forward disc tilt.*

3. **Factor Z.** Forward flight adds a horizontal component to the overall relative airflow experienced by the vertically descending rotor. The faster the forward flight, the greater this component. When the flow vector quantities are added together the angle of attack reduces (Figure 18-8). As in Factor Y, a decrease in the angle of attack ultimately decreases rotor thrust so that the effect of Factor Z is an increased rate of descent.

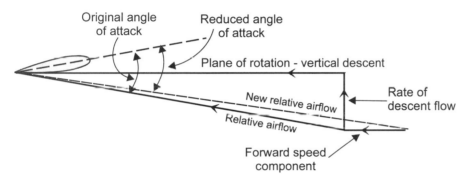

Figure 18-8. *Effect of forward speed on angle of attack.*

Combined Effect

As the vertical descent is changed into a forward autorotation, the tilt of the disc at slow flight is relatively small, so that Factors Y and Z combined are less than Factor X and the rate of descent slows. As forward speed increases and Factors Y and Z become more powerful, there comes a speed where their combined effect equals that of Factor X, which is when the helicopter is descending at its minimum rate of descent.

Further increases in airspeed enlarge the effects of Factors Y and Z. Sharp increases in parasite drag add to the requirement for more total rotor thrust. The consequence is that Factors Y and Z combined become more powerful than Factor X and the rate of descent increases.

A graph plotting changes in rate of descent against changes in airspeed shows a reducing rate of descent as airspeed increases from zero, reaching a minimum value at a given speed, beyond which the rate of descent increases again (Figure 18-9).

The rate of descent/TAS curve is almost identical to the horsepower-required curve. The horsepower-required curve should not be used for autorotation purposes because the flow pattern around the rotor is substantially different in an autorotation than in powered situations. Having noted that, however, both curves do *show the same trend*.

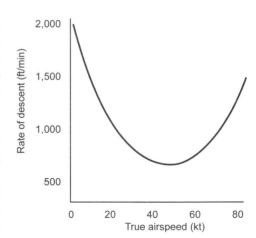

Figure 18-9. *Variation of rate of descent during autorotation with changes in airspeed.*

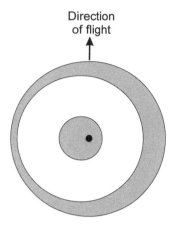

Direction
of flight

Figure 18-10. *Regions move towards the retreating side with increasing airspeed.*

The influence of airspeed changes on rate of descent in an autorotation is dramatic. If the pilot slows just 10 knots off the minimum descent speed in an autorotation, the rate of descent increases by almost 15%. If the speed is lowered 20 knots, the rate of descent increases by almost 45%.

Airspeed does not necessarily have to involve flight straight ahead – autorotations can be done in a circular or even backwards fashion. Remember though, whenever the helicopter is in a banked condition, the rate of descent is greater than when it is in laterally level-disc situations.

Effect of Forward Speed on the Three Regions

As soon as forward speed is gained, dissymmetry of lift and blow-back must be eliminated through flapping and cyclic. The advancing blade flaps up and decreases its lift coefficient while the retreating blade flaps down and increases its lift coefficient. The effect of these lift coefficient changes (through angle of attack changes) enlarges the stalled region on the retreating side and decreases it on the advancing side. This effect is fed through to the other two regions so that a pattern develops as shown in Figure 18-10.

Effect of Airspeed Changes on Rotor RPM

The effect of cyclic on rotor rpm was mentioned in Chapter 16 where it was explained that rearward cyclic alters inflow angles and orientates the total reaction in such a way that rotor drag reduces and rotor rpm increases. In similar fashion, forward cyclic causes rotor rpm to decrease.

Assuming the collective lever position is not changed, when airspeed is increased with forward cyclic during an autorotation, rotor rpm will fall off but return more or less to the original rpm value once the new, higher, airspeed has stabilized. Similarly, when reducing airspeed with rearward cyclic, rotor rpm increases but returns more or less to the original value when the new, lower, airspeed has stabilized.

Autorotation Range and Endurance

The TAS/rate of descent curve shows that the minimum rate of descent occurs at only one speed, located directly below the bottom of the curve. This is the helicopter's endurance speed which produces the longest time in the air. This speed *does not* produce the greatest distance moved forward, range, which is obtained at a slightly higher speed. These two speeds are normally stated in the aircraft Flight Manual, and it is important that pilots know them in order to carry out autorotations safely and effectively.

If the terrain beneath the aircraft is suitable for touchdown, then the TAS for endurance might be best to use because that gives the pilot the least rate of descent and maximum time in the air to plan and think. If the only satisfactory touchdown area is away from the aircraft, however, an autorotation at the speed for maximum range may be called for.

The speed for range in autorotation is found on the TAS/rate of descent curve (Figure 18-9) directly below the point where the tangent strikes the curve (in similar fashion as the tangent to the power required curve). Although the distance covered will then be greatest (ignoring the wind), the rate of descent is increased compared to the endurance speed.

The principles explained in Chapter 13, *Range and Endurance*, also apply to autorotation. Before summarizing these principles, rotor rpm must be mentioned. In many helicopters, best lift/drag ratio on the blades, required for best range, is enhanced by maintaining the rotor rpm *at the bottom of the green range*. For best endurance, however, the rotor rpm should be *at the top of the green range* in many, but not for all helicopters. (Consult your aircraft's Flight Manual for its proper operation.)

Effect of Altitude on Range and Endurance

The higher the altitude when the autorotation commences, the greater the initial rate of descent. The rate of descent slows as altitude is lost, provided the correctly adjusted TAS is used. The rate of descent, being ultimately determined by the shortfall in power, is high when the horsepower required is high under the influence of high altitude.

Thus to fly for endurance from a high altitude, the TAS for the minimum rate of descent at that altitude should be selected initially. The helicopter's rate of descent will slow as altitude is lost, in response to the pilot slowly reducing the TAS.

To fly for range from altitude, the published TAS for that altitude must be selected initially. The angle of descent will not alter, but the distance covered will be greater if the initial autorotation altitude is higher. The TAS must again be correctly slowed by the pilot as altitude is lost.

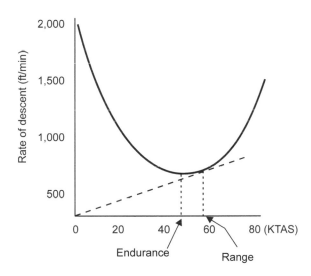

Figure 18-11. *Speeds for range and endurance during autorotation.*

Effect of Gross Weight on Range and Endurance

For endurance, changes in gross weight make only small differences to the rate of descent, provided the airspeed and rotor rpm are maintained in accordance with the aircraft's Flight Manual. The reason for this is that over the entire disc the three regions may shift their location and alter their size a little when different gross weights and airspeeds are in use, but the overall lift/drag ratio changes little. In principle, however, changes in weight produce slightly different rates of descent.

When autorotating for range, an increase in gross weight causes a small reduction in range (refer again to the summary for descending, end of Chapter 14). Since the horsepower-required curve moves up and to the right with increases in gross weight it follows that when heavier, the TAS for minimum drag is slightly higher than when light. These speeds are usually listed in the aircraft's Flight Manual. In the same listing it is common to see heavier weights coupled with increased rotor rpm to maintain range.

Effect of Parasite Drag and Slingloads on Range & Endurance

Parasite drag needs some total rotor thrust to overcome it. If range or endurance is critical, parasite drag should be reduced to a minimum. An autorotation would be best accomplished by releasing any slingload (terrain permitting), but the final decision for this action rests with the pilot.

Touchdown

If an aircraft is autorotating at a satisfactory forward airspeed and the terrain below the helicopter is smooth, level and long, a run-on landing might be a good option. In that case, it is essential that the disc be level with the surface on touchdown. The cyclic must not be moved aft subsequently in a mistaken belief that this maneuver will reduce the groundspeed more rapidly.

The cushioning response to a collective application is greater above translational lift speed. This makes the run-on landing somewhat less demanding than the almost zero speed landing following a flare.

If the terrain is not suitable for a run-on landing, the touchdown must be preceded by a flare and zero forward speed. The flare is initiated by aft cyclic, which points the total rotor thrust rearward so that the aircraft slows down. The high fuselage attitude during the flare adds substantially to parasite drag, which further assists in reducing airspeed.

Angles of attack and coning angles increase during the flare, causing rotor rpm and total rotor thrust to increase. This slows the helicopter's rate of descent. In some situations this may be further enhanced by up collective to stop the rotor rpm from exceeding its upper limit.

The outward movement of the three regions is one of the contributing factors towards increasing rotor rpm during the flare (apart from *Coriolis Effect*). The higher angles of attack, when cyclic moves aft, enlarge the stalled region which in turn forces the driving and driven regions out towards the blade tips (which might even push the driven region partly off the disc).

As the aircraft slows down to almost zero, the disc must be leveled with cyclic and, as the aircraft is about to make contact with the ground, the collective should be raised to cushion the touchdown as much as possible. The resulting rotor rpm decay during this up collective action must take second consideration to the need to land with the smallest possible rate of descent. Simply put, every ounce of energy is squeezed out of the rotating rotor in order to produce the greatest possible amount of work stopping the rate of descent.

A low inertia rotor readily increases its rotor rpm as the flare is initiated and this increase provides additional total rotor thrust apart from the total rotor thrust obtained from the increased angle of attack. As a result, the rate of descent decreases sharply. Admittedly, the rotor rpm falls off just as quickly shortly after, but if the flare began at an ideal height, this rotor rpm loss may well be acceptable.

A high inertia rotor, on the other hand, does not build up its rotor rpm to the same extent during the flare. During the initial phase of the flare, slowing the rate of descent is mainly achieved through increased angles of attack. The advantage of the system comes into play, however, when towards the end of the flare rotor rpm tends to maintain its value so that the pilot has more time to land the aircraft.

Loss of Power at Low Heights

If an engine fails at low heights (2 to 10 feet) during a hover or slow forward flight, there is no time to establish a proper autorotation. The main consideration then is to land the aircraft at the smallest possible rate of descent. Under those circumstances, a level disc attitude should be established and the collective raised smoothly, as required, to ensure a soft touchdown.

The anti-torque pedals and cyclic must be well-coordinated by the pilot because fairly substantial anti-torque (left pedal) was in use prior to the engine failure and some left cyclic may have been in use to correct for tail rotor drift. A sudden loss of power may therefore cause a brisk sideways movement (and yaw) to the left which must be corrected promptly. If the pilot fails to do this, the left yaw will cause skidding to the right which presents the right skid forward. If ground contact is made under these conditions it is possible that the helicopter will tip over (*dynamic roll-over*, to be discussed in Chapter 19).

Factors Influencing Rotor rpm Decay When the Engine Fails

The rate at which the rotor rpm decays when the engine fails depends largely on the blade angle in use at the time of failure. Any flight condition involving a high collective setting is conducive to a loss of rotor rpm, ignoring the rotor inertia factor. These conditions include:

- slow speed, especially hovering
- high speed
- high altitude or high density altitude
- steep, full-power climb
- steep angle of bank
- carriage of slingload and/or other external stores

Combinations of Airspeed and Height Best Avoided

One must have both height above ground level and time to establish a satisfactory autorotation when the engine fails. This is especially applicable when flying under the critical conditions mentioned in the previous paragraph. Whenever the helicopter is at a low height while the airspeed is low or high, it may be impossible to establish a satisfactory autorotation prior to contacting the terrain.

Manufacturers publish a *Height-Velocity diagram* in the aircraft's Flight Manual showing shaded areas that should be avoided as a combination of height and airspeed. These diagrams must be used with discretion because flight tests that determined the various combinations were carried out by highly experienced pilots who were mentally prepared for the engine failures. Although a safety factor has been included in most diagrams, pilots need to appreciate that the shaded areas are a guide, at best. Wise pilots add their own safety margin to the height-velocity diagram when computing climbs, descents and general operations.

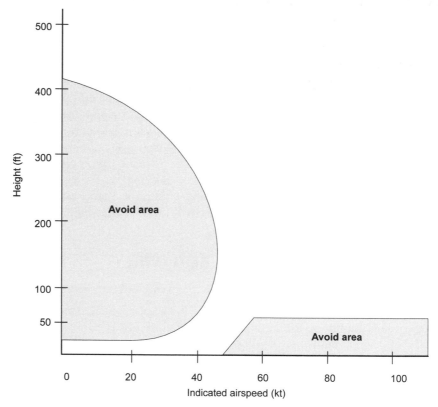

Figure 18-12. *Example of an autorotation avoid-areas graph.*

The larger shaded area involving low speed and low height is self explanatory, but the high speed/low height area requires explanation. There are three main reasons why high speed and low height should be avoided in case of engine failure:

1. Most aircraft cannot be landed safely at that speed because of landing gear strength limitations.

2. If an attempt is made to flare, it is likely that the helicopter may end up too high, facing a decreasing airspeed and a lowering rotor rpm, especially when cyclic is moved forward to level the disc. Reducing speed could place the aircraft in the low speed/low height shaded area of the diagram.

3. A flare attempt at too low a height may result in a tail boom strike when the nose pitches up.

Note: Just as flare effect increases total rotor thrust and rotor rpm while flaring for an engine-off landing, an over-zealous check forward produces a negative flare effect, with a dramatic decrease in total rotor thrust and rotor rpm. If this is done when leveling the skids for touchdown, the helicopter will quickly develop an increased rate of descent with little chance for recovery. The result may be a heavy landing.

The following factors enlarge the size of the shaded areas:

- increased gross weight
- increased altitude
- increased density altitude
- increased parasite drag, including carriage of a slingload

The reason for all these factors is the higher collective setting and higher pitch angles in use at the time an autorotation begins. The higher rate of descent in each case requires greater margins in height and time.

Review 18

Autorotation

1. When a helicopter's engine fails, rotor rpm will _____ if blade angles are not (increased/ reduced) through _____ of the collective lever.

2. The function of the freewheeling unit is to _____ the engine from the rotor so that engine components do not (retard/overspeed) the rotor.

3. When the engine fails there is, in most helicopters, a tendency for the nose to pitch (up/down) and for the aircraft to roll (right/left).

4. Rotor rpm is adversely affected by the stalled region of the disc near the blade (roots/tips) because inflow angles are (small/large) and the total reaction produces a component (in the direction of/against) rotation.

5. The driven region of the disc near the blade (tips/roots) have a (good/poor) lift/drag ratio resulting in a component of total reaction acting (in the direction of/against) rotation.

6. The driving region is normally found (near the hub/in the middle of the blades/ near the tips) and the total reaction provides a component (in the direction of/against) rotation.

7. In a vertical autorotation, rate of descent is (low/high) but it (increases/decreases) as forward speed is gained because angles of attack (increase/decrease) up to a given airspeed.

8. When a vertical autorotation is changed into forward-flight, the three regions of the disc move towards the _____ side so that the stalled region becomes smaller on the (retreating/ advancing side).

9. When you autorotate at the speed for minimum rate of descent and you realize you are under-shooting, you should (increase/ decrease) the airspeed and bring the rotor rpm towards the (bottom/top) of the green range in most light helicopters.

10. When changing from autorotation for maximum endurance to one for maximum range, the airspeed must be _____ and the rate of descent will (increase/decrease).

11. Rotor rpm during an autorotation is controlled with the (cyclic/collective) control.

12. Rotor rpm decay is likely to be severe when the helicopter's engine fails while the aircraft is at a (low/high) gross weight, (high/low) altitude and in a (steep/shallow) angle of bank turn.

13. The airspeed-height avoid areas expand when the helicopter is at _____ gross weight, _____ altitude and when the atmosphere is (dry/moist).

Hazardous Flight Conditions 19

Vortex Ring State
(Settling with Power)

Vortex ring state, or *settling with power*, is potentially hazardous because it places the helicopter into a descent at an increasing rate. What's worse, the recovery action from a vortex ring state may involve even more loss of height. Pilots must use considerable caution when operating at low height if conditions likely to lead to vortex ring state are present.

It doesn't take much to bring on a vortex ring state. Imagine a helicopter hovering at altitude. The relative airflow onto each blade section is dependent upon the induced flow and local rotational speed (Vr), both of which are greatest near the blade tip. Assuming that the ratio of rotational velocity to induced flow is more or less constant over the entire blade, then the direction of the relative airflow is about the same throughout the blade. Because of the higher blade angle at the root through wash-out, however, the angle of attack at the root is larger than that at the tip (Figure 19-1).

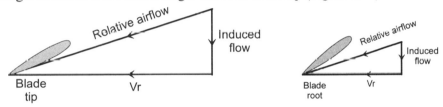

Figure 19-1. *Larger angle of attack and smaller induced flow at the blade root, - hover conditions.*

If collective is lowered slightly, the aircraft begins a slow rate of descent, which produces a minor rate of descent flow up towards the disc. Once established in the descent, this upward flow opposes the induced flow from above (which is less at the root and greater at the tip) and the effect of the rate of descent flow ceases to be equal over the entire disc (Figure 19-2).

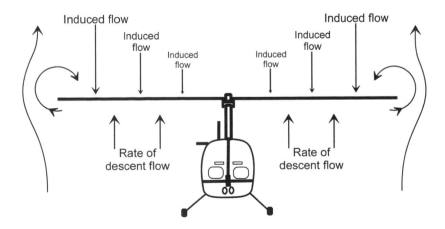

Figure 19-2. *Slow rate of descent, causing onset of vortex ring state.*

Effect on the Root Section of the Blade

As the rate of descent flow increases, it affects the root section more strongly, and a stage is soon reached where it is equal and opposite to the small induced flow that exists near the mast. The relative airflow is then in line with the plane of rotation (Figure 19-3). As the angle of attack becomes larger it eventually exceeds the maximum lift coefficient (C_{Lmax}), the blade root section stalls.

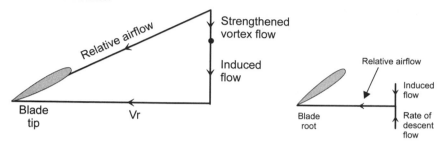

Figure 19-3. *Slow descent. Blade root section about to stall and tip section with reducing angle of attack.*

Effect on the Tip Section of the Blade

Strengthening of the customary vortex action around the tip adds to the induced flow along the outboard section of the blades so that the angle of attack becomes smaller (after allowance has been made for rate of descent flow). The combined effect is that the inner and outer sections of each blade produce less rotor thrust, resulting in an increased rate of descent. As the pilot further lowers collective a snowball effect develops that soon causes the root section to go deeper into the stall and the tip section to further reduce its lift coefficient (Figures 19-4 and 19-5).

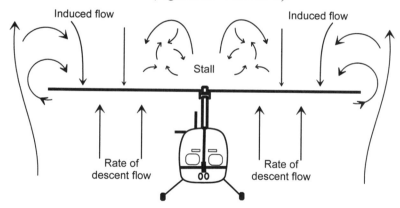

Figure 19-4. *Established vortex ring state.*

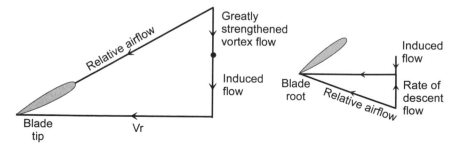

Figure 19-5. *Blade root section stalled. Tip section with greatly reduced angle of attack. Rotor established in vortex ring state.*

The only section of the blade producing effective rotor thrust at this point is the relatively small central area between the root and tip, which is clearly insufficient to support the weight of the helicopter. As a consequence, the rate of descent increases and, if collective is reduced further, a rate of descent that can approach 5,000 feet per minute, follows. The aircraft is now fully established in the vortex ring state.

Pay attention to the flow pattern around the disc as vortex ring state develops (Figure 19-4). The upward flow above the stalled region tends to merge with the induced flow over the center area of each blade so that a secondary vortex forms away from the center of the disc. Wind tunnel tests have shown that flow patterns around the disc during vortex ring state conditions are highly erratic and confused. Large and sudden changes to the angle of attack of individual blade sections produce severe dissymmetry of lift so that the helicopter pitches, rolls and yaws to no set pattern, making aircraft control difficult.

The main danger in vortex ring state is that the high rate of descent requires considerable height for recovery. If a helicopter enters vortex ring state too close to the ground, there is little that can be done before the helicopter impacts the terrain. Random pitching, rolling and yawing motions can lead to a total loss of control in flight.

Requirements for the Development of Vortex Ring State

Vortex ring state can develop when the helicopter has:

- a low or zero airspeed (below translational lift speed)
- some power in use (collective input)
- a rate of descent that is in the region of 400 to 800 ft/min, depending on aircraft type

The actual rate of descent factor is critical for the onset and development of vortex ring state. Many texts refer to a "high" rate of descent being required at the initial stage, but this seems to depend on the meaning of the term "high" rate of descent.

A helicopter's rate of descent is a function of airspeed and "shortfall" in power. For a given low power setting and low-to-medium airspeed (say 35 knots), the rate of descent increases and the angle of descent steepens as speed slows. If little power is being used and the airspeed is low (say 6 knots), associated with a very steep descent profile, the rate of descent is too high for vortex ring state to develop. Indeed, by removing all the power and entering autorotation the aircraft recovers from vortex ring state, if it has occurred.

Figure 19-6 provides some interesting conclusions. A steep descent with little power produces a rate of descent so large (close to 1,500 ft/min in this example) that the vortex ring state is avoided. A descent angle shallower than 30 to 40 degrees requires a power setting and airspeed that again avoids the vulnerable combination for vortex ring state.

> **If the airspeed is very low or zero and the power in use is such that the rate of descent is in the region of 400 to 800 ft/min., the stage is set for vortex ring state.**

In simplified terms, if the rate of descent is too little, the disturbed airflow in the vortex ring state wake lies below the disc, and if the rate of descent is too large, this disturbed wake is found above the disc. If airspeed is too high, the wake lies behind the disc.

> **There is a definite combination of airspeed and rate of descent, largely determined by the power in use, that produces vortex ring state conditions.**

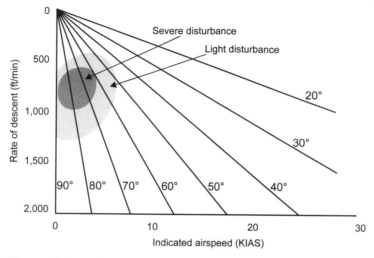

Figure 19-6. *Effect of airspeed and rate of descent on conditions required to develop vortex ring state.*

Flight Conditions Likely to Lead to Vortex Ring State

The combinations mentioned above are encountered under the following flight conditions. All of these flight conditions require that an induced flow be present, some power be in use and interference to the induced flow by an airflow from below the aircraft be present.

- a powered descent at low or zero airspeed at a "high" rate of descent
- loss of height during a harsh flare
- executing a quick-stop downwind
- a squashing recovery, when power is applied at the end of an autorotation
- a downwind approach

Any factors that involve high collective settings in the hover or slow flight, such as high gross weight, high altitude, high density altitude and maneuvers, encourages vortex ring state to occur sooner.

Symptoms of Vortex Ring State

Symptoms of vortex ring state are:

- aircraft vibration and cyclic stick shake
- random yawing, rolling and pitching
- increasing rate of descent
- reduction in cyclic stick effectiveness

During a steep descent in turbulent conditions, the aircraft vibrates and the stick shakes with regularity. To rule out vortex ring state, the pilot cross checks between his airspeed and rate of descent to distinguish between the turbulence and a possible developing vortex ring state.

The surest way to prevent vortex ring state from developing is to avoid those conditions that are likely to lead to it. For instance, an approach into a confined area should be planned and then carried out at a rate of descent less than that required to produce vortex ring state conditions. For additional insurance, always maintain translational lift speed until as close as possible to your landing spot.

Recovery from Vortex Ring State

If vortex ring state has developed, the pilot's first instinct may be to pull up collective to reduce the rate of descent. But the higher blade (pitch) angles cause greater angles of attack and the stalled regions of the blades increase, tip vortex activity increases and the rate of descent increases instead of decreasing.

The pilot's main consideration should be to remove the helicopter from the airflow condition that is producing the problem. The disc attitude must be changed and airspeed increased so that the induced flow is no longer opposed by the rate of descent flow to the same extent.

It is possible to recover from vortex ring state by entering autorotation. The problem with this recovery is that it may be impossible to prevent the rotor rpm from overspeeding, and the rate of descent that is bound to follow will be brisk.

The recommended recovery technique for vortex ring state is:

- cyclic forward (and/or slightly to one side) to increase airspeed
- brief pause, to allow the airspeed to build up
- apply power

Use of down collective during the vortex ring state recovery is recommended by some sources. It is acknowledged that down collective decreases blade angles of attack and may aid in the recovery, but the associated increased rate of descent may be counterproductive if height available is limited.

> **The key to recovery from vortex ring state is recognizing the condition and acting before it develops.**

Tail Rotor Vortex Ring State

Vortex ring state can also occur on the tail rotor if the tail rotor thrust is opposed by a sufficiently strong airflow. In helicopters with counter-clockwise rotating main rotors, tail rotor thrust is produced by air being drawn from the right and accelerated to the left. Thus if an airflow is present from left to right onto the tail rotor, vortex ring state can develop (Figure 19-7).

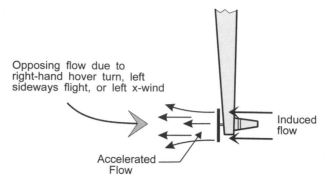

Opposing flow due to
right-hand hover turn, left
sideways flight, or left x-wind

Induced
flow

Accelerated
Flow

Figure 19-7. *Factors that may lead to tail rotor vortex ring state.*

Such an opposite airflow may occur when the aircraft is subjected to a high rate hover turn to the right, wind from the left, or sideways flight to the left. The problem shows up when the rate of turn to the right suddenly increases. If the pilot uses full left anti-torque pedal to stop the turn it may place substantial stresses on the drive system because the angles of attack on the tail rotor blades rapidly become exceedingly large. The recovery from a high-rate right-hand hover turn has to be accomplished as smoothly and timely as possible to avoid a loss of tail rotor effectiveness (see Chapter 9).

Ground Resonance

Ground Resonance is a vibration of large amplitude resulting from a deliberate or unintentional oscillation of a helicopter in contact with the ground or resting on the ground. The onset of ground resonance is recognizable by a slow rocking of the fuselage. If no remedial action is taken at an early stage, the degree of vibration may rapidly increase until the aircraft sustains major damage.

Causes of Ground Resonance

Vibrations are invariably present within the rotor disc most of the time. These vibrations may enter the fuselage through the rotor head, but they generally dissipate against the surrounding air. Most of these vibrations are inherent in the aircraft design and pose no great problem. A rotor vibration (caused by disc center of gravity position away from the center of rotation for instance) is potentially dangerous, however, when the helicopter is brought in contact with the ground.

The main rotor acts like a flywheel. The center of gravity of its total mass should be on the axis of rotation to ensure freedom from oscillations. Should the position of the center of gravity, for whatever reason, shift away from this axis, the rotor experiences a *wobble*, which is safe so long as the helicopter is kept off the ground. If ground contact is made (and particularly light contact), the wobble cannot dissipate. If the frequency of oscillation of the undercarriage (skids with dampers, or tires) is in sympathy with the rotor vibration, destructive vibrations develop in a matter of seconds.

Research has shown that ground resonance, or its avoidance, is a function of damping, both in the rotor head around the lead-lag (drag) hinges and in the undercarriage system.

One of the most critical conditions for resonance is just before the helicopter becomes airborne or just prior to placing the full weight of the aircraft onto the undercarriage on landing. At these stages the undercarriage components are fully extended and cannot provide all the damping required.

Rotors that have substantial in-plane stiffness and that are not fitted with lead-lag (drag) hinges, or their equivalents, are not susceptible to ground resonance and so require less damping in the rotor head or undercarriage.

Factors that May Cause Ground Resonance

• *Rotor Head Vibrations*

Rotor head vibrations are caused by factors involving the blades themselves or by items which are part of the rotor head construction, such as lead-lag (drag) dampers. Since the principal causes of ground resonance are displacement of the disc center of gravity away from the axis of rotation and faulty damping, it follows that any of the following factors can be potential causes:

Unbalanced Blades. Blades can be unbalanced for a variety of reasons, including uneven ice build-up, differential moisture absorption, damage to one blade and uneven dust accumulation. The total mass of the disc becomes unevenly distributed and the disc center of gravity moves off-center.

Incorrect Tracking. A blade tracking problem is usually felt as a low frequency beat in the cyclic stick and is not often the cause of ground resonance. The vibration "feels" vertical in nature. If tracking is seriously out of line, though, it produces the combination of factors that can result in ground resonance.

Faulty Lead-Lag Dampers. The angular difference between blades of a three-or-more bladed rotor must be equal if the rotor's center of gravity is to remain on the axis of rotation. For instance, a three-bladed system ideally has 120° between blades. If a lead-lag damper sticks so that the blade to which it is attached lags, the spacing between blades is upset and the disc center of gravity is displaced.

• *Fuselage Factors*

Hard or Mismanaged Landing. A hard landing may jolt the main rotor so that the disc center of gravity is forced away from the axis of rotation. The occurrence is aggravated by mismanagement of the cyclic stick. A run-on landing over rough ground may also cause ground resonance.

Uneven Oleo (or Tire) Pressures. Uneven tire or oleo strut pressures cause the fuselage to rest unevenly on the surface and undercarriage damping is affected. The same problem may arise when resting on sloping ground.

One-skid Landing. When landing on one skid the rotor is displaced to maintain a steady fuselage position and damping may be affected. The shifting weight of people entering or exiting the aircraft while in this precarious condition aggravates it.

Ship Operations. Any of the preceding factors may present themselves when operating on unsteady ship decks.

Ground Resonance Recovery Action

If the rotor rpm is such that the aircraft can fly, the pilot's immediate action in the face of ground resonance must be to get the helicopter airborne. The rotor rpm should always be held in the operating range until the final landing has been completed just in case there is a problem with ground resonance and a quick liftoff is necessary. If the rotor rpm is not within operational limits, there is little the pilot can do short of immediately shutting down by lowering collective fully, reducing power and applying the rotor brake (if fitted) and/or wheel brakes.

Pilot opinion varies as to the proper cyclic stick movement when ground resonance symptoms appear. The aircraft Flight Manual is the best reference for specific procedures.

Blade Sailing

Blade sailing is a problem when low rotor rpm during start-up or shutdown produces insufficient centrifugal force on the rotor blades and flapping, caused by the wind, becomes excessive. The problem is worse when the wind is gusting and variable.

> **Two-blade rotors are more vulnerable to blade sailing than three-or-more blade rotors.**

The slowly rotating blade into the wind experiences a relatively large increase in V and, in the absence of adequate centrifugal force, flaps up with great force. The same factor, but in the opposite sense, applies to the retreating blade. Blade sailing conditions are dangerous for anyone in the immediate vicinity of the parked aircraft and to helicopter components, such as rotor blades and the tail unit.

In conditions when blade sailing is a possibility it is essential that precautions are taken to reduce the risk to persons and equipment. If the aircraft is equipped with a rotor brake it should be engaged as quickly as possible during shutdown and rotor rpm should be increased at a faster rate during startup (if possible).

There are differences of opinion amongst pilots regarding the best way to use cyclic and how to park a helicopter when blade sailing is a risk factor. It is commonly accepted, however, that a small amount of into-the-wind cyclic helps avoid the phenomenon during the initial stages of shutdown. During the final stage, when the blades have slowed down considerably, cyclic is centered. In general, parking the aircraft with the wind coming from the right side (left side with clockwise rotating rotors) causes the blade approaching the tail to rise as it becomes the advancing blade. This technique reduces the risk of a wildly flapping blade striking the tail boom.

> **Follow the manufacturer's instructions for any type-specific method of avoiding potential blade sailing damage.**

Dynamic Rollover

When the helicopter rests on the ground on one skid or one wheel, the aircraft may begin rolling, and, under certain circumstances, it cannot be controlled. This rolling is known as *dynamic rollover*.

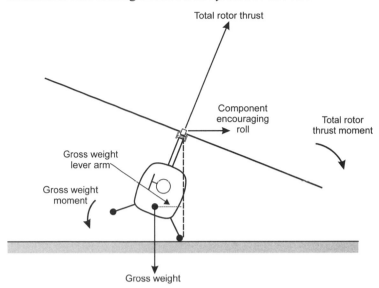

Figure 19-8. *Beginning of potential dynamic rollover.*

The forces involved in dynamic rollover are shown in Figure 19-8. A moment is produced by the horizontal component of total rotor thrust about the point of ground contact of the skid. This moment is opposed by the weight of the aircraft, positioned between the wheels or skids. This moment decreases as the aircraft is placed in progressively steeper banks.

If the angle of bank or roll is small, the horizontal component of total rotor thrust is small and the risk of rollover is insignificant. However, there is an angle of bank beyond which it is impossible to stop further roll, and if the helicopter is kept in contact with the ground, it will fall over. The angle beyond which this is likely to happen is called the *critical angle*.

Factors Influencing the Critical Angle

The rate at which the roll takes place influences the critical angle. The faster the rate of roll, the smaller the critical angle. When the right skid is on the ground, as distinct from the left skid, tail rotor drift to the right encourages further roll that results in the critical angle being smaller. A crosswind from the left which causes disc blow-back to the right, adds to the problem.

A lateral center of gravity to the right of the butt line encourages the right skid to remain in touch with the ground on lift-off. A left yaw input causes the helicopter to present its right skid forward.

A skid stuck in ice or mud can also shift the center of gravity just enough to begin dynamic rollover. The onset of rollover is not an uncommon occurrence when taking off from a sloped surface. If a little too much cyclic is held into the slope when the down-slope skid has been raised the aircraft may roll uphill

The occurrence of dynamic rollover is common when a skid or wheel inadvertently contacts the ground or an obstruction, or an animal, while flying sideways. Since the critical angle reduces sharply when contacting the ground at a reasonably high sideways speed, the resulting high rate of roll often has an inevitable, and sad, outcome.

> **Many of the factors associated with dynamic rollover relate back to the problem of tail rotor drift. Remember, tail rotor drift is to the right with counterclockwise rotating rotors and to the left with clockwise rotating rotors.**

When rollover starts and cyclic cannot stop the roll, the pilot must lower collective smoothly to place both skids on the ground again. If collective is lowered abruptly the helicopter may bounce onto the other skid and roll in the opposite direction (ground resonance is also a risk here).

If an operational rotor rpm has been attained and a safe takeoff can be completed, the pilot should get the helicopter airborne. If a takeoff cannot be undertaken for whatever reason, up collective only aggravates the situation because the increased total rotor thrust produces a larger horizontal component, which strengthens the moment about the skid contact point with the ground (Figure 19-9). Experience shows that the use of smooth collective is more effective in avoiding rollover problems than using cyclic.

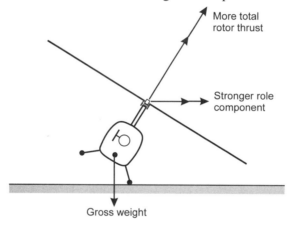

More total rotor thrust

Stronger role component

Gross weight

Figure 19-9. *Raising collective may increase the risk of rollover.*

Cyclic Limitations

There are a number of factors that limit the available cyclic both on the ground and in the air.

1. Operating on a slope with a downslope crosswind, less lateral cyclic into the slope is available. The pilot cannot accept as much slope at the landing site if a downslope crosswind is encountered.

2. Touching down with the left skid up-slope (counterclockwise rotor), provides less lateral cyclic to the pilot compared to touching down on the right skid, because the pilot needs some left cyclic to stop tail rotor drift.

3. Adequate lateral cyclic may not be available if passengers or freight are loaded or off-loaded while the aircraft is hovering or has one-skid in contact with the slope.

4. Exceeding the aircraft's center of gravity limits, both laterally and longitudinally, is dangerous because it requires corrective cyclic input. The pilot is left with less residual cyclic movement.

5. Ship-borne operations are particularly vulnerable to any of the factors mentioned above

Mast Bumping

Mast bumping is the result of poor pilot technique. The phenomenon occurs when the helicopter's main rotor hub is allowed to make contact with and deform the main rotor mast. The consequence: rotor separation from the mast. Mast bumping is peculiar to two-blade rotor systems that use the teetering hinge, such as many Bell and Robinson helicopters.

The hub making contact with the mast requires excessive flapping. Even under high speed, high gross weight and high altitude conditions, the degree of blade flapping is well within maximum allowable values and the risk of mast bumping is zero under all normal flight conditions when correct piloting techniques are maintained. However, incorrect techniques that cause excessive flapping set the stage for disaster.

A blade's flapping amplitude is increased by:

- gusty wind conditions
- sudden attitude changes caused by abrupt cyclic inputs
- sideways flight at or near the helicopter's maximum allowable speed
- flight under low, zero or negative 'g' conditions

Any of the above, or a combination of them, impose a risk of excessive flapping, but the low-g situation is the most dangerous for the development of mast bumping.

Airplane pilots who have recently transitioned to helicopters are at a higher risk for mast bumping accidents because reactions honed by years of airplane flying are not necessarily conducive to safe helicopter flying. For example, if the pilot must descend suddenly to avoid another object, say, a bird, helicopter technique is to rapidly lower collective. The airplane/helicopter pilot is prone to push the cyclic forward in the same situation, lowering the nose of the helicopter into a dive, as would the case in an airplane. Such a push-over is the exact formula for mast bumping.

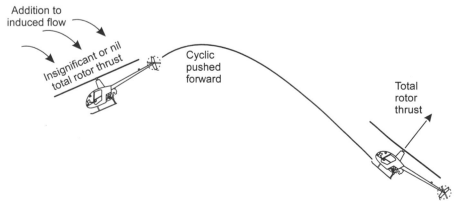

Figure 19-10. *Firm application of forward cyclic can cause low, zero or negative g and a severe reduction in total rotor thrust.*

Low g flight occurs when cyclic is moved forward rather firmly, such as during a push-over at the end of a zoom climb, especially if the pilot lowers collective at the same time. The effect of low, zero or negative g on total main rotor thrust production (Figure 19-10) is devastating.

Tail rotor drift (translating tendency) is typically balanced by a slight tilt of the main rotor disc in a direction opposite tail rotor thrust. With a counterclockwise rotor, the disc is tilted slightly to the left, so the horizontal component of main rotor thrust opposes drift, and through that it opposes yaw. The amount of main rotor thrust is reduced or even eliminated by a combination of reduced collective and forward cyclic. Forward cyclic decreases blade angles of attack as the helicopter's up and forward momentum increases the induced flow. A greatly reduced or zero total rotor thrust allows the tail rotor thrust to yaw the aircraft's nose to the left. The resulting skid to the right causes the fuselage to lag so that a right roll results. The tail rotor thrust also forms a right-hand turning moment around the aircraft's center of gravity, which is now much lower down than the tail rotor. As the aircraft continues to roll right (while cyclic is forward but not to the side) the clearance between the rotor head and the mast is reduced (Figure 19-11). This condition is not in itself dangerous, but incorrect flying techniques can make it so.

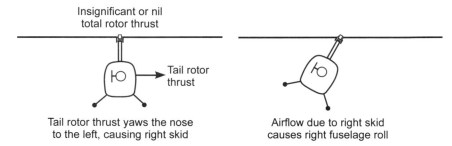

Insignificant or nil
total rotor thrust

Tail rotor
thrust

Tail rotor thrust yaws the nose
to the left, causing right skid

Airflow due to right skid
causes right fuselage roll

Figure 19-11. *Lateral cyclic neutral. Right fuselage roll reduces the clearance between the rotor head and shaft.*

The unwary pilot may instinctively use left cyclic to oppose the increasing right roll. This left lateral cyclic action causes upward flapping on the right-hand side of the disc, so that the clearance between the rotor head and the mast on the left-hand side lessens even more. Under normal, positive g conditions, this left cyclic input would have produced a horizontal component of total rotor thrust to the left, creating a moment that would have brought the aircraft back to the required attitude.

Under zero or negative g conditions, however, initial left cyclic fails to provide the restoring moment resulting from disc tilt and further left cyclic is similarly ineffective. The clearance between rotor head and mast becomes smaller still, and if not corrected, the two connect and the rotor may separate from the mast.

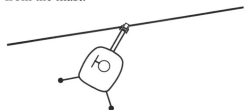

Figure 19-12. *Left lateral cyclic application reduces rotor head clearance. Mast contact may become inevitable.*

Avoiding Mast Bumping

Clearly, the answer to mast bumping is to avoid flight conditions that involve reduced or negative g. If a pilot inadvertently finds himself/herself in a zero or negative g state he or she must react with the correct instincts and particularly resist the natural tendency to move cyclic left when right roll starts.

Total rotor thrust must be restored. To do this the pilot must reload the disc by either moving the cyclic aft or increasing collective. Of the two techniques, increasing collective is less desirable because the associated increase in power tends to produce more yaw problems, particularly under low g conditions. Also, tests have shown a tendency for main rotor underspeed or gearbox over torque when the collective recovery technique is used.

Recovery from Low and Zero g

The most effective recovery technique from a low or zero g condition is:

- apply gentle rearward cyclic to reload the rotor (reintroducing a positive g situation), then
- use left cyclic to roll the aircraft level

Mast Bumping Summary

1. Avoid, low, zero or negative g situations especially when flying teetering hinge helicopters.
2. An unintended right roll may commence during low, zero or negative g conditions.
3. Left cyclic will not stop a right roll under low, zero or negative g conditions and can rapidly lead to mast bumping.
4. Total rotor thrust must be restored before lateral cyclic becomes effective.
5. Aft cyclic, applied gently, is the most effective way to reload the disc.

Exceeding Rotor rpm Limits

There are sound reasons why manufacturers insist that certain rotor rpm limits not be exceeded.

Reasons for High Rotor rpm Limits:

Engine Considerations

With both engine rpm and rotor rpm needles joined, engine rpm is invariably exceeded when the rotor rpm goes beyond the top of the green range.

Blade Attachment Stress

The mechanism that connects the root of the blades to the rotor head may be unable to absorb the stress forces if the rotor rpm exceeds the upper green range.

Sonic Problems

Exceeding the top rotor rpm limit causes the velocity of blade sections near the tips to approach, if not exceed, the speed of sound. The dramatic and rapid changes in drag experienced by the tip sections under those circumstances may cause unacceptably high vibrations.

Reasons for Low Rotor rpm Limits:

Insufficient Centrifugal Force

The coning angles of rotor blades are strongly affected by centrifugal force, which is dependent on rotor rpm. Insufficient rotor rpm produces large coning angles, which reduce total rotor thrust because the disc becomes smaller. Over-pitching is an associated risk when large blade angles (often present with low rotor rpm) prevent the available power from increasing the rotor rpm above the bottom of the green range.

Reduced Tail Rotor Thrust

The anti-torque rotor is totally dependent on main rotor rpm for its rotational velocity. If main rotor rpm drops below acceptable limits, the rpm of the tail rotor may be too low to produce the required tail rotor thrust. Once again, a potentially dangerous situation may develop when reduced anti-torque from low rpm is compensated by larger tail rotor blade angles (more left pedal), which bleeds off even more power. Furthermore, the high angles of attack on the tail rotor, caused by the low rpm, could stall the blades.

Rotor Stalls

When the helicopter is engaged in a powered descent it experiences a rate of descent flow in opposition to the induced flow across the disc. Inflow angles are reduced and the blades' angles of attack increase. The root sections of the blades historically have the weakest induced flow. During a powered descent the root sections may find their angles of attack increased such that they stall. The early rotor stall acts like the early stages of a vortex ring state. Provided the pilot keeps enough power to maintain rotor rpm and provided the aircraft is flown in a manner that avoids the development of vortex ring state, the descent continues normally.

If the pilot fails to identify and react to the early rotor stall's most prominent symptom, decaying rotor rpm, then trouble is just around the corner. Airplane pilots who have transitioned to helicopters, again, are at a higher risk for rotor stall accidents because of the differences in how airplanes and helicopters respond to control inputs. Airplane/helicopter pilots tend to push forward cyclic, increase collective and add power at the sound of the low rotor rpm warning horn (this drives the rotor rpm even lower).

The correct response to a developing rotor stall is to increase the throttle to maintain rotor rpm and lower collective simultaneously. Pilots flying helicopters equipped with high-inertia rotors have more time to react than pilots flying low-inertia rotor systems such as some Robinson helicopters (Chapter 6).

The decaying rotor rpm, brought on by the blade roots' stalling, results in less total rotor thrust, which increases the helicopter's rate of descent, which in turn increases the rate of descent flow and decreases the induced flow and inflow angles further. The consequence is that the stalled region at the blade roots spreads out towards the tips.

Slower blade velocities mean that centrifugal force drops off sharply, quickly leading to high blade coning angles, reducing the disc area and thereby further reducing the total rotor thrust. An inexperienced pilot, however, may simply pull more collective pitch in an effort to check the increased rate of descent, not noticing or responding to the lowering rotor rpm. All this action does is decay the rotor rpm further and places large portions of the blades deeper into the stalled condition.

Throughout this sequence the engine is operating at a fixed ratio rpm to the rotor rpm, which means that the engine power available falls off as rotor rpm diminishes. Consequently, the demand on engine torque to oppose further rotor rpm drop exceeds the engine's ability to do that particular job.

Eventually a complete rotor stall leads to a loss of directional control, severe blade flapping, possible blade failure from the coning angles, as well as a nose-down pitch as the longitudinal stability aligns the fuselage with the rate of descent flow. It's not a pretty picture.

Recovery from Low Rotor rpm

Pilots who find themselves in a low rotor rpm condition (leading to a possible rotor stall) must react quickly. The recovery procedure is simple:

- lower the collective to reduce blade pitch angles while simultaneously
- rolling on throttle to increase power output and rotor rpm

Rotor stalls, like vortex ring state and mast bumping, are entirely avoidable mishaps. The rotor rpm at which the stalled condition becomes critical is significantly below normal operating rotor rpm and should be easy for pilots to avoid. Proper pilot training and complete comprehension of the aerodynamics involved is all the cure that is needed. Fitting of governors has reduced the risk of unintended low rpm but like any mechanical component, a governor can fail and therefore pilots should know how to recover early from low rpm situations.

Review 19

1. The symptoms of settling with power are aircraft _____ and stick _____ while the helicopter is in a (autorotative/powered) descent at a (decreasing/increasing) rate of descent and (high/low) airspeed.

2. When settling with power has developed, (it is/is not) good practice to reduce the rate of descent with raised collective because the (higher/lower) blade angles cause the stalled region to (contract/expand).

3. To recover from a settling with power situation at low altitude you must use (collective/cyclic) to increase (rate of descent/airspeed) and after a brief pause re-apply power.

4. Settling with power of the tail rotor may be experienced during a high-rate hover turn to the (left/right).

5. When surrounding terrain forces you to approach a landing site downwind, you must be conscious of the risk of _____ particularly when you are at (high/low) gross weight, (high/low) altitude and (above/below) translational speed.

6. If you suspect that ground resonance is the cause of an increasing vibration you notice after touch-down, you should (in due course/immediately) lift the helicopter off the ground but if rotor rpm is insufficient, (raise/lower) the collective, (increase/reduce) power and apply the _____ brake, if fitted.

7. When closing down in strong and gusty wind conditions it is recommended that the rotor _____ be applied to stop rotor rotation as (slowly/quickly) as possible.

8. When lifting the downslope skid off a sloping surface you ease cyclic somewhat excessively into the slope and you notice the helicopter starts to roll. If unable to lift off you should (raise/lower) collective (quickly/smoothly).

9. If you have the choice of landing on a slope with the left or right skid up-slope in calm conditions, you will have more cyclic available if you place the (right/left) skid on the upslope.

10. To avoid a bird in flight you push cyclic forward and the helicopter starts a roll to the right. Your immediate action must be to _____ the disc with (aft/forward) cyclic and (do/do not) use left cyclic before rotor thrust has been (increased/decreased).

Helicopter Design and Components 20

Strict guidelines are involved in the design and production of helicopters. For example, helicopters certified in the United States must be designed to criteria laid out in the Federal Aviation Regulations (FAR) Part 27. These regulations note strict performance minima and stability requirements for helicopters, and explain how critical speeds such as best rate and best angle of climb, and best glide are to be determined in a new design.

Helicopters certified in other countries must conform to either International Civil Aviation Organization regulations (ICAO) or the specification of those particular countries' aviation authorities. Each country's rules vary, and it is important that helicopter operators study the regulations of the country they fly in.

Transmission

The transmission system transfers the work done by the engine to the main rotor, tail rotor and other components of the helicopter that rely on engine propulsion.

The major parts of the transmission system include the main rotor gear box, drive shafts, freewheeling unit, rotor brake (not installed in all light helicopters) and tail rotor gear box. The manufacturer decides how these components are arranged.

Main Rotor Gear Box

The main rotor gear box transfers engine power to the main rotor shaft and it also provides reduction gearing between the engine and the main rotor. If the rotor rotated at engine rpm, tip speeds would be faster than the speed of sound, blade strength would need to be increased and gyroscopic inertia would be extreme, to say nothing of the noise such a system would produce.

In most cases, rotor rpm is about 1/7th of engine rpm, but again, it varies from helicopter type to type. Turbine engines, rotating much faster than piston engines, require greater reduction gearing.

With two rpm values to monitor – engine and rotor – there must be two tachometers, which are typically combined in one instrument presentation.

Other functions of the main rotor gear box include the drive mechanism for the tail rotor, hydraulic and lubrication systems, rotor tachometers and other ancillary systems.

Freewheeling Unit

The freewheeling unit automatically disengages the engine from the main rotor when the engine rpm is less than the main rotor rpm, preventing engine "drag" from affecting the rotor rpm. There are a number of freewheeling unit designs, the most common being the sprag clutch type and the engine-to-gear-box centrifugal system.

Drive Shafts

The number of drive shafts depends on the aircraft's design. In general, when the transmission shaft takes a different direction, intermediate gear boxes and follow-on drive shafts are required. For example, a tail rotor positioned on a pylon requires an intermediate gear box and a number of drive shafts. Some helicopters, notably homebuilts, are equipped with a number of V belts or chain linkages to drive the tail rotor assembly instead of a drive shaft.

Tail Rotor Gear Box

In most installations, the tail rotor gear box contains gearing for tail rotor rpm and the tail rotor pitch control mechanism.

Rotor Brake

If the helicopter is equipped with a rotor brake it can slow down the main rotor rpm and tail rotor rpm quicker during shut-down. The brake may be a disc type or drum type. It is often hydraulically operated (on the Robinson series of helicopters it is manually operated).

Clutch

A clutch is an integral part of a transmission system.

The clutch allows the pilot to control the contact between the engine and the driveshaft.

In most helicopters it takes the form of either a belt-driven or centrifugal arrangement.

The belt-driven clutch is made up of a number of belts positioned between the engine drive shaft and the main rotor gear box. When disengaged, the belts are slack, but when engaged the belts tighten so that engine power is delivered to the main rotor system.

Most modern systems use a small electric motor to move an adjustable pulley (Figure 20-1) to tighten or loosen the belts. On older model helicopters you may find that belt adjustments are managed manually with a pilot activated lever.

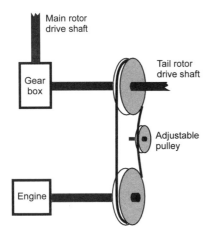

Figure 20-1. *Belt-driven clutch arrangement.*

The centrifugal clutch's spring-loaded shoes control contact between the inner part and outer part of the clutch. The inner part is connected to the engine while the outer part is connected to the main rotor drive shaft (Figure 20-2). At low engine rpm, the shoes are held away from the outer part of the clutch by the tension of the springs but as engine rpm increases, centrifugal force moves the shoes out and contact is made with the outer part. During the engaging stage the clutch experiences some slip. This clutch also acts as the freewheeling unit so that the engine is disconnected from the rotor if the engine stops.

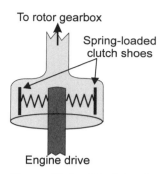

Figure 20-2. *Principle of the centrifugal clutch.*

Chip Detectors (Or Magnetic Plugs)

When bearings or other transmission parts wear and metal particles shed off, the metal chips are transported within the lubrication fluid. *Chip detectors* (which attract those chips) positioned at strategic points within the transmission system activate warning systems so that the pilot can take the appropriate remedial action without delay.

The detector consists of a magnetic core separated from the outer casing by insulating material (Figure 20-3). Metal chips, when attracted by the magnet core, lie across the insulating gap, "shorting" the outer casing and the core. The action closes an electrical circuit so that a light or other warning signal is activated. Some chip detectors are designed to activate warning signals while others can be unscrewed and inspected visually during maintenance or pre-flight inspections.

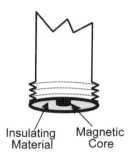

Figure 20-3. *Principle of the chip detector.*

Governors

The fitting of a governor in helicopters to maintain engine rpm (normally near the top of the green operating range) is designed to ease pilot workload with regard to rpm control. It should be noted that during normal powered flight, rotor rpm is controlled by engine rpm via the transmission train (free-wheeling unit – gearbox – drive shaft). Thus the mention of engine rpm effectively means rotor rpm as well.

When a governor senses changes in engine rpm it instantly adjusts the throttle (in piston engines) and fuel flow (in turbine engines) to oppose the change with the result that engine/rotor rpm remain constant. Whilst this arrangement certainly prevents unintentional loss of engine/rotor rpm due to pilot inexperience or inattention, it may lead to a false sense of security under certain conditions.

In the case of a climb in piston engine helicopters for example, when the collective lever is raised progressively as altitude is gained the required increase in power is produced by the collective lever action, whilst the governor sees to it that engine rpm is kept constant. When full throttle height is reached however, even the governor is not able to make the engine produce more power than it has at that altitude.

If the pilot then raises the collective further in an attempt to climb higher, the increase in aerodynamic rotor drag will cause engine/rotor rpm to decay. At that stage the condition can become hazardous if the pilot fails to lower the collective lever as required to restore rpm. This recovery action will generally result in some height loss.

Thus a pilot who has not been trained adequately in manual rpm control and has become totally reliant on the governor 'safety net' may not be able to cope as well with a low rpm warning horn as the pilot who treats the governor as an aid in maintaining rpm.

It should also be noted that some governors require an electrical supply. Therefore, if the battery runs down due to alternator failure for example (a not uncommon occurrence unfortunately), the governor will cease to operate.

Swashplate (or Control Orbit)

The swashplate consists of two "stars" (also known as orbits or plates) that transfer pilot cyclic and collective inputs to the blades. It controls the main rotor disc orientation and the amount of rotor thrust produced (Figure 20-4). The pilot control linkage system is connected to the lower (stationary) star which does not rotate but has the freedom to move up or down and tilt in any direction.

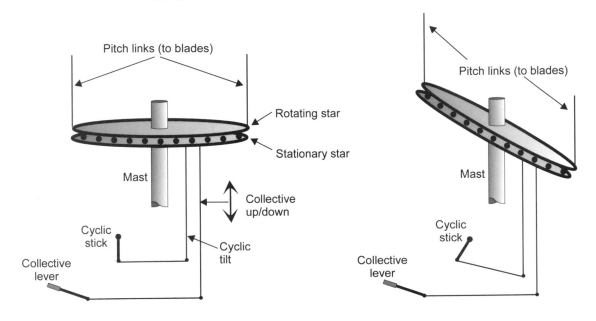

Figure 20-4. *The mechanics of the cyclic and the collective controls.*

A bearing, such as a ball bearing race, is fitted between both plates so that movement of the pilot-activated stationary plate is transferred to the blades via the rotating plate.

In the right-hand diagram the cyclic has tilted the swashplate and if the collective lever had been raised or lowered at the same time, the swashplate would have moved vertically in the same tilted position (up or down, or down and up, depending on where the pitch links are attached to the blades).

The rotating star above the stationary lower star is attached to each blade via a pitch link to the pitch horn.

The pitch horn is an attachment at the leading edge or the trailing edge of each blade. If a pitch horn is attached to the trailing edge of a blade, moving the pitch horn up reduces the blade angle, and if it is attached to the leading edge of the blade, moving the pitch horn up increases the blade angle. Therefore, raising the collective lever does not necessarily mean that the swashplate goes up; it depends on whether the pitch link is attached to the leading or trailing edge of the blade. This is shown in Figure 20-5 where it is assumed that the collective lever is raised. This action should result in an increase in blade angles on all blades simultaneously.

In "A" the pitch horn is on the leading edge of the blade and to increase the blade angle, the pitch link must push the pitch horn up; therefore the swashplate must move up. In "B" the pitch horn is on the trailing edge of the blade and to increase the blade angle, the pitch link must pull the pitch horn down; therefore the swashplate must move down. Thus it depends on the rotor head design as to how the swashplate responds to raising or lowering of the collective lever.

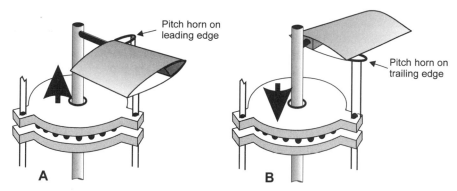

Figure 20-5. *The position of the pitch horn determines whether the swashplate moves up or down when moving the collective lever.*

Phase Lag

The operation of the cyclic control was explained in Chapter 12 where it was stated that if the rotor disc is to be lowest over the nose of the helicopter, the greatest input in flapping down must be made 90° beforehand, that is, minimum pitch angle midway on the advancing side. The principle of gyroscopic precession then causes the cyclic input to act 90° further on in the direction of rotation.

Thus a cyclic input causes the disc attitude to change, the blade reaching its highest and lowest position 90° later than the point where the maximum increase and decrease of cyclic pitch are experienced. This phenomenon is known as *phase lag*.

Advance Angle

If moving the cyclic control causes the swashplate to tilt in the same direction and if, in response to changes in pitch angles, the rotor disc tilts 90° out of phase, then the disc will also be 90° out of phase with the cyclic stick movement. For instance, forward cyclic would cause a roll to the right or left depending on main rotor rotation.

To overcome this problem, the orientation of the swashplate and attachments of the pitch links are altered in such a way that forward cyclic always causes the main rotor to tilt forward and a similar response applies for flight in any direction.

Using forward cyclic for forward flight, the pitch angle of the blade on the pilot's right must be at its minimum on counterclockwise rotating main rotors. The leading edge of that blade (at that position) is lowest down (or the trailing edge highest up). If the swashplate has the same tilt as the main rotor, then the pitch link must be attached to the front of the rotating plate. The lowest position of the swashplate then pulls the leading edge of the advancing blade lowest down.

The angular difference between the centre of the swashplate and the point on the swashplate where the pitch link is attached in advance of the blade to which it relates is known as *advance angle*.

Figure 20-6 further explains the phenomenon. In A, the swashplate is on the page, while the top of the main rotor mast and the attached blade are some inches out of the page towards the reader. The pitch link from the front of the rotating plate to the leading edge of the blade slants up, out of the page.

> **The advance angle is the angular difference between the attachment point of the pitch link on the swashplate and the blade to which it refers.**

Thus the advance angle in this case is 90°.

Forward cyclic causes the swashplate to have its low point at the front (and the high point at the rear), as shown in B. The pitch link pulls the leading edge of the blade on the pilot's right (the advancing blade) as low as it can go (minimum pitch angle). The 90° precession (phase lag) rule then causes the main disc to orient down in front (and up at the back). The tilt of the main rotor, the tilt of the swashplate and movement of the cyclic stick are in the same sense, fully compensating for phase lag.

If the same 90° advance angle is used, but the pitch link is attached to the back of the swashplate, then the top of the pitch link acts at the trailing edge of the blade (see C).

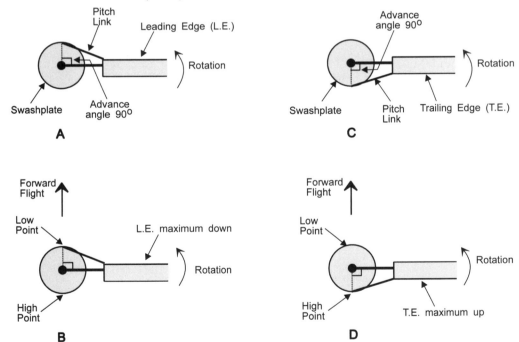

Figure 20-6. *An advance angle of 90° with pitch links attached to the leading or trailing edge of the blade, compensates fully for phase lag.*

Forward cyclic (D) requires the trailing edge of the advancing blade to be at its maximum up, so the swashplate has to have its high point at the back (and the low point at the front). Again, the swashplate, the cyclic stick movement and the main rotor disc move in the same sense.

We can therefore conclude that no matter whether the pitch links are attached to the leading edge or trailing edge of the blades, with an advance angle of 90°, the orientation of the swashplate and the main rotor is the same and in sympathy with cyclic movement, and full compensation is made for phase lag.

If the cyclic stick movement is not in sympathy with the swashplate tilt, then the advance angle has to be adjusted. If the cyclic is 45° out of phase with swashplate orientation, the advance angle has to be 45° to fully compensate for phase lag.

Rotor Blades

Early helicopter blades were manufactured the same way as airplane wings, with steel tube spars, ribs and plywood or fabric skins. These blades suffered in high moisture and temperature extremes. Besides these factors, the high speed at which the blades travel through the air caused ongoing and sometimes serious problems.

Aluminum alloy blades, introduced in the 1960s, used hollow leading edge spars (similar to the D-spar arrangement in many wings) allied with a light trailing edge construction. Most modern blades are made of fiberglass reinforced plastic and stainless steel rather than aluminum, which has a lower fatigue life. Trailing edge compartments are stiffened with light honeycomb-like materials that add to the stiffness of the blades. The use of carbon fiber, a strong and light material, increases the stiffness of the blades even more, which helps reduce vibration and increases their resilience to corrosion and damage. Robinson, one of the world's leading light helicopter manufacturers, makes its rotor blades with stainless steel leading edge spars and aluminum honeycombed filler that is bonded to aluminum skins. The Robinson tail rotor has aluminum blades.

Blades are attached to the rotor head many different ways. A commonly used construction is alloy forging that is bolted to the blade root end and attached to the rotor head by a pivot bolt (Figure 20-7).

Attachment areas are strengthened by bonding laminates or doublers on the upper and lower surfaces of blade root sections to distribute the high stress forces as far along the blade as possible.

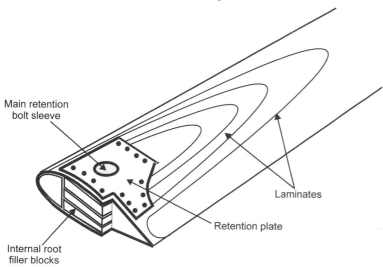

Main retention bolt sleeve

Laminates

Retention plate

Internal root filler blocks

Figure 20-7. *Example of rotor blade attachment construction.*

Chordwise Blade Balancing

If the axis on which the blade center of gravity lies is behind the aerodynamic center axis (on which lift from each blade section occurs), twist forces may become excessive. Use of counter-balance weights attached internally to the leading edge spar provides the mass balance needed to prevent the associated unwanted flutter or blade oscillation.

Spanwise Blade Balancing

In most cases, spanwise balancing is achieved through balancing the individual trailing edge skin sections and through fitting balance weights at the blade tips (see Figure 20-8).

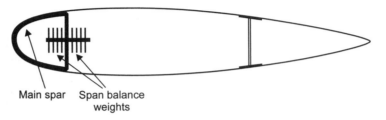

Main spar   Span balance
weights

Figure 20-8. *Blade tip and span balance weights.*

Both chordwise and spanwise balancing is carried out by the manufacturer against a *master blade* and, in some two-bladed systems, sets of blades must remain as sets. During subsequent maintenance, re-balancing is occasionally required. Checking for spanwise balance is normally more common than for chordwise balance.

Trim Controls

Helicopters do not have trim tabs such as fixed-wing aircraft. Instead, trimming is generally achieved through either of the following.

Bias Control

Bias control involves increasing or decreasing the tension at will in one or more of the linkages leading from the pilot controls to the blade control mechanism. For instance, by increasing the tension in the linkage system leading to the swashplate so that it provides a slight amount of left cyclic, the cyclic stick is automatically held in that position so that less pilot input is needed.

Electronic Servo Systems

Computer-based inputs to the hydraulic actuating arms ensure that the aircraft is kept in a desired configuration without further pilot actions. Thus the helicopter autopilot can be seen as a type of trim control.

Tail Rotors

Most tail rotors are constructed using the semi-rigid (teetering hinge) rotor principle. Lead-lag hinging is normally not required except for some modern helicopters which use multi-blade fully articulated rotor systems.

The tail rotor hub is attached to the horizontal drive shaft, often via a Delta-3 hinge to reduce flapping amplitude. A type of swashplate moves away from the tail cone or towards it by way of a bell crank operated by the pilot through the foot pedals (Figure 20-9). The action of the swashplate is then transmitted to the tail rotor blade by a pitch link connected to the trailing edge or leading edge (depending on the maker's preference).

When power increases and main rotor torque increases in proportion, more anti-torque is required from the tail rotor, requiring an increase in tail rotor blade angles. In counterclockwise rotating main rotor systems, increasing left pedal is necessary as more torque is experienced. Left pedal increases the pitch angle of the tail rotor blades and right pedal decreases these pitch angles. In Figure 20-9, left pedal moves the swashplate into the tail cone (to the right viewed from the rear) and right pedal moves the swashplate away from the tail cone (to the left viewed from the rear). This would be reversed if the pitch links are attached to the blades' trailing edges.

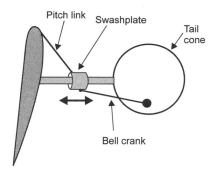

Figure 20-9. *Simplified diagram of a tail rotor mechanism.*

Tail Rotor Flapping

Tail rotors must flap to overcome dissymmetry of lift in forward flight. The flapping amplitude is reduced by using the *Delta-3 hinge*, which causes the pitch angle to decrease as the blade flaps up and the pitch angle to increase as the blade flaps down. A conventional hinge does not change its pitch angle through flapping (refer to Chapter 12, Figure 12-8). The Delta-3 hinge works because the hinge line is set at an angle other than 90° to the feather axis of the blade. Since flapping amplitude is reduced by the Delta-3 hinge, the tail rotor can be placed closer to the tail boom or empennage, improving structural strength.

Tail Rotor Rotation

For reasons not totally understood, tests have shown that better performance is obtained from the tail rotor if the upgoing blade is nearest the main rotor. In other words, if you are facing the left side of the helicopter, the tail rotor should rotate clockwise. In spite of this knowledge, many helicopters have the tail rotor rotating in the opposite direction because of factors peculiar to their individual design features, such as a high tail-rotor position.

Helicopter Vibrations

With as many rotating parts as a helicopter has, we must expect it to vibrate. These vibrations are caused by out of balance forces resulting from uneven rotor mass distribution, aerodynamic forces associated with incorrect blade tracking and forces resulting from unbalanced components such as drive shafts.

Pilots need to understand the cause and effect of helicopter vibrations, since higher than normal vibrations result in premature component wear and in the case of severe vibration, even structural failure.

Types of Vibrations

Vibrations fall into two categories, those that are *non-correctable* and those that are *correctable*.

Non-Correctable Vibrations are essentially those that the manufacturer cannot eliminate completely. They are generally caused by aerodynamic forces that "excite" natural resonance in blades and other helicopter components. The age of the helicopter, normal wear of components and loose parts aggravate the degree of non-correctable vibration it experiences. The problem can be managed by proper maintenance, but it cannot be eliminated.

Non-correctable vibrations are normally related to the number of blades that make up the rotor system, commonly referred to as *"n-per-rev,"* where "n" equals the number of blades. A five-blade rotor system would experience a "five-per-rev" vibration, which is evident if all the other "correctable" vibrations are eliminated. The *two-per-rev* vibration in many Bell helicopters, with their semi-rigid rotor systems, is familiar to many pilots.

Correctable Vibrations are predominantly caused by out-of-track blade(s) and/or by uneven mass distribution within the rotor system. A blade is tracking correctly when its path of travel is the same, or nearly so, as the preceding blade. Even mass distribution is obtained when the center of gravity of the overall mass of the spinning rotor is precisely located on the axis of rotation. Correctable vibrations caused by inadequacies in tracking or balance are either "vertical" (at right angles to the plane of rotation) or "lateral" (parallel to the plane of rotation).

Vertical Vibrations

When a vibration is caused by an out-of-track blade (an aerodynamic cause), the result is a one-per-rev vertical vibration. A faulty trailing position of the trim tab or wear in pitch link bearings can cause incorrect tracking. The problem can also show up when an old blade or a repaired blade is installed among new blades.

A pilot can easily detect vertical vibrations by resting the forearm on the knee and allowing the wrist to relax. Vertical vibrations move the relaxed hand up and down at the rate of one shake per revolution of the rotor. Another good tell-tale sign is the vertical movement of the (rod-type) HF antenna that is often mounted horizontally forward from the nose cone of some helicopters.

Blade tracking can be a tedious process, particularly when the rotor consists of more than two blades. Correction for tracking is normally done by adjusting pitch links and trim tabs positioned at the trailing edge of blades. Having tracked the blade into the correct plane while in the hover, it is likely that it will be out of track again at a given forward speed. Thus the blades must be checked (normally through the use of strobe lights and blade markers) while the helicopter flies at different speeds.

The final correction is always a compromise of the least out-of-track condition in the greatest range of airspeed. Most manufacturers stipulate a limit for the degree of out-of track vibration.

Lateral Vibrations

The steering wheel of a car vibrates if the mass of each front wheel is not correctly distributed. We solve the problem by attaching small weights to the rim of each wheel so that the center of gravity of its total mass is as close to the center of rotation as possible. The same principle applies to spinning rotors. When the mass of the rotor is not evenly distributed, it causes a "lateral" *one-per-rev* vibration, which shakes the helicopter from side to side.

There are many reasons for lateral vibrations, including blade damage, an uneven coating of ice or dust, shedding from one blade of blade tape (which helps prevent corrosion), or peeling paint, all of which produce an imbalance in weight distribution. A mechanical cause can be faulty drag dampers, which cause the angular difference between blades of a three-or-more blade rotor to be unequal. For instance, if the angular difference between blades of a three blade rotor is not 120°, the total mass of the rotor shifts off center. Similarly, drainage of grease from one bearing near the hub and not from others produces imbalance.

Lateral vibrations are eliminated by placing the correct amount of lead weight on or near the rotor hub or at a position determined by the manufacturer.

Combined Vertical and Lateral Vibrations

The interaction between vertical and lateral vibrations is complicated. When a helicopter becomes subject to lateral vibrations (balance problem), the introduction of a vertical vibration (tracking problem) only aggravates the situation. Pronounced "bumps" are experienced under those circumstances.

When correcting for vibrations, tracking problems ("vertical" vibrations) come first, and then weight distribution ("lateral" vibrations).

Both vertical and lateral vibrations associated with the main rotor can cause considerable discomfort to pilot and passengers because the low vibration rate is close to the natural frequency range of the human body (resonance of organs such as eyeballs and internal organs). The low vibration rate and relatively low forces, however, keep the vibrations from damaging the helicopter to any great degree.

The amount of lateral and vertical vibration is proportional to how of out-of-balance and out-of-track it is, and it is also proportional to the pitch link/trim tab and weight changes required to fix the problem.

It is sometimes difficult to differentiate between lateral and vertical vibrations. As a general rule, a vertical is a "bounce" and a lateral is a "rock." When your sunglasses slide down your nose the problem is vertical, and when they move from side to side the problem is lateral vibration. Vertical vibrations are also speed-sensitive, they get worse as speed increases. Laterals, on the other hand, are not affected by speed, but may be aggravated by stronger verticals with increasing airspeed.

High Frequency Vibrations

High frequency vibrations are caused by out-of-balance components that rotate at higher rpm, such as the tail rotor, cooling fans and components of the drive train, which includes gear boxes, drive shafts, bearings, pulleys, and belts.

Tail rotor vibrations are detected in most cases through the anti-torque pedals. Under certain conditions the pilot's feet go numb from these vibrations.

The tail rotor blade imbalance, bearing wear, drive shaft imbalance (possibly from the loss of the manufacturer's balance weights) and associated high frequency vibrations are extremely harmful to the helicopter. High frequency vibrations can cause cracks to develop and rivets and components to work loose. The main reasons for this are the long lever arm over which the destabilizing forces act on the airframe and the stronger forces involved with higher rpm.

Engine Vibrations

There is a normal degree of high frequency vibration from the engine in piston-engine helicopters. This is aggravated when plugs foul or break down for whatever reason. Vibrations caused by incorrect mixture or carburetor icing are difficult to detect.

Unbalanced cooling fans in piston-engine helicopters can cause cracking of the fan itself as well as the cracking of engine components, such as the exhaust manifold.

Vibrations in turbine engines are often hard to detect. If detected, the situation is serious and should be reported without delay.

Remedial Action by the Pilot

Low frequency vibrations, although uncomfortable to pilot and passengers, are not immediately threatening to the helicopter. High frequency vibrations, however, are a different matter and should be investigated immediately. It is the pilot's decision whether to land the aircraft under these circumstances or whether to proceed to a maintenance facility.

Control Functions

Collective

When collective is raised, the increasing rotor drag tends to reduce rotor rpm. To prevent this from happening, a cam-linkage (correlation unit) is positioned between the collective and the engine throttle butterfly so that pulling up collective coincides with opening the butterfly, which produces more manifold pressure and vice versa.

Thus the principal function of the collective, as it relates to engine performance, is to control manifold pressure and power output. However, collective movement has some effect on rotor rpm.

Twist-Grip Throttle

The twist-grip throttle is also connected to the throttle butterfly, but its main purpose is to adjust and fine tune rotor rpm and engine rpm. Thus the principal function of the twist-grip throttle is to control rotor rpm, but it also has some direct influence on manifold pressure. The correlator handles all the big power change commands automatically, which is why the twist-grip is the fine-tune instrument (but this function is generally taken care of by the governor, if fitted).

Coordinated use of collective and twist-grip throttle produces the required engine power output at a given engine and rotor rpm.

In turbine engine helicopters, the principle of the two controls is the same, but instead of throttle butterfly adjustments, the fuel flow is altered.

The following table shows the action to take if manifold pressure or rotor rpm require adjustment. By "throttle" is meant the twist grip control. As mentioned, the function of manual throttle control is taken care of by the governor.

Manifold Pressure	Rotor rpm	Solution
Low	Low	Increase throttle
High	High	Decrease throttle
Low	High	Raise collective
High	Low	Lower collective

In the first combination, a low manifold pressure and a low rotor rpm, raising the collective increases the manifold pressure, but the rotor rpm drops further because of the associated increase in pitch angles on all rotor blades.

If high rotor rpm (combination number three) is corrected by a decrease in throttle, the associated small reduction in manifold pressure further reduces the already low manifold pressure.

Engine Cooling

Most piston-engine helicopters' engines are cooled by an engine-driven fan that blows outside air over the finned engine cylinders. Forward speed has relatively little effect on cooling.

It is important that the fan is inspected regularly for balance because an out-of-balance fan can vibrate and fracture other engine components, such as exhaust manifold and engine support braces. Small weights placed at strategic places on the hub of the fan blades balance them in similar fashion as mass balancing of the main rotor blades.

Carburetor Icing

The standard symptoms of carburetor icing are loss of power and a rough running of the engine.

Normal vibrations in most helicopters tend to over-shadow the rough running symptom of carburetor icing, leaving the pilot with only a loss of manifold pressure and/or engine rpm to detect the phenomenon. Most piston engine helicopters are fitted with a carburetor air temperature gauge that displays the actual temperature in the vicinity of the throttle butterfly.

By intelligent use of carburetor heat, the risk associated with carburetor icing can be avoided. At temperatures below approximately −15°C (5°F), the ice formed is dry and unlikely to adhere to carburetor parts such as walls or the butterfly. Applying carburetor heat when the carburetor temperature gauge shows values colder than −15° C may encourage the formation of carburetor ice.

Small throttle butterfly openings, commonly associated with low manifold pressures in a descent for example, increase the risk of carburetor icing. Close monitoring of the carburetor temperature gauge is then essential and carburetor heat applied as required. Flight Manual instructions on minimizing the danger of carburetor icing must be studied and obeyed.

Dual Tachometer Instruments

Helicopters use a dual tachometer to display engine and rotor rpm on one instrument. There are many designs in use, but all are based on the principle that both needles are joined at all times except when power is reduced below specific values, such as during an autorotation. Figure 20-10 shows various display combinations that apply at different rotor rpm and/or different power settings.

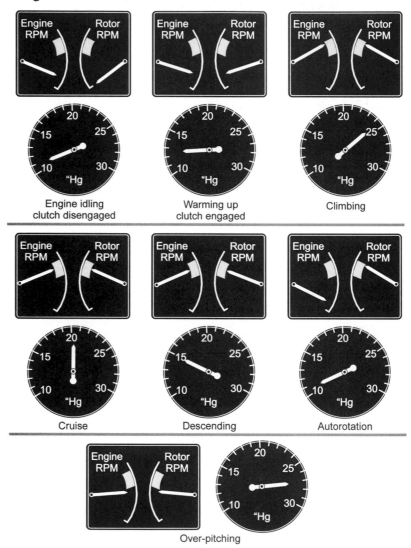

Figure 20-10. *Examples of engine and main rotor instrumentation.*

It should be noted that in some helicopters a mechanical linkage arrangement is employed to show engine and rotor rpm readings. However, in many helicopters the instrument indications are electrically controlled which means that a total electrical failure will zero both rpm needles.

Rotor Stabilizing Design Systems

Some rotor systems have been designed to reduce the effects of turbulence (and similar factors) on disc attitude and indirectly, on fluctuations in rotor rpm.

The Bell Stabilizing Bar

The *Bell stabilizing bar* consists of a bar with heavy weights at each end connected at right angles to the main rotor system and rotating at rotor rpm (Figure 20-11). The bar acts as a gyro so that the rigidity attained through rpm is utilized to stabilize the main rotor. Any disturbance of a blade caused by turbulence, for instance, is corrected by the tendency of the bar to remain in its plane of rotation. Mixing levers between the bar and rotor pitch links provide the necessary correcting input to an offending blade.

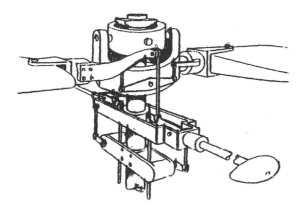

Figure 20-11. *The Bell stabilizing bar system.*

The Hiller System

Two airfoil-shaped paddles are mounted at 90° to the rotor blades (Figure 20-12). Cyclic pitch movement alters the pitch of the paddles which in turn, alters the plane of rotation of the rotor disc. If a blade moves because of a disturbance, the aerodynamic action of the paddles tends to put the blade back in its original position.

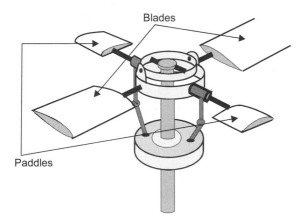

Blades

Paddles

Figure 20-12. *The Hiller stabilizing system.*

The Underslung Rotor System

The *underslung rotor system* involves attaching the blades to the rotor head lower than the top of the rotor mast. This design reduces vibrations within the rotor and minimizes lead-lag tendencies, thereby reducing stress on rotor head components.

Flapping up or down affects the position of a blade's center of gravity from the axis of rotation. For instance, flapping up brings the center of gravity in closer to the axis of rotation and, through conservation of angular momentum, the particular blade speeds up, moving forward on the lead-lag hinge (Coriolis effect) if such a hinge is fitted. The underslung rotor system tends to reduce the effect and, through that, it reduces stress on lead-lag links, or on the fore-aft strength of the blades and attachments. (On some two-blade rotor systems, the flexibility of the mast also assists in reducing the effect of lead/lag forces.)

In Figure 20-13, on the left, a blade attached to the head of the mast speeds up or down depending on the degree of flapping. When the disc is tilted, positions A and B move to the left in such a way that distance A-to-hub becomes larger and B-to-hub becomes smaller. As a consequence, conservation of angular momentum affects the rotational velocity of each blade per revolution.

On the right in Figure 20-13, the underslung system shows the blades attached at positions C and D. When the disc is tilted and blades flap as shown, the tendency for A/B to shift to the left is countered by the design function of C/D shifting to the right. The overall effect of flapping on position of blade center of gravity relative to the axis of rotation is reduced or eliminated. Through this the underslung system reduces the influence of conservation of angular momentum (Coriolis) effect.

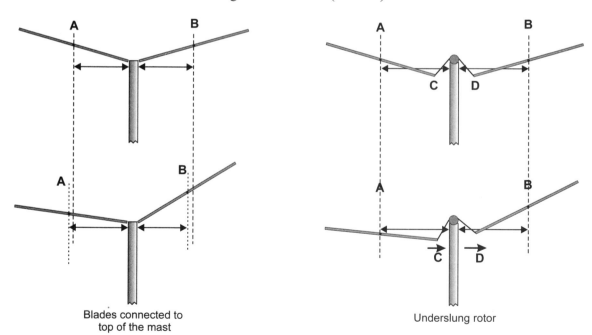

Blades connected to top of the mast

Underslung rotor

Figure 20-13. *The underslung rotor reduces or eliminates the effects of conservation of angular momentum.*

Most underslung systems involve two-bladed rotors, but there is no reason why the design cannot be used in multi-bladed rotors.

Restricting the inward and outward movement of blade center of gravity during flapping retains an even distribution of the total mass of the rotor around the axis of rotation. Vibrations from uneven mass location are therefore reduced.

Rotorless Anti-Torque System

Some helicopters are equipped with anti-torque systems that do not use the conventional tail rotor. An example is the NOTAR helicopter produced by McDonnell Douglas (MD).

Although this book does not dwell on specific types of helicopter, the only "*no tail rotor*" anti-torque system available appears to be that used on the MD520N. Accordingly, these explanations are based on the main rotor rotating anti-clockwise when viewed from above, and thus during powered flight the anti-torque force will be required to act towards the right when viewed from behind the aircraft.

Advantages of the NOTAR System

There are a number of features in the NOTAR system that improve on the conventional tail rotor design such as:

- elimination of the hazards associated with tail rotor strike
- elimination of foreign object damage to the tail rotor
- elimination of tail rotor blade stall and improved control in crosswind conditions
- reduced vibration

Components

The MD NOTAR anti-torque system has the following components:

- An air intake at the top rear of the fuselage
- A fan, driven from the main gearbox, which forces low pressure air from the intake into and through the tail boom
- Two slots along the right-hand side of the tail boom that allow some of the fan-driven air to escape so that this air can energize the boundary layer of the main rotor downwash on that side (see Figure 20-14)
- A tail thruster cone which permits high speed fan-driven air to exit through a "direct jet thruster"
- Fixed baffle plates which turn the fan-driven flow of air more or less at right angles before exiting through the rotatable direct jet thruster cone

In addition to the above there are two movable vertical stabilizers which come into play during forward flight.

Finally, the 520N has a *strake* along almost the entire length of the tail boom on the opposite side to the slots, ie, on the left-hand side.

Air Intake

The air for the fan is drawn in through a large opening on the top of the rear fuselage. Protection against foreign object ingestion is provided by a fine-mesh screen.

Engine-driven Fan

The fan is located just aft of the transmission at the rear of the fuselage near the attachment of the tail boom. The pitch angle of the fan blades can be adjusted through a bell crank and pushrod arrangement to increase or decrease the volume of air being processed. For example, if more anti-torque is required, the pilot pushes the left pedal which, ignoring other reactions, increases the pitch angle of the fan blades and a larger volume of air is forced through the tail boom.

The fan rpm is controlled directly by the main rotor gear box which ensures that directional control is maintained at all times including during autorotation.

Slots

The *slots* on the right-hand side of the tail boom direct fan air tangentially downwards so that it energizes the boundary layer of downwash flow from the main rotor on that side. At the same time, the downwash flow on the left-hand side is 'spoiled' by the effect of the strake fitted to that side. The net effect is that the downwash is accelerated on the right-hand side and retarded on the left, generating an anti-torque (lift) force to the right (see Figures 20-14 and 20-15).

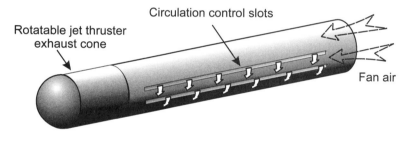

Figure 20-14. *Circulation control slots provide boundary layer control.*

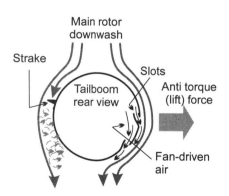

Figure 20-15. *The slots and the strake produce a force to the right.*

The slots (and strake) are most effective during the hover when they are capable of providing in excess of 50% of the required anti-torque force. As forward speed is gained, or in windy conditions, the main rotor downwash starts to angle away from the tail boom so that the amount of anti-torque from this source diminishes.

Direct Jet Thruster

The *direct-jet thruster cone* rotates around a stationary unit made up of a series of baffle plates more or less at right angles to the fan-driven air. The baffle plates assist in deflecting the air sideways.

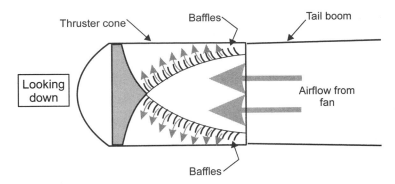

Figure 20-16. *Fan-driven air is re-directed by the baffle plates. The thruster cone rotates around the stationary baffle plate arrangement.*

The rotatable thruster cone has a rectangular opening through which the fan-driven air escapes. Pedal inputs by the pilot can orientate this outlet through almost 180° so that the required left or right anti-torque force can be provided for all normal flight conditions.

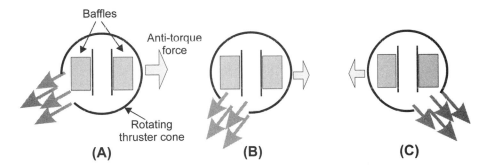

Figure 20-17. *Rear view of the thruster cone.*

Viewed from the rear, the high speed air from the fan escapes like a jet blast. Figure 20-17 (A) shows that when left pedal has been applied, the direct thruster expels air to the left and the reaction to this on the opposite wall of the tail boom forces it to the right. Figure 20-17 (B) is typical in cruise flight and shows that when the vertical stabilizers provide most of the required directional control; the direct thruster will point more downwards than sideways depending on required pedal position. Figure 20-17 (C) is typical of autorotation when the tendency of the fuselage to turn with the main rotor may require right pedal. This situation could also be present to varying degrees during a strong crosswind from the left (causing left yaw) when the tail boom may need to be forced to the left, and the nose to the right.

Vertical Stabilizers

Vertical stabilizers are attached to each end of the horizontal stabilizer. The pitch angle of these stabilizers is independently controlled as follows.

The pitch angle of the left stabilizer is increased or decreased in unison with the rotation of the direct jet thruster. For example, if left pedal is applied and the jet thrust is directed towards the left (anti-torque to the right), the left stabilizer increases its pitch angle to provide added anti-torque. Clearly, the effect of the vertical stabilizer is nil during the hover but will become progressively more effective as forward speed is gained.

During autorotation when right pedal may be required, the direct jet thruster would be directed to the right and the pitch angle of the vertical stabilizer would be reversed to provide the required anti-torque to the left (and nose right).

The right vertical stabilizer is essentially a "*yaw damper*". It is controlled by computer and when sensing left/right yaw in turbulence for instance, it adjusts the pitch angle of the stabilizer to counter unwanted yaw. The computer can be switched off and an immediate decrease in directional stability is then commonly noticed.

Undercarriages

The type of undercarriage, skids or wheels, that is fitted to helicopters is largely determined by the size of the helicopter and the role for which it has been designed. For example, most light helicopters are fitted with a *skid-type undercarriage* which, although not ideal from the ground handling perspective, is simple and light. On the other hand, the *wheeled-type undercarriage* is generally preferred for large helicopters considering the problem of ground handling and aspects such as taxiing and running take-offs which often can more easily be accomplished with wheels than with skids. For ship-borne operations where space is limited, the wheeled type is often preferred.

Skids

Skids are predominantly of simple tensile steel construction. The fitting of damping devices depends largely on the type of helicopter and especially the rotor: − fully articulated rotors and the associated risk of ground resonance normally require skid damping. The main advantages and disadvantages of skids are:

- simplicity of construction
- resistance to movement when the helicopter is parked on a slope
- suitable for attaching racks or pods so that freight or cargo can be carried externally
- skids may not be as suitable as wheels for running take-offs and landings but this would depend to some degree on the type of surface
- ground handling is somewhat more difficult

Wheels

When a heavy helicopter is fitted with skids it is generally necessary to bring the aircraft to the hover prior to lift-off; − this goes hand in hand with huge volumes of high velocity downwash air affecting the surrounding area. The problem is reduced when a wheeled undercarriage is fitted which enables the aircraft to be taxied clear of busy areas while using greatly reduced rotor thrust.

Similarly, the improved ability to use the running take-off technique enables the aircraft to be brought to translational speed while the weight is still partly on the undercarriage, hover OGE problems are thereby reduced.

Another advantage of wheeled type undercarriages is that they can be retracted so that parasite drag is reduced and better advantage can be taken of total rotor thrust.

Disadvantages of wheeled type undercarriages are:

- increased risk of inadvertent movement on sloping terrain

- complexity and weight of supporting equipment such as brake and hydraulic systems

- added maintenance requirements

Oleo (Shock) Struts

Many wheeled-type undercarriages use *oleo-pneumatic shock struts* which use compressed air and hydraulic fluid to absorb the shock loads. Oleo-pneumatic means 'oil-air', and such struts are often referred to simply as *oleo legs*.

There are a number of oleo shock strut designs which have many mechanical arrangements in common. A common form of oleo-pneumatic shock strut is shown in Figure 20-18. The strut consists of two tubes which 'telescope' together. The upper tube is called the *cylinder* and contains a type of hydraulic oil. The lower tube is called the *plunger tube* (or *piston*) and mostly contains compressed air, but with provision being made for oil to enter through the top of the tube (when it is forced upwards) through orifices and a flutter valve. The oil and air are kept apart by a separator which is able to slide up and down inside the plunger tube. The two tubes are joined by torsion links which, although allowing them to telescope, prevents the plunger tube from rotating inside the cylinder. The wheel axle is fitted at the bottom of the plunger tube. The principle of operation is illustrated in Figure 20-19:

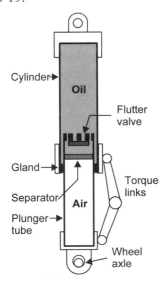

Figure 20-18. *The main components of an oleo shock strut system.*

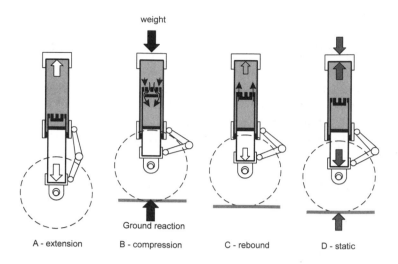

weight

Ground reaction

A - extension   B - compression   C - rebound   D - static

Figure 20-19. *The principle of operation of an oleo shock strut.*

Diagram A shows the oleo in an extended position, e.g. when airborne. With no weight on the oleo leg, the compressed air inside the plunger tube is able to expand and, with this air pressure acting against the separator and the column of oil, the plunger tube extends downwards until it is stopped from going any further by the torque links.

Diagram B shows the oleo under compression, e.g. during the touchdown on landing. The weight of the aircraft on the top of the strut, and the ground reaction on the wheel at the bottom, telescopes the tubes together. The air in the plunger tube becomes compressed (i.e. reduces in volume). To allow this to happen, as the plunger head penetrates the oil column, the flutter valve opens to allow oil to flow in at the top.

Diagram C shows the oleo in the rebound (or damping) mode. While the initial shock of compression is being absorbed, there is a tendency for the air to become 'over-compressed', i.e., greater than that required to support the aircraft weight. (Air can be considered as having a natural 'springiness'). To prevent the oleo from suddenly extending again (rebounding), once the plunger tube begins to reverse direction, the flutter valve, assisted by spring pressure, closes. This reduces the outflow of oil to small orifices which are not covered by the valve, thus reducing the rate of extension and providing damping.

Diagram D shows the oleo in static mode on the ground, e.g., with the aircraft parked. The pressure of the air and the oil inside the oleo is equalized, creating a force which tends to expand the strut. This is balanced by the force created by the weight and ground reaction which tend to compress it.

Note that in the diagrams, it is the air which provides the shock absorption – by compressing and expanding (changing its volume) when required. With oleo struts therefore, the helicopter could be said to be riding on a cushion of air when on the ground. The column of oil in the strut does not change its length (i.e. volume) to any great extent. As a liquid, the oil in the strut is for all practical purposes, incompressible, although any changes in air pressure in the oleo are transmitted to the oil by the separator. The function of the oil in the strut is therefore to provide a damping medium, a means of sealing and lubricating the sliding parts, and heat absorption when the air in the leg is being compressed.

Review 20

1. The principal function of the main rotor gear box is to transfer power from the ____ to the main rotor and to provide ____ gearing to ensure main rotor rpm is (less/more) than engine rpm.

2. When the engine rpm becomes less than rotor rpm, the ____ unit (engages/disengages) the engine from the rotor.

3. When a chip detector light comes on in flight it indicates a (non-serious/serious) situation and urgent investigation is (essential/not essential).

4. Phase lag means the transfer of a cyclic input ____ degrees (in the direction of/at right angle to) direction of rotation.

5. If there is a 90° advance angle between the blade feathering axis and the pitch link attachment point on the swashplate, forward cyclic will cause the swashplate to tilt (in the same direction as/at 90° to) the tilt of the main rotor.

6. Many tail rotors are fitted with a delta-3 hinge which (increases/reduces) flapping amplitude because as the blade flaps, it also (lead-lags/feathers).

7. You note that rotor rpm is low and manifold pressure is high. To correct this situation you should (roll on throttle/lower collective).

8. The principal means of providing engine cooling of helicopter engines is through (airspeed/engine driven fan).

9. An underslung rotor system (restricts/encourages) movement of blade centre of gravity from the (mast axis/axis of rotation) during flapping.

Principles of Helicopter Flight

Stability 21

Stability is the characteristic of a body to return to its original state after it has been disturbed, without any corrective control input from a person. For instance, if a helicopter pitches its nose up from a disturbance and then pitches its nose down again when the disturbance has ceased without any pilot input, the helicopter has a degree of stability. FAR 27.171 lists the minimum stability requirements for helicopters designed for the U.S. (and many other countries') market.

Stability is classified in two main categories, *static stability* and *dynamic stability*. (Neutral stability is insignificant and will be mentioned only once or twice.)

Static Stability

> **Static stability deals with the tendency of an object to return to its original position after a disturbance.**

The function does not consider how, or if at all, the object finally manages to return to original, it simply depicts the behavior of the object immediately after the disturbance.

In Figure 21-1 three objects are faced with the same disturbance.

Object A shows a tendency to return to the track it was following initially and therefore it is statically stable. How A finally succeeds in returning to original is not a question here.

Object B wants to deviate further from track and is therefore statically unstable.

Object C shows a tendency to retain the new direction, that is, it does not wish to return to original and neither does it wish to deviate further. C is statically neutral.

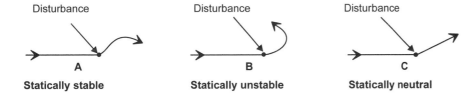

Figure 21-1. *The three categories of static stability.*

Dynamic Stability

Dynamic stability reflects the success, or lack of success, of a *statically stable* object to return to its original state after a disturbance. This verifies that there can be no dynamic stability if there is no static stability.

An object that is statically stable displays one of the following three characteristics of dynamic stability:

- it succeeds in returning to the original direction, which means that it is dynamically stable, or

- it overshoots the original direction and the oscillation becomes worse, meaning that it is dynamically unstable, or

- it overshoots the original direction and the oscillation continues at a constant magnitude, getting no worse or better, making it dynamically neutral

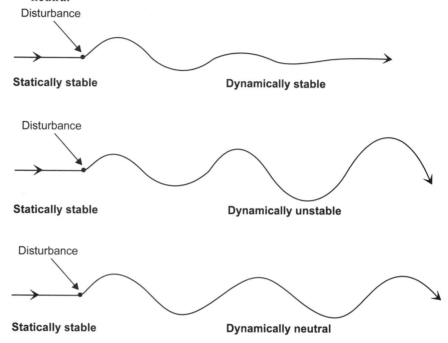

Figure 21-2. *The three categories of dynamic stability.*

Dynamic stability indicates how successful the object is in finally returning to its original track. It either succeeds, it fails and gets worse, or it fails while not getting better or worse.

Dynamic stability is often referred to in terms of amplitude in oscillation (phugoid). For instance, static and dynamic stability produce a convergent phugoid (convergence), static stability and dynamic instability produce a divergent phugoid (divergence), while static stability and dynamic neutral stability produce a neutral phugoid.

Stability in aircraft is a matter of design. Some designers get it right and there are others who simply don't.

Stability In The Three Planes Of Movement

Static and dynamic stability apply to each plane of movement of a helicopter. Thus the aircraft may be statically and dynamically stable in the rolling, pitching and yawing planes. How helicopter stability functions in these three planes of movement depends to a large degree on whether the aircraft controls are held by the pilot or if they have been released. These two situations are referred to as *stick held* and *stick free*.

In general, most helicopters *stick held* are statically stable but dynamically unstable. These aircraft display *divergence*. An unwanted roll (without the pilot moving the control) tends to correct itself, but in so doing, the resulting oscillation becomes progressively worse (dynamic instability).

Stick free, most helicopters are statically unstable and, as stated, there can then be no dynamic stability function. With the cyclic stick released, the aircraft may roll, yaw and pitch without any tendency to regain the original flight path.

The following paragraphs deal with stability or lack of stability in the three planes of movement. A *stick held* situation is assumed.

Longitudinal Stability

Longitudinal stability deals with the behavior of the helicopter in the pitching plane around the lateral axis – the straight-line axis tip-to-tip at right angles to the fuselage.

In a hover, the aircraft is statically stable, but dynamically unstable.

A hovering helicopter being struck by a gust from straight ahead experiences blow-back, which causes the disc to tilt downwind so that the aircraft begins to move backwards. While moving backwards it experiences an airflow from the rear that makes the disc flap-forward, but the aircraft momentum forces the fuselage to continue traveling rearward for a few seconds after the initial wind gust dies down. The disc tilts forward while the fuselage lags behind. As the sequence repeats itself, the oscillation becomes progressively worse and a clear case of dynamic instability presents itself.

In forward flight, the same characteristic shows up. For instance, a gust from straight ahead causes the disc to blow back. The airspeed slows, but the momentum of the fuselage causes the nose to pitch up, which further tilts the disc back. As the aircraft stabilizes at a lower speed, the fuselage begins to pitch down through pendulosity, the disc flaps forward and a dynamically unstable cycle develops as the helicopter loses height.

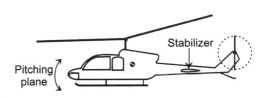

Figure 21-3. *Longitudinal stability in the pitching plane around the lateral axis.*

> **At best, helicopters are statically stable and dynamically unstable in the longitudinal plane**.

Longitudinal Stability Aids

Stabilizers. Stabilizers are flat-plate or airfoil shaped surfaces attached horizontally to the tail boom or to the rear of the fuselage. Their main function is to stabilize the fuselage to prevent follow-through pitching movements when flap-back occurs.

A gust from straight ahead during forward flight causes blow-back, so the disc tilts back and the fuselage pitches up. This pitch up produces an increased angle of attack on the stabilizer, which results in greater lift production at the rear of the aircraft. As a consequence, the nose is prevented from pitching up further and in some designs, it is actively encouraged to pitch down to some degree. Thus stabilizers tend to dampen dynamic oscillations by stabilizing the fuselage and the disc.

Stabilizers are helpful for longitudinal stability in forward flight, but they can be detrimental to rearward flight. When flying backwards the stabilizer accentuates longitudinal oscillations and a dangerous situation can develop in a short period of time.

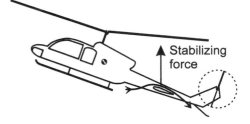

Figure 21-4. *Lifting force from the stabilizer assists in pitching the nose down.*

Stabilizers are fitted to some helicopters at odd angles because the angle of attack on the stabilizer is influenced by the airflow from forward flight as well as that from rotor downwash slanting rearward in forward flight. Design tests are usually conducted to determine where, and at what angle, to place the stabilizer to make the best use of its functions. Stabilizers are generally set up to function best at normal forward cruise speeds.

Synch Elevators. Synch elevators are stabilizers, but instead of being rigidly attached to the fuselage empennage, they pitch up and down with *fore/aft* cyclic movements (they are "synchronized"). Synch elevators strengthen the degree of response from the stabilizer at varying airspeeds.

Synthetic Stabilizing. It is difficult to provide satisfactory longitudinal stability even with the best designed stabilizers. Modern helicopters are therefore equipped with electronic stabilization, such as gyro-controlled autopilots and computers, which provide inputs into the main control linkage system.

Lateral Stability

Lateral stability deals with the behavior of the helicopter in the rolling plane around the longitudinal axis, which is the straight-line axis from the nose of the aircraft to the tail. Stability in this plane is similar in principle to that described in longitudinal stability.

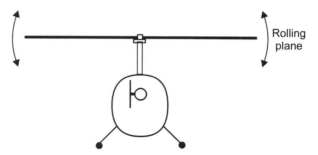

Figure 21-5. *Lateral stability in the rolling plane around the longitudinal axis.*

> **In the rolling plane, helicopters are generally statically stable but dynamically unstable.**

The movement of the aircraft in one plane affects its behavior in another plane, which complicates matters. This phenomenon is known as *cross coupling*.

When a helicopter is subjected to a gust of wind from the left in forward flight, blow-back causes the disc to tilt to the right, forcing the aircraft to roll right out of balance. The resultant slip acts on the fuselage in such a way as to cause a yaw to the right, the degree depending on the airspeed of the aircraft at that time. Cross coupling in this case produces an adverse affect in the yawing plane when the rolling plane was the original offender.

Lateral stability is typically achieved in helicopters through electronic means, such as gyro stabilization systems and autopilots.

Directional Stability

Directional stability involves the yawing plane around the normal axis, which is the axis at right angles to the other two. In the calm hover the normal axis is in line with the axis of rotation.

In a hover, most helicopters are (directionally) statically stable but dynamically unstable.

If a helicopter with counterclockwise main rotor rotation is struck by a gust from the right the aircraft will start to move to the left when the disc blows (flaps) back, but it will also weathervane into the wind, to the right. This is partly because the gust from the right effects tail rotor thrust production. To produce tail rotor thrust, the tail rotor must draw air from the right and accelerate it to the left. The air being drawn in from the right may be seen as induced flow, which ultimately determines the thrust produced by the tail rotor. A gust from the right increases the induced flow on the tail rotor, which reduces its angle of attack and consequently produces less tail rotor thrust. For a constant power delivery to the main rotor, less tail rotor thrust causes a yaw in the direction of torque, to the right (Figure 21-7).

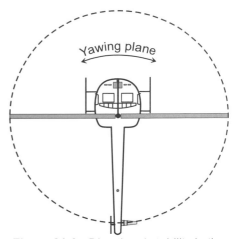

Figure 21-6. *Directional stability in the yawing plane around the normal axis.*

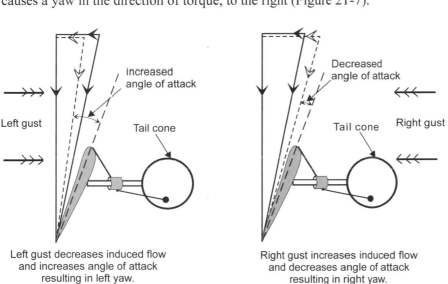

Figure 21-7. *Effect of side gust on directional stability.*

Even though the gust ends, the aircraft still travels to the left because of its momentum. The induced flow on the tail rotor reduces sharply, angles of attack on the tail rotor blades increase and more tail rotor thrust is produced, yawing the aircraft to the left. This right, then left yawing repeats itself with increasing amplitude, demonstrating the helicopter's innate dynamic instability. The same sequence occurs if a gust strikes the helicopter from the left during a hover.

Beyond a given airspeed in forward flight the helicopter becomes statically and dynamically stable directionally.

The airflow from forward speed provides a sufficiently strong side force on the fuselage, empennage and tail rotor, to assist in overcoming any unwanted yawing movement from air disturbances. The greater the flat vertical area of the fuselage behind the aircraft center of gravity, the further back the tail rotor and the larger the tail rotor, the more directional stability the helicopter has (and at lower forward airspeeds).

Directional Stability Aides

Any design that strengthens the weathervane action of the fuselage and empennage obviously improves a helicopter's directional stability in forward flight. Vertical fins, both dorsal and ventral, add to directional stability. Placing these fins further back from the aircraft center of gravity further enhances directional stability due to a longer lever arm.

Twin rotor helicopters such as the Chinook suffer from a lack of directional stability, especially at low forward airspeeds, because their vertical fuselage areas are almost equidistant forward and aft of the aircraft center of gravity. As forward airspeed increases, the influence of the vertical components of the forward pylon is reduced by spoilers so that the rear pylon can produce the weathervane effect required to give the Chinook a reasonable degree of directional stability.

Cross Coupling with Lateral Stability

Any yaw in forward flight, whether intended or not, causes the helicopter to skid in the opposite direction. For instance, a yaw to the right makes the aircraft skid to its left. As soon as a skid occurs, a number of factors come into play:

1. Increased parasite drag slows the aircraft down and flap forward causes a longitudinal stability problem as the nose pitches down.

2. Blow-back from airflow from the skid direction causes the disc to tilt away from the skid, creating a lateral stability problem as the aircraft rolls.

3. The slip resulting from the unbalanced roll produces an airflow from the direction of the initial yaw, causing the helicopter to roll in the opposite direction (through blow-back away from the slip).

This underlines the need for electronic means (for example, an autopilot) to fly the helicopter safely in instrument conditions.

Offset Flapping Hinges

Stability shortcomings are often the result of *pendulosity forces* swinging the fuselage excessively beneath the rotor. Any design that assists in maintaining the fuselage parallel with the disc improves stability. The effectiveness of the cyclic control in achieving changes in fuselage attitude is known as *control power*. The more control power a helicopter has, the less problems with stability and pendulum action it has. Different kinds of rotors, hinges and blades have been designed to accentuate control power in helicopters.

A rotor that has its blades flapping from the hub itself (as in the case of the teetering hinge of the semi-rigid rotor) may have large unwanted fuselage swings in all but totally non-accelerated flight conditions. The helicopter's center of gravity position further complicates the problem.

If the aircraft center of gravity position is slightly aft of neutral on liftoff, the tail of the aircraft sinks, the rotor tilts rearward and the aircraft starts to fly backwards as soon as hover flight is established. To prevent rearward flight, the pilot must add forward cyclic to hold a hover position. The forward cyclic forces the disc more or less level while the fuselage hangs tail down, creating a substantial attitude difference between the rotor disc and the fuselage. Load the center of gravity further aft still and you aggravate the situation even more.

There are great control power advantages in a rotor design that encourages the fuselage to remain more or less parallel with the disc even when the aircraft center of gravity position is near its fore or aft limits. Although horizontal stabilizers extend a helicopter's usable center of gravity range at higher speed, they do not do so in a hover or at low speeds. The *offset flapping hinge* rotor does help, however.

Figure 21-8 shows the mast as a large T with the flapping hinges well away from the hub. When cyclic is used so that one blade flaps up while the other flaps down, a couple is produced (A - A1) by the vertical components of centrifugal force (X - X) acting in the tilted plane of rotation. The A - A1 couple is instrumental in aligning the "T" (and therefore the fuselage to which is attached) with the rotor disc. The right-angle components (primarily centrifugal force) acting along B - B1 pull out from the mast attachment points and hinges. The construction of the rotor head must be sufficiently strong to overcome these outbound forces, which can approach ten times the power of the rotor thrust alone.

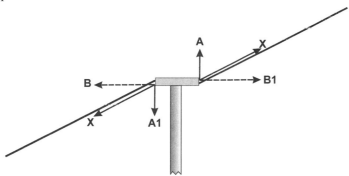

Figure 21-8. *Action of offset flapping hinges encourages the fuselage to remain parallel with the rotor disc.*

Some modern blade designs that do not have flapping hinges use the principle of offset hinges by constructing the first three or four feet of the blades as rigidly as possible, while the extended portions to the tip are more flexible.

The benefits of offset flapping hinges compared to flapping hinges at the mast are:

- longitudinal and lateral stability are improved (less pendulum action)
- the aircraft has wider center of gravity limits
- the aircraft can go faster in forward flight

Offset flapping hinges (or blade designs that produce the same results) improve *control power* by keeping fuselage and disc attitudes in sympathy.

When compared to each other, the truly rigid rotor imparts the most control power to a helicopter, while the articulated rotor has slightly less control power and the semi-rigid rotor has the least control power.

Review 21

Stability

1. When an object is disturbed and returns to its original path but in so doing starts to oscillate at an increasing rate it is said to be statically _____ and dynamically _____.

2. A dynamic stability function can exist only if there is _____ stability.

3. Most helicopters, stick held, are statically _____ and dynamically _____. Stick-free, most helicopters are statically _____ and there (can/cannot) be a dynamic function under those circumstances.

4. Longitudinal stability is in the _____ plane around the (longitudinal/lateral/ normal) axis. Lateral stability is in the _____ plane around the (longitudinal/lateral/normal) axis. Directional stability is in the _____ plane around the (longitudinal/ lateral/normal) axis.

5. Stick-held, when a gust of wind strikes a helicopter on the nose during the hover, dynamic (stability/ instability) will cause it to oscillate forward and back at a (reducing/ increasing) rate.

6. The main function of a stabilizer is to dampen out (static/dynamic) oscillations. In rearward flight it has a (positive/ negative) influence on longitudinal stability.

7. Synch elevators (can/cannot) pitch up/ down, they respond to cyclic (fore-aft/left-right) movements only.

8. Beyond a certain speed in forward flight, most helicopters are directionally statically _____ and dynamically _____.

9. Control power is a function of the effectiveness of (collective/cyclic) to achieve changes in fuselage attitude. Generally, the rigid rotor has (most/least) control power, the semi-rigid rotor has (most/least).

10. Offset flapping hinges (do/do not) assist in keeping the fuselage parallel with the rotor disc and they allow a (wider/narrower) range of centre of gravity position.

Special Helicopter Techniques 22

Out-of-Wind Takeoffs and Landings

Sometimes it is not possible to take off or land into the wind. Before tackling crosswind or downwind takeoffs or landings, the pilot needs to understand how wind affects a helicopter under the conditions.

Crosswind Factors

The following factors are involved when taking off or landing crosswind:

- lateral blow-back (flap back) of the disc
- weathervane action of the fuselage
- effect on tail rotor thrust

Lateral Blow-Back (Flap-Back)

The crosswind component causes the rotor disc to flap back "downwind," that is, a crosswind from the left causes the disc to tilt to the right. On takeoff the cyclic stick must be held into the wind prior to becoming airborne to counteract anticipated aircraft sideways movement from blow back (flap back) after liftoff.

Aside from blow back, to hold constant ground position in a crosswind, the hovering aircraft must fly sideways at exactly the wind speed.

Weathervane Action

Depending on fuselage design, there is a tendency for the nose of the helicopter to yaw into the wind as the aircraft leaves the ground. Appropriate tail rotor pedal should be used from the start to counter this yaw. The principles of LTE (loss of tail rotor effectiveness) explained in Chapter 9 apply here.

Effect on Tail Rotor Thrust

A crosswind from the left opposes the induced flow onto the tail rotor blades (from the right) thereby increasing the angle of attack on the blades (Figure 21-7, Chapter 21). For a given pedal position, the tail rotor thrust increases and the nose yaws to the left, in the same direction as the weathervane effect. Left pedal must be reduced to provide the correct tail rotor thrust to maintain directional control.

A crosswind from the right, however, may pose a directional control problem when the induced flow onto the tail rotor blades increases, reducing the angle of attack on the blades. For a given pedal position, tail rotor thrust decreases and the nose yaws in the direction of main rotor torque, to the right. This direction coincides with the weathervane effect so lots of left pedal may be needed to maintain directional control.

The intent of this textbook is to state and explain the aerodynamic factors associated with helicopter flight, it is not meant to be a book on how to fly a helicopter. Having said that, there are a number of special flying techniques that exhibit unique aerodynamic aspects. The following text in no way endeavors to support or contradict the teaching methods used by instructors or the operating methods of qualified pilots. It merely explains the theory associated with certain flying techniques.

It is possible, in a strong right crosswind at a high gross weight or high altitude that the pilot may run out of left pedal, making it impossible to operate the helicopter in that crosswind condition.

Different Types of Takeoffs and Landings

Downwind Takeoffs and Landings

Downwind operations should be carried out only when there is no possible alternative because most helicopters have less rearward cyclic available than forward cyclic. If the helicopter must stop after the lift-off and initial departure, rearward cyclic may be impaired to the degree that the helicopter cannot hover. The same problem may arise when approaching the hover prior to landing, especially in strong tailwind conditions.

An approach to a restricted landing area (generally the main reason for landing downwind) often involves a steep approach angle. In downwind conditions, the risk of *vortex ring state* is present unless the rate of descent is strictly controlled.

When the tailwind is gusty and changeable in direction, the directional stability of the helicopter may be impaired. Abrupt and possibly large movements of the tail rotor pedals may be needed to maintain control, this problem is aggravated in helicopters fitted with stabilizers. As explained in Chapter 21, longitudinal stability is somewhat eroded by stabilizers when flying backwards. A tailwind approach at slow speed or hover is essentially the same and overall control of the aircraft may be difficult.

The area ahead of the helicopter must be clear of obstructions and suitable for touchdown because a downwind takeoff that results in a loss of aft cyclic control may require an immediate landing.

Running Takeoff

When there isn't enough power to bring the helicopter to the hover prior to climbing out on takeoff you should seriously consider abandoning the takeoff (unless you are flying a wheeled helicopter). Nevertheless, if a departure is essential, a running takeoff is one of your limited options. The surface ahead of the aircraft must be smooth and the undercarriage must be designed for running takeoffs. Since acceleration will be slow, particularly in the early stages of the takeoff, it is imperative that the area ahead is clear of obstructions.

In a running takeoff the pilot places the helicopter into wind and smoothly applies full allowable power, holding slightly forward cyclic. Once the helicopter accelerates to near translational lift speed it can be flown off the ground in ground effect, then through translational lift. The pilot may notice a pitch-down tendency when the aircraft becomes light on its undercarriage, and a roll to the left or right after lift-off, both of which need to be corrected with cyclic.

Principles of Helicopter Flight

In a running takeoff climb power may be limited during the early stages of the climb, so it is essential that the pilot's cyclic movements are gentle, otherwise the aircraft may lose height and re-contact the ground. Depending on obstructions ahead, the pilot may need to initiate the climb at best angle of climb speed and revert to normal climb speed when obstructions have been cleared.

Cushion-Creep Takeoff

When power is available to hover at one or two feet above the ground, but insufficient power is available to complete the transition into normal forward flight, the cushion-creep takeoff may be appropriate.

Essentially, the technique converts the benefits of ground effect into benefits of translational lift. The helicopter is brought to a low hover using full power and cyclic is then used very gently to obtain forward speed. Should the helicopter descend at any stage during the initial phase, cyclic should be used to bring the disc almost level and when height has stabilized again, gentle forward cyclic can again be used to increase speed once more. Depending on the obstructions in the takeoff corridor, the pilot may again need to increase speed to best angle of climb speed before selecting normal climb speed.

Confined Area Takeoff (Towering Takeoff)

When confronted with a takeoff from a confined area that prevents any forward movement to gain translational lift, pilots use the *confined area takeoff (towering takeoff)* technique. This procedure ignores the cautions of the height/velocity charts and should be used only when absolutely necessary. There is danger in this type of takeoff should the engine fail while ascending vertically. This is an extreme maneuver that should be avoided as much as possible.

From a low hover, maximum power is applied and the helicopter climbs out vertically. As the lowest obstacle is passed, the vertical motion is converted into forward flight by the pilot's gentle use of forward cyclic. The high power used during a confined area takeoff forces the pilot to pay attention to directional control because translating tendency (tail rotor drift) may cause the aircraft to drift to the right. When all obstructions are cleared, the climb reverts to normal climb out speed.

As the aircraft looses ground effect the power surplus and rate of climb decay and may even cease. It is imperative that the pilot accurately judges the helicopter's performance margin correctly. Rate of climb must be converted to forward airspeed (and translational lift) before the rate of climb is lost, otherwise height will be lost while accelerating. In this regard bear in mind that towering takeoffs usually offer little in the way of emergency landing areas ahead if translational lift cannot be achieved in time.

Maximum Performance Takeoff

The maximum performance takeoff is more typical than the confined area takeoff. It is used for the same reasons as the confined area takeoff, but the restricted area allows some forward speed during the initial climb.

The aircraft should be positioned for a departure that takes best advantage of any favorable winds, lower barriers, and possible emergency landing sites in the departure path. Before beginning the takeoff the pilot plans the line of climb from the takeoff point to the top of the highest barrier that must be cleared. After applying full power, the cyclic is eased forward and speed is gained as the aircraft climbs away. As in the previous case, tail rotor drift to the right must be prevented. The climb speed selected should allow for easy clearance of the nearest obstructions. If it appears that this clearance cannot be assured the pilot should slow down immediately. Use the best angle of climb speed until clearing the highest obstructions, at which time transition to normal flight configurations can be made.

Running Landing

A *running landing* is used when it is unlikely that the helicopter can be brought to a hover in ground effect prior to touchdown. The airspeed at which the aircraft is run on depends on the power margin – the smaller this margin the higher the airspeed. It is essential that the run-on speed does not exceed the figure stated for the procedure in the helicopter's Flight Manual.

Again, if you are landing in conditions where you cannot hover, you should examine your options closely because it is unlikely that you can leave the landing site without being forced into offloading weight, waiting until the temperature cools off, the wind picks up, and/or the humidity drops, or performing a running takeoff.

The landing area for a run-on landing must meet the following criteria:

- flat and sufficiently smooth
- long enough for the speed used
- clear of overshoot obstructions
- clear of approach obstructions so that a shallow approach can be made

The landing area must be inspected thoroughly. The pilot should determine a height below which it would be dangerous to overshoot (commit height). The reason for this is that if insufficient power is available for the landing and this becomes apparent to the pilot unexpectedly at low heights, the rate of descent will dramatically increase when the helicopter's speed falls off. A heavy landing may result or the pilot's attempt at an overshoot may result in over-pitching.

The initial approach is made at a gradually reducing airspeed that does not fall below translational lift airspeed (approximately 15 to 20 kt) and surplus power must be available until the predetermined commit height is reached. If the pilot needs full power just to maintain the descent path to the commit height, the approach must be aborted. As soon as the commit height is reached, the pilot begins to slow the helicopter down as much as power available allows while controlling the rate of descent to ensure a smooth touchdown.

Once on the ground the helicopter slides on its undercarriage. The pilot maintains directional control and keeps the rotor disc level (parallel) with the fuselage or slanted slightly forward.

The Zero-speed Landing

The *zero-speed landing* falls in the same category as the running landing except that terrain restricts the helicopter from forward movement after touchdown.

Once the pilot determines the landing spot, the approach is made at a gradually lowering airspeed and reducing rate of descent. More power is required as the landing spot comes nearer because translational lift decreases and also because the rate of descent must be decreased. When the helicopter descends to ground effect height, the rate of descent must be small enough for the ground effect to essentially stop the final descent. At this stage full power (or close to it) will be in use. The landing proceeds as normal from this point.

If at any stage during the approach (prior to reaching in ground effect height) full power is required to reduce the rate of descent or to compensate for a reduction in translational lift, the approach should be abandoned.

Zero-speed landings require a high degree of pilot judgment. Once this has been developed, many pilots prefer the zero-speed landing to the running landing because it is easier on the undercarriage and it avoids possible damage from running into potholes or boulders that may be impossible to see from the air.

Operations on Sloping Surfaces

The degree of slope that can be used for a safe landing is fairly small. Since it is often not possible to ascertain the exact slope angle prior to touchdown, especially when operating into confined areas, great caution must be exercised throughout the maneuver.

Figure 22-1 shows the aircraft brought to a hover with the up-slope skid placed onto the surface. During this stage the aircraft heading is kept constant and the disc level or as required to maintain position over the touchdown point. (The degree of slope is exaggerated for clarity.)

The weight transfer from the disc to the landing gear is made by downward movement of the collective while at the same time cyclic is eased "into the slope" to stop the rotor disc from following the fuselage movement. (If cyclic reaches its full stop when the down-slope skid is not yet on the ground, the helicopter may roll downhill.) Once the entire undercarriage is on the ground, collective may be lowered smoothly, unless the aircraft starts to slide down hill. Should this occur, the risk of ground resonance increases rapidly. The pilot's only recourse then is to get the helicopter airborne again immediately.

Operational rotor rpm must be maintained until the landing is completed so that an immediate takeoff can be made should this be required at any stage. When the landing is safely completed, cyclic may be centered, provided this does not initiate a downhill slide.

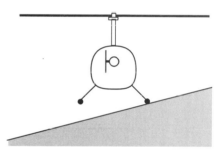

Disc horizontal and fuselage horizontal. Cyclic stick central or as required to maintain position.

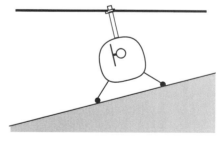

Disc near horizontal and fuselage inclined parallel to the surface. Cyclic stick displaced to maintain disc attitude.

Figure 22-1. *Landing on a sloping surface.*

Some slopes prevent the pilot from completely lowering collective. Loading or offloading passengers or freight may be possible, but great care must be taken while in contact with the ground since the conditions that may lead to ground resonance or roll-over are present.

If the pilot sits on the downhill side of the aircraft and offloading involves items from the uphill side, there is a risk that insufficient cyclic will be available for takeoff.

Control of persons in the immediate vicinity of the aircraft during slope operations cannot be over-emphasized. While it may be possible to walk under the rotor disc when the aircraft is parked on level ground, the vertical clearance between the disc and the surface is less on the upslope side, making it a dangerous area for ground personnel.

Sling Operations

Helicopters can lift and transport items many times their size. Sling operations in the U.S. are highly regulated and require a special operations permit from the Federal Aviation Administration (FAA) issued under Part 133 of the FARs. Each helicopter that conducts slingload activity must carry a copy of the operator's permission certificate on board during such operations, and each pilot must be trained and certified for slingload operations by the FAA. Pilots looking for slingload certification in the U.S. must first obtain an ATP rating, and then pass both an oral and flight examination. Pilots who fly slingload operations in the U.S. must also abide by stringent recurrent training rules laid down in FAR 133. Aviation authorities in most other countries stipulate similar requirements

This section aims to summarize a number of principles that have proved effective in the conduct of safe sling operations, but in no way substitutes for a thorough understanding of FAR Part 133 if you intend to conduct external load operations in the U.S. It goes without saying that the helicopter used for slingload operations must be capable for the task in all respects. The pilot must take density altitude, gross weight and environmental factors into serious account and precisely plan all aspects of a sling operation before making a flight.

The Equipment

Specialized equipment such as a cargo hook, load strap (strop), swivels or shackles should be preflighted by the pilot and found in good condition. The type of cables or straps and the method of retaining the load must match the nature of the load. In the U.S. FAR 133 designates several different types of external loads, classifying them as Load Class A through D.

1. Class A rotorcraft and load combination means one in which the external load cannot move freely, cannot be jettisoned, and does not extend below the landing gear.

2. Class B rotorcraft and load combination means one in which the external load is jettisonable and is lifted free of land or water during the rotorcraft operation.

3. Class C rotorcraft and load combination means one in which the external load is jettisonable and remains in contact with land or water during the rotorcraft operation.

4. Class D rotorcraft and load combination means one in which the external load is other than a class A, B, or C and has been specifically approved by the FAA administrator for that operation (human slingload operations fall within Class D).

Pilots must always be aware of the position of the load and its behavior. Helicopter doors may need to be removed to facilitate this. Electrically manipulated mirrors help the pilot watch the load during flight. Mirror placement depends on the helicopter type. Helicopters equipped with wheels usually have mirrors attached to the foremost part of the fuselage, whereas helicopters fitted with skids can have mirrors attached to the skid toes. Mirror positions also depend on what it is the pilot wishes to see. If it is the cargo hook that requires close monitoring, then the mirror location is as far forward as possible so that the entire underside of the aircraft is visible to the pilot. This placement allows the pilot to see precisely where the sling is in a low hover so he can avoid snagging the load.

A number of specially designed mirrors have been developed in recent years. One type is slightly convex at the upper part and hemispherical at the bottom so that both the load and the underside of the fuselage are constantly visible to the pilot. Another system consists of twin mirrors, one for the load and the other for the underside of the fuselage.

Although not all countries require mirrors as mandatory slingload equipment, they are a prerequisite for safe slingload operations. When properly fitted and used correctly, mirrors can safely be used for cables up to 60 feet (about 20 meters) in length.

Another item of equipment that requires close attention is the cargo hook fitted to the helicopter. The ready availability of second-hand hooks makes it possible to fit a 1,000-pound hook to an aircraft that can (and often will) lift 2,000 pounds. Make sure that the hook you use is certified to the maximum lift weight capacity of the helicopter. Your preflight inspection must verify that the hook is suitable for the aircraft concerned and before each slingload operation it is imperative that the hook be tested for proper electric and manual release.

The external load attaching means for Class B and Class C rotorcraft/load combinations in the U.S. must include a device to enable the pilot to release the external load quickly during flight. This quick release device, and the means by which it is controlled must be installed on one of the pilot's primary controls and must be designed and located so that it may be operated by the pilot without hazardously limiting his/her ability to control the rotorcraft during an emergency situation. In addition, a manual mechanical control for the quick release device, readily accessible either to the pilot or to another crew member, must be provided. The quick release device must function properly with all external loads up to and including the maximum external load for which authorization is requested. A placard or marking must be installed next to the external load attaching means stating the maximum authorized external load.

Some slings incorporate a hook at the lower end of the cable for quick turn-around missions. Some of these hooks can be operated electrically from the helicopter while others are operated manually from the ground. It is important that these hooks have a proper safety catch.

The Sling

The type of sling or cable used depends to a large degree on pilot preference and the regulations of the country in which the slingload operation is performed. For large and/or heavy loads there is no alternative to high tensile steel rope or high tensile chain. Although these items may be relatively heavy and often difficult to stow inside the helicopter there is no doubt that they provide the strongest means of support. Wire cables and chains must be checked regularly for kinks or damage and *rejected* if fraying, rusting or distortion is evident. Again, many countries have explicit regulations regarding the types of slings to be used in particular slingload operations.

If chain is used to wrap around a load the links may interlock or bind, which presents a risk of the chain becoming loose should the links unlock. For that reason it is recommended that chains be used only when they have "*reeving thimbles*" at either end, similar to dog choker chains (Figure 22-2). If the wire or chain does not have reeving thimbles, then the use of suitably rated shackles will do the same job. Always check that the shackle pins are firmly in place prior to lifting. In the same context, there is a definite risk of the load becoming loose when wrapping chain twice around a load so that chain-on-chain contact is made, which prevents tightening. Don't do it.

Synthetic rope is suitable for light loads and light helicopters and is often used for "chokers." Care must be taken, however, with certain nylon ropes which are prone to moisture absorption, substantial stretching and ultraviolet damage. There is no doubt that woven polyester material (similar to car seat straps) is the best available in the range of synthetics because it does not come apart if twisted. Hemp ropes are unsuitable for any slingload operation because of their tendency to decay, unravel and stretch.

Regarding strength of cables or straps, the following rules of thumb apply:

1. When using wire, steel or chain, ensure that the minimum certified strength is equal to four times the maximum allowable load.

2. When using synthetic materials, ensure that the equivalent strength is seven times the maximum allowable load.

To illustrate, for a maximum load of 1,000 pounds carried by wire ropes, the minimum certificated safe working load is 4,000 pounds, and in the case of synthetic ropes, the safe working load is 7,000 pounds. These factors allow for a good safety margin when the load is subjected to additional g forces such as in turbulence, while at the same time allowing for a small degree of wear and tear.

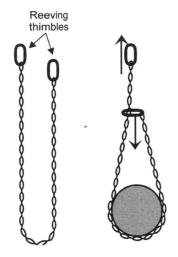

Reeving
thimbles

Figure 22-2. *A choker chain.*

Slings should not be attached to the aircraft hook other than via a D-ring, shackle or metal eyelet. No load is ever totally steady beneath the helicopter; the inevitable swinging to and fro of a rope attached directly to the aircraft hook causes fraying and unacceptable wear where the hook makes contact with the rope. Most cables can also twist up on the aircraft hook and make it difficult, if not impossible, to release the load.

Loads must have an ability to revolve independently from the helicopter. A swivel joint must be located within the line either at the aircraft attachment end or the load end, unless the aircraft hook has its own built-in swivel mechanism (Figure 22-3). Swivels must be lubricated regularly if they are to work reliably.

Synthetic rope or webbing is often used for multiple slings or chokers during lifting operations. These ropes or webbing straps are hooked to the bottom end of the main (or master) sling and then to the load and often around the load. Many pilots who prefer steel rope or chain for the master cable are quite satisfied with synthetic cables for chokers because they are pliable and fit firmly around loads (Figure 22-4). One advantage of using this combination is that it reduces the risk of static electricity passing through ground handlers when the load is delivered. Helicopters are notorious for substantial static electricity potential because of the many rotating components such as main rotor, swashplate, bearing assemblies, engine, tail rotor and gear box. The matter is aggravated by the differences in rpm at which most of these items rotate, which can cause differences in electrical potential even within the helicopter itself. Synthetics rarely conduct static electricity unless very wet, but wire rope or chain pass this energy with ease. Using synthetic cables for the lower part of the sling isolates the helicopter from the ground.

The length of the main sling is important, particularly when it is intended that the line remains attached to the helicopter between loads. A generally accepted rule is that the cable length should be 25% less than the *radius* of the helicopter rotor. For instance, the Hughes 500, with a rotor *diameter* of approximately 28 feet, should use a cable of .75 x 14 = 10.5 feet. This prevents the unloaded main sling from reaching the tail rotor should it oscillate or trail in an aft position. It also provides sufficient length to minimize the "pendulum effect" of swinging loads. When flying the sling without a load it is essential that a weight of at least 10 pounds (about five kilograms) is attached at the lower end to ensure that the cable trails well.

Ground Handling

The general loading and receiving area must be clear of non-essential equipment and objects that could snag the load on takeoff and approach or be blown about by the helicopter's downwash. In particular, watch for corrugated iron and plastic wrapping or bags commonly used to cover loads before lifting commences.

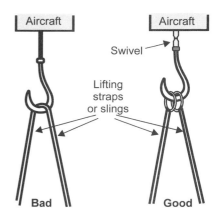

Figure 22-3. *Use eyelets, shackles or D-rings to attach a load to the hook.*

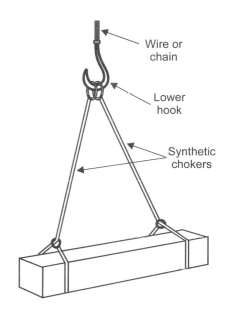

Figure 22-4. *Synthetic chokers attached to a wire or steel master sling.*

Personnel must be totally familiar with the particular operation and be trained and briefed on tying loads, rigging, hook-up signals and safety procedures. In the U.S., FAR 133 specifies the required training and certification for ground personnel. All ground personnel should wear adequate protective clothing, including goggles, gloves and ear muffs. They must never stand beneath a load or between a load and an immovable object such as a solid wall. If the load is to be checked for security prior to the aircraft's departure, it is vital that hands be kept clear of areas where the ropes are likely to be tightened as the helicopter takes the strain on the load. Be absolutely clear on the direction of exit from under the helicopter in the event of an engine malfunction.

Individual load items must be tied such that the knots do not come undone or tighten up so that they cannot be untied at the receiving station. The "bow line" knot is by far the most efficient and effective. Most Boy Scout books explain all there is to know about this knot.

When receiving a load in conditions that encourage high static electricity potential within the helicopter, such as rain, snow or dusty conditions, it is vital that the helicopter, its cable and load be "grounded". A simple grounding method is to have a length of chain attached to a steel rod at one end that is pushed into the ground. At the other end of the chain is a four-foot steel probe. An insulated handle on the probe allows the ground handler to touch the cable or load with the probe so that a safe discharge is accomplished instantly (Figure 22-5). Once this has been completed, the cable and load are safe for handling. Ship-borne operations are particularly vulnerable to static electricity.

Some pilots attach a length of chain or a steel cable to the load or master cable in such a way that it touches the surface before the load and thereby "ground" the load. This works well, but there are risks of snagging the chain on fences or similar obstructions.

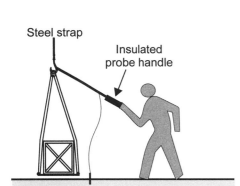

Figure 22-5. *Bonding probe equalizes electrical potential between the helicopter, the load and the ground.*

Steel strap

Insulated probe handle

Flying Techniques

Many loads are difficult to fly because of spinning or oscillation or because of aerodynamic qualities developed by the load in forward flight. There is no golden rule that allows you to predict how a particular load will behave, but the following points go some way in avoiding serious problems.

Snagging of Cable or Strap on the Undercarriage before Lift-off

When the cable or strap has been attached to the helicopter hook it is most important to ensure that the cable does not pass over a skid or undercarriage leg. As the aircraft rises and the strain is taken on the load, this could cause a serious rolling sequence. Use the mirror or look directly at the cable. Sadly, non-compliance with this simple rule continues to cause problems.

Never Exceed Speed (V_{ne})

The load's V_{ne} is always lower than the V_{ne} of the helicopter. By accelerating away from the loading area in the smoothest possible manner and maintaining a close watch on the load's behavior, its V_{ne} can be established readily. Once established, it is counter-productive to go faster. A good rule of thumb is: at the onset of first load swing, note the IAS, reduce your airspeed by 10 knots and then proceed.

Preflight Rigging

Thorough load preparation (number of straps, tying of individual items etc) far outweighs the cost in time involved. Trouble is rarely encountered when sound and professional attention is paid to preflight preparation.

Length of Cable or Strap

The longer the cable (within reason of course), the less the likelihood of serious oscillation of the load or its effect on the helicopter. Figure 22-6 shows a short and a long cable attached to a similar load. For a given longitudinal or lateral load movement (say 10 feet), the short cable acts at the helicopter hook through an angle of, say, 15°, which results in a given tendency for the aircraft to swing (A). In the case of the long cable, the same 10 feet of load movement produces a much smaller angular effect at the helicopter hook (say 10°) so that the aircraft remains steadier in flight (B). An added plus with the long cable is that a load disturbance is distributed through a much greater distance, so that its effect is greatly reduced at the aircraft attachment point(s).

Number and Type of Slings

Two cables are preferable to one, three are better than two and four are better than three. Multiple cables create additional fulcrums or pivot points within the load and these tend to self-correct any tendency of the load to oscillate. It is important to note, however, that cables must be of equal length. There are exceptions to the multi-cable rule, however, such as vertical slinging of logs.

Nets

Using suitable nets to transport a number of items in one lift is preferable to tying the items together with rope and then attaching the rope to the master sling. There is no argument that nets offer one of the best and safest means of slinging, particularly for odd-shaped and/or awkward items.

If sharp-edged items are carried in nets it is essential that the sharp edges are covered. Use a tarpaulin as inside lining for small items that could escape through the net's mesh. When preparing the load on the ground, ensure that the center of gravity of the load remains as close to the center and as low down as possible when the net is lifted up.

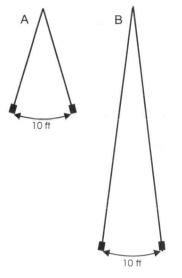

Figure 22-6. *The horizontal movement in A produces a larger angular effect at the hook than in B for the same movement.*

Pallets

Next to nets, pallets offer an excellent base on which to place loads. When using pallets it is essential that a cable is attached at each corner in such a manner that the strain is applied evenly below the pallet. If necessary, place steel or strong wooden beams or bars under the pallet and attach the slings to each protruding end, making sure that the beam supports cannot shift under any circumstances.

The use of spreader bars either above the fore and aft attachment points (Figure 22-7.[i]), or between the attachment points (Figure 22-7.[ii]) reduces the risk of cable shift. Using pre-loaded pallets makes quick turn-arounds, while at the same time they create a strong base for most loads.

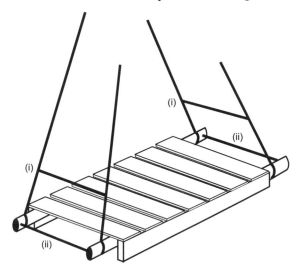

Figure 22-7. *Pallet supported by steel bars which must be secured (by spreader bars for instance) to prevent inward movement.*

Load Center of Gravity

The load's center of gravity must be as low as possible to prevent the load from tipping over or becoming unbalanced. This applies equally to loads carried individually, in nets or on pallets.

Pilot Action in Case of Helicopter Oscillation

Accurate flying is required to avoid load and aircraft swinging. If, in spite of this, the aircraft starts to oscillate, it is normally counter-productive for the pilot to try and oscillate the helicopter in an opposing sense. In most cases the situation simply becomes worse.

Should a swing become severe, there are three fundamental options:

1. Reduce speed, preferably by gentle flare and/or slight climb.
2. Put the helicopter in a steady turn in the opposite direction to the swing of the load.
3. If neither action produces the desired effect and the oscillation threatens the safety of the helicopter, consider jettisoning the load.

If turning the aircraft has succeeded in bringing the oscillation under control, it is then possible to continue the flight by smoothly turning say 30° right, followed by 30° left. This puts the pilot in control of the load.

The Approach

A steady speed reduction to the hover rather than a fast approach and harsh flare is the best way to control the load and maintain its stability throughout the approach phase of flight. Although the pilot must maneuver the helicopter, he or she should do this in relation to the load. In other words, "fly the load" and ensure that it arrives over the release area at the required height and at zero speed.

Common sense (and regulations in many countries, particularly the U.S.) dictates that whenever possible, fly the slingload away from or around populated areas. Although this may occasionally involve a few more minutes per flight, it is well worth the increased options the pilot gains in case an unstable load situation develops.

Types of Slingload

There are basically three types of loads:

- horizontal loads
- vertical loads
- unusual loads

Horizontal Loads

Horizontal loads include major construction-related components such as bridge beams, water or drilling pipes, casing, rig masts, construction steel and portals. These loads must be carried by at least two chokers to the master cable or two cables directly from the helicopter. In the case of cables or chokers, their lengths must be no less than 1.5 times the distance between the cable or choker attachment points at the load (Figure 22-8). In general, these items cause relatively few problems in flight provided they have been properly rigged and provided they are flown below their V_{ne}.

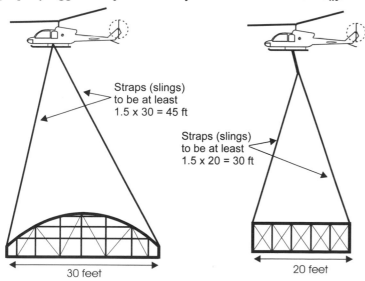

Figure 22-8. Relationship between length of load and length of straps.

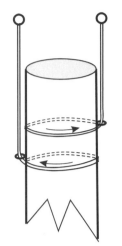

Figure 22-9. *Two choker chains positioned within the top 10% of the pole.*

Vertical loads are also invariably construction-related but may include logs in forestry operations (and similar) or items such as radio masts, power and telegraph poles. The main reason why these items are not often carried horizontally is that most are meant to be positioned or installed vertically after arrival.

For the steadiest possible flight, vertical load items should be attached to two choker cables within 10 percent of the top. For instance, a 30 foot pole should have the slings attached within the top 3 feet of the pole with one choker cable or chain going clockwise and the other counter-clockwise around the pole (Figure 22-9). This ensures that the load hangs as vertically as possible with the least degree of oscillation.

Choker chains ensure that the heavier the load, the tighter the chains grip it. When the tension comes off the chains, the choker automatically loosens, disengaging the load.

Unusual Loads

Unusual loads include items such as building materials, including floor boards, roofing iron and wall siding. Also within this category are small buildings, boats, framing, swimming pools, signs, tanks and similar items, which, if not prepared carefully, can be difficult to control in flight.

Any flat load, flown horizontally, flies like a wing once airspeed increases. Such a load can actually climb up to the helicopter and some tales have it that it can even ascend above helicopter height. Every effort must be made to ensure the load remains stable and unable to provide its own lift. Apart from its desire to fly of its own accord, a bundle of boards may separate at the front like a pack of cards.

A load of boards can be flown horizontally or vertically. If flown horizontally, it is essential that the lift-potential (C_L) of the load is destroyed by placing any number of irregularly shaped articles on top of the horizontal load. Building materials invariably include bales of insulating material. These bales, placed on top of the load, act as efficient destroyers of lift. Alternatively, secure aircraft seat cushions, nail boxes, empty drums (Figure 22-10), or similar items to the top of the load. "Secure" is the operative word!

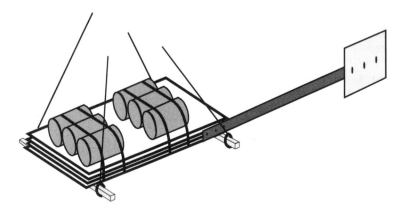

Figure 22-10. *Irregularly shaped objects will spoil lift while a simple fin adds directional stability.*

Principles of Helicopter Flight

When the pilot elects to fly a load vertically, the load may start to oscillate and swing. Instead of orienting itself edge-on to the direction of travel, it turns broadside and even at relatively low airspeeds the load becomes quite unstable. To avoid problems under these circumstances, it is possible to produce directional stability of the load by attaching a *drogue* or, if not available, a simply constructed fin from a piece of plywood on a pole. Figure 22-10 shows such a fin for a horizontal load. The principle is the same for vertical loads. A drogue must trail behind the load at least three times the length of the load. If the load is 10 feet long, the drogue must trail at least 30 feet behind. A parachute-like contraption is likely to cause more instability because of the need for air caught within the parachute to spill out. If a make-shift drogue is constructed, make a hole large enough for air to pass through in a restricted fashion (Figure 22-11). A marine sea anchor is ideal, as is a "spare" windsock.

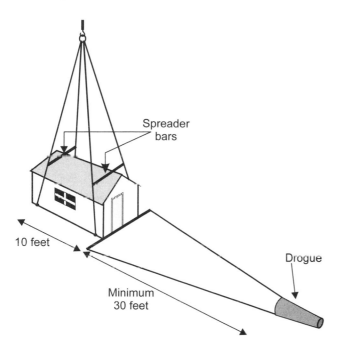

Figure 22-11. *A stabilizing drogue should trails at least three times the length of the load to which it is attached.*

Construction pipes carried in bundles pose a problem if only one cable is used because the bundle probably will not fly horizontally. Inevitably the pipes in the middle of the pack slide out. The best way to handle this type of load is to use two choker cables, one clockwise and the other counterclockwise around the bundle, so that the action of the cables twist the pipes together (Figure 22-12).

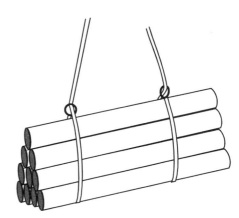

Figure 22-12. *One choker strap clockwise and another counterclockwise will twist a stack of pipes together.*

Crates or similar containers must never be suspended solely from anchor points on top. If an anchor fails the boxes skew and the load inside then depends on the strength of the box sidewalls, which are more prone to fail than the floor. Webbing straps passing around the container is the only method of strapping that provides the required lifting strength. The straps must also be prevented from sliding towards the center of the box during lifting. This can be achieved through the use of lateral straps, as shown in Figure 22-13.

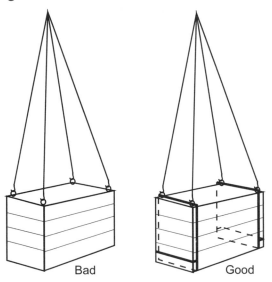

Bad   Good

Figure 22-13. *Use of webbing straps supporting the load from underneath makes the load safe.*

Figure 22-14. *Drum hooks.*

Fuel drums are often carried in slingloads. Nets are the safest way to carry heavy, hazardous drums. If nets are not available, then use drum hooks as shown in Figure 22-14. These hooks are designed so that as the strain comes on the main cable, the jaws of the hooks press more firmly into the rims of the drum. A single cable wrapped around the middle of the drum, no matter how well attached, is not recommended because it is impossible to determine where the center of gravity of the drum will be. Inevitably the drum will hang down and risks slipping out.

Swimming pools and small boats are difficult to lift. Imagine standing in a large bucket and trying to lift oneself off the ground. Rotor downwash creates a nuisance for these types of load. The only way to ensure adequate lifting performance is to use cable lengths at least three times the rotor diameter between the aircraft and load. Load V_{ne} can be critical and as a general rule, 30 knots is the maximum safe speed, irrespective of aircraft type or lift capability.

Salvage operations are probably one of the more difficult types of sling operations. Conditions are invariably poor and speed is of the essence. The number one rule for salvage is to separate the aircraft from the load by the longest manageable sling available. This caveat keeps the pilot away from immediate danger and buys time in flight if the load develops any unusual tendency towards formation flying.

Longline operations, involving a technique commonly referred to as "vertical reference," has the pilot leaning out of the aircraft seat to observe the load during lifting, placement, and quite often, in transit.

It is accomplished either by removing the pilot door or by using a door suitably modified and generally incorporating a bubble window. Continuous logging, ship load/unload, electricity towers and jungle seismic support are examples of roles requiring exacting placement and continuous load monitoring by the pilot.

Longlining is generally regarded as a sling over 60 feet (20 meters) in length. Flying techniques remain the same but control of the load is accomplished by observing the continuous relationship between the ground or target (placement area), and the item being transported. The transition from cockpit to load and back to cockpit is initially unsettling for some pilots and may result in a tendency to over-control the helicopter, particularly laterally. Pilots can loosen their shoulder harness, lower their seat position and keep the cyclic hand on the knee to overcome the tendency toward overcontrolling. The key to longlining is to be comfortable at the pilot position and to always mentally be "down, flying the load." Small, smooth control inputs are important.

Conclusion

Slingload operations are an integral part of helicopter flying, but they invariably require the assistance of trained and certified personnel at either or both ends of the flight and so introduce an external factor that requires continuous monitoring by the pilot.

Any load has the potential to cause disaster, both in the air and on the ground. A well-planned exercise that has anticipated every possible contingency inevitably results in a successful flight and a satisfied customer.

Review 22

1. A helicopter can tolerate a strong crosswind from the (right/left) better than from the (left/right) because from the (left/right) the tendency to yaw will be in the same direction as main rotor torque.

2. Downwind take-offs and landings are not recommended partly because the amount of (rearward/forward) cyclic is less than (rearward/forward) cyclic and in a strong downwind condition there may be insufficient _____ cyclic to bring the helicopter to a hover.

3. When flaring during a downwind approach there is a risk of (recirculation/settling with power).

4. Helicopters fitted with stabilizers are (more/less) difficult to handle in a downwind take-off or landing situation than those without stabilizers.

5. When faced with a marginal take-off obstruction clearance you should select the best (rate of climb/angle of climb) speed as soon as possible and revert to _____ climb speed when obstructions have been cleared.

6. If during a zero-speed landing approach you require full power to control rate of descent, you should _____ the approach because there (will /will not) be sufficient power to _____ the rate of descent just prior to touch-down.

7. Passengers vacating a helicopter parked on sloping ground must avoid the (uphill/downhill) area below the spinning rotor.

8. During sling load operations, it (is/is not) good practice to wrap chain twice around a load.

9. Sling loads (must/must not) have an ability to revolve independently from the helicopter and this requires a _____ joint either at the aircraft or load end of the sling.

10. Your helicopter has a disc diameter of 40 feet. If a sling is intended to remain attached to the helicopter between loads, the length of the sling must be no (longer/ shorter) than _____ feet and a weight of at least _____ lb (or _____ kg) must be attached to the (lower/upper) end of the sling.

11. If a sling load starts to oscillate, you should (increase/decrease) airspeed and/or turn the helicopter in the (same/opposite) direction to the swing.

12. When carrying a pack of floor boards horizontally as a sling load it is essential that the _____ potential of the load is destroyed by attaching irregular objects (on top of/below) the load.

Mountain Flying 23

There is more to mountain flying than just considering the density altitude and helicopter performance factors. Wind flows and thermal flows require special attention, particularly when operating in or around pinnacles, valleys and ridgelines.

In the mountains the airflows match the wildness of the terrain. When planning a mountain flight the pilot must consider:

- updrafts and downdrafts

- thermal currents

- katabatic and anabatic winds

- mechanical turbulence, including wave action and rotor streaming

Updrafts and Downdrafts

An updraft can force a helicopter into an ascent when the vertical airflow approaching the disc from below produces an opposition to the induced flow. Inflow angles reduce, angles of attack increase and the total reaction becomes more vertical. The consequences are:

- more total rotor thrust is produced because of the new orientation of the total reaction

- rotor rpm increases as rotor drag decreases

- greater coning angles are created from increased blade rotor thrust

- a further increase in rotor rpm results from Coriolis effect as blade coning angles increase

If the pilot lowers collective, preventing the helicopter from climbing in an updraft, the reduced pitch angles further encourage the rotor rpm to rise. The stronger the updrafts, the greater the manifestation of these factors.

The reverse applies when downdrafts from above add to the induced flow, decreasing total rotor thrust due to reducing angles of attack and tilting of the total reaction further away from the axis of rotation. The associated increase in rotor drag reduces rotor rpm. If the pilot raises collective to correct the descent, inflow angles are further increased so that the rotor thrust /rotor drag ratio is once again eroded.

Up and downdrafts must not be confused with turbulence, in spite of the fact that both phenomena are invariably associated with mountain winds. Drafts can be large scale, both up and down and may even be entirely smooth. They can be found at either side of a mountain range. For instance, a westerly wind onto a range oriented north-to-south often produces smooth updrafts on the windward (western) side and downdrafts, possibly accompanied by turbulence, on the lee (eastern) side. In some situations the drafts can extend many thousands of feet above the highest peaks.

The vertical velocity of downdrafts is sometimes so large that all the surplus power available for climbing is insufficient to overcome their effects. Herein lies danger. A pilot, having flown across a mountain range downwind in ascending air on the windward side (which may have been quite smooth) descends in a downdraft on the lee side. This downdraft goes unnoticed because of the pilot-induced descent. At this point the pilot is misled into believing that the return flight will be just as uneventful until the downdraft region is entered while climbing out. As rate of climb diminishes and rising ground gets closer, the stage is reached where nothing but a 180° turn can avert disaster. Even if the turn is exercised at a late stage, the reduced total rotor thrust while banked may be insufficient to complete the turn at a safe height above the terrain.

The moral is to have at least some surplus altitude above the highest elevation prior to crossing a mountain range into a strong wind. Always cross ridges at an oblique angle, so that if a strong downdraft is experienced while still on the lee side, a small turn is all that is necessary to make a safe departure from the danger zone.

The effect of flying higher in amongst the mountains adds to the up/downdraft problem because with height, control responses decrease in the reduced air density. At high altitudes collective and cyclic require larger pilot inputs. The fact that collective is already high in order to produce the angles of attack required to compensate for the reduced density doesn't make the pilot's job any easier. Finally, the tail rotor requires larger pedal inputs. At maximum gross weight and high density altitude conditions, this may involve pedal inputs to their full stops. Tail rotor stall conditions may be encountered, as well.

The pilot must pay greater attention to the rotor rpm control at altitude because the correlation unit does not function with as much efficiency as at lower altitudes. The reason for this is that a given collective movement associates with a given throttle butterfly (or fuel flow) alteration. At sea level a small adjustment in butterfly may change the manifold pressure by a given amount, but at high altitudes a larger butterfly adjustment is required for the same change in manifold pressure.

Most modern helicopters are fitted with a governor which, with few exceptions, maintains engine and rotor rpm at a required value.

Chapter 14 explained how high altitude and/or high density altitude reduce the power available from the engine. This, coupled with the need to employ higher blade angles to provide the required rotor thrust, seriously erodes the helicopter's performance. Eventually the pilot runs out of power and altitude cannot be maintained, even if no downdrafts are present.

Finally, the aircraft's built-in stability, small as this may be, is adversely affected by altitude because of reduced rotor damping (static and dynamic stability).

Thermal Currents

In bare rock mountain environments, strong heating during the day may add considerably to air disturbances. Even bush-clad slopes can cause thermal updrafts and disturbed air. In cold, snow-covered high mountain slopes, the cold, dense air near the surface can cause downdrafts to form within the last 100 feet, or so, near the surface.

In general terms, the severity of thermal up-currents is determined by:

1. The degree of instability of air caused by surface heating; - the higher the surface air temperature, the stronger the up currents

2. Height above terrain; – thermal intensity decreases with height depending on the degree of instability

3. The presence of meteorological phenomena such as inversions, which limit the extent of thermal waves

Because the nature of mountainous terrain can change dramatically in short distances, thermal waves can be erratic. Although flight through these waves is bumpy and unpleasant, their potential danger lies in the approach to land phase and the initial climb out after lift off, both times when ground clearance is limited. This is accentuated when operating at maximum gross weight, near the aircraft's service ceiling and particularly when external stores are carried. Under these circumstances it may be wiser to do a number of lightly loaded flights rather than one flight with the helicopter too heavy for the conditions.

Always be alert for windshear, which is the rapid change in wind speed and/or direction with height or with horizontal distance. It is possible to experience vertical windshear or horizontal windshear both from thermal or mechanical causes. For instance, a helicopter pilot approaching a landing zone that is in the lee of a large and steep mountain side may find that there is no wind at the landing site. Prior to entering this zone, the prevailing wind assists in providing translational lift, particularly as airspeed is reduced during the initial approach. As the helicopter crosses the shear boundary where the prevailing wind suddenly changes to calm conditions, translational lift is severely impaired and the rate of descent increases. This is a case of horizontal shear where, with horizontal distance, the speed of the wind abruptly changes from a given value to little or calm.

Alternatively, consider an early morning approach to a landing site high in the mountains in a prevailing wind. The cold surface at the site enhances the stability of the air so that an inversion forms a few hundred feet above the surface. Beneath the inversion the wind is calm. As the helicopter descends at decreasing airspeed, relying partly on translational lift from the wind, on passing through the inversion it loses translational lift and, as a result, its rate of descent increases rapidly. This is a situation of vertical wind shear where with altitude, the speed of the wind abruptly alters.

In both examples the loss of translational lift at a critical time during the approach phase requires quick pilot action to avert a heavy landing. The conditions can be anticipated to some degree by assessing the shadow effect of mountain sides and by realizing that any landing site that can be expected to be cold will invariably be covered by an inversion.

Katabatic and Anabatic Winds

Towards the end of day, when mountain slopes cool (quite abruptly in some situations), the adjacent air is cooled through contact with the cold slopes and a large scale descent of air may result. The wind caused by the descending air is called a *katabatic wind*, and can become quite strong if the slopes are smooth and steep. Katabatic winds are not necessarily restricted to night time conditions. Since the phenomenon is based on differential heating, it can also be found when relatively cold valley air is encouraged to flow onto warm adjacent plains. Under these conditions, katabatic winds persist into the day. Generally speaking, this effect is more pronounced in autumn and spring.

Flight conditions are not generally hazardous in katabatic winds except during takeoffs and landings. The approach to a landing zone on a hillside can be uneventful from a distance, but as the katabatic downdraft area is entered, a rapid increase in the rate of descent close to the ground may ensue. This is aggravated by the fact that at this point in the approach the pilot has reduced airspeed which calls for increased power requirements.

A similar problem may arise on takeoff from a confined area where it is impossible to obtain a degree of translational lift through horizontal flight. Descending katabatic flow interferes with the pilot's ability to obtain the required rate of climb.

After sunrise when mountainsides exposed to the sun are warmed, the reverse wind can occur. Adjacent air rises so that an *anabatic wind* develops. Large scale updrafts develop, the strength of which depend on the nature of terrain and locality. Gravity opposes the updrafts, generally making this wind less significant than its katabatic counterpart. Nevertheless, some valleys around the world can have temperature differences of some 25°C between the valley floor and mountain tops, allowing strong anabatic winds to develop.

Mechanical Turbulence

There is a fine line between the characteristics of up/downdrafts and mechanical turbulence because often the two are encountered together. Whereas drafts are only up or down and often involve relatively large blocks of air, turbulence is caused by erratic wind patterns involving rapid changes in both speed and direction in a short distance. Turbulence can cause air to approach the helicopter from up and down, left and right, fore and aft at amazingly quick intervals. Induced flow, inflow angles, total rotor thrust and rotor rpm may fluctuate wildly in turbulence, resulting in obvious control problems.

Helicopters are somewhat less uncomfortable in turbulence than fixed wing aircraft because the flexibility within rotor blades, hinge arrangements of blades and relatively low airspeeds transfer less upsets from the rotor to the fuselage. While fixed-wing aircraft may be subjected to gusts that can overstress the wing and wing attachments, the helicopter is not endangered to the same extent. Apart from possible risks of short-lived negative g, turbulence does not often pose threatening situations en route, even though the flight may be uncomfortable.

The potential danger of turbulence lies in the takeoff and landing phase, when power requirements are high and ground clearance is low. Pilot inputs must be timed and adequate for the conditions. When operating near mountain tops, at altitudes where control effectiveness is reduced and surplus power is limited, moderate to severe turbulence can be dangerous.

Most helicopters are dynamically unstable both longitudinally, laterally and even directionally at low speeds. During takeoffs and landings control of the aircraft receives little or no assistance from stability features that may be part of the aircraft design.

Pilots can predict mechanical turbulence near the ground by assessing:

- wind strength
- the size and shape of the mountains
- the stability or instability of the air
- wind direction relative to mountain orientation

Wind Strength

Winds up to 15 to 20 knots rarely produce significant turbulence. Depending on the mountain's shape, it is possible that stationary eddies are present on both the windward and leeward side. With stronger wind speeds, turbulence becomes more intensified and stationary eddies no longer exist. Frictional eddies form repeatedly in the vicinity of ridges or individual hills and drift downwind for miles (Figure 23 1).

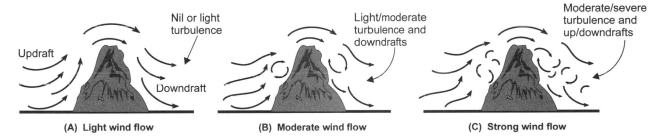

Figure 23-1. *Effect of different wind speeds on drafts and turbulence.*

The worst turbulence, associated with strong winds, is found at or below mountain height on the leeward side, where, under certain circumstances, rotor action can be present close to the slopes (Figure 23-2). On approach to a landing site on the lee side a headwind and downdraft can suddenly change to a tailwind and updraft. In the worst situation, a helicopter may be forced into the slope in spite of corrective pilot action.

The effect of valley orientation on turbulence is dramatic. A 20-knot wind (with little turbulence to be concerned about) may increase substantially if a valley is deep and oriented at a slight angle to the prevailing wind direction so that a venturi effect develops. Turbulence, especially near valley exits, can become locally moderate to severe under these conditions.

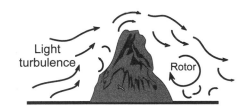

Figure 23-2. *Lee rotor action in strong wind flow conditions.*

Size and Shape of Mountains

Turbulence produced by an isolated mountain depends on the wind strength. Most of the disturbances can be avoided by careful route planning. Pilots are best off if they plan on remaining clear of the lee wind until well downwind of the mountain. Similarly, mountains or hills with rounded tops and gentle slopes rarely produce more than light to moderate turbulence unless the wind is strong.

The most common feature of rolling country is the presence of updrafts on the windward side and downdrafts on the lee. This pattern can be upset, however, if a series of ranges are closely spaced. In such an environment the downdraft from the preceding ridge can cover the windward side of the next one, where an updraft was expected. In general, pilots can avoid problems by choosing to fly at altitudes that are 1,500 to 2,000 feet above ridge height. Even takeoffs and landings on the lee side should pose no great difficulty provided the pilot remains alert to the possibility of minor downdrafts. If a choice of landing sites is available, those on the windward side are obviously preferred.

When mountain tops are irregular and sharp, the effect on turbulence and drafts intensifies. Even 20 to 25 knot winds can produce severe turbulence and downdrafts on the lee side, preventing safe low level and slow flight operations. Under these conditions, restrict takeoff and landing operations to the windward side. If the slopes are steep, however, the approaches may have to be downwind or very steep, conditions likely to lead to vortex ring state.

Stability or Instability of Air

Generally speaking, the more unstable the air, the more intense the turbulence for a given wind strength and the higher its vertical extent. Humid air is more prone to instability than dry air. When operating in the mountains in the presence of substantial cumulus cloud, it is fair to assume that moderate turbulence may be encountered between the top of the high ground and the base of the cumulus cloud. Updrafts can cause spiraling of air and takeoff and landing operations in the immediate vicinity of these clouds may involve unpredictable wind directions and strengths.

The worst turbulence and drafts can be expected during the hottest time of day. The least turbulence is to be expected in the early hours of the morning. Remember that the low density altitude conditions prevailing during the cold early morning hours soon change to high density altitude conditions as the day warms up. The aircraft performance that enabled large loads to be carried at the start of the day generally evaporates by mid-morning, and a thoughtful pilot will adjust expectations from the helicopter accordingly.

Wind Direction Relative to Mountain Orientation

If the wind blows humid air (especially unstable, humid air) more or less at right angles to a substantial mountain range, updrafts and precipitation are found on the windward side, while dry and gusty conditions with moderate to severe turbulence are present on the lee side. Provided various meteorological pre-requisites are met, this condition often produces wave action as well as the warm and dry föhn (foehn, chinook) wind on the lee side.

The föhn wind's effects invariably spread many miles downwind from the mountain range. Low-level and slow-flight helicopter operations close to the mountains on the lee side should not be attempted when these conditions exist. Downdrafts, severe turbulence and rotor action can overwhelm even the most powerful helicopters.

Under föhn wind conditions it is not unusual to witness gale force winds exiting valleys, carrying with them vast amounts of dust and even large stones. Helicopters flying in the vicinity of these outlets at low levels risk damage akin to hail damage, not to mention the detrimental effects of sand and dust in their engine intakes.

A variation to the föhn wind occurs when 20 to 30 knot winds decrease sharply with altitude, in which case rotor streaming may develop on the lee side (possibly worse than wave action). The wind is funneled through saddles and valleys, resulting in severe to extreme lee turbulence. Flight in these conditions is not recommended.

Summary

The main hazards in mountain flying under adverse wind conditions are:

- updrafts and downdrafts that jeopardize control of the helicopter
- rapid changes to total rotor thrust during the landing phase that may contribute to a hard touchdown or force the helicopter back onto the ground on liftoff
- rapid and unpredictable changes to translational lift values
- the possibility of retreating blade stall in vertical gusts or updrafts
- risk of mast bumping in severe updraft (negative g) situations

Valley Flying

> **When following a valley en route, fly on the updraft (i.e. on the downwind) side at an altitude high enough to avoid possible turbulent eddies.**

The advantages of the updraft side are:
- the updrafts reduce the requirement for power, leaving more reserve in hand
- should a reversal turn be necessary, a turn into the wind requires a smaller radius than one downwind

Take note, power lines often abound in valleys, and they are difficult to see. When flying within valley confines it is often easier to fly at low speeds. A reasonable margin above translational lift speed should be maintained, however.

This book is not designed to specify the detailed helicopter handling techniques necessary when a pilot is confronted with adverse meteorological conditions in mountainous terrain. Good and thorough training and above all, alertness to the risks enhance safe flying. The following tips can help pilots determine the best way to stay out of trouble in the mountains.

Monitor the IAS closely when flying at low altitudes because there is a dangerous tendency to fly a constant ground speed. This trend is aggravated by the fact that there is no natural horizon, which may lead to the pilot unconsciously selecting the high ground ahead as the attitude reference, allowing the speed to fall off. Should this happen, translational benefits reduce, power requirements increase and in downwind conditions there is a definite risk of vortex ring state developing.

When transporting heavy loads it is wise to fly on the warm or sunny side of the valley at relatively low altitudes. Strong winds rarely blow across valleys at low altitude on sunny days and considerable lift is obtained on the warm side. Usually, winds blow up- or down-valley until about two-thirds the height of the valley walls is reached. Above that height the wind orients itself more to the regional prevailing or geostrophic wind.

Ridgeline Flying

Fly on the windward side when flying parallel to a ridge if the wind is not in line with the ridge. If you must fly on the lee side, anticipate downdrafts and turbulence. The inevitable saddles and depressions in the ridge line often cause the wind to funnel, creating additional turbulence. When a series of close ridges are involved, as explained in a previous paragraph, the presence of downdrafts on the windward side of the ridges is possible.

Cross ridges in moderate to strong winds at an angle other than 90°. The angled crossing leaves room for the helicopter to make a small turn away from the ridge if downdrafts are encountered.

The "Standard" Mountain Approach

The word "standard" is emphasized because there is no standard approach that always holds good in mountainous terrain operations. Standard is used to identify basic mountain approach considerations that influence the selection of an appropriate approach profile.

> **The standard approach consists of an approach directly into the wind using the constant angle landing technique.**

The landing is normally preceded by a hover, but zero-speed or run-on landings are alternatives. Landings on mountain ridges into the wind may place the aircraft on the lee side of the ridge during the approach, in which case the steepness of the approach angle should be adjusted as shown in Figure 23-3.

If the wind or turbulence prevents the standard approach, the approach can be made along the ridge, angled or from the upwind side. In all cases a reconnaissance should be flown along the ridge at a slow but safe speed to establish the best final approach direction and to check for obstacles. A helicopter approaching from the windward side risks drifting into the downdraft area after crossing the ridge itself when turning into the wind towards the landing site.

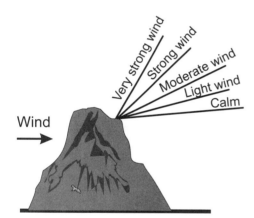

Figure 23-3. *Approach angle variations with different wind speeds.*

In all but light wind conditions (less than 10 knots), one need only approach from the lee side of a ridge when landing on a saddle that has steep or high walls. In other situations, an approach at up to 90° to the wind with a turn into wind at the site is preferable. The turn should not require additional tail rotor thrust, so the direction of the approach should be selected accordingly.

An approach to a pinnacle in strong wind conditions can be angled to avoid turbulence and downdrafts so that a steep approach profile is not essential. Alternatively, the approach can be made from the upwind side, as described for ridges.

There are some important points to constantly be alert for during pinnacle approaches.

1. An absence of peripheral clues both ahead and laterally deprives the pilot of visual information about the rate of the approach. Unless the site is familiar to a pilot, a short trial approach is advisable.

2. Turbulence is often pronounced on the lee side.

3. Ground effect is slow to come into play and approaches should not be protracted on the lee side of the pinnacle with resulting demands for high power.

4. The slope of the surface of a pinnacle is not as easy to assess as sites with adjacent ground features. Pilots should be prepared to abort landings where slopes exceed undercarriage and mast/hub limits.

Pilots must ascertain (through adequate reconnaissance) the best method in which the task can be completed and most importantly, to have a planned escape route. Do not hesitate to use the escape route if things don't work out the way they were planned. Some experienced pilots wish they had obeyed this golden rule.

General Comments on Mountain Approaches

High Altitude Approach Considerations

In Chapter 3 the principles of the airspeed indicator, and the IAS/TAS relationship, were clarified. One topic explained how, *for a given* TAS, the IAS falls off with height as density of air reduces.

The generation of lift at a given angle of attack is dependent on the IAS (ie, the product of TAS x density). Hence with increasing altitude at a constant TAS and angle of attack, lift generation of an airfoil will fall off as the IAS decreases.

In practical terms it can be said that rotor rpm is more or less constant which means that the TAS of blades can be considered constant. Now if a pitot tube were to be placed on a rotating blade, the true airspeed of the blade remains constant as altitude is gained but the "indicated airspeed" of the blade, and therefore lift produced, will decrease. Since lift is dependent on the angle of attack and IAS, it follows that if total rotor thrust must continue to provide the force to support the weight, a decreasing "IAS" (of the blade) with altitude must be compensated by an increase in angle of attack. And, as we well know, there is a limit to which the angle of attack can be increased.

In preceding chapters it was explained that higher angles of attack place a restraint on maneuvers which rely on the availability of extra total rotor thrust, for example steep turns.

Other consequences of high angles of attack are:

1. A reduction in V_{ne} because retreating blade stall will be experienced at slower forward speed.

2. An increased risk of vortex ring state (and rotor stall for that matter) because the already high angles of attack can tolerate less upward flow through the rotor disc before the stall spreads out from the blade root sections. The risk of vortex ring state must be kept in mind at altitude – a helicopter is particularly vulnerable when flaring during an approach in this respect.

3. An increased risk of over-pitching when the effect of high rotor drag, associated with high angles of attack and high inflow angles, is not adequately monitored or controlled.

The momentum of a helicopter is another factor to be considered when operating at altitude or in low density conditions. *Momentum = mass x velocity* where the velocity is TAS. An important aspect to remember is that when momentum is high, the force required to change momentum is high, eg, at a high TAS is takes a greater force to slow the helicopter down than would be the case with a low TAS. This is of little concern to pilots who fly mostly at low levels because they can relate momentum to the reading on their airspeed indicator considering that IAS is more or less equal to TAS near sea level. But operations at increasing altitudes require more attention to the problem of momentum.

With reference to the surrounding air, momentum is proportional to TAS but when referenced to obstacles or points on the ground, it is proportional to groundspeed, ie, in wind-still conditions *TAS = groundspeed = the same momentum*. Thus in any situation where a pilot needs to make judgments with reference to a ground feature, the IAS/TAS/groundspeed relationship must be remembered.

Considering calm conditions, most pilots have little problem with a high speed approach to a landing site near sea level but they may be in for a surprise when they use the same technique approaching a site at high altitude. The increased TAS for a given IAS, and the high groundspeed mean a high momentum which, as explained, requires a greater force to bring the helicopter to a halt.

This is highlighted in Figure 23-4. The lower diagram shows a helicopter approaching a landing site at sea level. During the last 500 meters the aircraft is flared in such a way that the tilted disc provides the required rearward component of total rotor thrust to bring the aircraft to the hover over the site. The upper diagram shows the same helicopter approaching a site at altitude aiming to come to the hover in the same 500 meter distance. In both cases it is assumed that there is no wind and that the IAS is reduced smoothly from a cruising configuration to zero within the stated distance. It can be seen that at altitude, the higher TAS/ groundspeed, and the greater momentum, demand a higher nose attitude and more disc tilt to generate a greater rearward component of total rotor thrust.

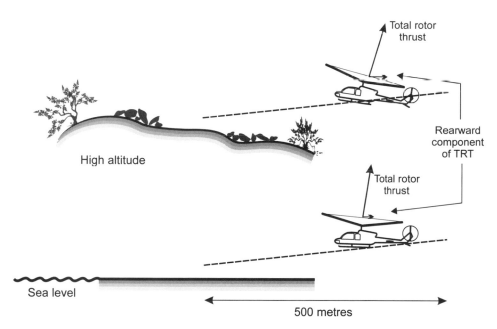

Figure 23-4. *Assuming nil-wind conditions, a larger rearward component of total rotor thrust is required to slow a helicopter down in the same distance at altitude compared to at sea level.*

This illustrates the need for pilots to bear in mind the aerodynamic and engine considerations during an approach and touch-down at elevated sites. High collective settings, large inflow angles and high angles of attack go hand in hand with poor lift/drag ratios which result in the total reaction leaning well back from the axis of rotation.

As a consequence, rotor thrust/rotor drag ratios become very poor which require high power settings to maintain rotor rpm. Clearly, if the power available is not sufficient to bring the helicopter to the hover out of ground effect, the end result could well be a rapidly decreasing rotor rpm and a very heavy landing due to overpitching. Or worse, a pilot who suddenly realizes at a late stage during the approach that the helicopter is not going to stop in the remaining distance could be tempted to flare severely which might put the aircraft in a vortex ring state situation.

Precautions to be considered prior to making an approach to a high altitude site should include:

- a power check
- a thorough reconnaissance
- assessment of the wind to be expected during the final approach*
- presence of turbulence
- planning for the shallowest possible approach profile
- approach distance long enough to permit a smooth decrease in speed

    * The importance of making high altitude approaches into-wind wherever possible cannot be overstated.

Most of these are probably standard practice but there are a few negative aspects that must be remembered when carrying out long and shallow approaches such as:

- flight below translational speed is a little longer than one might like
- if the approach is over uneven terrain (often covered by boulders and energy-absorbing vegetation), ground effect is likely to be erratic
- ground clearance may be compromised if turbulence is encountered during the approach
- if the approach is over snow covered surfaces, reduced visibility due to swirling snow is likely

Transition

Towards the end of any mountain approach, avoid making rapid or excessive changes to the rotor disc attitude that cause dissipation of total rotor thrust. The transition from the approach to the hover should be a smooth deceleration so that the downwash is immediately effective for building up the best possible ground effect.

Ground Effect Considerations on Mountain Sites

Mountain landing sites are often on ridges, saddles or on brief breaks on a mountain slope. These surfaces are invariably irregular, sloping and covered in a variety of absorbent and airflow-dissipating ground cover, including snowgrass, alpine vegetation, clumps of grass or rocks. In addition, landing sites often have small areas that can provide recirculation.

The absence of (or reduced) ground effect benefits means that the end of the approach should be completed over the selected set-down site. Approaches that end short of the landing site require high power to move through an area where ground effect may be negligible.

Lift off and departure from sites where ground effect benefits are erratic requires special care. It is possible to have the front part of the disc in ground effect and the remainder in free air, in which case the helicopter experiences a rapid rolling effect. To offset this possibility, achieve translational lift as soon as practically possible and anticipate any tendency to roll as it occurs.

Determining Wind Change during Critical Phases

There are a number of obvious indicators of wind flow in the mountains, such as the movement of trees, grassy clumps and snowgrass, blowing dust and snow and of course, the aircraft drift.

When approaching high altitude sites at reduced speed and power, wind changes and reversals often occur because of rapid changes in ground features. The most serious wind shift is the change to a positive tailwind during the latter stages of an approach. This manifests itself as a tail rotor instability usually in the form of irregular "twitching".

As the helicopter is in the high power and low speed configuration, there is always the possibility of vortex ring state when larger than normal main rotor disc changes are demanded to accelerate the aircraft as it approaches the landing site in a tailwind.

Should tail rotor twitching be encountered, it is recommended that the approach from the given direction be abandoned and an alternative direction to the site selected away from the area where the tailwind was encountered.

Landing Site Selection

Mountain landing sites should have features that permit a reasonable approach path at angles that permit the helicopter to lift off and depart by the same route. Sites with a single approach and departure path need a safe maneuvering area bordering the landing area to permit the aircraft to be turned clear of all obstructions such as trees and rocks prior to its departure from the site. Where adequate performance is still available, the helicopter can use rearward or sideways flight prior to assuming normal takeoff once clear of obstructions.

Surface of Sites

Care is necessary in selecting and testing surfaces in the mountains. In areas of considerable water collection such as bogs and concealed streams, surfaces are likely to be uneven and the collective control lever should not be lowered completely until the landing gear has settled within its fore and aft and lateral limits.

Where skid undercarriages are used, care should be taken when water and soft ground covers one skid, but not the other. During takeoff, a considerable amount of suction can be experienced on the covered skid with the resulting tendency for roll at liftoff. To control this, apply cyclic to accentuate a nose-down pitch attitude and break the rear of the skid out of the suction area. In extreme cold conditions one skid might freeze to the ground, also creating conditions for dynamic roll-over on takeoff.

In areas where surfaces are covered in fine sand, grit and snow, care is needed to avoid limiting the visibility in blowing dust, and so on, during the landing. It is often wise to sweep such sites by a low pass, to remove much of the loose material. If this is not effective and a landing is essential, the zero-speed landing technique should be used. Once in ground contact, the reducing rotor pitch angles no longer kick up debris.

In uneven areas, where sloping or rough sites are the only ones available, care has to be exercised to prevent dangerous dynamic roll-over conditions. Skid-equipped helicopters may experience mast bumping on slopes as control limits are reached. The landing should immediately be aborted at the first onset of a twice-per-revolution vibration. Wheel equipped helicopters are prone to ground resonance on rough or sloping ground and should the pronounced bouncing symptoms occur, the aircraft should immediately be lifted from all ground contact.

Helicopters fitted with dynamic or centrifugal droop stops have problems on sloping ground where the divergence between rotor disc attitude and the mast does not permit consistent operation of the stops. This is usually experienced as a one-per-revolution vibration. If this occurs, the landing should be aborted.

All mountain landing sites should be clear of obstructions to allow adequate clearance for tail rotors during in flight maneuvering and during ground contact of the helicopter landing gear. Obstructions beyond the set-down area should be at least a helicopter length away to provide safe tail rotor maneuvering.

Flight in Areas Covered in Snow and Ice

When snow cover is predominant in mountain operations, care is needed during takeoff, climb out and approaches to landing sites that have little bare ground, rock or shadows. Frequent reference to airspeed and attitude information is needed. Progress towards a landing site requires more attention than in conditions where abundant peripheral information is available.

Sunglasses should be worn in continuous snow covered terrain and care exercised when turning into valleys or glacier approaches with strong sunlight behind the helicopter. Continuous operations to the same site in snow can often be improved by dropping a bag of dye in the snow about 200 yards downwind from the landing site so that it is visible during the approach.

Survival Equipment

In addition to the mandatory emergency equipment carried in helicopters such as an emergency locator beacon, first aid kit, fire extinguisher and ax, pilots, crew and/or passengers engaged in mountain operations should take or wear some basic items in case of a mishap in hostile environments.

A personal checklist should include:

- a lined parka worn or simply carried
- footwear suitable for wet and broken country
- a foil survival blanket that fits in a parka pocket
- a knife
- waterproof matches and a small mug
- a flashlight or torch
- two red flares and two red smoke generators
- packet of barley sugar or glucose tablets, instant tea or coffee bags
- sun or snow glasses

Most of these items are sufficiently compact to fit in a parka. Fuel from the disabled aircraft can be used for making fires.

Review 23

Mountain Flying

1. When experiencing a strong updraft, total rotor thrust is (increased/decreased) because induced flow is briefly (increased/decreased), inflow angles (increase/ decrease) which results in a (rise/fall) of rotor rpm.

2. When crossing a mountain ridge into a strong headwind you should have sufficient clearance height (before/after) you cross the ridge and cross the ridge at a (90°/oblique) angle.

3. If there is an inversion above your planned cold mountain landing site, you should anticipate that translational lift will (increase/decrease) as you descend through the inversion.

4. In strong wind flow conditions, low level operations on the (lee/windward) side of a mountain are likely to encounter rotor action which can be associated with (severe/weak) turbulence.

5. Whenever possible, fly on the (downwind/upwind) side of a valley because on that side there are likely to be (up/down) drafts and a (greater/smaller) radius is involved should a reversal turn be necessary.

6. Approaching a pinnacle, it is (easier/more difficult) to assess the slope of the surface and ground effect becomes effective (earlier/later) during the approach.

7. If you have to land on a high-level landing site surrounded by irregular features, you should aim to complete the approach (short of/over) the site.

8. If your landing area is snow-covered, you (should/should not) plan a lengthy hover because ground effect will be (improved/diminished) and there is a risk of disorientation due to _____ snow.

Helicopter Icing 24

Ice forms when humidity is high and temperatures are at or below 32°F (0°C). Icing can also occur at temperatures slightly above freezing in regions where pressure reduces because of increased flow velocity, such as in the deflected airflow above rotating blades. Reduced pressures cause temperatures to decrease and provided the original temperature is not too far above the freezing mark, ice can form on the upper blade surfaces.

Humidity can take the form of precipitation, clouds or fog.

Ice Accretion

The rate of ice accretion varies with:

- temperature and size of water drops
- water content of air
- kinetic heating
- shape of airfoils and other aircraft components
- mechanical flexion and vibration

Influence of Temperature and Drop Size

Most icing encountered under normal conditions is produced by freezing of supercooled water droplets. These are water droplets at temperatures below freezing, but still in the liquid state. Any disturbance to the droplets, such as a rotating blade striking them, solidifies part of the drops instantaneously while the remainder flows back over the blade, freezing as it moves. In general, the larger the drop size and the closer its temperature to the freezing mark, the smaller the portion that turns to ice on impact and the larger the amount that flows back, freezing as it goes. The type of ice produced through this process is known as *clear ice* (also known as *translucent ice*), it is mostly formed when the temperature is between 0°C and approximately −15°C (32°F to 5°F). It is hard and often difficult to dislodge. If it does fly off, it can be in relatively large portions and become dangerous flying debris. The irregular shedding of such ice from the blades can also cause severe, potentially destructive vibrations.

Smaller droplets, and those at temperatures colder than −15°C (5°F) involve greater portions freezing instantaneously on impact and less water flowing back along the blade, freezing as it flows. Ice produced under these conditions is rather porous and referred to as *rime ice* (also known as *opaque ice*). Although this type is easier to break, its irregular shape can upset the aerodynamic qualities of a blade.

At close to −40°F (−40°C), water can no longer exist in the supercooled liquid state and only ice crystals can be found at and below those temperatures. Since these crystals are dry, they do not adhere to surfaces and no icing problems will therefore be encountered.

Below approximately −20°C (−4°F) and towards −40°C (−40°F), the size of droplets is likely to be small and the portion solidifying instantaneously is relatively large, which again leads to reduced icing problems for helicopters.

Aircraft icing of either type is potentially threatening if no anti-ice equipment is available to combat it. Nevertheless, it is generally felt that clear ice is worse than rime ice.

Water Content of Air

Regardless of a droplet's size and temperature, the amount of water contained in air has an overriding influence on the rate at which ice can form and build up. Clouds and precipitation resulting from orographic causes (mountains), generally contain much water. The combination of flight at higher altitudes plus the high water content produce a severe risk of icing in mountainous areas.

Other meteorological conditions that can produce high rates of ice accretion are thunderstorms, active cold fronts and under certain conditions, unstable warm fronts.

A very dangerous and almost instantaneous total coverage of ice can be encountered in freezing rain which is sometimes found just under the freezing level on the cold side of the frontal boundary of a warm front. No degree of anti-icing can cope with the rate of ice build-up encountered in freezing rain conditions.

Ironically, the relatively low water content of air in polar regions and the very cold temperatures found there produce smaller rates of ice accretion than in tropical regions where the water content of the air is notoriously high. In low latitudes (towards the equator) however, helicopters have to fly at 15,000 to 20,000 feet to be affected by icing because the freezing level is higher.

Kinetic Heating

Blade sections traveling at high speeds produce heat through friction between air or moisture and the surface of the blades. Ice is often discouraged from forming near the tip regions of blades because of the high local velocities. This notwithstanding, some high-rotor-rpm blades of small radius rotors accumulate ice faster than those rotating at low values.

Shape of Airfoils and Other Aircraft Components

Ice forms quickly on thin objects such as the sharp leading edges of blades, antennae and similar items. Supercooled water can readily penetrate the thin boundary layer associated with these shapes and adhere to their surfaces, whereas blunt shapes, with their thicker boundary layers, tend to oppose skin and drop contact. High-performance blades and those operating at high rotor rpm are more vulnerable to icing than high-lift blades, with their larger leading edge radius.

Tail rotors suffer from icing too, but relatively few problems have been encountered from tail rotor icing.

Fuselage components such as windshields ice up when flying in supercooled water or in sleet. Snow, especially dry snow, does not stick to any great degree except in certain fuselage areas. Condensation settling on the inside of windshields that are colder than freezing temperature often turns to ice.

Mechanical Flexion and Vibration

Ice formed on rotor blades is subjected to natural shedding forces that are always present to some degree but are reinforced by vibration and flexing of the helicopter's blades. Tests have shown that the latter forces are at their maximum about one-third out from the root end of blades. High-lift and flexible blades are better at shedding ice than high performance and stiffer blades. A certain amount of ice must have built up before natural shedding can occur. The outside air temperature has a strong influence on the process.

Although shedding may be seen as a measure of de-icing, by no means do all blades shed their ice equally. Thus an unbalanced rotor may cause destructive vibrations; an immediate landing in those circumstances, is the best course of action. The rotor rpm does not have to be up to operational values for uneven shedding to cause unacceptably high vibrations; it can occur during start up in icing conditions.

Ice Formation on Blades at Different Temperatures

The manner in which ice builds up depends to a large degree on the air temperature.

In the temperature range of 0°C to approximately −6°C (32°F to 20°F), ice will form on the leading edge of blades from the root to approximately 70% out toward the tip. The last 30% of the blade remains clear due to kinetic heating. The chordwise extent of the icing is about 20% from the leading edge rearward. Maximum build up occurs in the middle of the affected area and near the blade root where localized turbulence has a strong influence.

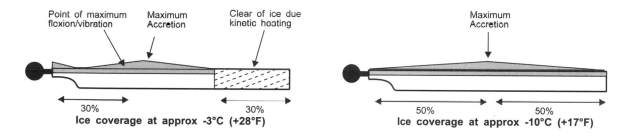

Figure 24-1. *Icing coverage at different temperatures.*

As temperatures decrease from −6°C (approximately 20°F) down to approximately −17°C (0°F), the influence of kinetic heating near the blade tips reduces so that the entire leading edge will become covered with ice. At temperatures colder than −17°C (0°F), the air becomes relatively dry and the rate of ice build-up decreases as a result.

The shape of the ice build-up depends to a large extent on the size of droplets and temperature. Large drops at just below freezing temperature are likely to produce clear ice that is characterized by a concave depression shape at the leading edge, where the initial small portions of the drops turn instantaneously to solid ice. The remaining rearward flow, which freezes as it flows, then produces smooth lobes of ice.

Drops (and especially smaller drops) at temperatures colder than approximately −10°C have a larger portion freeze on impact at the leading edge and a rounded ice shape appears as a result. The remaining rearward flowing (and freezing) water again produces jagged ice lobes (Figure 24-2).

Smooth shape of clear ice   **Jagged shape of rime ice**

Figure 24-2. *Characteristics of clear ice and rime ice.*

Electrical Anti-Icing

Heat, produced by electrical elements fitted inside the leading edge of blades, is phased in different sectors and timed to coincide with the natural shedding cycle, once sufficient ice has built up to begin the shedding cycle. Ice shedding initiated before there is enough accumulated ice on the blades can result in incomplete shedding. A problem also occurs when the heat supply and shedding cycle go out of phase. Under those conditions, ice accretion can actually be encouraged when supercooled water flow-back is facilitated. The electrical demand of a blade anti-icing system is high, limiting the amount of the blade that can be heated.

Windshield anti-icing is usually accomplished through thin electric elements inside the (perspex) windshield. This method has proved effective for avoiding ice without using up too much power.

Consequences of Ice Accretion

Ice build up causes:

- changes to the shape of the blade airfoil, and therefore changes to its lift coefficient
- an increase in the blade's drag coefficient
- an increase in the aircraft's gross weight

The first two factors influence the helicopter's lift /drag ratio, which in turn degrades the rotor thrust/rotor drag ratio when the total reaction leans further away from the axis of rotation.

Icing then can initially be detected by the need for more power as rotor rpm falls off when increased rotor drag begins to take its toll. Since ice accretion is almost always uneven throughout the disc, the resulting vibration gives the pilot an additional warning of ice buildup.

If natural shedding occurs and the blades are briefly cleared of ice, the helicopter's power requirement returns to its original value and the vibration ceases. The next cycle soon commences, however, and continues so long as the helicopter remains in icing conditions.

In the absence of anti-ice equipment, a pilot who ignores the symptoms of icing would do well to remember that although in normal powered flight ice does not readily adhere to the outside sections of the blades where a large proportion of lift is being produced, in an autorotation the situation is drastically different. As explained earlier, the driving region of the blade is more or less in its middle, which is likely to be effected by ice accretion. Thus the pilot's ability to carry out an autorotation is jeopardized by blade icing.

The weight of accumulated ice does not usually pose a serious problem except when it causes a shift in the blades' center of gravity position. Under those circumstances the associated twist and stress forces produce vibrations that may become unacceptable.

Engine Intake Icing

Since most helicopter engine intakes are mostly not exposed to direct ram airflow, intake icing is not generally a problem. The nature of some helicopter operations, such as landing in blowing snow, may present problems such as snow accumulation on intake filters.

Review 24

Helicopter Icing

1. Flying a helicopter in rain a few feet below the freezing level (can/cannot) result in ice forming on the rotor blades because the area of (reduced/increased) pressure above the blades is associated with (higher/lower) temperatures than the environment temperature.

2. When the environment temperature is between 32°F (0°C) and 5°F (−15°C) and cloud droplets are large, _____ ice is likely to form and when temperatures are much colder and/or droplets are small, _____ ice will form.

3. A (major/minor) risk of rotor blade icing is the resulting unbalancing of blades which can cause (recirculation/ground resonance) problems on landing.

4. The initial build-up of ice normally occurs in the (tip/middle) region of blades and since this is the blade's (driven/driving) region during an engine-off descent, it follows that a safe autorotation (may/may not) be possible.

5. Above approximately 20°F (−6°C), the tip regions of blades are generally (covered by/clear of) ice because of _____ heating resulting from (high/low) local speeds.

6. Generally, ice accretion is (quicker/slower) on sharp objects and (quicker/slower) on blunt objects.

7. Flying in sleet (is/is not) unsafe because visibility through the windshield (will/will not) reduce when _____ forms.

Helicopter Performance 25

Helicopter Performance Factors

There are a number of factors that influence a helicopter's performance in flight. The most significant of these are:

- altitude, including pressure altitude and density altitude
- moisture content of the air
- aircraft gross weight
- external stores
- the wind

Altitude

One of the overriding factors in aircraft performance is the density of the air, which decreases with a gain in altitude. Lift production by the rotor relies heavily on the available air density, and is adversely affected as the aircraft ascends. Since rotor thrust is dependent on lift, helicopter performance ultimately decreases with an increase in altitude.

For a given total rotor thrust production, a decrease in air density requires a compensating increase in the angle of attack of the blades, which reduces the lift/drag ratio. The ratio of total rotor thrust to rotor drag is upset because of the increased angles of attack, with the result that total rotor thrust production incurs increased rotor drag. More power is then required to overcome this in order to maintain a given performance.

Power production in a helicopter varies, depending on type of engine. The unsupercharged piston engine loses performance from sea level on up, while supercharged piston engines maintain a given power output to a certain altitude, above which a fall-off in performance must be expected. The turbine engine, typically de-rated, will perform well up to much higher altitudes than a piston engine, but again, above a given altitude, its performance falls off as well.

> All engines inevitably reach an altitude above which power production falls off. The increasing power demand from the anti-torque rotor with gain in altitude has a considerable adverse influence.

Gross weight may have to be reduced, hovering and climbing vertically may not be possible and slingloads may be impossible to carry as altitude is increased. Performance prediction with altitude is figured on graphs that combine the various criteria. Unfortunately, the use of altitude (height above mean sea level) to calculate performance is not feasible because the density of air at any given altitude is subject to change according to the following variables:

- atmospheric pressure
- air temperature
- moisture content

By allowing for atmospheric pressure and air temperature it is possible to calculate *pressure altitude* and *density altitude*, two essential values in performance graphs. There is no simple formula which allows for the influence of moisture content.

Pressure Altitude

Pressure altitude reflects the influence of atmospheric pressure values when they are different from the "average" pressure at sea level under standard (ISA) conditions, which is 29.92 in.Hg (1013 hPa). If the sea level pressure (QNH) is less than 29.92 in.Hg (1013 hPa), air molecules from sea level on up are further apart, making the air density less, and aircraft performance is adversely affected. If the sea level pressure is higher than 29.92 in.Hg, the air may be more dense, and performance at altitude can be expected to be better. Most Flight Manual performance graphs use pressure altitude rather than just altitude as one of the main grid values, so it is important that you clearly understand the concept and are readily able to convert one to the other.

Pressure altitude is the altitude indicated on the aircraft altimeter when the Kollsman window (pressure or sub-scale window) on the altimeter has been set to 29.92 in.Hg (1013 hPa). If the day's barometric pressure setting also happens to be 29.92 in.Hg, the instrument displays pressure altitude as the exact height above sea level.

At this stage it is necessary to clearly define the difference between the term altitude and pressure altitude. Altitude means the vertical distance (height) above sea level, it can also be called "elevation." This value is shown on the altimeter when the correct sea level pressure (whatever that may be) is set on the Kollsman window. Pressure altitude, however, is the indicated height value on the altimeter when the Kollsman (sub-scale) window is set to 29.92 in.Hg (1013 hPa). Since the barometric pressure is often other than 29.92 in.Hg, a correctly referenced altimeter (to the current sea level barometric pressure) does not often read pressure altitude.

Most of the following calculations involve converting sea level pressure to standard pressure and vice versa. In the U.S. these pressures are stated in inches of mercury (in.Hg) whereas in many other countries they are stated in hectopascals (hPa, formerly known as millibars). Both units of measurement will be used in this chapter and to convert from one to the other remember that 1 hPa = 0.03 in.Hg. Appendix 3 at the end of this book contains a conversion table showing the relationship between hPa and in.Hg.

If the sea level barometric pressure is 30.10 in.Hg and this value is set on the altimeter pressure window, the instrument reads its exact height above sea level (altitude), but this height does not reflect conditions found there under standard (or ISA) conditions. Since the sea level pressure in this example is more than 29.92 in.Hg the atmosphere on this occasion is more "compressed" and the associated pressure altitude is lower than the altitude showing on the altimeter (because more "compressed" air is normally found lower down).

By allowing a certain value of height per inch of pressure (or per hPa), it is possible to calculate pressure altitude. The average value is *1 inch per 1,000 feet of altitude* (or *30 feet per hPa*).

For example, if the sea level pressure is 30.92 in.Hg, the atmospheric pressure is 1 inch more than standard, which equates to (1 x 1,000) = 1,000 feet of altitude. Therefore, a helicopter operating at 2,500 feet above sea level will perform as though it is 1,000 feet lower, 1,500 feet above sea level because greater pressure relates to lower altitudes. Under these conditions, the helicopter operates at a pressure altitude of 1,500 feet.

In similar vein, if the sea level pressure (QNH) is 1003 hPa, the atmospheric pressure is 10 hPa less than average (1013), which equates to (10 x 30) = 300 feet of altitude. A helicopter operating at 2,000 feet above sea level performs as though it is 300 feet higher, 2,300 feet above sea level because lower pressure relates to higher altitudes. Under these conditions, the helicopter operates at a pressure altitude of 2,300 feet.

The same information can be obtained without calculations by using the mechanics of the altimeter. Regardless of sea level pressure, if the sub-scale is turned to 29.92 in.Hg (or 1013 hPa), the altimeter reads pressure altitude. No matter where one may be, by selecting 29.92 (or 1013), the pressure altitude value is at hand.

The diagram in Figure 25-1A shows the correct reading of the altimeter when the aircraft operates at 2,000 feet above sea level and the prevailing sea level pressure of 1023 hPa is set in the sub-scale (Kollsman) window. By turning the sub-scale to the standard atmosphere pressure, (25-1B) the altimeter instantly shows 1,700 feet pressure altitude which is the correct pressure altitude value under these conditions (2000 − 10x30 = 2000 − 300 = 1,700 feet).

Similarly, when operating at 2,000 feet above sea level when the prevailing sea level pressure of 1003 hPa is set on the sub-scale (25-1C), the altimeter indicates 2,000 feet, but when 1013 hPa is set, the altimeter reads 2,300 feet pressure altitude, as calculated earlier.

In Figure 25-1E - H the same readings are shown based on in.Hg in the Kollsman window.

Thus it is a quick and simple matter to obtain pressure altitude values by setting 1013 hPa (29.92 in.Hg) in the Kollsman (sub-scale) window. It must be noted, however, that it is easy to forget to reset the window to the correct sea level pressure again. Always reset the local barometric pressure after 1013 hPa (or 29.92 in.Hg) has been selected briefly to determine the pressure altitude.

Figure 25-1. *Pressure altitude can be determined instantly by setting 1013 hPa (or 29.92 in.Hg) in the Kollsman (subscale) window.*

Barometric pressure is felt more or less evenly throughout the lower atmosphere. A helicopter operating off a helipad at 5,000 feet above sea level when the barometric pressure is 1030 hPa performs as if the altitude was lower because the pressure is 17 hPa greater than standard. This equates to 510 feet (30 x 17) and since greater pressures are associated with lower altitudes, it follows that the pressure altitude is 4,490 feet (5000 – 510). Its performance relates to a pressure altitude of 4,490 feet.

Summarizing, and ignoring humidity and temperature:

- a high barometric pressure produces a low pressure altitude and performance is improved

- a low barometric pressure produces a high pressure altitude and performance is degraded

The following two examples consolidate these principles:

Example 1. A helicopter operates at an elevation of 7,500 feet, with a sea level barometric pressure (QNH) of 1005 hPa. What is the pressure altitude?

1013 – 1005 = 8 hPa, which equates to 240 feet. Since pressure is less than 1013 hPa the aircraft may be assumed to be at a higher altitude where pressures are normally less. Thus the pressure altitude is 7,500 + 240 = 7,740 feet. Performance responds to this higher altitude value.

Example 2. A helicopter operates at an elevation of 6,350 feet, the sea level pressure is 30.10 in.Hg. What is the pressure altitude?

30.10 – 29.92 = 0.18 inches, which equates to 180 feet. Since the barometric pressure is more than standard, the aircraft may be assumed to be at a lower altitude where pressures are normally greater. Thus the pressure altitude is 6,350 – 180 = 6,170 feet.

Density Altitude

This term reflects the influence of temperature at pressure altitude, compared to what the temperature is assumed to be at pressure altitude in standard conditions (U.S. terminology) or according to the International Standard Atmosphere (ISA).

Most helicopter performance graphs use degrees Celsius. To facilitate converting Fahrenheit (F) to Celsius (C), a conversion table is provided in Appendix 2 at the end of this book.

Standard atmospheric conditions assume a sea level temperature of 15°C (59°F) and a temperature lapse rate of 1.98°C (near enough to 2°C) (or 3.5°F) per 1,000 feet of altitude. Once the lapse rate is known, one can calculate what the temperature should be at any pressure altitude.

For example, the temperature at 4,000 feet pressure altitude should be: 15°C – (2 x 4, because every thousand feet loses 2°) = 15 – 8 = +7°C. If the actual temperature at 4,000 feet pressure altitude is +9°C it follows that the temperature at this time and altitude is 2° warmer than it ought to be. This is expressed as ISA +2 or 2° warmer (or more) than standard.

As another example, the pressure altitude of 6,500 feet should have a temperature of $15 - (2 \times 6\frac{1}{2}) = +2°C$ under ISA conditions. If the actual temperature there is 0°C it follows that the temperature at this time and altitude is 2° colder than it ought to be. This is expressed as ISA −2 or 2° colder (or less) than standard.

The terms ISA +2 and ISA −2 in the above examples produce what is known as *ISA deviation* or *deviation from standard conditions*. It is this deviation that is used to calculate the effect of temperature on pressure altitude to establish density altitude.

Calculations have shown that each degree Celsius of deviation from standard conditions equals a height of approximately 120 feet. If the deviation from standard is +2°C it means that density altitude is $(2 \times 120) =$ 240 feet higher than the pressure altitude. The reason for a higher density altitude in this example is that warmer temperatures imply less dense air, equal to that usually found at greater altitudes. If the deviation is −2°C from standard it means that the density altitude is $(2 \times 120) = 240$ feet lower than pressure altitude because colder temperatures imply more dense air, equal to that normally found at lower altitudes.

Summarizing :

- colder than standard temperatures produce a density altitude lower than the pressure altitude

- warmer than standard temperatures produce a density altitude higher than the pressure altitude

Example 3. Assume the pressure altitude is 5,500 feet where the actual temperature is +10°C. Calculate the density altitude.

At 5,500 feet pressure altitude the temperature ought to be $15 - (2 \times 5\frac{1}{2})$ = +4°C. Since the actual temperature is +10° C it follows that this can be expressed as 6° warmer than standard (ISA+6). With a deviation of 6° (warmer) it follows that density altitude is $5,500 + (6 \times 120) = 5,500 + 720 = 6,220$ feet.

Combined Effect of Pressure and Density Altitudes

When allowance has been made at any altitude above sea level for the deviation from standard pressure, the pressure altitude is known. When this pressure altitude is corrected for any temperature deviation from standard conditions, the density altitude is known.

There is a substantial altitude correction for temperature deviation as compared to the correction for standard pressure deviation. Warmer or colder temperatures in general have a stronger influence on helicopter performance than pressure deviations (ignoring exceedingly high or low sea level pressure deviations).

The higher the density altitude the worse the performance and the lower the density altitude the better the performance.

Moisture Content of Air

The mass of a molecule of moisture is less than the mass of a molecule of "dry" air. If a large amount of moisture is present in air, the total mass per volume (its density) is less. The consequence of this is that performance is degraded. By the same token, dry air and particularly cold dry air (as in the Arctic and Antarctic) is good for aircraft performance because it is denser than humid, warm air. The moisture content in the air has a significant impact on helicopter performance, but there is no rule-of-thumb formula that allows a pilot to calculate the effect of moisture content in terms of altitude above sea level, as with pressure altitude and density altitude calculations. It is important then that pilots develop a natural sense of how "wet" the air is so that their performance expectations from the helicopter are reasonable. The humidity factor often has a far greater influence than pressure and temperature factors.

Aircraft Gross Weight

Increases in aircraft gross weight go hand in hand with requirements for higher angles of attack and demand for more power. Any high gross weight situation limits the helicopter's performance. This is particularly important when considering flight at high altitudes, where the power in use is already relatively high. The limited surplus power available when at high gross weight places a great restriction on the helicopter's ability to hover, do steep turns, vertical climbs and maneuvers.

The high power requirement in the hover when at high gross weight also affects the required performance from the anti-torque (tail) rotor. It is possible that a large left pedal deflection may be needed to produce the required anti-torque. Under such conditions the takeoff needs to be preceded by a check for adequate directional control. If any yaw occurs with the left pedal fully forward when the helicopter becomes light on the skids, some weight should be offloaded. Operations at high altitudes accentuate this problem.

High gross weight situations also affect the maximum height that the helicopter can operate in ground effect for a given power availability. Under these conditions, the heavier the aircraft, the lower the maximum hover height (refer again Figures 11-1 and 11-2, Chapter 11).

External Stores

Any loads carried externally on skid platforms or as slingloads increase parasite drag. Since power is required to overcome additional parasite drag, reserve power is decreased. As a consequence, helicopter performance is degraded by external loads, which is particularly noticeable at high altitudes.

The Wind

Previous text has made many references to the beneficial influence of the wind on power available over power required, especially when the helicopter operates in the low speed, low height, high gross weight envelope and when the helicopter is flown with reference to a ground feature. (Carefully note that "low height" refers to a small vertical distance between the helicopter and the ground, which may apply at any altitude.) Increased translational lift values are applicable when the wind blows and especially when it blows strongly. By the same token, the reverse holds true as well, and a decreasing wind reduces the overall benefit of translational lift and through that, possibly limits the helicopter's performance.

Power Check

Many landings are preceded by a hover. Since power required to hover is greater than that required during forward flight, special care is required for landings in high altitude/high gross weight situations where power use is already high.

Figure 25-2 shows an example of a typical situation at altitude where level flight and climbing is possible only when the helicopter is flown at speeds between 12 and 90 knots. It is assumed that the horsepower-available curve shown is the maximum possible at that altitude. When approaching a high level helipad (under these conditions) it is not difficult to be duped into believing that since the aircraft is performing well the imminent hover and landing can be carried out safely. The graph, however, shows quite clearly that at speeds below 12 knots, the aircraft cannot fly level. This means that on initial approach, everything looks good, and the rate of descent can be controlled, but as the airspeed is reduced to 12 knot and less, the rate of descent increases. Even if this is not of critical importance at this time, the truth comes home when collective is raised to stop the rate of descent just prior to commencing the hover. Even with full up collective, the power output cannot be improved beyond what the engine can deliver at that altitude and, as shown in the graph, this is insufficient for hover. The aircraft continues to descend rapidly to a hard landing.

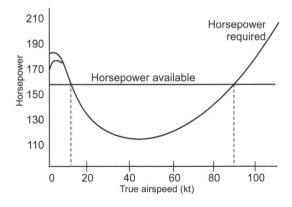

Figure 25-2. *The horsepower available/horsepower required curves showing that flight at speed below about 12 knots cannot be level.*

All Flight Manuals contain graphs that indicate maximum altitudes at which the helicopter can hover under various gross weight and environmental conditions. The information must be considered prior to operating at high altitude locations. In addition to this information, it is advisable that prior to approaching a landing area at altitude, a power check be carried out to ensure that adequate power will be available during the hover prior to touchdown. The check must be carried out in relatively still air, in straight and level flight and with landing rotor rpm selected. Initially the helicopter is flown at endurance speed (minimum power for straight and level flight) and the manifold pressure (or fuel flow in turbine aircraft) is noted. While maintaining the rotor rpm, full power is briefly applied and the change in manifold pressure or fuel flow is noted again. During this power increase it is not essential that the airspeed is maintained because the purpose is to ascertain the maximum power available, which is independent of airspeed.

Having obtained the difference between the two values (the power margin), it is possible to determine the helicopter's slow flight capabilities by referring to the aircraft graphs or tabulations in the Flight Manual. Since these graphs or tabulations do not take the wind into consideration, any wind will be an added advantage.

In extreme situations, such as during an approach to a high altitude ridge or pinnacle at high gross weight, bring the helicopter to the hover alongside the landing area. If hover power is not available, it is then possible to veer away when the aircraft loses altitude as the airspeed decreases. A landing at a lower elevation is then obviously one of few alternatives.

Performance Graphs

There are many performance graphs included in helicopter Flight Manuals, and while it is impractical to cover every facet of all graphs, it is possible to explain the common principles employed in most.

Before attempting to use any graph examine the total meaning of the graph. For instance, look at the X-axis (the bottom horizontal line) and note what the axis represents. Then look at the Y-axis (the side vertical line) and see what it represents. Look at the differently shaped or slanted curve lines within the graph and determine their meaning(s). Finally, absorb the trend of the graph using the values obtained from the X-axis, the Y-axis and curve lines.

The graphs used in this chapter are representative of most light helicopters in service today. Both piston and turbine engine helicopter types are included. Note that the graphs do not apply to a specific helicopter. Since most graphs use pressure altitude, good knowledge of how to convert elevation (or altitude) to pressure altitude is essential.

Temperature is normally in terms of degrees Celsius, which can be used directly on graphs that use that unit of measurement. Standard atmosphere or ISA conversions are required for those graphs that use the standard atmosphere (ISA) grid to determine density altitude. A temperature conversion chart in Appendix 2 helps smooth the transition from Fahrenheit to Celsius for U.S. pilots.

There are a few simple rules for plotting temperatures on graphs:

1. If the ambient temperature (the temperature in the immediate vicinity of one's position) is given or is available, plot that temperature on the degree Celsius baseline or curve line and follow the graph's grid straight up or across, as the case may be.

2. If a random temperature at some altitude is given, convert this either to ISA (standard atmosphere), or convert it to the anticipated temperature at the required elevation using an average lapse rate of 2°C per 1,000 feet throughout the atmosphere. In practice, this is accurate enough.

3. For many standard atmosphere/ISA graphs, the curve lines are slanted so that the main square grid of the graph is not in line with the standard atmosphere lines. In this situation, parallel the standard atmosphere (ISA) lines.

Units of Measurement

Most American-built helicopter graphs use the pound as the unit of measurement for weight, but European helicopter graphs commonly use the kilogram. It is therefore important that the correct conversion is used, for example, 1 kg = 2.2 pounds. The hectopascal (previously called the millibar) is used for atmospheric pressure in these charts, though the majority of American-built helicopter graphs use in.Hg when describing barometric pressure settings. A conversion table hPa to in.Hg is provided in Appendix 3.

Hover Ceiling Graph

Many different types of graphs are employed to determine hover ceiling. The example used in Figure 25-3 represents the common features of most. The purpose of this graph is to show the relationship between the helicopter's ability to hover in ground effect or out of ground effect versus atmospheric factors and gross weight.

A higher gross weight and warm temperatures decrease the helicopter's ability to hover. Looking at the graph it is easy to see the substantial difference in altitude between the hover ceiling out of ground effect compared to in ground effect, some 6,000 feet in this example.

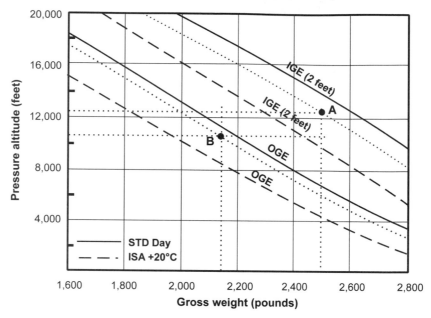

Figure 25-3. *Hover ceilings.*

Example 4. What is the maximum elevation the helicopter can hover in ground effect if the gross weight is 2,450 pounds, the temperature at sea level is +22° C and the sea level pressure is 1003 hPa?

Solution: Since the graph uses standard (ISA) values, first convert 22° C at sea level to standard. Since sea level temperature under ISA conditions is +15° C and the actual temperature is +22° C it follows that in ISA terms the temperature can be expressed as ISA+7. Plot this value as a parallel line to the standard (ISA) lines (through necessity the line has to be approximate).

Plot the gross weight line straight up, 2,450 pounds in this case. Where the ISA line and the gross weight cross (point A), draw a horizontal line to the left, which crosses the pressure altitude leg at approximately 12,200 feet. Again, the values have to be approximate given the scale of the graph.

The question asked for *elevation* and therefore 12,200 feet *pressure altitude* must be converted. Since the barometric pressure given is less than standard, the pressure altitude must be higher, which means that the elevation must be lower. The difference between 1003 and 1013 is 10 hPa. It follows that the correction is 10 x 30 feet = 300 feet lower.

Answer: The pressure altitude of 12,200 − 300 = elevation of 11,900 feet.

Example 5. The landing site for a planned flight has an elevation of 11,000 feet. Temperature at the site has been reported as −3°C and the sea level barometric pressure is 30.25 in.Hg. What is the maximum gross weight that can be carried for this flight if the helicopter is required to hover out of ground effect prior to landing ?

Solution: First convert 11,000 feet elevation to pressure altitude. Since the barometric pressure is greater than standard, pressure altitude must be lower than elevation.

30.25 − 29.92 = .33 x 1,000 = 330 feet.

11,000 − 330 = a pressure altitude of 10,670 feet.

Next convert the ambient temperature of −3° C at 10,670 feet (nearest to 10,500 feet) into ISA values. Under ISA the temperature at 10,500 feet should be 15 − (2 x 10½)= −6° C. Since the actual temperature is −3° C, the temperature is ISA+3 (from −6 to −3 is +3).

Now plot the pressure altitude of 10,670 on the vertical graph leg (the Y leg) and from that point draw a horizontal line to the right. Then draw the ISA+3 line parallel to the ISA lines out of ground effect (approximately).

Answer: From where the two lines intersect (point B), draw a line vertically down, it strikes the gross weight line at about 2,150 pounds.

Takeoff Distance over a 50-foot Obstacle

When the available power is insufficient for a vertical, or near vertical, climb, the horizontal distance required for the climb angle depends on the variables shown in Figure 25-4. (It is acknowledged that this graph is not often used under operational conditions but it has good practice values).

This graph assesses the relationship between gross weight, pressure altitude and temperature on the horizontal takeoff distance required should a vertical climb not be possible.

When operating at high altitudes the takeoff distance increases for a given gross weight. Alternatively, if only a certain distance is available, the gross weight may have to be reduced with increasing altitude or with increasing outside air temperatures.

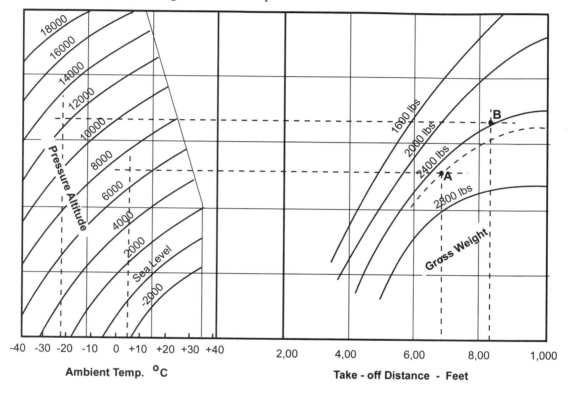

Figure 25-4. *Take-off distance over a 50 foot obstacle.*

Example 6. What is the required takeoff distance to cross a 50 foot obstacle if operating from a site of elevation 7,380 feet where the ambient temperature is +5°C and the aircraft gross weight is 2,500 pounds? The local sea level barometric pressure is 1029 hPa.

Solution: First convert the elevation to pressure altitude. The sea level barometric pressure is better than standard, so the pressure altitude is lower than the elevation.

1029 − 1013 = 16 hPa (x 30 feet) = 480 feet

Elevation 7,380 feet − 480 = a pressure altitude of 6,900 feet

Start at +5° C at the X-axis and draw a line straight up to intersect the pressure altitude of 6,900 feet. From that intersection, draw a horizontal line to the right into the weight guide lines. Trace an approximation of the 2,500 pounds line relative to the total distance between 2,400 and 2,800 pounds. From where the two lines intersect (point A), draw a vertical line down.

Answer: The vertical line intersects the X-axis at approximately 690 feet, therefore that is the horizontal distance required for takeoff.

Example 7. The area around the takeoff zone allows just 820 feet of forward distance. The elevation of the site is 12,800 feet, with a local sea level barometric pressure of 30.01 in.Hg and an outside temperature of −22° C. What is the maximum gross weight that can be carried during this takeoff in order to clear a 50 foot obstacle?

Solution: First calculate the pressure altitude:

30.01 − 29.92 = 0.09 in.Hg (x 1,000) = 90 feet.

The barometric pressure is high thus the pressure altitude is low, so 12,800 − 90 = a pressure altitude of 12,710 feet.

Plot the temperature of −22°C straight up and from where this line intersects the pressure altitude of 12,710, draw a horizontal line through the gross weight guide lines. Draw a vertical line up from 820 feet and note where this intersects the dotted line from the left, point B.

Answer: Point B is slightly above the 2,400 pounds line, towards 2,000 pounds. Interpolation shows that the maximum gross weight for the conditions described above is approximately 2,380 pounds.

Turbine Engine Power Check

This graph (Figure 25-5) indicates the percentage torque (power) that must be available for satisfactory engine performance at a given altitude and ambient temperature and barometric setting. It is noted that this graph is an engine performance graph and it's purpose is mainly to establish the health of the turbine engine, therefore it could be seen as a maintenance engineer's graph. The shape of the curves on the graph indicates that the higher the turbine outlet temperatures and/or the colder the outside air temperature at a given pressure altitude, the greater the percentage power required for satisfactory engine performance.

Example 8. A helicopter is in the hover at an elevation of 7,790 feet, the area sea level pressure is 29.56 in.Hg (= 1001 hPa). The ambient temperature is +12°C and the turbine outlet temperature shows 755°C. What is the minimum percentage torque (power) that can be accepted as satisfactory?

Solution: First convert elevation to pressure altitude:

29.92 – 29.56 = 0.36 (x 1,000) = 360 feet.

(or 1013 - 1001 = 12 x [30] = 360 feet).

Since the barometric pressure is less than 29.92 in.Hg (less than 1013 hPa), the pressure altitude is higher than the elevation.
Therefore, 7,790 + 360 = a pressure altitude of 8,150 feet.

Now draw a line vertically up from +12°C and from where this intersects a turbine outlet temperature of 755°C (point A), draw a horizontal line to the right through the pressure altitude part of the graph. Note where this intersects a pressure altitude of 8,150 feet (point B).

Draw a vertical line down from the pressure altitude intersection (point B), this touches the X-axis at 98%. This means that if the actual power check shows that at least 98% torque is available, the power check can be accepted as satisfactory. If the power check shows less than 98% power available, the engine performance is not acceptable for flight.

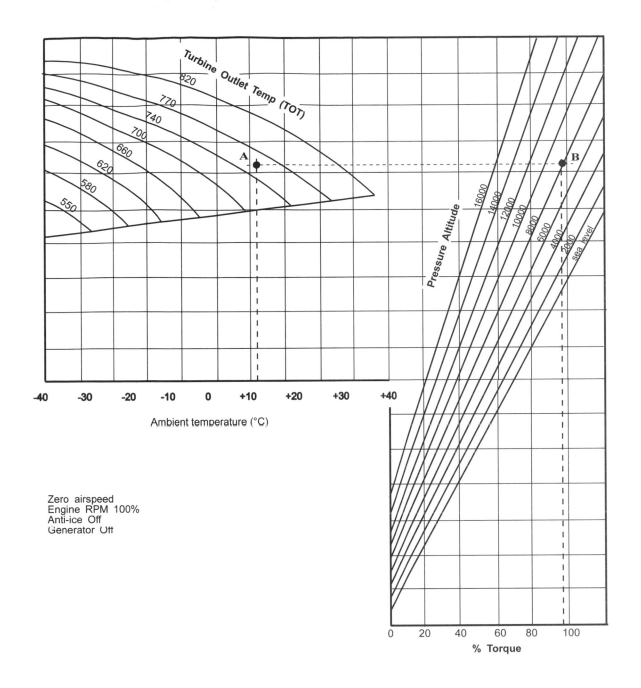

Figure 25-5. *Turbine Engine power check chart*

Maximum Gross Weight for Hovering

This graph (Figure 25-6) gives similar information as the Hover Ceiling graph in Figure 25-3, but this time the graph uses a baseline. The graph establishes the effect of pressure altitude, temperature and the wind on the maximum gross weight that can be carried in ground effect at a skid height of two feet.

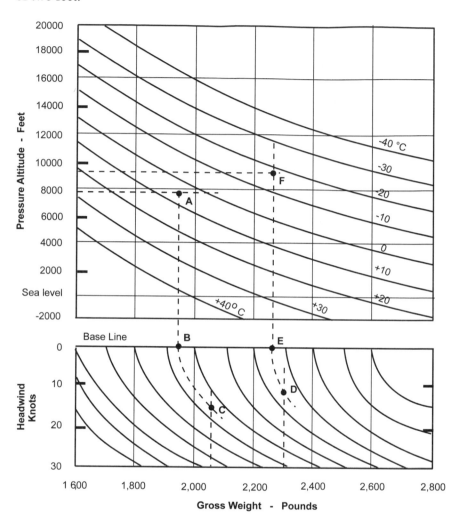

Figure 25-6. *Maximum gross weight for hovering – takeoff power, skid height 2 feet.*

Example 9. What is the maximum gross weight for hovering at two feet if the helicopter is to operate at an elevation of 7,980 feet, temperature has been reported as ISA+6, there is a 15 knot headwind blowing and the barometric sea level pressure is 30.07 in.Hg (1018 hPa)?

Solution: First it is necessary to convert the elevation to pressure altitude. The barometric pressure is 30.07 (1018 hPa), therefore:

30.07 – 29.92 = 0.15 (x 1,000) = 150 feet

(or 1018 – 1013 = 5 x [30] = 150 feet).

7,980 – 150 = 7,830 feet pressure altitude

The ISA temperature needs to be converted to degrees Celsius because the graph does not have ISA lines. ISA+6 means that the temperature in the atmosphere at this time is 6°C warmer than it ought to be at pressure altitude. It is therefore necessary to establish what the temperature ought to be at a pressure altitude of 7,830 feet (nearest to 8,000 feet) allowing 2°C per 1,000 feet:

$$15 - (2 \times 8) = 15 - 16 = -1°C$$

Since the temperature today is 6° warmer (ISA+6) than it ought to be, it follows that the actual temperature at 7,830 feet is +5°C (−1 + 6).

From 7,830 feet on the Y-axis draw a horizontal line into the temperature curve lines and where this intersects +5°C, mark A. Then draw a vertical line straight down to the base line where it intersects point B. From this point, parallel the headwind guide lines until the 15 knot value is reached, point C. From this point, draw a line vertically down to the gross weight axis.

Answer: The maximum gross weight under the stated conditions for hovering at a two-foot skid height is approximately 2,050 pounds.

Example 10. The aircraft gross weight is 2,300 pounds. Is it possible to fly this helicopter to a landing site of elevation 8,500 feet and hover there at the two-foot skid height when conditions at the site are an outside air temperature of −18°C, barometric sea level pressure of 1005 hPa (29.68 in.Hg) and a wind of 12 knots.

From the X axis at 2,300 pounds, draw a line vertically up until it intersects the 12 knot wind value (point D). From that point, parallel the wind guide lines to the base line where it intersects at point E. Draw a line vertically up until a temperature of −18°C is met at point F and then draw a horizontal line to intersect the Y axis. This indicates a pressure altitude of 9,500 feet.

Since the example asked for an elevation, it is necessary to convert 9,500 feet pressure altitude using the sea level pressure of 1005 hPa (29.68 in.Hg). A low sea level pressure means a high pressure altitude and thus a lower elevation. Therefore:

$$1013 - 1005 = 8 \times 30 = 240 \text{ feet}$$

(or 29.92 − 29.68 = [0.24 × 1000] = 240 feet)

deduct this from pressure altitude: 9,500 − 240 = 9,260 feet elevation

Answer: Since the graph showed that this helicopter at a 2,300 pounds gross weight can hover at a two-foot skid height at 9,260 feet elevation, it can clearly operate satisfactorily lower down at the proposed landing site of 8,500 feet elevation.

Climb Performance

The graph in Figure 25-7 confirms, in practical terms, the theory explained in Chapter 14. This graph depicts the best rate of climb that can be expected for varying temperature conditions while the aircraft is at a given gross weight (8,000 pounds in this example). The graph on the far right indicates the associated indicated airspeed (IAS) per pressure altitude necessary to enable a helicopter to maintain its best rate of climb.

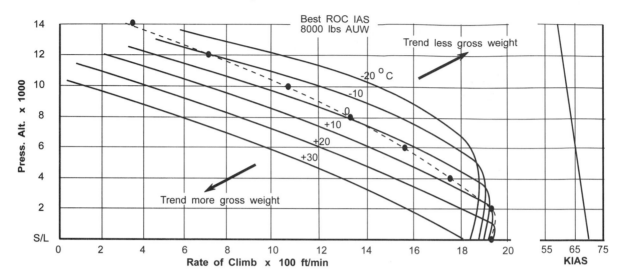

Figure 25-7. *Climb performance – maximum continuous power.*

The IAS decreases progressively with each increase in pressure altitude. The manufacturer must have established that the increasing true airspeed (TAS) where the vertical gap between the horsepower required and horsepower available curves remains greatest with altitude matches the lowering values of IAS (using standard or ISA conditions). The dashed line represents ISA temperatures with altitude, which provides a quick reference in flight for the pilot to ascertain whether the readings of the outside air temperature gauge are higher or lower than standard.

Assuming standard conditions, the graph shows that the rate of climb from sea level to 2,000 feet pressure altitude is slightly in excess of 1,900 feet per minute (fpm) provided the IAS averages 68 knots. From 2,000 to 4,000 feet pressure altitude the rate of climb reduces to an average of 1,820 fpm provided the IAS is reduced to an average of 67 knots. IAS values for subsequent altitudes can be read off in similar fashion.

Above 14,000 feet pressure altitude the rate of climb drops to an average of 200 fpm (with an associated IAS of close to 55 kts), which implies that the helicopter's service ceiling is not far above that pressure altitude. The helicopter's service ceiling is the altitude at which it no longer has enough power available to climb at a steady rate of 100 fpm.

Should actual temperatures be colder than standard, the temperature curve lines shift slightly up and to the right, indicating better rates of climb. Under warmer conditions, the temperature curve lines shift down and to the left indicating reduced rates of climb.

The aircraft Flight Manual provides similar graphs for different gross weight values. The example graph includes "trend arrows" for less or greater gross weight situations. For example, a reduced gross weight shifts all the temperature curve lines up and to the right, indicating better rates of climb.

Range

The graph shown in Figure 25-8 is based on the range performance of a light piston-engined helicopter. It indicates the likely range in nautical miles (nm) in zero-wind conditions and under varying values of gross weight and TAS.

The maximum range of close to 250 nm is achieved when the gross weight is lowest (1,750 pounds in this example) and when the helicopter is flown at 74 knots TAS at 5,000 feet. Flight at lower altitudes reduces this range value, which confirms the theory explained in Chapter 13. In similar vein, an increased gross weight lowers the curve so that less range is achieved. Range is significantly reduced when flying at speeds faster or slower than best range speed.

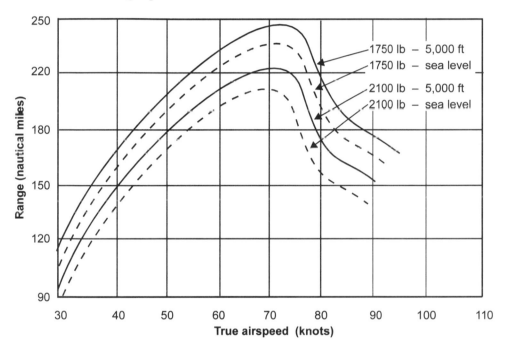

Figure 25-8. *Range – standard day temperature, zero wind.*

For a given gross weight (which may require interpolation between the gross weight curve lines) the maximum range and the required TAS can be determined. Since the altitude to fly is often determined by cloud or wind conditions, the graph provides for different altitudes, again through interpolation between the gross weight to altitude curve lines.

The example graph does not allow for temperature deviations, so anticipated range must be slightly reduced in warm conditions.

Endurance

Figure 25-9 shows a typical endurance graph similar to the range graph on the previous page. It is designed to indicate the likely endurance in hours and parts thereof when operating at varying altitude, gross weight and TAS values. Altitude and gross weight have an influence on endurance. The longest time in the air (some 3 hours 45 minutes) is achieved when at a low gross weight and at sea level provided that the TAS is at or about 50 knots. There is quite a dramatic reduction in endurance as TAS increases towards V_{ne} values.

The graph does not allow for altitude "in hand," which may improve endurance. Also, no allowance is made for temperature deviation from standard, but one can assume that the time in the air is reduced when temperatures are warmer than standard. For a given gross weight (which may require interpolation between the gross weight curve lines), maximum endurance can be determined per TAS and altitude. As in the range graph, interpolation between the altitude curve lines is required if endurance is flown at an altitude other than indicated on the graph.

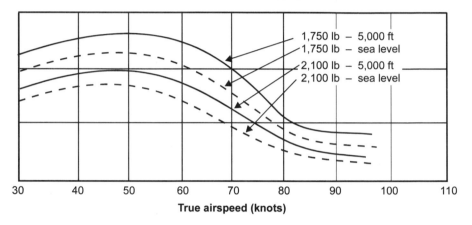

Figure 25-9. *Endurance – standard day temperature.*

Review 25

1. Your altimeter is set to the prevailing sea level pressure (QNH) of 30.03 in.Hg (1017 hPa) when you land at a site of 2,500 feet elevation. Your altimeter will read _____ feet after landing.

2. When you fly at 4,500 feet indicated on your altimeter with the prevailing sea level pressure of 30.03 in.Hg set on the Kollsman (subscale) window, the pressure altitude is _____ feet.

3. When you wish to establish what the pressure altitude is without calculating it, you can find the answer by turning the Kollsman (subscale) window to _____ in. Hg (or ___ hPa) but you must not forget to _____ to the prevailing _____ afterwards.

4. The outside air temperature gauge in your helicopter shows +21°C while you cruise at 2,500 feet and the sea level pressure is 29.92 in.Hg (1013 hPa) which you have set in the Kollsman (subscale) window. The density altitude is ____ feet.

5. When you do your pre-start checks in your light piston engined helicopter, you turn the Kollsman window setting to 29.92 in.Hg (1013 hPa) and the altimeter reads 1,200 feet. When you set the known elevation of 1,500 feet in the window, you expect the reading to be _____ in.Hg (_____ hPa).

6. Following on from question 5, the outside air temperature gauge reads +28°C. You calculate the density altitude to be ____ feet.

7. Following on from question 6, you note that the air is very humid and there is no wind. What will be the influence of the density altitude and high moisture content on the take-off performance of your helicopter ?

8. You plan to land at a high altitude pinnacle landing site and prior to making your approach you decide to check your helicopter's performance by slowly flying alongside the area. As your airspeed reduces to about 20 knots you note you are using full power to maintain level flight. Is it possible to bring your aircraft to the hover out of ground effect over the landing site and land there?

(continued on next page)

9. Use the hover ceiling graph in Figure 25-10. You plan to use a landing site at an elevation of 8,800 feet when your helicopter gross weight is 2,350 pounds and the sea level [pressure is 29.62 in.Hg (1003 hPa). From information supplied, you calculate that the temperature is ISA+8. Can you fly to the landing site and hover out of ground effect prior to touch-down?

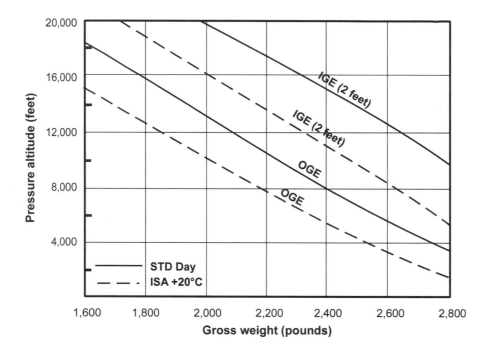

Figure 25-10. *Hover ceiling graph (see Figure 25-3 for guidance).*

Weight and Balance

26

Helicopter loading is important. Both aircraft performance and the aircraft's center of gravity position depend on the proper calculation of the helicopter's gross weight and the proper balancing of that weight.

Definitions

Before weight and balance can be discussed the following basic terms and definitions need to be clear:

arm (also referred to as **moment arm).**

The horizontal distance from a reference datum to the center of gravity of each item is known as the arm. For longitudinal (fore/aft) considerations the arm is termed positive if measured aft of datum and negative if forward of datum. For lateral (left/right) center of gravity considerations, the arm is termed positive if measured to the right of the *butt line* and negative if measured to the left of the *butt line (*a line through the symmetrical center of the helicopter fore/aft).

datum.

The datum is an imaginary line from which all measurements of arms are taken. The reference datum can be placed at any point and is determined by the aircraft manufacturer. For instance, datum can be a line positioned at the nose of the helicopter for longitudinal center of gravity position and (commonly) the butt line for lateral center of gravity position.

moment.

Moment is the product of the force and the perpendicular distance from datum to the line of action of the force (*weight x arm = moment*). Moment can be seen as the turning effect of an item around datum. All moments that produce *clockwise rotation* are termed **positive** whereas moments that produce *counterclockwise rotation* are termed **negative**. The **total moment** is the total weight of the helicopter multiplied by the distance between the datum and the aircraft's center of gravity.

center of gravity.

The point through which all the weight of the aircraft is said to act is the center of gravity, it is the *balance point* of the helicopter. The position of center of gravity is expressed as a distance from datum. If moments are taken about this point, then all the clockwise moments equal the counterclockwise moments, therefore total moments are zero.

center of gravity range and limits.

Center of gravity range and limits are determined by the manufacturer in terms of distance from datum within which the center of gravity must be positioned to keep the helicopter safe and balanced correctly for flight. The range is determined by a forward limit which denotes the most forward position of center of gravity and an aft limit which denotes the most rearward position of center of gravity. In similar vein, there is a right limit and a left limit for lateral center of gravity positions.

Although not generally applicable to light piston engine helicopters, most large helicopters have vertical center of gravity limits for slingload operations, not for on-board loading. The larger the distance between the rotor head and the slingload (hook) attachment at the aircraft the greater the need for vertical center of gravity limits.

station.

Station is the same as *arm*. For instance, Station 44 means that the item is positioned 44 units (of distance) aft of datum while Station –44 means that the item is positioned 44 units (of distance) forward of datum.

index units.

Some moments are numerically large. To make these difficult-to-manage figures easier to work with, the moments can be divided by a factor such as 10, 100, or 1000. For instance, 4000 x 200 = 800,000. By using a factor of 1000, the final answer can be expressed as 800 IU (index units).

empty aircraft weight.

The empty aircraft weight includes the entire aircraft structure, powerplant(s) and equipment (as detailed in the aircraft Flight Manual). It also includes unusable fuel, full oil and full systems fluids (e.g. hydraulic oil).

empty aircraft center of gravity position.

The empty aircraft center of gravity position is the center of gravity of a helicopter in its empty weight configuration as calculated by a qualified maintenance engineer. The information is found in the "Loading Data" section of the aircraft Flight Manual.

basic operating weight (or aircraft prepared for service weight).

The helicopter's basic operating weight includes the empty aircraft weight, pilot and crew, crew's baggage, food, water etc., i.e. total load except payload and fuel.

payload (or commercial load).

The helicopter payload includes passengers, their baggage, freight, cargo etc. from which revenue may be derived.

zero fuel weight.

Zero fuel weight is the basic operating weight plus payload.

ramp weight.

Ramp weight is the zero fuel weight plus fuel.

take-off weight.

Takeoff weight is ramp weight less fuel for run-up and taxi.

landing weight.

Landing weight is takeoff weight less the fuel consumed (or load offloaded) during flight.

center of gravity envelope.

The center of gravity envelope is a graphical method to determine whether the center of gravity is within prescribed fore/aft and left/right limits. If the calculated center of gravity position falls inside the envelope, or on its outline, then the center of gravity position is satisfactory (see Figure 26-2.).

Weight

The manufacturer provides specific limiting information on items such as maximum certificated takeoff weight, maximum zero fuel weight, maximum hook weight, and maximum payload. The amounts of these items are based on structural considerations as well as power availability and under no circumstances must these limitations be exceeded.

Chapter 25 discussed the adverse effects of high density altitude on the maximum takeoff weight. Under conditions other than sea level values this weight may be considerably less than those stated in the operating handbook.

Balance

Even though the weight of a helicopter may fall within prescribed limits, if the distribution of this weight is not correct the helicopter's center of gravity may be outside authorized limits, in which case the aircraft's balance is unsatisfactory and the aircraft is unsafe for flight.

The center of gravity of a body can simply be defined as the point through which weight acts. It is the point of balance of the aircraft. If a helicopter is placed on a fulcrum (support) in such a way that the aircraft center of gravity is exactly above the fulcrum, the aircraft tips neither forward or back, left or right. Similarly, when the main rotor is suspending the aircraft in the calm hover, the helicopter hangs level beneath the rotor, provided the rotor mast and the center of gravity position are in line vertically.

As pilot(s), crew, payload and fuel are either added to or subtracted from the aircraft, the point of balance (center of gravity) moves and the helicopter no longer hangs horizontally beneath the rotor. Instead it hangs nose up or nose down depending on the weight distribution. This pitching movement causes the disc to be displaced and the aircraft moves forward, back or to one side. To compensate for a re-positioned center of gravity, cyclic inputs are required. An aft center of gravity needs forward cyclic, while a forward center of gravity needs aft cyclic, the amounts depending on the center of gravity distance from datum.

The same principles also apply to lateral center of gravity positions in that center of gravity movement either to the left or right requires lateral compensating cyclic inputs. This factor is worthy of note particularly for aircraft equipped for hoist operations where lateral center of gravity positions become very important and because of that, maximum permissible hoist loads are invariably stipulated in the aircraft Flight Manual.

There comes a center of gravity position where no more cyclic input is available and the helicopter becomes uncontrollable. To avoid this situation, the manufacturer of the aircraft pre-determines the allowable amount of center of gravity movement that can be safely accepted. This information is published in the aircraft Flight Manual in terms of distance from the datum line, fore and aft, and left and right center of gravity limits (Figure 26-2.).

Some helicopters have the longitudinal datum coincidental with the rotor mast, in which case the center of gravity limits are expressed in units of distance forward and aft of datum. Since this arrangement involves positive and negative turning moments and since it is easy to make mistakes adding these different values, few helicopters use this arrangement.

A more common datum is one located at the front of the skids, in which case the center of gravity limits are expressed in units of distance aft of datum only. Some helicopters have datum located three feet or more in front of the skids. This arrangement makes all moments positive because all weights acting aft of datum produce a clockwise turning moment (which is positive).

Lateral datum is usually the butt line running through the center of the aircraft from nose to tail. To calculate lateral center of gravity position it is impossible to avoid positive and negative moments because various weight items are on either side of the butt line.

Beyond The Center of Gravity Limits

Excessive Forward Center of Gravity

The further forward the center of gravity, the further aft the required movement of cyclic to maintain a certain disc attitude. In the hover it may be impossible to hold a given position, especially when many helicopters have less aft cyclic than forward cyclic available.

A helicopter with a center of gravity beyond its forward limit may not be able to flare, requiring a greater landing distance (which may not be available). Worse still, it may become impossible to control the low nose attitude for a level-skid landing.

In most helicopters the fuel tank configuration is such that as fuel is used up the center of gravity moves forward. Pilots must ensure that when a flight is undertaken (especially one of long duration) the center of gravity remains within authorized limits for the entire flight. Any loading or unloading of passengers or cargo can cause the same problem. Preflight planning is essential.

Excessive Aft Center of Gravity

Forward cyclic is needed when the center of gravity is too far aft. When the pilot runs out of forward cyclic, the tail boom and tail rotor may strike the ground.

Assuming you are hovering into wind, the effect of the wind is more critical with a center of gravity beyond the aft limit than beyond the forward limit. In an excessive aft center of gravity situation, blow back (flap-back) caused by the wind requires forward cyclic, and this may already be at or near its forward limit. In an excessive forward center of gravity situation (cyclic aft), the same blow-back allows the rearward cyclic to be moved forward towards the neutral position, so the wind effect is not quite as bad.

Fuel burn, passenger or cargo loading all affect excessive rearward center of gravity position in similar fashion as excessive forward center of gravity position. Again, sound planning is essential.

Excessive Lateral Center of Gravity

Limits for lateral center of gravity are often quite small and, especially in the case of light helicopters, great care must be exercised to remain within lateral limits. Depending on fuel tank location, the pilot may have to occupy a seat on the opposite side when flying solo to ensure that lateral limits are not exceeded. (The pilot's operating handbook for the specific helicopter model being flown should always be obeyed.) The consequences of excessive lateral center of gravity are similar to those for longitudinal center of gravity.

Summary

The longitudinal and lateral center of gravity positions are both important for the safe operation of a helicopter. Thorough calculations must be made prior to flight to ensure that limits are not exceeded

Calculating the Center of Gravity Position

Determination of center of gravity position can be done using simple formulas.

Weight x Arm = Moment and

$$\frac{Total\ Moment}{Total\ Weight} = Center\ of\ Gravity\ position\ measured\ from\ datum$$

Using an example based on an imaginary helicopter, Figure 26-1, center of gravity positions can be calculated and plotted on the limit graphs of Figure 26-2. Weights are pounds, arms in inches and moments in inch-pounds.

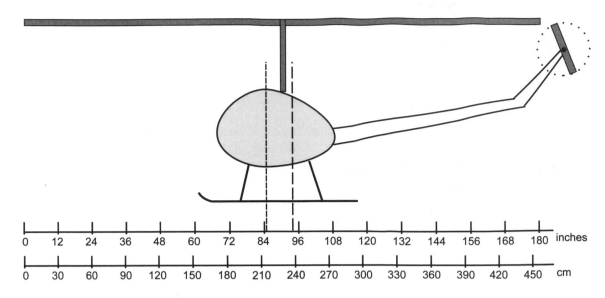

Figure 26-1. *Datum forward of the aircraft. Longitudinal forward limit 84.8"
(215.4 cm) and aft limit 94" (238.8 cm) behind datum. Lateral limits as shown
in Figure 26-2).*

In Figure 26-1 the datum is in front of the helicopter for longitudinal center
of gravity position, while the butt line through the mast is the datum for
lateral center of gravity position. Any weight applied at any station produces
a clockwise moment (positive) for longitudinal center of gravity calculations,
but positive and negative values have to be used for lateral center of gravity
calculations.

The following data apply to the imaginary helicopter concerned:

Item	Weight (lb)	Longitudinal Center of Gravity	Lateral Center of Gravity
Empty weight	1020	93.1	+ 0.3
Pilot	150	72.0	+12.2
Passenger	160	72.0	−12.1
Fuel, full tank	148	95.2	− 9.3
Maximum certificated gross weight	1480		

Assume for this example that the flight time is calculated at 2 hours 30
minutes at an average fuel consumption of 49 lb/hr (31 liters per hour).

First it is necessary to calculate all the moments for the longitudinal
center of gravity. Since all stations are aft of datum they all produce positive
moments:

Aircraft empty weight	1020	x	93.1	94962
Pilot & passenger weight	310	x	72.0	22320
Fuel weight	148	x	95.2	14089
Takeoff Gross Weight and Total Moment	1478			131371

To Calculate Longitudinal Center of Gravity Position

$$\frac{\text{Total Moment}}{\text{Total Weight}} \quad \frac{+131371}{1478} = \text{Center of gravity 88.8 inches aft of datum}$$

Transferring this information to Figure 26-2 on the next page, you can see that a horizontal line from 1478 pounds intersects a vertical line from 88.8 inches (A) inside the limit envelope, making the aircraft safe for takeoff from the point of view of longitudinal center of gravity.

For the landing phase, allowance must be made for a fuel burn of 2.5 hours at 49 lb/hr = 122.5 pounds. At that point the calculations are repeated:

Aircraft empty weight	1020	x 93.1	94962
Pilot & passenger weight	310	x 72.0	22320
Fuel weight	25.5	x 95.2	2427
Landing Gross Weight and Total Moment	1355.5		119709

$$\frac{\text{Total Moment}}{\text{Total Weight}} \quad \frac{+119709}{1355.5} = \text{Center of gravity 88.3 inches aft of datum}$$

This shows that the center of gravity has moved forward but is still well within allowable limits (Figure 26-2B).

To calculate the longitudinal center of gravity position if the pilot flies solo:

Aircraft empty weight	1020	x 93.1	94962
Pilot weight	150	x 72.0	10800
Fuel weight	148	x 95.2	14089
Takeoff Gross Weight and Total Moment	1318		119851

$$\frac{\text{Total Moment}}{\text{Total Weight}} \quad \frac{+119851}{1318} = \text{Center of gravity 90.9 inches aft of datum}$$

When this is plotted on the longitudinal limit graph it shows that the center of gravity is within limits (Figure 26-2C) and has moved rearward which makes sense because the passenger weight aft of datum has been deleted.

To Calculate the Lateral Takeoff Center of Gravity Position

Aircraft empty weight	1020	x	+0.3	+306
Pilot weight	150	x	+12.2	+1830
Passenger weight	160	x	−12.1	−1936
Fuel weight	148	x	−9.3	−1376
Takeoff Gross Weight and Total Moment	1478		+2136	−3312 = −1176

$$\frac{\text{Total Moment}}{\text{Total Weight}} \quad \frac{-1176}{1478} = \text{Center of gravity } -0.79 \text{ inches (left) of datum}$$

When this is plotted on the lateral center of gravity limit chart, Figure 26-2D), the lateral takeoff center of gravity is within its left limit.

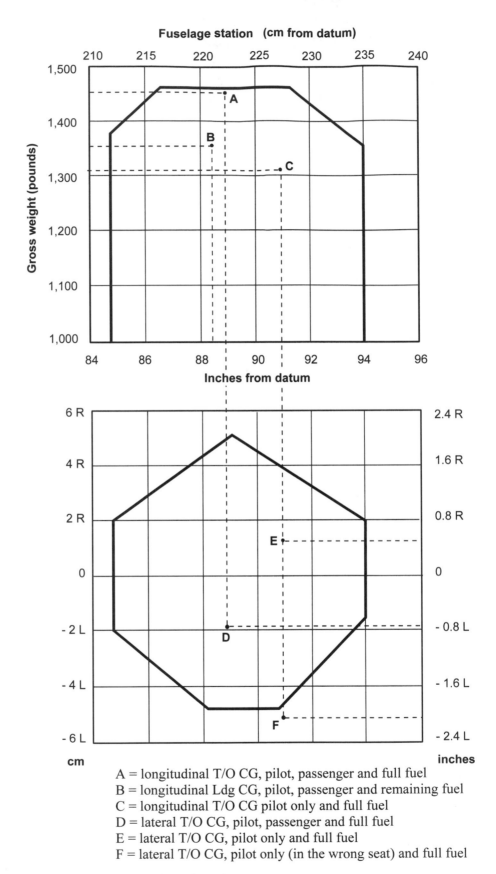

Figure 26-2. *Center of gravity limits.*

If the pilot flies solo from the right-hand seat and the remaining information is unaltered, calculations show:

Aircraft empty weight	1020	x	+0.3	+306	
Pilot weight	150	x	+12.2	+1830	
Fuel weight	148	x	−9.3		−1376
Takeoff Gross Weight and Total Moment	1318			+2136	−1376 = +760

$$\frac{\text{Total Moment}}{\text{Total Weight}} \quad \frac{+760}{1318} = \text{Center of gravity} +0.57 \text{ inches (right) of datum}$$

Again, this lateral center of gravity is within limits (Figure 26-2E).

When the pilot occupies the wrong seat and flies from the left:

Aircraft empty weight	1020	x	+0.3	+306	
Pilot weight	150	x	-12.1		−1815
Fuel weight	148	x	−9.3		−1376
Takeoff Gross Weight and Total Moment	1318			+306	−3191 − −2885

$$\frac{\text{Total Moment}}{\text{Total Weight}} \quad \frac{-2885}{1318} = \text{Center of gravity} -2.1 \text{ inches (left) of datum}$$

The lateral center of gravity is outside its left limit (Figure 26-2F), and the helicopter is unsafe for flight.

Summary

The foregoing calculations were kept as simple as possible and avoided using formulas that could have reduced the amount of work involved. All Flight Manuals contain tabulations for weight and balance such as the ones used in the above examples and all you need is a calculator to complete the information.

Effect of External Loads on Center of Gravity Position

If the hook attachment on the aircraft is positioned precisely beneath the center of gravity of a light helicopter, the slingload affects the gross weight of the aircraft, but not the longitudinal center of gravity position.

In many cases the hook attachment is positioned close vertically beneath the main rotor mast because that is where the center of gravity is often positioned. But fuel burn, passenger or freight configuration can shift the center of gravity away from the mast line and, in that case, the aircraft's attitude is affected by slingloads. For instance, it is common for the helicopter to adopt a rather unusual nose up or nose down attitude (depending on aircraft type) with a slingload attached when the fuel quantity becomes low.

When hoist loads are carried it is important that the maximum allowable hoist weight is not exceeded and that the weight distribution within the aircraft is such that lateral limits are not infringed.

Finally, in most large helicopters the vertical center of gravity position is invariably affected by slingloads.

In all three cases discussed in this section, longitudinal, lateral and vertical center of gravity positions and maximum allowable weights, it is important that you follow the manufacturer's instructions and government regulations for the aircraft you fly.

Conclusion

There are a number of formulas that are used to calculate the amount of weight to be offloaded, changed in position or added as ballast in order to keep the center of gravity within stipulated limits. These formulas and workings are beyond the scope of this book.

Although many pilots treat weight and balance on a "fly it and try it" basis, this is no substitute for thorough preflight planning. Most countries have explicit regulations concerning the calculation of aircraft weight and balance before flight. A pilot who does not figure weight and balance is flying illegally and recklessly. The helicopter may fly reasonably well under takeoff conditions, but landing may be a challenge after prolonged flights. A little time spent on the ground, calculating the center of gravity position(s) for the entire operation enhances the safety of any flight.

Review 26

Weight and Balance

1. To determine the center of gravity position of your helicopter you divide the total _____ by the total _____.

2. Your helicopter's center of gravity position is at its forward limit. Is this more critical or less critical than an aft center of gravity position, should you wish to hover in a headwind?

3. Your helicopter is at its maximum gross weight and fuel tanks are full. You calculate that the center of gravity position is near its forward limit. If the planned flight is likely to use most of the fuel on board, where will the center of gravity be at the end of the flight and how is this likely to affect the attitude of the helicopter during the hover prior to touch-down?

4. Use the information in Figures 26-1 and 26-2. The following details are given:

Item	Weight (lb)	Long CG	Lat CG
Empty weight	1080	89.8	+ 0.4
Pilot	145	71.0	+11.8
Passenger	125	71.0	−12.0
Fuel, full tank	126	94.6	− 6.8
Max. Certificated gross weight	1480		

Assume the flight is planned to take 1 hour 50 minutes at an average fuel consumption of 35 lb/hr.
Is the center of gravity within prescribed limits prior to takeoff, both longitudinally and laterally?

5. What is the center of gravity position on landing?

6. Is the gross takeoff weight within allowable limits?

Appendix 1

Practice Examination

Unless otherwise specified, all questions are based on a counterclockwise rotating rotor when viewed from above.

1. While in forward flight you jettison a sling load and maintain the same airspeed as before. Considering momentum and inertia of the helicopter, the result of your action is that:

    a. momentum remains constant but inertia reduces.

    b. inertia remains constant but momentum reduces.

    c. both momentum and inertia remain constant.

    d. both momentum and inertia reduce.

2. Which of the following combinations of atmospheric pressure, temperature and humidity is likely to cause the worst performance from your helicopter?

    a. Low pressure, high temperature, high humidity.

    b. Low pressure, low temperature, low humidity.

    c. High pressure, low temperature, low humidity.

    d. High pressure, high temperature, high humidity.

3. The lift coefficient of an airfoil is determined by its:

    a. shape and area.

    b. airspeed and angle of attack.

    c. shape and angle of attack.

    d. airspeed and area.

4. The airflow in tip vortices has an upward and a downward component. Which of these affects induced drag?

    a. Both.

    b. Neither.

    c. Only the downward component, as it increases downwash behind the blade.

    d. Only the upward component, as it serves to increase the angle of attack.

5.   The purpose of the "wash-out" design is to:

a.   increase the blade angle from root to tip in order to reduce angles of attack towards the tip sections.

b.   decrease the blade angle from root to tip in order to reduce angles of attack towards tip sections.

c.   increase the blade angle from root to tip in order to increase angles of attack towards tip sections.

d.   decrease the blade angle from root to tip in order to increase angles of attack towards tip sections.

6.   Consider the digram below. Which choice correctly identifies items 1 to 4 in the tabulated columns?

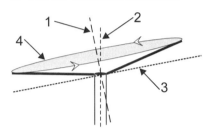

	1	2	3	4
a.	axis of rotation	shaft axis	plane of rotation	tip path
b.	shaft axis	axis of rotation	plane of rotation	tip path
c.	axis of rotation	shaft axis	tip path	plane of rotation
d.	shaft axis	tip path	plane of rotation	axis of rotation

7.   Examine the diagram below.

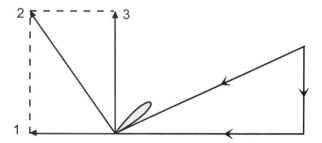

What happens to force 1 and force 3 if the inflow angle is reduced while the pilot maintains a constant angle of attack by lowering collective? (Assume rotor rpm constant.)

a.   Force 1 increases while force 3 decreases.

b.   Force 1 decreases while force 3 increases.

c.   Both force 1 and force 3 increase.

d.   Both force 1 and force 3 decrease.

8. The helicopter shown in the diagram below will enter ground effect as it very slowly moves towards the landing site. The pilot makes no adjustment to the collective lever position as ground effect is entered. Which of the following choices correctly states changes to induced flow, angles of attack and aircraft height over the landing site?

Landing site

a. Induced flow will increase, angles of attack will decrease and the helicopter will sink towards the ground.

b. Induced flow will increase, angles of attack will increase and the helicopter will rise.

c. Induced flow will decrease, angles of attack will increase and the helicopter will rise.

d. Induced flow will decrease, angles of attack will decrease and the helicopter will sink towards the ground.

9. This question is based on a helicopter which has the rotor rotating clockwise when viewed from above.

If the engine fails when you are proceeding at a skid height of 5 feet towards the takeoff area, what pedal and cyclic inputs should you make to avoid touching down sideways?

a. Left pedal and right cyclic.

b. Left pedal and left cyclic.

c. Right pedal and left cyclic.

d. Right pedal and right cyclic.

10. Consider the swashplate assembly in the diagram on the right. How does the assembly respond, and what happens to total rotor thrust, when you lower the collective lever?

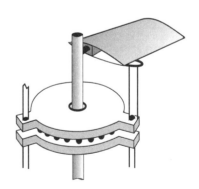

a. both stars go down, total rotor thrust increases and tilts in a different direction.

b. both stars go up, total rotor thrust decreases and tilts in a different direction.

c. both stars go down, total rotor thrust decreases.

d. both stars go up, total rotor thrust decreases.

11. You are in the hover when the wind changes from calm to 6 knots crosswind from your right. To maintain a constant heading and position and without changing power, you require right cyclic and:

a. less left pedal, the helicopter tends to descend.

b. more left pedal, the helicopter tends to climb.

c. less left pedal, the helicopter tends to climb.

d. more left pedal, the helicopter tends to descend.

12. This question relates to a helicopter fitted with a clockwise rotating rotor.

    When flying sideways to your right, the blade will flap down at the greatest rate when it is:

    a.   over the nose.

    b.   on your right.

    c.   over the tail.

    d.   on your left.

13. You maintain a constant indicated airspeed of 5 knots while flying straight and level in a 20 knot tailwind (thus your groundspeed is 25 knots). Under these conditions, will you have the benefit of translational lift?

    a.   Yes, any speed over approximately 15 knots provides translational lift benefits.

    b.   Yes, provided the wind strength remains constant.

    c.   No, any tailwind rules out translational lift benefits.

    d.   No, translational lift is dependent on airspeed.

14. Considering range and endurance, when you fly into a headwind while maintaining the appropriate true airspeed for each:

    a.   range is reduced but endurance is not affected.

    b.   endurance is reduced but range is not affected;

    c.   both range and endurance are reduced.

    d.   neither range nor endurance are affected.

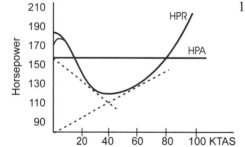

15. The horsepower required (HPR) and horsepower available (HPA) curves shown on the left apply to your piston engine helicopter.

    Which choice correctly identifies the information that can be deduced from the graphs during a climb?

    a.   The rate of climb will be maximum at 40 knots, and the angle of climb will be the steepest possible at 28 knots.

    b.   The rate of climb will be maximum at 40 knots and the angle of climb will be the steepest possible at 40 knots.

    c.   The rate of climb will be maximum at 60 knots and the angle of climb will be the steepest possible at 28 knots.

    d.   The rate of climb will be maximum at 40 knots and the angle of climb can be vertical (at 0 knots).

16. Identical helicopters A and B are flying straight and level in a narrow valley. A is at maximum gross weight and B is lighter. Both helicopters fly at the same airspeed. If the helicopters need to turn 180° and do so in level flight and at identical angles of bank, how does the rate and radius of turn of A compare to that of B?

    a.   A and B will have the same rate and radius of turn.

    b.   A will have a larger radius and less rate of turn than B.

    c.   A will have the same radius but less rate of turn than B.

    d.   A will have the same rate of turn but a larger radius than B.

17. The nose of your helicopter pitches up when you experience retreating blade stall. If you use forward cyclic to arrest the pitch-up:

    a.   the pitch angle of the advancing blade will increase and the stall will spread to the advancing blade.

    b.   the pitch angle of the retreating blade will decrease and the pitch-up will become worse.

    c.   the pitch angle of the blade over the nose will increase and the pitch-up will become worse

    d.   the pitch angle of the retreating blade will increase and a larger section of the retreating blade will enter the stall.

18. Which of the three helicopters below shows the correct relationship between gross weight and total rotor thrust (TRT) during a vertical autorotation at a constant rate of descent?

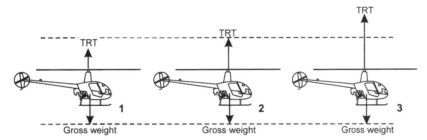

    a.   1

    b.   2

    c.   3

19. You are flying at the speed for maximum endurance during an autorotation and realize you may not be able to reach your planned landing site. How can you improve your prospects of reaching the site?

    a.   Increase your airspeed to fly for range and accept a slightly increased rate of descent.

    b.   Decrease your airspeed to reduce your rate of descent and improve your range.

    c.   Increase your airspeed to fly for range and benefit from a reduced rate of descent.

    d.   Decrease your airspeed to fly for range, this will not alter the rate of descent.

20. Your instinctive reaction when vortex ring state develops is to raise collective in an effort to reduce the rate of descent. This will cause the rate of descent to increase because:

   a. the stall spreads out further from the blade roots, and tip vortex intensity is likely to increase.

   b. the increased pitch angles will stall the blade tips so that both the inner and outer sections of the blades are stalled.

   c. the stall spreads further inward from the blade tips towards the unstalled inner sections of the blades.

   d. the added power with up-collective will decrease the induced flow and cause the stall to spread inward from the blade tips.

21. When crossing a mountain ridge in a two-blade helicopter you push cyclic firmly forward and the aircraft rolls to the right. Your immediate actions should be to:

   a. stop the roll by using left cyclic, and simultaneously raise the collective lever.

   b. restore total rotor thrust by loading the disc with gentle use of aft cyclic before using lateral cyclic.

   c. lower the collective lever and simultaneously roll the disc level with gentle use of left cyclic.

   d. restore total rotor thrust by unloading the disc with gentle use of forward cyclic and then use left cyclic.

22. The helicopter in the diagram above is:

   a. Statically stable and dynamically unstable.

   b. Statically unstable and dynamically unstable.

   c. Statically stable and dynamically stable.

   d. Statically unstable and dynamically unstable.

23. You are on approach for a zero-speed landing on a small landing site. When about 200 feet agl, and with the airspeed reducing to 20 knots, you have to use full permissible power to prevent the rate of descent from increasing. At this stage you should:

   a. continue the approach as planned.

   b. flare the helicopter so as to reduce the rate of descent.

   c. maintain translational lift until you enter ground effect.

   d. discontinue the approach.

24. The fundamental purpose of the offset flapping hinge design is to:

   a.   permit greater freedom for the blades to flap and feather.

   b.   encourage the fuselage to remain more or less parallel with the main rotor disc.

   c.   reduce the tendency for the fuselage to remain parallel with the main rotor disc.

   d.   alter the pitch angle of the blades when the blades flap up or down.

25. Examine the diagram below which shows a helicopter about to touch down on a slope affected by an anabatic wind.

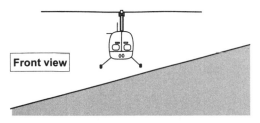

   Would the pilot have more into-slope cyclic available touching down on the left skid as shown or would touching down on the right skid provide more into-slope cyclic?

   a.   Touching down on the left skid provides for more into-slope cyclic.

   b.   Touching down on the right skid provides for more into-slope cyclic.

   c.   The amount of into-slope cyclic available will be the same touching down on the left or the right skid.

   d.   With an anabatic wind it would be better to touch down on both skids facing uphill.

26. You plan to land on a high altitude site using the same approach profile and distance, the same disc attitude, and starting with the same indicated airspeed, as you would employ when approaching a low altitude site. Assuming identical weather conditions, it is almost certain that:

   a.   you will reach the pre-touchdown flare height short of the landing site.

   b.   your airspeed will decay more rapidly.

   c.   you will need to flare more harshly prior to touch-down.

   d.   your angle of approach will be steeper.

27. During flight in light rain you note that the outside air temperature gauge shows +1°C (34°F). Does this mean that there is a risk of ice forming on the rotor blades?

    a. Yes, the reduced pressure above the blades can lower the temperature there to below the freezing point.

    b. No, there is no risk of icing whenever the outside air temperature is above the freezing point.

    c. Yes, rain will normally turn to ice when the temperature approaches the freezing point.

    d. No, rain will remain supercooled liquid to temperatures well below the freezing point.

28. Based on the instrument readings below, which choice correctly states the pressure altitude and the density altitude?

	Pressure altitude	Density altitude
a.	2,790 feet	3,510 feet
b.	3,000 feet	3,720 feet
c.	3,210 feet	3,930 feet
d.	3,210 feet	3,510 feet

29. Use the Hover Ceiling graph below.

What is the maximum elevation the helicopter can hover out of ground effect (OGE) if the gross weight is 2,500 pounds, the sea level temperature is +20°C and the sea level pressure (QNH) is 1028 hPa (30.36 in.Hg)?

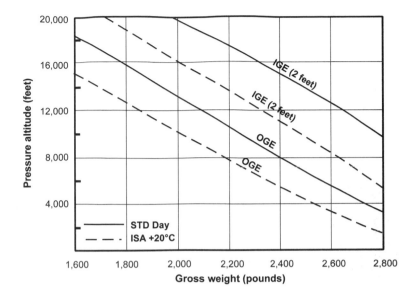

30. Use the following Weight & Balance data and the center of gravity envelope published in the aircraft Flight Manual (see next page).

Item	Weight Pounds	Longitudinal Center of Gravity	Lateral Center of Gravity
Empty weight	1150	90.5	+0.4
Pilot	185	74.8	+11.7
Passenger	190	74.8	−11.4
Fuel full tank	165	94.6	−8.8
Max certificated Gross weight	1800		

a. What is the longitudinal center of gravity position?

b. Is the longitudinal center of gravity within published limits?

c. What is the lateral center of gravity position?

d. Is the lateral center of gravity within published limits?

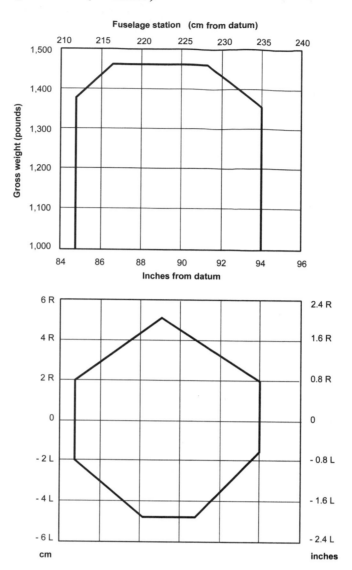

Principles of Helicopter Flight

Appendix 2

Temperature Conversion

Degrees Fahrenheit to Degrees Celsius

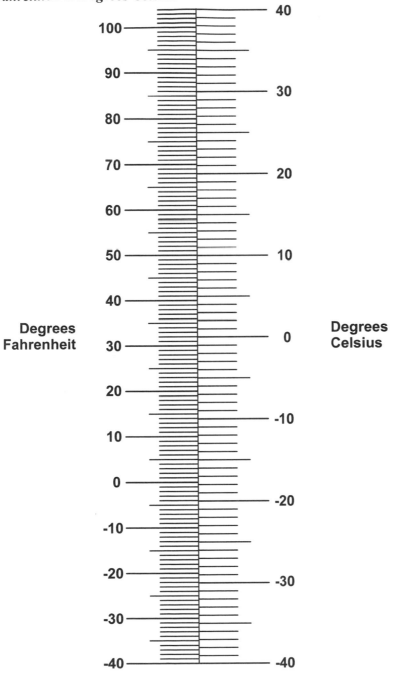

Principles of Helicopter Flight

Appendix **3**

Altimeter Setting Conversion

Hectopascals (hPa) to Inches of Mercury (in.Mg)

hPa (mb)	0	1	2	3	4	5	6	7	8	9
	Inches Mercury									
970	28.64	28.67	28.70	28.73	28.76	28.79	28.82	28.85	28.88	28.91
980	28.94	28.97	29.00	29.03	29.05	29.08	29.11	29.14	29.17	29.20
990	29.23	29.26	29.29	29.32	29.35	29.38	29.41	29.44	29.47	29.50
1000	29.53	29.56	29.59	29.62	29.65	29.68	29.71	29.74	29.77	29.80
1010	29.83	29.86	29.89	29.92	29.95	29.97	30.00	30.03	30.06	30.09
1020	30.12	30.15	30.18	30.21	30.24	30.27	30.30	30.33	30.36	30.39
1030	30.42	30.45	30.47	30.50	30.53	30.56	30.59	30.62	30.65	30.68
1040	30.71	30.74	30.77	30.80	30.83	30.86	30.89	30.92	30.95	30.98

Examples

1017 hPa = 30.03 in.Hg

29.65 in.Hg = 1004 hPa

Principles of Helicopter Flight

Appendix 4

Review and Examination Answers

Review 1

1. mass, do not
2. does not, increases
3. greater
4. is, direction
5. are, is not
6. does not, weaker, less
7. greater
8. two, rotation
9. increased
10. quadruples

Review 2

1. pressure, temperature, moisture
2. weight, datum
3. reduces, reduce
4. from below
5. decreases, increase
6. decrease
7. 29.92 (1013.2), 59 (15), 3.5 (1.98)
8. high, low, low, good

Review 3

1. chord line, plane of rotation
2. blade (or pitch) angle, feathering
3. total reaction
4. acting at right angles, parallel
5. decreases, streamlined
6. the same
7. shape and angle of attack
8. C_{Lmax}, stalling
9. chord line, aerodynamic forces
10. remains steady
11. aerodynamic center

Review 4

1. shape, angle of attack, zero
2. parasite, profile, induced
3. nine
4. shaping
5. boundary, retarded, relative airflow
6. thin, little, is
7. thick, much, is not
8. transition

9. increases, forward, thickens
10. pressure, directly
11. decreases, increases
12. decrease
13. decreases, blade angle
14. high, decreases, increases

Review 5

1. as small as possible
2. cannot
3. improves, closer to
4. shape, angle of attack
5. small
6. is not, minimum

Review 6

1. rotor head, right angles
2. tip path plane, is not, coning
3. gross weight, disc area
4. vertical, plane of rotation
5. forward/aft, plane of rotation
6. does not, lead-lagging
7. two, lead-lagging
8. rotation, induced flow, aircraft speed
9. always, plane of rotation
10. most of which
11. increases, decrease
12. component, cannot
13. in line with, axis of rotation
14. total rotor thrust
15. plane of rotation, decrease
16. improves, less
17. best, low
18. greater, worse
19. increase, increase, power
20. less, easier, less quickly

Review 7

1. larger, smaller
2. symmetrical, on, feather
3. wash-out, decrease
4. wash-out, lift
5. long, high
6. higher, higher

Review 8

1. increased, increase, deterioration
2. more
3. smaller, smaller, decreased
4. decreases, increase, climb
5. the same, smaller, less
6. angles of attack, increase

Review 9

1. directly
2. yaw, left, increased, right
3. right, right, left
4. main rotor
5. decreased, less
6. decrease, increased
7. left, left
8. strong, high, low
9. tilted, left
10. decreasing, rolling tendency
11. more, more difficult, does not
12. yaw, right, decrease

Review 10

1. fall, increases
2. will, will not
3. will not, tilt, individual blades, blade angle
4. stationary, rotating
5. increase, less
6. in towards, increase, forward Coriolis
7. angles of attack

Review 11

1. greater, higher
2. less, the same
3. higher
4. reduced
5. roll, to the right
6. higher, higher
7. increase, increase, reduce
8. less, increase, translational, abandon

Review 12

1. thrust, parasite drag, vertical, weight
2. weight, parasite drag, gravity
3. smallest, do not
4. tail
5. greater, less, retreating
6. flapping, decreases, angle of attack
7. smallest, smallest
8. flapping, dissymmetry of lift
9. retreating, are not
10. climb, translational lift
11. low, greater, roll, advancing side

Review 13

1. lowest, includes
2. increasing, weight
3. parasite
4. decreases, increases, increases
5. increases, up
6. drag, tangent
7. higher, reduced
8. reduced, increased
9. is not, bottom
10. does not, should not
11. drag, power

Review 14

1. the same as
2. increases
3. is not
4. decrease, shallower
5. is, is not
6. cannot
7. will not, steeper
8. increasing, equal to
9. decreased, decrease
10. will not, steeper
11. decreases, greater

Review 15

1. total rotor thrust, tilted
2. three, second
3. increase, steeper
4. $(6 + 7) = 13°$
5. less, smaller
6. steeper, greater
7. total rotor thrust, increases
8. two, greater, weight
9. greater, power, induced drag
10. less, shallower
11. the same, the same
12. tail, nose

Review 16

1. rearward, upward, height
2. decreases, below
3. smaller, increase, climb
4. increase, greater, coning, towards, increases
5. lowered, right, raising, left
6. will not, decay

Review 17

1. retreating, greater, increased, down
2. tip
3. roughness, vibration, up, rolls
4. is not, increases
5. decreases, increases, worse
6. high, high, turbulent
7. decreases, lower, high
8. lower

Review 18

1. decay, reduced, lowering
2. disengage, retard
3. down, left
4. roots, large, against
5. tips, poor, against
6. in the middle of the blades, in the direction of
7. high, decreases, increase
8. retreating, advancing
9. increase, bottom
10. increased, increase
11. collective
12. high, high, steep
13. greater, increased, moist

Review 19

1. vibration, shake, powered, increasing, low
2. is not, higher, expand
3. cyclic, airspeed
4. right
5. settling with power, high, high, below
6. immediately, lower, reduce, rotor
7. brake, quickly
8. lower, smoothly
9. right
10. load, aft, do not, increased

Review 20

1. engine, reduction, less
2. freewheeling, disengages
3. serious, essential

4. 90° in the direction of
5. in the same direction as
6. reduces, feathers
7. lower collective
8. engine driven fan
9. restricts, axis of rotation

Review 21

1. stable, unstable
2. static
3. stable, unstable, unstable, cannot
4. pitching, lateral, rolling, longitudinal, yawing, normal
5. instability, an increasing
6. dynamic, negative
7. can, fore-aft
8. stable, stable
9. cyclic, most, least
10. do, wider

Review 22

1. left, right, right
2. rearward, forward, rearward
3. settling with power
4. more
5. angle of climb, normal
6. abandon, will not, arrest (or reduce)
7. uphill
8. is not
9. must, swivel
10. longer, 15, 10 pounds (5 kilograms), lower
11. decrease, opposite
12. lift, on top of

Review 23

1. increased, decreased, decrease, rise
2. before, oblique
3. decrease
4. lee, severe
5. downwind, updrafts, smaller
6. more difficult, later
7. over
8. should not, diminished, swirling

Review 24

1. can, reduced, lower
2. clear, rime
3. major, ground resonance
4. middle, driving, may not
5. clear of, kinetic, high
6. quicker, slower
7. is, will, ice

1. 2,500 feet
2. Sea level pressure high, pressure altitude. is low. 30.03 - 29.92 = 0.11 x 1000 = 110 feet. 4,500 - 110 = press. alt 4,390 feet
3. 29.92 (1013), re-set the subscale, sea level pressure
4. Sea level pressure equals standard value, thus 2,500 feet is also the pressure altitude. At 2,500 feet, ISA temperature is 15 - (2x2.5) = 15 - 5 = 10°C. The reported temperature is +21°C which is 11° warmer than in the standard atmosphere = ISA+11. 11 x 120 = 1320 and since warmer temperature gives higher density altitude it follows that density altitude = 2,500 + 1,320 = 3,820 feet.
5. Pressure altitude = 1,200 feet which is 300 feet lower than elevation of 1,500 feet, thus sea level pressure is greater than 29.92 in.Hg. 300 feet = 0.3 in.Hg. Thus Kollsman window should show 29.92 + 0.3 = 30.22 (= 1023 hPa)
6. Pressure altitude = 1,200 feet where the temperature should be 15 - (2 x 1) = 13°C. The actual temperature is +28°C = ISA+15. 15 x 120 = 1,800, up. Thus density altitude is 1,200 + 1,800 = 3,000 feet.
7. Moisture makes density altitude higher still, thus take-off performance will be strongly degraded.
8. 20 knots means you still have translational lift. Since you are using maximum power simply to hold altitude it follows that you will be unable to hold height when airspeed reduces below translation. Thus you cannot hover out of ground effect over the site.
9. First calculate pressure altitude. Pressure is low = pressure altitude high. 29.92 - 29.62 = 0.3 = 300 feet. 8,800 + 300 = pressure altitude 9,100 feet. Draw this value horizontally on the graph. Estimate the ISA+8 (OGE) line and where this crosses the horizontal line you just drew, draw a line vertically down. It crosses the x-leg at about 2300 pounds. Your actual gross weight of 2,450 pounds is too heavy for the conditions and so you cannot do the flight and hover out of ground effect at the landing site with the current gross weight.

Review 26

1. moment, weight
2. Less critical. You need back cyclic to allow for the forward centre of gravity. Thus you have plenty of available cyclic to compensate for a headwind. With the centre of gravity at its aft limit you need forward cyclic and less cyclic movement is available to compensate for a headwind.
3. Center of gravity usually moves forward as fuel is used up. Thus on landing the center of gravity may well be at or near its forward limit and the helicopter will have a nose-down attitude during the hover prior to landing.
4. Taking the above information to the loading envelope it shows that, on takeoff, the longitudinal center of gravity at 86.7 inches aft (A) is within limits. Similarly, the lateral center of gravity position at 0.14 inches left (B) is within limits.
5. On landing, the longitudinal center of gravity at 86.4 inches aft (C) is within limits and note, this confirms that using fuel in flight moves the center of gravity forward. The lateral center of gravity has moved to the right side of the butt line and at 0.15 right (D) is also within limits.
6. The gross weight on takeoff at 1,476 pounds is within limits by 4 pounds.

Take-off –
Longitudinal center of gravity

1080	x	89.8	=	96984
145	x	71	=	10295
125	x	71	=	8875
126	x	94.6	=	11919
1476				128073

$\dfrac{128073}{1476}$ = 86.7 inches aft

Take-off –
Lateral center of gravity

1080	x	+0.4	=	+432
145	x	+11.8	=	+1711
125	x	-12.0	=	-1500
126	x	-6.8	=	- 856
1476			+2143	-2356
		=		-213

$\dfrac{-213}{1476}$ = 0.14 inches left

Landing –
Longitudinal center of gravity

1080	x	89.8	=	96984
145	x	71	=	10295
125	x	71	–	8875
62	x	94.6	=	5865
1412				122019

$\dfrac{122019}{1412}$ = 86.4 inches aft

Landing –
Lateral center of gravity

1080	x	+0.4	=	+ 432
145	x	+11.8	=	+1711
125	x	-12	=	-1500
62	x	- 6.8	=	- 421
1412			+2143	-1921
		=		+222

$\dfrac{+ 222}{1412}$ = 0.15 inches right

Review 26 (continued)

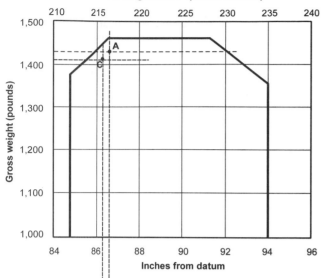

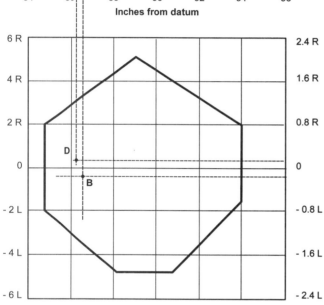

Question 29 - Hover ceiling graph

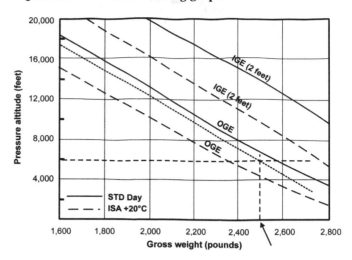

Question 30 - Center of gravity envelope

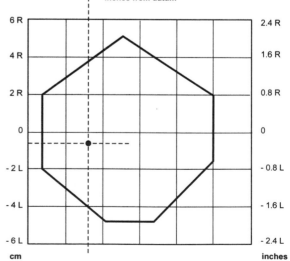

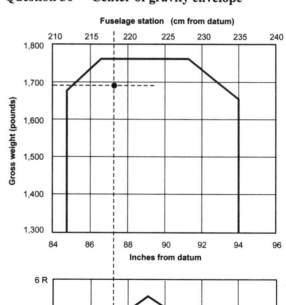

Answers to Practice Examination questions

1.	d.	page 1	18.	b.	page 146
2.	a.	page 13	19.	a.	page 150
3.	c.	page 19	20.	a.	page 161
4.	c.	page 31	21.	b.	page 169
5.	b.	page 33	22.	c.	page 196
6.	a.	page 43	23.	d.	page 207
7.	b.	page 50	24.	b.	page 201
8.	c.	page 50, 63	25.	b.	page 224, 207
9.	b.	page 70	26.	c.	page 231
10.	d.	page 77, 177	27.	a.	page 237
11.	d.	page 68	28.	c.	page 244, 246
12.	c.	page 93	29.		6,300 ft ± 300 ft
13.	d.	page 100			page 252
14.	a.	page 110, 111	30a.		87.4 inches aft
15.	a.	page 115	30b.		Yes
16.	a.	page 128	30c.		− 0.58 (left)
17.	d.	page 139			

Glossary

Advancing blade. -- The blade in that half of the rotor disc where rotation is in the same direction as the movement of the helicopter. If the helicopter is moving forward, the advancing blade will be in the right half of the rotor disc; if moving backward, it will be in the left half; if moving sideward to the left, it will be in the forward half; and if moving sideward to the right, it will be in the rear half. Reverse these regions for clockwise rotating rotors.

Airfoil. -- Any surface designed to obtain a useful reaction from the air through which it moves.

Angle of Attack. -- The angular difference between the chord of the blade and the relative air flow.

Anti-torque pedals. -- The foot pedals used by the helicopter pilot to control the pitch of the anti-torque rotor (tail rotor) of a single rotor helicopter. The anti-torque pedals allow the pilot to control movement of the helicopter (yaw) about its vertical axis.

Aspect ratio. -- The ratio of length of a helicopter blade (its span) to the width (its chord).The aspect ratio of a tapered blade is found by dividing the square of the blade's span by its total area.

Axis of rotation. -- The line through the rotor head at right angles to the plane of rotation. The blades rotate around this axis.

Blade Angle. -- The angular difference between the chord of the blade and the plane of rotation. This angle may be altered by the pilot through movement of the collective control lever or through the cyclic control. Blade angle is also known as pitch angle.

Blade Area. -- The total area of all the rotor blades of a helicopter. Blade area is a constant for each helicopter.

Blade damper. -- A device (spring, friction, or hydraulic) installed on the vertical (lead-lag, or drag) hinge to diminish or dampen blade oscillation (hunting) around this hinge.

Blade loading. -- The load placed on the rotor blades of a helicopter, determined by dividing the gross weight of the helicopter by the combined area of all the rotor blades.

Center of gravity. -- The imaginary point at which the total weight of a body can be considered to be concentrated and to act through.

Center of pressure. -- The imaginary point on the chord line through which the resultant of all aerodynamic forces on an airfoil can be considered to act.

Centripetal force. -- The force required to make a body follow a curved path. It acts towards the center of the curve.

Chord (line).--The straight line between the blade's leading edge and its trailing edge.

Coefficient of lift (C_L), also referred to as lift coefficient. -- The dimensionless number representing the lifting ability of an airfoil. The coefficient of lift (or lift coefficient) is determined mainly by the airfoil's shape and angle of attack.

Collective pitch control. -- The method of control by which the pitch angle of all rotor blades is varied equally and simultaneously. The collective pitch control lever can be moved up, down or held steady by the pilot to control total rotor thrust.

Coning Angle. -- The angular difference between the blade's feathering axis and the plane of rotation or tip path plane.

Coriolis effect. -- The tendency of a mass to increase or decrease its angular velocity when its radius of rotation is shortened or lengthened, respectively.

Cyclic pitch control. -- The control which changes the pitch angle of the rotor blades individually during a cycle of revolution to control the tilt of the rotor disc, and therefore, the direction and velocity of flight. The pilot exercises cyclic pitch control via fore/aft/left/right movements of the upright cyclic stick.

Density altitude. -- Pressure altitude corrected for standard atmosphere temperature deviation.

Disc area. -- The area of the tip path plane, which is swept by the blades of the rotor. The tip path is a circle with its center at the hub. The coning angle of the blade influences the disc area.

Disc loading. -- The gross weight of the helicopter divided by the disc area, expressed as lb/sq inches or kg/m2. Since the disc area is not a constant in flight, it follows that disc loading is not a constant.

Dissymmetry of lift. -- The unequal lift (or rotor thrust) across the rotor disc resulting from the difference in the velocity of air over the advancing blade half and retreating blade half of the rotor disc area.

Drag coefficient (CD).-- The dimensionless number which represents the drag characteristics of an aerodynamic body. The drag coefficient of an airfoil is determined mainly by its shape and angle of attack.

Feathering. -- The movement of the blade about its feathering axis (which results in pitch angle changes).

Feathering Axis. -- The straight-line axis between the root of the blade and its tip, about which the blade can alter its blade (or pitch) angle.

Fineness Ratio. -- the thickness of the airfoil as a percentage of its chord length.

Flapping. -- Movement of a blade in the vertical sense relative to the plane of rotation.

Flapping Hinge.-- The hinge with its axis parallel to the rotor plane of rotation, which permits the rotor blades to flap up or down to equalize lift (or rotor thrust) between the advancing blade half and retreating blade half of the rotor disc.

Freewheeling unit. -- A component part of the transmission or power train which automatically disconnects the main rotor from the engine when the engine stops or slows below the equivalent of rotor rpm.

Fully articulated rotor. -- A common system for most rotors with more than two blades that allows the blades to flap, feather and lead/lag (drag or hunt), usually through hinges or bearings.

Ground effect. -- A beneficial gain in lifting power when operating near the surface - caused by the rotor downwash field being altered from its free air state by the presence of the surface.

Gyroscopic precession. -- A characteristic of all rotating bodies. When a force is applied to a rotating body parallel to its axis of rotation, the rotating body will tilt in the direction of the applied force 90 degrees later in the plane of rotation.

Hovering in ground effect. -- Hovering at such an altitude (usually less than one rotor diameter above the surface) so that the influence of ground effect is realized.

Hunting. -- The tendency of a blade to oscillate (or "hunt") ahead of or behind a position which would be determined by centrifugal force alone.

Induced flow. -- The mass of air forced down by rotor action. Most of the induced flow passes through the rotor disc.

International Standard Atmosphere (ISA). -- See Standard atmosphere

Lateral axis. -- The straight line axis at right angles to the fuselage around which the helicopter can pitch its nose up or down. Lateral axis is also known as pitch axis.

Lead-lag (dragging). -- Movement of a blade forward or aft in the plane of rotation. Lead-lag is facilitated by a lead-lag (or drag) hinge in the rotor system or through rubber-like bearings that allow individual rotor blades to move back and forth in their plane of rotation, which minimizes vibration. The drag brace resists the movement of the blade around its lead-lag hinge on a semirigid rotor system.

Longitudinal axis. -- The straight line axis from the nose of the helicopter to its tail about which the aircraft can roll left or right. Longitudinal axis is also known as roll axis.

Normal axis. -- the axis at right angles to the lateral and longitudinal axes. The helicopter can yaw around this axis. Normal axis is also known as the yaw axis or the vertical axis (to the other axes).

Pitch angle. -- See Blade angle.

Pitch axis. See lateral axis.

Pitching. --Movement of the helicopter about its lateral (or pitch) axis. Forward and aft movement of the cyclic control causes the nose of the helicopter to move down or up respectively, pivoting around the pitch, or lateral, axis.

Relative (or Resultant) airflow (RAF). -- The velocity vector of the airflow approaching the blades. The relative airflow is dependent on a number of component flows, e.g. induced flow, flow due to rotor rpm, and others.

Retreating blade stall. -- The stalled condition of the retreating blade when it operates beyond its critical (stall) angle. The condition is generally (but not only) associated with high speed flight.

Rigid rotor. -- A rotor system with blades fixed to the hub in such a way that they can feather but cannot flap or lead-lag (drag). Lead-lag and flapping stresses are absorbed either within the blades, in rubber-like bearings at the hub, or through other means.

Rotor brake. -- a brake that is engaged to stop the rotation of the rotor blades when the engine is being shut down on the ground.

Roll axis. -- See longitudinal axis

Semirigid rotor. -- A rotor system in which the blades are fixed to the hub, generally by a teetering (see-saw) hinge, allowing blades to flap and feather but not lead-lag (drag).

Shaft axis. -- The line consistent with the rotor shaft (mast). Only when the plane of rotation is exactly perpendicular to the shaft axis will the axis of rotation coincide with the shaft axis.

Solidity. -- The ratio of total blade area to disc area. Solidity is a function of the blade's ability to absorb power from the engine and potential to provide rotor thrust.

Standard atmosphere. -- Atmospheric conditions in which it is assumed that:
1. the air is a dry, perfect gas;
2. the temperature at sea level is 59°F. (15°C.);
3. the pressure at sea level (or reduced to sea level) is 29.92 inches of Hg (1013 hPa); and
4. the temperature gradient is approximately 3.5° F. (1.98°C.) per 1,000-foot change in altitude. Standard Atmosphere is also known as the International Standard Atmosphere (ISA).

Tip path. -- The circular path described by the tips of the rotor blades.

Tip path plane. -- The plane within which the tips of rotor blades travel. It is parallel to the plane of rotation, which acts through the rotor head. A pilot may alter this plane through movement of the cyclic control.

Tip speed. -- The rotational speed of the rotor at its blade tips.

Torque. -- The moment of a force or combination of forces that tends to produce rotational motion.

Translational lift. -- The additional lift (or rotor thrust) obtained through airspeed because of increased efficiency of the rotor system, whether it be when transitioning from a hover into forward flight or when hovering in a wind.

Velocity (V). -- True Air Speed (TAS), the speed at which the airfoil flies through the air. Ignoring aircraft speed, in helicopter terms V represents the rotor rpm because it is the angular velocity of the blade that determines the speed at which the air passes each given section of the blade. (Velocity appears in many formulas as a squared function, ie V^2)

Wash-out. -- a design that decreases the blade angle from root to tip by twisting it, which maintains the associated angle of attack or, in many cases, reduces it. Wash-out controls the coefficient of lift from root to tip to ensure even, or controlled, lift production throughout the length of the blade.

Yaw. -- Movement of the aircraft around its normal (or vertical) axis.

Yaw axis. -- See normal axis.

Index

ground effect, 61 - 62, 81 - 83, 100, 207, 209, 235
ground resonance, 162 - 164, 192, 236
groundspeed, 109, 120, 135, 233
gyroscopic inertia, 173
gyroscopic precession, 91, 177

headwind, effect on
    angle of climb, 118
    angle of descent, 121
    rate of climb, 118
    rate of descent, 121
hectopascals, 7
height/velocity charts, 154, 207
helicopter vibrations, 181
high density altitude, 81, 115, 132, 139, 160, 224
high frequency vibrations, 183, 184
high inertia blades, 54, 170
Hiller stabilizing system, 187
Hookes joint effect, 79
horizontal stabilizer, 135
horsepower available, 83, 114 - 117, 251
    angle of climb and, 116
    lowering, effect of, 116 - 117
    rate of climb and, 116
horsepower required, 83, 105, 107
    endurance and, 111
    range and, 108
    total horsepower required curve, 105 - 107
hover, 34, 68, 74, 100, 133, 199, 206
    ceiling, 14
    height, 82
    in ground effect, 81
    power, 81
    turn, 68, 162
humidity, 11
hydraulic systems, 143

IAS, 21, 230
IAS/TAS relationship, 231
ice, 163
ice accretion, 239
ice crystals, 239
icing
    in freezing rain, 240
    mechanical flexion and, 241
    orographic causes for, 240
    shape of airfoils and, 240
    in thunderstorms, 240
in ground effect, 63, 100
inches of mercury, 7

induced drag, 28, 31 - 35, 41, 57, 126
induced flow, 2, 34, 41, 82, 84, 85, 126, 134, 160, 205, 223
    airspeed, effect of, 47 - 48
    climbing and, 113
    descending and, 118
    directional stability and, 201
    horizontal flow, 99
    in ground effect, 62 - 63
    induced power and, 104
    lift coefficient, effect of, 32
    perpendicular flow, 99
    rotor drag, effect on, 61
    rotor thrust/rotor drag ratio and, 50 - 51, 65
    translational lift and, 64, 99 - 100
    in vortex ring state, 157
induced power, 104, 105, 107
inertia, 1, 2, 6, 10, 55
inflow angle, 50 - 51, 61, 99, 105, 113, 134, 150
    in autorotation, 149
    climbing and, 113
    descending and, 118
    in ground effect, 62 - 64
    power and, 104
    rotor drag, effect on, 61
    updrafts/downdrafts, effect of, 223
inflow roll, 101
in-ground effect, 106
in-ground effect hover ceiling, 84
International Standard Atmosphere, 12, 246, 248
inversion, 225
ISA deviation, 249

katabatic wind, 226
kinetic heating, 240 - 241
Kollsman window, 246

lateral axis, 199
lateral center of gravity, 271
lateral stability, 200, 202
lateral vibrations, 183

lead-lag, 44, 71
    damper, 163
    hinge, 78, 162, 188
    tendencies, 188
leaning (of mixture), 115
lift, 48, 53, 92
    basic concept, 15 - 16
    envelope, 22, 59
    formula, 18, 20

lift /drag ratio, 39 - 41
    in autorotation, 144
    best (or maximum), 40, 41
    icing, effect on, 242
    in ground effect, 62 - 64
    rotor drag, effect on, 61
lift coefficient, 19, 20, 35, 39, 97
    airspeed, effect of, 137
    altitude, effect of, 53
    flapping, effect on, 92, 93
    ice accretion, effect of, 242
    in vortex ring state, 158
    induced drag, effect on, 33
    of slingloads, 218
    of symmatrical airfoils, 59
    reverse flow and, 98
    stalled region in autorotation, 144
load factor, 126, 139
load strap, 210
longitudinal axis, 200
longitudinal stability, 199, 202, 206
longitudinal stability aids, 199
loss of tail rotor effectiveness, 69, 205
low
    density altitude, 115, 228
    frequency vibrations, 184
    inertia rotor, 152
    rotor rpm, 164, 170
    rpm warning horn, 175
    g situation, 167
    inertia blades, 55
    inertia rotor, 170

main rotor
    disc, 176
    gear box, 173
    rpm, 68
    torque, 67
maneuvers, 123 - 132
manifold pressure, 184, 185
mass, 1, 4, 7, 20, 54, 123, 163, 181, 182, 183, 232
mass balance, 180
mast bumping, 167 - 169, 236
    recovery technique, 169
maximum performance takeoff, 208
maximum straight and level speed, 114, 116
maximum-rate turn, 127
mean lag position, 78
mechanical turbulence, 223, 226
minimum
    drag, 108, 109
    drag speed, 120
    radius turn, 127